The Real Utopias Project

Series editor: Erik Olin Wright

The Real Utopias Project embraces a tension between dreams and practice. It is founded on the belief that what is pragmatically possible is not fixed independently of our imaginations, but is itself shaped by our visions. The fulfillment of such a belief involves 'real utopias': utopian ideals that are grounded in the real potentials for redesigning social institutions.

In its attempt at sustaining and deepening serious discussion of radical alternatives to existing social practices, the Real Utopias Project examines various basic institutions – property rights and the market, secondary associations, the family, the welfare state, among others – and focuses on specific proposals for their fundamental redesign. The books in the series are the result of workshop conferences, at which groups of scholars are invited to respond to provocative manuscripts.

Volume I
ASSOCIATIONS AND DEMOCRACY
Joshua Cohen and Joel Rogers

Volume II
EQUAL SHARES: MAKING MARKET SOCIALISM WORK
John E. Roemer

Volume III
RECASTING EGALITARIANISM: NEW RULES FOR COMMUNITIES, STATES AND MARKETS
Samuel Bowles and Herbert Gintis

Volume IV
DEEPENING DEMOCRACY: INSTITUTIONAL INNOVATIONS IN EMPOWERED PARTICIPATORY GOVERNANCE
Archon Fung and Erik Olin Wright

Volume V
REDESIGNING REDISTRIBUTION: BASIC INCOME AND STAKEHOLDER GRANTS AS ALTERNATIVE CORNERSTONES FOR A MORE EGALITARIAN CAPITALISM
Bruce Ackerman, Anne Alstott and Philippe Van Parijs

Gender Equality

Transforming Family Divisions of Labor

The Real Utopias Project
VOLUME VI

JANET C. GORNICK
MARCIA K. MEYERS

with contributions by

Barbara Bergmann
Johanna Brenner
Harry Brighouse
Scott Coltrane
Rosemary Crompton
Myra Marx Ferree
Nancy Folbre
Heidi Hartmann
Shireen Hassim
Lane Kenworthy
Vicky Lovell
Cameron Macdonald
Peter McDonald
Ruth Milkman
Kimberly Morgan
Ann Orloff
Michael Shalev
Erik Olin Wright
Kathrin Zippel

Edited with a preface by

Erik Olin Wright

VERSO
London • New York

First published by Verso 2009
© in the collection Verso 2009
© in individual contributions the contributors 2009
All rights reserved

The moral rights of the authors and the editors have been asserted

1 3 5 7 9 10 8 6 4 2

Verso
UK: 6 Meard Street, London W1F 0EG
US: 20 Jay Street, Suite 1010, Brooklyn, NY 11201
www.versobooks.com

Verso is the imprint of New Left Books

ISBN-13: 978-1-84467-326-1 (hbk)
ISBN-13: 978-1-84467-325-4 (pbk)

British Library Cataloguing in Publication Data
A catalogue record for this book is available from the British Library

Library of Congress Cataloging-in-Publication Data
A catalog record for this book is available from the Library of Congress

Typeset by Hewer Text UK Ltd, Edinburgh
Printed and bound in the USA by Maple Vail

Contents

Preface
Erik Olin Wright — vii

Part I—AN INSTITUTIONAL PROPOSAL

1 *Janet C. Gornick* and *Marcia K. Meyers*, "Institutions that Support Gender Equality in Parenthood and Employment" — 3

Part II—PRINCIPLES

2 *Barbara R. Bergmann*, "Long Leaves, Child Well-Being, and Gender Equality" — 67

3 *Harry Brighouse* and *Erik Olin Wright*, "Strong Gender Egalitarianism" — 79

4 *Shireen Hassim*, "Whose Utopia?" — 93

5 *Nancy Folbre*, "Reforming Care" — 111

6 *Ann Shola Orloff*, "Should Feminists Aim for Gender Symmetry? Why a Dual-Earner/Dual-Caregiver Society Is Not Every Feminist's Utopia" — 129

Part III—DESIGNS: MODIFICATIONS, SPECIFICATIONS, ALTERNATIVES

7 *Peter McDonald*, "Social Policy Principles Applied to Reform of Gender Egalitarianism in Parenthood and Employment" — 161

8   Johanna Brenner, "Democratizing Care"   177

9   Lane Kenworthy, "Who Should Care for Under-Threes?"   193

10 Kathrin Zippel, "The Missing Link for Promoting Gender Equality: Work–Family and Anti-Discrimination Policies"   209

11 Heidi Hartman and Vicky Lovell, "A US Model for Universal Sickness and Family Leave: Gender-Egalitarian and Cross-Class Caregiving Support for All"   231

Part IV—TRANSFORMATIONS: OBSTACLES, OPPORTUNITIES, THE POLITICS OF IMPLEMENTATION

12 Michael Shalev, "Class Divisions among Women"   255

13 Myra Marx Ferree, "An American Road Map? Framing Feminist Goals in a Liberal Landscape"   283

14 Kimberly J. Morgan, "The Political Path to a Dual-Earner/Dual-Caregiver Society: Pitfalls and Possibilities"   317

15 Ruth Milkman, "Class Disparities, Market Fundamentalism and Work–Family Policy: Lessons from California"   339

16 Rosemary Crompton, "The Normative and Institutional Embeddedness of Parental Employment: Its Impact on Gender Egalitarianism in Parenthood and Employment"   365

17 Scott Coltrane, "Fatherhood, Gender and Work–Family Policies"   385

18 Cameron Macdonald, "What's Culture Got to Do with It? Mothering Ideologies as Barriers to Gender Equity"   411

Part V—CONCLUSION

19 Janet C. Gornick and Marcia K. Meyers, "Further Thoughts"   435

Index   451

Preface
Erik Olin Wright

There was a time not so long ago when a majority of married women with young children in economically developed countries were full-time caregivers with husbands who worked outside the home to provide the family income. This was the era of the male-breadwinner/female-caregiver model of the family. While this model was never universal—poor women often worked to bring income into the household even when they had young children—it was pervasive, both as a normative ideal and as a practical reality.

That era has passed irretrievably. We now live in a world where most women in the developed economies of the world work in the paid labor force, even when they have small children. Role differentiation between men and women within employment has significantly declined, and at least some change is also observed within the family: men do more housework and child care than in the past. Yet gender inequality still persists, both in the family and in employment. Women continue to bear a disproportionate burden of family caregiving responsibilities; they do most of the housework; and, when the time spent on these activities is added to their time in paid employment, many married women have significantly less free time than their spouses. Within employment, while opportunities have expanded and inequalities reduced, the family responsibilities women face frequently undermine their career prospects and reinforce other gender-based discriminatory practices by employers. The result of these developments is a very widespread experience of "time-binds" and tensions between work life and family life for both men and women in contemporary families.

The chapters in this book were first presented at a conference in the Real Utopias Project on the design of public institutions that could significantly mitigate these pressures and create conditions that would facilitate much more deeply egalitarian gender relations within the family over both caregiving and employment. The conference was anchored by Janet Gornick and Marcia Meyers' essay "Institutions that Support Gender Egalitarianism in Parenthood and Employment." They argue that in order to reconcile in an egalitarian manner the interests of men, women, and children within the emerging dual-earner/dual-caregiver model of the family, three clusters of institutional innovations are needed: 1) a generous mechanism of paid parental leaves for caregiving activities which is allocated to mothers and fathers individually, thus requiring fathers to "use or lose" their paid leave time; 2) effective working-time regulations that limit full-time work hours and raise the quality and availability of reduced-hour work; and 3) an expansive, universal program of early childhood education and care. The other chapters interrogate these proposals, examining their ramifications and possible limitations, elaborating alternatives, and exploring their relationship to the broader problem of emancipatory social change.

PART I
An Institutional Proposal

1

Institutions that Support Gender Equality in Parenthood and Employment*

Janet C. Gornick and Marcia K. Meyers

I. INTRODUCTION

Parents in the rich countries of the world are navigating new realities in the organization of family and market work. Women's labor force participation is approaching that of men's in many industrialized countries and is rising in several newly industrializing countries in the northern and southern hemispheres. In much of the industrialized world, the majority of children now live in families in which both or the single parent are employed and most mothers, as well as fathers, combine employment with caregiving responsibilities at home.

Changing patterns of parenthood and employment have created new opportunities and unprecedented prosperity for many. These changes are also creating new problems of "time-poverty" for parents, exacerbating long-standing gender inequalities, and exposing many children to unstable and poor-quality child-care arrangements. These

---

* Throughout this essay, we draw heavily on our prior publications. On several topics, we direct the reader to more detailed discussions presented in our book, *Families That Work: Policies for Reconciling Parenthood and Employment* (Gornick and Meyers, 2003). We also revisit two recent book chapters—one in a collection edited by Janet Giele and Elke Holst (Gornick and Meyers, 2004) and the other in a volume edited by Jody Heymann and Christopher Beem (Gornick and Meyers, 2005). Please see the reference list for the complete citations.

problems are often framed in terms of tradeoffs between the interests of women, men and children. Children can have more time with their parents, some observers suggest, only if women scale back their employment commitments and achievements. Or women can join men in the public spheres of employment and civic life, but only if the care and rearing of children is outsourced to non–family members.

We, the two authors of this essay, came to this collaboration as interdisciplinary social scientists with a shared interest in social welfare policy. Our backgrounds also differed in ways that mirrored these larger divides: one of us was steeped in feminism, the other had a longstanding concern with the care and well-being of children. Not surprisingly, we clashed over several issues, and especially those related to maternal employment, in particular when children are very young. One of us worried about symmetry between women's and men's engagement in the world outside the home, arguing that women's emancipation depends on reaching parity with men in the public spheres of employment and politics. The other worried about poor quality care for children, pointing out that children need their parents' time and that, in many families, that might be incompatible with full-time maternal employment when children are young.

The challenge of reconciling these apparent tradeoffs is at the heart of the analysis in this essay. In suggesting a blueprint for institutions that support gender-egalitarian caregiving, we argue that tradeoffs between gender equality, family time, and child well-being are not inevitable. The interests of men, women and children are not fundamentally at odds with one another. Rather, the interests of each—and our shared social interests in raising healthy children while promoting women's full equality with men—are at odds with contemporary workplace practices and social policies that have failed to respond to changing social and economic realities. Male-breadwinner/female-homemaker family arrangements that were common in the early twentieth century are increasingly rare in industrialized countries. But workplace structures and social policies in most of the industrialized world are still based on the assumption that men will commit themselves to full-time employment while women provide unpaid domestic work and caregiving in the home.

In this essay we envision a different social arrangement for the future: a dual-earner/dual-caregiver society. This arrangement—the Real Utopia at the heart of this volume—is a society in which men and women engage symmetrically in employment and caregiving, and all parents have realistic opportunities to combine waged work with the direct provision of care for their children. A dual-earner/dual-caregiver society is one that supports equal opportunities for men and women in employment, symmetrical contributions from mothers and fathers at home, and high-quality care for children provided both by parents and by well-qualified and well-compensated non-parental caregivers.

Building on these principles, we outline a package of work–family reconciliation[1] policies that would support dual-earner/dual-caregiver arrangements in industrialized countries. We concentrate our analyses and policy recommendations on a group of high-income market economies—a group that mainly includes the countries of western, northern, and southern Europe, as well as some non-European countries, including Canada and the US.[2] We do this for two reasons. First, as the earliest to industrialize, these countries exemplify the contradictions between historical assumptions about female caregiving and the contemporary demands and opportunities of industrial and postindustrial economies. Second, as the first to develop welfare-state protections, several of these countries also provide the most fully developed models for policies that reconcile market and family demands. Although our framing of these policies as the institutional blueprint for a dual-earner/dual-caregiver society is novel, the policies themselves have been partially or fully developed in many countries, mostly in Europe. None of these countries have achieved the ideal of full gender equality. Nor have they fully resolved competing demands on parental time and attention. But many have achieved high levels of economic productivity while providing substantial support to parents and children and promoting gender equality. Policy designs from these countries provide both general and specific lessons for institutions that could support our Real Utopia of gender-egalitarian caregiving that makes room for mothers and fathers both in the home and in the market.

We also concentrate on one dimension of caregiving, which is parental care of dependent children. Many of our arguments are relevant to other forms of caregiving that have historically been provided by families, including care for disabled children and adults, and for aging parents. More broadly, some observers argue that "time to care" is equally important for self-care and the full development of one's own human capabilities. We believe, however, that the care and rearing of children is a special case because of the profound and enduring impact of childrearing on gender specialization and the public benefits that result from time invested in caring for children. Nearly all adults are involved in childrearing at some point in their lives, and childbirth (or adoption) is the moment at which men's and women's working lives begin to diverge most radically. The care and rearing of children are also expensive and the arrival of children is the point at which the economic fortunes of households begin to diverge most markedly by family structure. Although most of the costs of raising children are private, the benefits of healthy, well-nurtured children, who become engaged citizens and productive workers in adulthood, are broadly shared by society. In this sense, well-nurtured children are a public good, and the case for government intervention is particularly strong.

Throughout this essay, we focus primarily on hetrosexual couples in our analyses and examples because we are especially interested in gendered divisions of labor within families. Single parents face additional challenges to their economic security and more acute competition for their time. Issues of gender equality are also particularly acute in the case of single-parent families from which fathers may opt out or be forced out as economic and care providers. The issues raised in this essay are also relevant to same-sex couples. In fact, same-sex couples raising children often exemplify the dual-earner/dual-caregiver model, in that paid and unpaid work hours are usually not allocated, within couples, according to traditional gendered expectations. Although we often refer to the birth and rearing of children, our analyses and policy recommendations are equally relevant to the care of adopted children.

The remainder of our essay is organized as follows. In section II we describe in somewhat greater detail the social and economic changes that are contributing to contemporary problems of work–family conflict, gender inequality, and risks to children's healthy development. We emphasize commonalities across the industrialized countries, drawing on data for the OECD countries as a whole or, in some cases, on examples from specific countries. In section III we draw on feminist welfare-state scholarship to outline our conceptual model and clarify the end vision of the dual-earner/dual-caregiver model of family and social arrangements. In section IV we present a blueprint for work–family reconciliation policies that would support these arrangements, drawing on existing models in six European countries that we have selected because each has developed one or more elements of a policy package that supports the dual-earner/dual-caregiver model. We make the case for government provisions and then summarize principles for policy design in three areas—paid family leave provisions, working time regulations and early childhood education and care. In section V, we describe in much more detail these work–family reconciliation policies as they have been developed in Denmark, Finland, Norway, Sweden, Belgium and France. In section VI, we compare these countries to the US, as an exemplar of limited government intervention, on indicators of gender equality, time for parental caregiving, and parents' experience of work–family conflict. Finally, in section VII, we discuss three areas in which we might be particularly concerned about the unwanted or costly consequences of these policies.

II. THE PROBLEM

Although the language of "work–family conflict" is contemporary, the conflict itself is rooted in longstanding contradictions in economic, social and gender arrangements in industrialized societies. In the late nineteenth century, industrialization and the rise of waged labor in western Europe and North America sparked a massive economic and social reorganization, although at different rates and with different institutional consequences in different regions. As most men—but few women—moved their labor from the agricultural to the industrial and commercial sectors, a male-breadwinner/female-homemaker family came to be defined as the ideal family. Men and women assumed increasingly separate work roles, with men engaging in paid work and women taking responsibility for unpaid work, most especially the work of caring for children.

This arrangement remained fairly stable through the first half of the twentieth century, but began to unravel later in the century in the face of rapidly changing social and economic realities. One of the most dramatic of these changes was the increase in women's labor-force participation. In the latter half of the twentieth century, women throughout the OECD countries entered waged work in large numbers, making a social and economic transition that their male counterparts had engaged in nearly a century earlier. The increase was particularly dramatic, and an especially significant change in many countries, for women with children. Across the thirty current OECD countries, 71 percent of mothers with one child and 62 percent of mothers with two or more children are now employed. Only one European country, Spain, has maternal employment rates lower than 50 percent. In the US, the maternal employment rate stands at nearly 70 percent, and in countries with high female employment, such as Sweden and Denmark, rates exceed 80 percent.

Patterns of family formation were also changing in the industrialized countries during the closing decades of the twentieth century. In most high-income countries, cohabitation became more common, births outside of marriage increased substantially, and divorce rates rose. More children were being raised in lone-parent families, and these families were overwhelmingly headed by mothers. In several countries, single parenthood is now a more common economic risk among working-age women than either disability or unemployment. By the close of the twentieth century, as the early industrializing countries were evolving into postindustrial economies, new family structures and patterns of maternal employment had profoundly altered family life. The majority of children no longer lived in the mid-century "ideal" of a male-breadwinner/ female-homemaker family—they lived in a family in which all adults were combining parenthood with employment.

Incomplete transformations

Although much has changed for families in the industrialized countries, much has also remained the same. The historically dominant male-breadwinner/female-homemaker model rested on a nearly complete specialization of economic roles within those families that could afford to have a full-time homemaker. To a greater or lesser extent across the industrialized countries, it has been replaced by a new arrangement in which most men invest their time primarily in earning, working long hours in full-time jobs, while many women split their time between earning and caregiving, by taking intermittent breaks from employment and/or holding part-time or "soft sector" jobs. In economic terms, in most of the OECD countries, total gender specialization has been replaced by partial specialization. Women have joined men in the public spheres of commercial and civic activity; but they continue to have primary responsibility for the private sphere of the home as well. Men have failed to make a corresponding shift in the amount of time and attention that they devote to caregiving.

The world is only partially transformed in another important respect: in many of the industrialized countries, labor market and social policy institutions continue to assume traditional divisions of labor. In the absence of direct government interventions, employers have largely absorbed the labor of women without reducing their reliance on, or contributing directly to the costs of replacing, women's uncompensated domestic and caregiving labor in the home. Unless compelled by labor laws or collective bargaining, employers in increasingly competitive global markets have taken steps, not to ease time demands on the growing proportion of workers who have dual commitments to employment and caregiving, but to demand even more effort, hours of work, and workplace productivity. Parents across the OECD countries are managing greater demands on their time and energy, but they are doing so, to a large extent, in the context of working arrangements and workplace policies that do little to make their lives more compatible with caring for dependent family members.

Social policy institutions have also been slow and uneven in their response to the changing realities of work and family life. By the middle of the twentieth century, many rich countries had developed a core of welfare-state protections designed to reduce economic risks and equalize outcomes for their citizens: old-age, disability, and survivors' pensions, as well as health, sickness, and unemployment benefits. These countries have been slower, and much more varied, in their adoption of policies that provide support for family caregiving and mitigate the gendered costs of providing this care, including maternity and paternity leaves, parenting leaves, public child care, services for the elderly, and family allowances.

Consequences for gender equality, family time and child well-being

The incomplete transformation of gender relations, labor markets, and social institutions has exacerbated long-standing gender inequalities and created new time pressures and possibly problematic consequences for children's well-being.

Gender inequalities. Increasing rates of female employment have narrowed the gender gap in labor force participation. But they have not dissolved other fundamental disparities, and these disparities remain particularly large for parents. In all of the OECD countries, mothers' employment rates lag behind the rates of 90 percent or higher reported among fathers. When mothers are employed, compared to fathers they average fewer hours in paid work, and they are more likely to take leaves and/or career breaks to care for children or other family members. Due in large part to employment interruptions associated with bearing and caring for children, employed mothers are less likely than their male counterparts to work in upper-echelon occupations or jobs, and they command lower earnings.

Mothers' career breaks, periods of part-time employment, and parenting-related occupational and job choices, along with employer discrimination on the basis of parental status, exact a substantial "mommy tax." The extent of this "mommy tax" varies considerably across the OECD countries. In none, however, have women with children reached parity with their male partners. Using one measure of labor-market equality—the share of total family earnings contributed by mothers in dual-parent families—we find that mothers' share of total parental earnings is as low as 18 to 19 percent in Germany and the Netherlands, and as high as 34 to 38 percent in only the highly egalitarian Nordic countries of Denmark and Sweden. The US ranks roughly in the middle of the OECD countries by this measure, with mothers commanding about 28 percent of total parental earnings.

Gender inequalities in the labor market are mirrored by continuing gender inequalities at home. Although men's engagement in domestic work and caregiving has increased in some countries, nowhere has this increase matched women's influx into paid employment. Comparative time-use studies suggest that employed fathers in most OECD countries devote fewer than one-quarter of the hours devoted by their female partners to routine housework, and less than half as much time to caring for their children as do their female partners. As with labor-market outcomes, gender inequalities at home vary across the OECD countries. But even in gender-egalitarian Sweden, fathers spend only about 56 percent as much time as their female partners do caring for children.

Family time. Increases in women's labor force participation have reduced but far from eliminated persistent gender inequalities. Changing employment patterns have had less ambiguous consequences for the time that parents have available to care for their children. As families have moved more adults into the workforce, they have had to forfeit much of the time that parents—overwhelmingly mothers—traditionally devoted to caregiving and other domestic labor. The rise in maternal employment is creating an increasingly acute "time-crunch" for many families in the industrialized countries.

In many industrialized countries, long employment hours—especially among men—compound the time pressures associated with the increased prevalence of maternal employment. Although annual hours of work have declined in some countries, due in part to the influx of women working part-time hours and to modest reductions in annual working days, men's weekly hours of work remain very high in many industrialized countries. In a number of high-income countries, men of prime age (from twenty-five to fifty-four) average well over forty hours per week in paid work; in several countries—including the US, the United Kingdom, Ireland, Belgium, Greece and Spain—they log an average of forty-five hours per week at their jobs. Even with reductions in annual working days, the persistence of long weekly hours among male workers is a formidable obstacle to greater involvement in the daily tasks of caring for children. Ironically, fathers' average working hours are even greater than the average for all men in these countries, because they typically work longer hours than their childless counterparts.

Both mothers and fathers have reason to complain about the competing time demands of employment and caregiving and the economic and social tradeoffs that it forces. But the gendered nature of contemporary partial specialization between fathers and mothers creates particularly acute demands on women, who are far more likely to combine major commitments to employment and caregiving. In most of the OECD countries for which we have comparable data, employed mothers still spend from five to seven hours a day in housekeeping and primary child care activities—twice the number reported by men. Where do women get this time? Some time-use studies in the US suggest that mothers' increasing hours of employment have not come entirely at the expense of hours devoted to direct care of their children (Bianchi, 2000). Instead, employed mothers do less of everything else: in comparison to their non-employed counterparts, they spend seven fewer hours per week on housework, six fewer hours sleeping, five fewer hours on personal care, and twelve fewer hours on leisure activities.

The social costs of increasing time demands on parents in the OECD countries are reflected in their own assessments of satisfaction with their time allocations. In surveys conducted in several OECD countries, one half or more of mothers report that they would like to have more time with their children. Nearly all mothers (90 percent) in time-starved American families report that they would like "a little or a lot" more time with their families. More strikingly, perhaps, fathers in these countries are even more likely to report that they feel time-poor with respect to family: 80 percent or more in most countries, and 95 percent in the US, express a preference for more time with their families.

Parental time and child well-being. The social costs of the time crunch for parents may also be exacted from children. Researchers have examined the effects of maternal employment on child well-being for several decades under the assumption that maternal absence, or the use of other caregivers, may jeopardize children's healthy growth and development. Early findings from this research suggested that maternal employment had generally positive effects on both the mental health of mothers and the well-being of children. These studies often failed to disentangle the contributions of maternal employment per se from the effects of increased family income. Unfortunately, this research has also focused almost exclusively on maternal employment; there is little research examining the question of how fathers' employment affects child well-being. In the absence of such studies there is little reason to believe that, outside the period surrounding birth and breastfeeding, maternal care is superior to paternal care on average.

Generalizing from the research on maternal employment, the most recent work suggests a complex and nuanced story about parental absence and substitute care. In an extensive recent review, a panel of researchers commissioned by the National Research Council and the Institute of Medicine (2003) suggest that the effects of parental employment vary with the characteristics of parents' working schedules and jobs, with the quality of substitute care, and with the developmental needs and temperaments of children. Employment arrangements that greatly reduce parents' time and attention for their children appear to pose the greatest risk to child well-being. For the youngest children, for example, employment arrangements that limit mothers' ability to breastfeed, or that place children in substitute care for long hours during the first year of life, have been linked to poorer health and developmental outcomes. For school-aged children, parental employment in nonstandard-hour jobs has been associated with poorer academic performance and more problem behaviors. For parents with adolescent children, employment that limits their oversight and monitoring of children's time appears to place children at heightened risk for engaging in dangerous and illegal behaviors.

For children of all ages, the quality of substitute care is a critical intervening variable between parental employment and child well-being. The stability of the caregiver and quality of the adult–child interaction are particularly crucial for the healthy development of young children. For school-aged and adolescent children, the proximity of adult supervisors is important, along with the quality and diversity of supervised activities. The quality of non-parental care has particularly important consequences for socially and economically disadvantaged children.

III. CONCEPTUALIZING AN INSTITUTIONAL RESPONSE

After more than a decade of research on work–family reconciliation policies, we have become keenly aware of several overlapping but surprisingly distinct conversations about work and family life in the industrialized countries. These parallel but nonintersecting conversations converge in recognizing that there is a problem. They diverge substantially, however, in their definition of the problem and in their proposed policy solutions.

One conversation has evolved out of growing concerns about parental time in the home and the well-being of children. Child development research, including important new findings about early brain development, has focused much of this discussion on the importance of parental availability and care during the earliest months and years of children's lives. Although the factors that promote healthy early development are multiple, a growing body of research suggests that compromises in the quality of children's care, particularly in the first year of life, can have lasting consequences for their healthy development. Other research suggests that a lack of close adult supervision is placing some school-aged and adolescent children at risk for poor academic, health and social outcomes. Evidence that children benefit from consistent and attentive caregiving resonates with parents' intuitive beliefs that children need their parents, and with the desire of many parents to be the primary caregivers for their children. And it raises concerns among many about the absence or diminished attention of parents who are more deeply engaged than ever in responsibilities outside the home.

A second conversation has been animated by rapid changes in women's engagement in the labor market. Following the sharp rise in mothers' employment during the 1960s and 1970s, a somewhat different group of social scientists, policy analysts, and advocates began a conversation about "work–family conflict." This conversation has focused on the problems of working parents whose conflicting responsibilities in the workplace and at home leave them penalized at work and overburdened and exhausted at home. Although not exclusively focused on the problems of women—men too complain about a lack of time with their families—it is mothers who are viewed as most burdened and conflicted by multiple roles. Some strands of this conversation, advancing a "women's caregiver" perspective, are explicitly feminist in their call for radical new conceptions of care, paid work, social citizenship rights, and welfare-state obligations (see, for example, Knijn and Kremer, 1997). More commonly, however, this conversation is situated within a "work and family life" perspective that is largely divorced from feminism in its emphasis on helping women balance competing demands within existing social and gender arrangements.

A third conversation has grown out of the second wave of the women's movement. Since the 1960s, when activists began to argue that "the personal is political," many feminists have taken a hard look at the role of the nuclear family in the subjugation of women. Feminists concerned with the family have concluded that persistent gender inequality in the labor market is both cause and consequence of women's disproportionate assumption of unpaid work in the home. This conversation revolves around the ways in which men's stronger ties to the labor market carry social, political, and economic advantages that are denied to many women, especially those who spend substantial amounts of time caring for children.

There has been surprisingly little meeting of the minds among participants in these separate but related conversations, which seem most at odds when they propose solutions to the problem. Research on child well-being stresses the importance of parents' availability, and many interpret this research to suggest the need for policies—such as child tax credits and maternity leaves—that would allow mothers of young children to opt out of labor-market attachments. Much of the work–family literature also locates work–family conflict in women's lives and focuses on arrangements that allow women to balance time between the workplace and home, such as part-time work, job-sharing, telecommuting, and flextime. In contrast, many feminists have identified the problem as women's weak and intermittent connection to employment. Feminists argue that women will not and cannot achieve parity with men as long as they shoulder unequal responsibilities for unpaid care work. Along with policies that reduce employment barriers and discrimination, feminists typically advocate for alternatives to maternal child care, including more and better-quality out-of-home child care.

Although they differ in naming the problem and in the solutions they propose, these conversations have two things in common: they all focus on women, and do little to question assumptions about the organization of men's employment and caregiving activities. And they suggest that the interests of men, women and children are essentially in conflict: children can have more time with their parents only if women reduce their employment commitments and career prospects; women and men can achieve greater equality in their employment only by reducing their time spent caring for their children.

Reconciling earning, caring, and gender equality: the dual-earner/dual-caregiver society

The challenge of reconciling these apparent tradeoffs is at the heart of our recent book and this Real Utopias exercise. To reconcile these tradeoffs we argue that scholars and social activists need to move beyond existing conceptualizations of the problem as one of child well-being *or* work—family balance *or* gender equality. The most

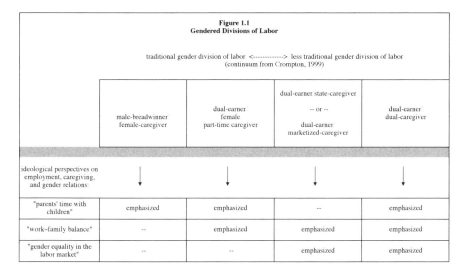

pressing conflicts of interest arise not between men and women, nor between parents and children, but between the needs of contemporary families and current divisions of labor, workplace practices, and social policies. To resolve these conflicts we do not need to choose sides, but rather to focus our attention on an end vision of what an earning, caring, egalitarian society that promotes the well-being of children might look like.

Fortunately, a number of feminist welfare-state scholars have articulated such an end vision—a dual-earner/dual-caregiver model that honors the importance of earning and caring, and that prioritizes both gender equality and parental care for children. In the following sections we develop the framework for this model and outline a set of policies that would support and enable it.

British sociologist Rosemary Crompton (1999) describes the dual-earner/dual-caregiver model as part of a continuum of social arrangements and gendered divisions of labor. She emphasizes that "the point of this exercise is not to provide a matrix, or static taxonomy, within with nation states may be precisely located. Rather, the aim is to develop a flexible framework through which change may be conceptualized" (1999: 204). This framework also serves as a useful tool for illustrating contemporary and idealized social and economic arrangements. In Figure 1.1 we present Crompton's continuum and (as extended by us) its relation to the issues of parents' time with children, work–family balance, and gender equality that animate current debates about work and family policy.

The first point on the continuum is the fully specialized traditional family, which prevailed across the industrialized countries from the late nineteenth century until the middle of the twentieth century. The pure form of this family arrangement—men in waged work, women caring for children at home full-time—is now relatively rare in the OECD countries. Mothers of infants constitute an exception to the demise of this fully specialized arrangement, as many mothers still exit the labor force during their children's youngest years.

The middle points on the continuum describe contemporary family political economies in most high-employment industrialized countries. The dual-earner/female part-time caregiver model is common in countries such as the United Kingdom and the Netherlands, where many mothers combine primary responsibility for family care with employment in part-time jobs with low weekly hours. Because mothers are free to spend time with their children, this model values parental caregiving. Given appropriate policy supports, such as caregiver stipends, it can be consistent with rewarding women as caregivers and reducing the competing demands of the home and market. It does little, however, to reduce gender divisions of labor in caregiving and market work.

The third point on the continuum—the dual-earner model with substitute caregivers—stresses gender equality in earning by moving more of the care of children outside the home, and by freeing mothers as well as fathers for employment that is continuous and full-time. The "state-caregiver" version, in which children are cared for in public child-care settings, characterizes arrangements in countries with high rates of full-time maternal employment and extensive public child-care systems. This arrangement was common in the state socialist countries during the 1980s; today it operates, to a degree, in Finland. In the "market-caregiver" version, most fully developed in the US, a large share of mothers are employed full-time, and families make extensive use of private market care arrangements.[3] By commodifying care and moving it out of the home, both options could be consonant with gender equality in the labor market. Yet both of these dual-earner/substitute-caregiver arrangements can also have gender-inegalitarian consequences if full-time employed women retain primary responsibility for unpaid caregiving at home—a double burden that can impoverish women's time and erode the quality of both their caregiving and labor market attachments. These arrangements also do little to value or protect parents' rights to care for their own children. They recognize the value of substitute caregiving labor by compensating privately or publicly subsidized child-care providers, while undervaluing caregiving labor provided by parents. Over time, the failure to support parents' caregiving labor both devalues and reinforces the gendered distribution of such labor, which is provided overwhelmingly by women in both publicly subsidized and market-based child-care systems. This gender-inegalitarian outcome is compounded, in private systems, by the extremely low wages paid to women who work in child-care settings.

The fourth point on the continuum illustrates a distinctly egalitarian social arrangement that honors both parental caregiving and market work: "the dual-earner/dual-caregiver model" (henceforth the earner–caregiver model). This model differs from the others in two key respects. First, unlike the first two arrangements, it envisions a social and economic outcome in which men and women engage *symmetrically* in both paid work and in unpaid caregiving; it is thus fundamentally gender-egalitarian. Second, unlike arrangements that shift substantial responsibility for caring for children outside the home, it assumes that parents have the right to choose whether they will care for their own children or rely on substitute forms of care. Both mothers and fathers in an earner–caregiver society would have realistic opportunities to combine employment and caregiving and to adjust their hours of paid work to allow time to care for children. To these characteristics, suggested by Crompton, we add a third distinction: the state would support both parental and non-parental care for children, socializing the costs of caring for children and equalizing access to quality care across families of different means.[4] Thus amended, the earner–caregiver model resolves many of the apparent tradeoffs in contemporary work–family debates: it is gender-egalitarian, values both caregiving and market labor, and supports both parental and non-parental care arrangements that contribute to the well-being of children.[5]

IV. THE INSTITUTIONAL DESIGN OF POLICIES THAT SUPPORT AN EARNER–CAREGIVER SOCIETY

The earner–caregiver society is clearly utopian. It has the qualities of a *Real* Utopia, however, because it is possible to imagine the social, institutional, and structural transformations through which it could be realized. First, by definition, it requires the dissolution of remaining gendered divisions of labor in employment and at home. The achievement of gender symmetry, together with high-level parental care, can come about only if men, on average, shift substantial portions of time from the labor market to the home. At the same time, it envisions a virtual end to full-time homemaking as it makes a place for all women in the world of employment. Second, an earner–caregiver society would require major transformations in the workplace because it imagines that fathers, along with mothers, would have the right to reduce their employment hours to care for children, particularly when their children are young. As Crompton observes, "full-time work as we know it might be superceded" (1999: 208). Third, the realization of an earner–caregiver society would require that the state take an active role in protecting parents' rights to have time for caregiving without undue economic sacrifice, and in assuring that families have access to affordable, high-quality substitute child care.

In this essay we focus on this third transformation. We outline policies in the areas of *family leave*, *working time regulation*, and *early childhood education and care* that are consonant with the earner–caregiver model and have been well tested in other rich, industrialized countries. In the short term, these policies would provide men and women with greater options to equalize their allocation of time between the market and caregiving in the home, while ensuring that their children are well cared for. In the longer term, by altering incentives and creating new social norms, we believe these policies can contribute to a more fundamental transformation of the prevailing gendered divisions of labor and current devaluation of caregiving work.

In the remainder of this section, we provide the "blueprint" for a package of gender-equalizing work–family reconciliation policies. This blueprint summarizes the principles that we have derived from a more detailed study of model policy designs in six countries that serve as exemplars for all or part of our proposed policy package: Denmark, Finland, Norway, Sweden, Belgium and France. There is little that is controversial about our selection of countries; several empirical studies have established that these six form a relatively cohesive policy cluster. They are the main, and arguably the only, European countries that provide working time, child-care, and income supports that are both (relatively) generous and (relatively) consonant with gender-egalitarian divisions of labor.

We summarize the policy design principles in this section, and in Section V we provide the institutional details of current practices in these six countries. Before turning to the institutional story, however, we address a fundamental question that is often raised by our proposal: why should government be involved?

The case for government

Our policy blueprint envisions substantial government intervention to support parents, children, and non-parental caregivers. We believe that the fundamental promise of the earner–caregiver model cannot be delivered without state policies that regulate labor and child-care markets and that redistribute resources across households and enterprises, and over the life cycle. Among all but the most privileged families, parents cannot realistically choose to reduce or reallocate employment hours, even temporarily, in the absence of policies that protect their employment status and replace some of their earnings. Parents cannot count on safe and affordable child care in the absence of policies that regulate the quality of care in child-care settings and help defray costs of providing that care. Adults working in child-care settings cannot command decent wages and working conditions if they are negotiating individually with parent–consumers whose own resources are limited. To provide these rights and opportunities the state would need to intervene through both regulatory and redistributive policies.

Is this level of government intervention really necessary? We believe it is, because leaving the costs of child-rearing almost entirely to parents is unlikely ever to produce optimal social and economic outcomes, because the costs that parents incur on behalf of their children—including time, energy, forgone earnings, expenditures on children's consumer goods, and investments in child care and education—produce benefits that are widely dispersed. In other words, as Nancy Folbre and Paula England have argued, children are public goods, in the sense that their capabilities benefit society as a whole. In economic terms, children's capabilities are public goods in that others can reap the benefits without paying, and one person's enjoyment does not diminish another's (Folbre, 1994; England and Folbre, 1999a).[6]

Although the conclusion that children are public goods derives from mainstream economic principles, the bearing and rearing of children is still viewed in most of the industrialized world as largely a private concern. The decision to have children is understood to reflect the utility, or pleasure, that parents derive from the caregiving experience; the monetary, time, and other costs they incur are assumed to be offset by the happiness they derive and/or the future benefits they reap—for example, care during their own later and more dependent years. Of course, parents do derive benefits from raising their children. But, as Folbre and England have observed, children are not pets. Parents' reproductive and caregiving work, most of it performed by women, also contributes social and economic benefits to individuals and institutions that do not share its costs. All members of society benefit when parents invest more heavily in the "production" of well-nurtured children—children who are this generation's healthy playmates, creative peers, and well-behaved students, and who become the next generation's productive workers, social insurance contributors, and civic participants.

To the extent that family caregivers pay the costs of "producing" children, while others benefit, there are at least two persuasive arguments for government interventions. First, expanding public supports for child rearing would raise the likelihood of achieving economically efficient and socially optimal outcomes. Well-cared-for children generate positive externalities and, absent government supports, goods that generate positive externalities generally receive levels of private investment that are suboptimal. As a result, society as a whole may eventually pay a collective price in the form of children who, at best, fail to achieve their full potential, or, at worst, become a drain on public programs. Although the industrialized countries have historically invested in public schooling for children starting at age five or six, in some countries—the US is a prime example—public investments in younger children are much more limited. Government programs that help to ensure high-quality care for children below school-age, such as paid family leave and high-caliber substitute care, constitute needed investments in today's children and tomorrow's adults.

The second argument in favor of government support of young children's care is a normative one, and it concerns equality. Extending government investments has implications for equality among children, especially among children from families at different points along the income distribution. To the extent that we rely on parents' private resources, children in low-income families receive far less than their affluent counterparts.

Programs that spread the costs of caregiving also have major implications for gender equality because women do the majority of caregiving. Because caregivers can neither exclude others from sharing the fruits of their labor nor recover the costs of their work, others are able to free-ride on their unpaid work. As Budig and England argue, "a general equity principle is that those who receive benefits should share in the costs . . . Those who rear children deserve public support precisely because the benefits of child rearing diffuse to other members of society" (Budig and England, 2001: 221). Policies that shift some of the costs of childcare-giving from parents to taxpayers, and to employers, are equitable because they require that all who benefit make a contribution.

Some participants in the "work–family debates" agree that many employed parents need more institutional supports, in the form of leave rights and benefits, formal options for work schedule flexibility, and subsidized child care. But they argue that these measures should be left to employers to provide. According to this perspective, with sustained educational campaigns, persuasive bargaining, and considerable moral suasion, large numbers of employers can and will be enticed to add workplace benefits.

We are deeply skeptical that voluntary employer provisions will ever be sufficient, especially for low-wage workers. Employers could initiate crucial changes in workplace practices and offer supplementary work–family programs and benefits—and some employers do. But, overall, employers cannot individually and voluntarily provide the full range of work–family reconciliation supports for their own employees, and should not be expected to do so. In fact, the incentives for employers to do so are often weak or entirely absent. While some employer-provided services, such as flex-time and limited sick leave options, are relatively inexpensive and understood to "pay for themselves," others, such as high-quality child care and substantially compensated family leave, are simply too expensive for most employers to fully finance. Where few local employers offer work–family benefits, no one employer has the incentive to do so, especially when labor markets are loose. Although some employers do offer generous work–family options, especially employers with highly skilled workers with firm-specific skills, employers with largely low-skilled workforces have weak incentives to provide supports because employee replacement costs are fairly low. Workplace regulations and benefits that apply to a large swath of the labor force, and to diverse enterprises and workforces, are crucial, as are financing structures that spread the costs. Only the state can assume these roles.

The policy blueprint

In the remainder of this section we lay out the broad contours or principles of public policies that, in the short term, would enable families who wish to organize their work and care along earner–caregiver lines to do so. In the longer term, these institutional arrangements would be consonant with, and could encourage, more far-reaching transformations in the direction of gender-egalitarian employment and caregiving arrangements. We focus on three areas of policy that can help parents—as Francine Deutsch evocatively phrases it—to "halve it all," by sharing equally in the costs and benefits of earning and caring: paid family leave, regulation of working time, and early childhood education and care. In the next section, we will provide more institutional details for these policies as they have been developed in parts of Europe.

Paid family leave.
Family leave provisions would grant parents the right to take time off to care for children without losing their jobs, and provide cash benefits to compensate for lost wages during periods of leave. Leave policies should include short-term maternity leave rights and benefits, short-term paternity leave rights and benefits, longer-term parental leave for both parents, and temporary periods of paid leave—often referred to as "leave for family reasons"—that allow parents to respond to routine and non-routine caregiving demands. To reduce gender differentials in paid and unpaid work, gender-egalitarian leave policies would extend benefits to both men and women, and create incentives for men to take up the benefits to which they are entitled.[7] Gender-equalizing family leave policies would have several key features.

First, all employed mothers and fathers, and other primary caregivers of children, would be granted the right to take six months of paid leave, with job protection, following childbirth or adoption. The six-month duration reflects the length of earnings-related leave—from the perspective of a couple—that is currently in place in a number of the Nordic countries; that is, couples today are generally granted about one year of leave, to be shared.[8] Furthermore, we would cap the per-person leave at six months, because the accumulating evidence suggests that that duration lies within the leave length that is advantageous, and not harmful, to women's labor-force attachment and longer-term employment trajectories.[9]

Second, and crucially, each employed parent would have his or her own *entirely* non-transferable leave entitlement, meaning that recipients may not transfer their entitlements to their partners. While non-transferability potentially restricts some individuals' options—mothers may not take up "both shares"—it substantially increases incentives for fathers' participation.[10]

Third, employees would receive 100 percent wage replacement during these leave periods, with an earnings cap on benefits to incorporate progressivity and to contain costs.[11] A social insurance fund would be used to finance wage replacement through employer and/or employee payroll contributions. To minimize discrimination against potential leave-takers, employers would not be expected to replace the wages of their own workers when they took leave. Social insurance premiums would not be experience-rated at the enterprise-level; that is, they would not reflect the share of employees who actually draw benefits.

Fourth, flexibility in paid leave entitlements would allow parents to take up their benefits either full-time or in combination with part-time employment, and to draw down their six-month entitlements incrementally, over several years. In other words, each (employed) new parent would be granted a six-month allotment of leave time and permitted to flexibly choose how and when to "tick the clock down," throughout a period that could be as long as eight years. To accommodate staffing needs, employers would have the right to require substantial notification periods before workers exited the workplace and prior to their return. Governments would provide additional help for employers—particularly small employers—by making referrals between potential workers seeking employment or training opportunities and employers seeking to hire temporary replacement workers.

Fifth, mothers and fathers would have the right to some time off, with pay, to attend to short-term and unpredictable needs that arose throughout their children's lives. Parents need to be granted a reasonable number of days each year to attend to short-term needs—such as a child's routine illness, a disruption in childcare, or a school-related emergency—without fear of job loss or lost pay. Publicly financed "leave for family reasons" would secure children's access to their parents when unpredictable needs arose and extend benefits to low-wage workers, whose jobs and employers typically grant the fewest options for parents who need to make short-term changes in work scheduling.

The regulation of working time.
The regulation of working time is often ignored in discussions of family policy. But labor market policies that enable parents to reduce and reallocate employment hours for caregiving are an essential form of support for earner–caregiver families. Some feminist scholars argue that shortening (full-time) work hours might be the most promising tool for achieving a gender-egalitarian redistribution of domestic labor (see for example Mutari and Figart, 2001). Working time policies can limit the standard work week and grant rights to minimum numbers of paid days off, for both men and women. Policies

that raise the availability and quality of reduced-hour and part-time work are equally if not more important for earner–caregiver families. In the absence of public policies that prohibit discrimination in wages and other employment conditions, workers are likely to pay high economic and career penalties if they elect to reduce their working hours even temporarily to care for children. In practice, working-time regulations are distinct from family leave and childcare policies in that they typically apply to all workers, rather than being selectively designed for parents. Working time measures that increase parents' options for high-quality reduced-hour work would include the following provisions.

First, working time measures would limit weekly employment hours, setting normal full-time weekly hours in the range of 35 to 39 hours per week—as is standard in several European countries today. Limiting the standard full-time week to below 40 hours would grant parents more time for children on a daily basis. Limiting men's time in the labor market, in particular, would raise the likelihood of more gender-egalitarian time allocations between partners. Implementing reductions economy-wide would increase parents' opportunities to seek employment that is "full-time" but at less than 40 hours, across a broad range of firms, occupations, and industries. Overtime regulations would both offer compensation for those who worked longer hours and protect workers against compulsory overtime at excessively long hours.

Second, policies for paid time off would assure workers a substantial number of paid days off each year. Public measures would grant workers at least one month of paid time off annually; in practice, that means that the normal work year would be defined as 48 weeks of work per year. The right to paid time off of at least one month per year would alleviate some of the burden of arranging childcare coverage during summer school breaks, and would grant parents needed periods of uninterrupted family time.

Third, part-time workers would have the right to pay and benefit parity—in comparison to full-time workers performing similar work in the same enterprise. Such protections would be aimed at preventing discrimination against part-time workers. Improving the quality of part-time work would increase economic security for part-time workers and their families, and provide incentives for more men to participate in part-time employment.

Fourth, all workers would have the right to formally request a shift to reduced-hour or flexibly scheduled work, subject to employer agreement. Employers would have the right to refuse "on business grounds," but their refusals would be subject to government review.

To accommodate the needs of small employers, these general rights to work-hour changes would be restricted to workers in enterprises of a minimum size, but the minimum would be set relatively low.[12]

Early childhood education and care.
High-quality, publicly subsidized early childhood education and care[13] is a third critical component of policies to support earner–caregiver arrangements. Parents cannot fully engage in employment unless they can secure alternative arrangements for their children while they are at the workplace. Public financing of all of these care arrangements is essential both to reduce the burden on parents and to equalize out-of-pocket expenditures by families across different income levels. High-quality care is critical to supporting both children's healthy development and gender equality. In the absence of high-quality options, parents—particularly mothers—face more difficult tradeoffs in their employment decisions. And in the absence of stringent standards for professional training and compensation, child-care professionals—overwhelmingly women—command little status and low pay. To avoid penalizing children, and discouraging parents from using care, this care must be available for all children regardless of their parents' income and employment status. Care can and should be provided in a variety of settings—settings which could be fully public, or private but publicly subsidized. Such a system would have the following elements.

First, government would establish child-based entitlements to early care and education at the national level. Given entitlement status, the onus of assuring the availability of care would fall on government. With the provision of paid family leaves and greater flexibility in working hours, we assume that many parents would choose to be the primary caregivers during the first months after childbirth or adoption, and to arrange working schedules to provide substantial amounts of care beyond the first year. Some parents might choose to use alternative care within the first year, however, and all parents would be likely to use more non-parental care as their children approached school age and were more likely to benefit from social and early educational experiences. Unless local public schools provided extended-day or before- and after-school care, parents whose work schedules did not match their children's school schedules would also need care during these hours. These assumptions suggest the need for limited amounts of care for infants under the age of one, modest amounts of toddler care for children until the age of two-and-a-half or three, more extensive all-day care for three- and four-year-old preschool-aged children, and before- and after-school care after children enter school at age five or six.

Second, the government would finance early care and education, and before- and after-school care, at the national level. National financing is crucial for equalizing both access to care and the burden of out-of-pocket costs for families. To contain public costs, government could assume 80 percent of total costs (about the European mean), paid for through general revenues. The remaining 20 percent of costs would be covered through a uniform system of parental fees, adjusted to family income and exempting the poorest families entirely. Care could be financed directly, through public programs staffed by public caregivers and teachers, or through subsidies to private child-care, preschool, and after-school programs.

Third, care would be provided though multiple venues, which would give parents a broad choice of arrangements and caregivers. Parents' preferences for care arrangements vary with the ages of their children and with their own family and cultural beliefs. A fully developed system of care would allow parents to choose between small, family-like settings, center-based programs, and school-like educational programs. To maintain high standards of quality across diverse settings, government would set and actively monitor compliance with quality standards. As the European models suggest, national standards for service quality and program content can be combined with local, community- or program-level adaptations to provide consistent quality that is responsive to family preferences. The most crucial inputs into program quality are staff education and training, and commitment to caregiving work. These caregiver features are, in turn, dependent on wages, benefits, and working conditions that attract and retain high-quality workers. Along with protection of health, safety, and, where appropriate, program content, consistent and high standards for compensation and working conditions are essential.

Fourth, child-care, preschool and school schedules would be matched to parents' working hours. Schools and early childhood education and care services meet the needs of children and parents only when they fit the working hours of employed parents. For parents working a standard-hour week, the continuity of the day and the hours of operation for child-care centers and schools are crucial. For parents working non-standard hours and shifts, alternative forms of service delivery would be an essential component of a diverse delivery system. Children in these families would still benefit from participation in educationally oriented services provided during regular working hours.

V. FROM CONCEPTION TO PRACTICE: POLICY CONFIGURATIONS IN SIX EUROPEAN COUNTRIES

As we noted in the introduction to this essay, we have studied and compared work–family reconciliation models in detail in a number of rich countries, and across the fifty US states as well. We have assessed work–family policies in considerable detail in fourteen countries, including the US, Canada, and several European countries. In other research projects, we have studied elements of work–family reconciliation policies in nearly twenty-five countries. For this essay, we focus on six countries—Denmark, Finland, Norway, Sweden, Belgium and France—which have policies that serve as models for our policy blueprint.

Although our overarching aim here is to consider policy designs free of the constraints of existing practices, we consider the details of policy design in these six countries for two reasons. One is simply to demonstrate that policy elements that support our Real Utopia are in the realm of possibility. While our proposed policy package is not fully operational anywhere, elements of it are in place in all of these countries. The second is to illuminate the importance of the details of policy design. If "god is in the details" anywhere, it is surely in work–family policy design. A generous family leave policy could encourage or discourage gender equality in take-up, depending on its eligibility, benefit structure, and financing designs. A working-time policy that raised the quantity, but not the remuneration, of part-time work could inadvertently worsen working parents' financial outcomes. A child-care policy that made child care widely available but neglected its quality could have harmful effects on children and child-care workers alike. In this section, we synthesize the policies operating in these six countries, in order to sharpen our understanding of the realities of policy provision in these three crucial areas. In the accompanying exhibits, we include the US, with its limited provisions, as a seventh comparison case. We return to the case of the US in the subsequent section on variations in outcomes.

Before we turn to the details of policy designs, it is important to stress that the nature and generosity of work–family policies operating in these countries, and in all countries, may have been adopted for a variety of reasons. We focus on the potential for these policies to reconcile concerns about work, family and gender equality, but many were adopted to address other goals—such as raising fertility, alleviating labor shortages, attaining full employment, or preventing poverty. In many countries, the factors that motivate family policy

28   GENDER EQUALITY

formation lack political cohesion and shift over time. We do not imply that observing these policy designs in practice, at one point in time, reveals the social and political forces that led to their enactment.[14] We argue instead that these policies can have positive effects on gender equality and on work and family balance, regardless of the political motivation for their initial adoption.

Paid family leave

All six of these countries have national laws governing paid family leave. While the systems vary in a number of ways, they share several common features. First, in all of these countries, national maternity leave policies grant nearly all employed mothers several weeks or months of job security and wage replacement around the time of childbirth or adoption. Second, maternity leave benefits are supplemented by parental leaves that provide both mothers *and* fathers with periods of paid leave during children's preschool years. Third, leave policies promote gender equality by securing some rights and benefits for fathers and—with the arguable exception of France— by incorporating policy elements that encourage fathers to use the benefits to which they are entitled. Finally, in each of these countries, these leave schemes are financed through social insurance mechanisms, in order to distribute the costs across society, to minimize the burden on individual employers, and thus to lessen incentives for employers to discriminate against potential leave-takers.[15]

The Nordic countries—Norway, Sweden, Denmark and (to a lesser extent) Finland—provide generous paid leave benefits for mothers. Figure 1.2 synthesizes the program rules (reported in Appendix Table 1) into total weeks of full-time wage replacement available to mothers, assuming that mothers take all of the leave available to them through both maternity and parental leave. Family leave policies in these countries offer mothers the equivalent of about 30 to 42 weeks of leave with full pay, typically up to an earnings cap.[16] These countries achieve high levels of provision through various mechanisms. In Norway and Sweden, maternity and parental leave are blended into a single program that grants couples an allocation of about a year to be shared between them; wage replacement is high for the whole period, at between 80 and 100 percent. Finland and Denmark offer eighteen weeks of maternity pay (at about two-thirds pay, on average), followed by separate parental leave options that couples may allocate to the mother if they choose. In Denmark, collective agreements compel many employers to "top up" public benefits so that, in practice, most workers receive their full pay.

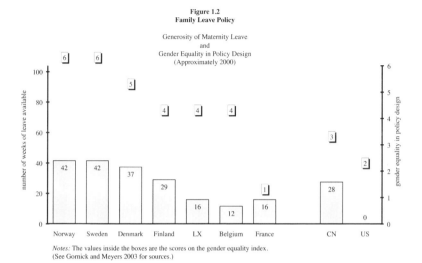

Figure 1.2
Family Leave Policy

Generosity of Maternity Leave and Gender Equality in Policy Design (Approximately 2000)

Notes: The values inside the boxes are the scores on the gender equality index.
(See Gornick and Meyers 2003 for sources.)

To contain costs, benefits are limited or capped for the highest-earning mothers. Finland, for example, reduces the replacement rate stringently as earnings rise. Norway and Sweden place caps on covered earnings, but the caps are set high—respectively, at about 1.9 to 2.2 times average earnings among mothers of working age, including both part-time and full-time workers. Earnings caps result in a progressive benefit structure and restrain program expenditures; when caps are set high, most mothers and their families are protected from substantial losses in economic security during leave periods.

More modest but still substantial public leave benefits are available to mothers in Belgium and France, which grant employed mothers in the range of 12 to 16 weeks of full-time pay. In these countries, maternity benefits are generally paid at high rates—80 to 100 percent of wages—and for about three to five months. These countries also set caps on maximum covered earnings; in France, for example, maternity pay is capped at about 1.2 times average mothers' earnings. (Mothers' total leave rights and benefits lag behind those granted in the Nordic countries largely because the parental leave options that they can draw on are more limited.)

In relation to parental leave, the Nordic countries provide especially generous rights and benefits. Most employed parents have the right to take relatively long periods of leave—from one to three years—and, through social insurance funds, they receive about two-thirds or more of their wages during most or all of their leave periods (again, subject to caps for high earners). Parental leave policies in the Nordic countries also afford parents substantial flexibility; parental choice is valued and codified in the law. Denmark and Sweden allow parents to take their allotted paid leaves in increments until the child is eight years old. Norway and Sweden allow parents to combine prorated leaves with part-time employment, and Finland and Norway permit parents to use a portion of their leave benefits to purchase private child care instead. Although parental leave periods are relatively long in Belgium and France as well—especially in France, which pays portions of a three-year leave—wage-replacement rates are much lower than in the Nordic countries. In these countries, parents may claim relatively modest, flat-rate benefits.

Policy development at the European level, meaning within the policy-making bodies of the European Union, has played a role in standardizing and expanding parental leave programs across these countries. In 1995, the EU enacted a Directive on Parental Leave and Leave for Family Reasons.[17] This directive required that member countries enact measures that provide men and women workers with at least three months of parental leave (paid or unpaid), as distinct from maternity leave, following the birth of a child until a given age of up to eight years. The directive also required that workers be protected against dismissal on the grounds of applying for or taking parental leave, and that they have the right to return to the same or a similar job.

Although none of the countries in our study have achieved gender equality in leave usage, several are taking steps to increase fathers' use of leave benefits. Two strategies appear particularly promising. First, high wage-replacement rates are the most straightforward instrument. Because men tend to have higher wages than women, in the absence of full wage replacement it often makes economic sense for couples to decide that the mother should withdraw from the labor market. Second, non-transferable rights can be created by granting fully individual rights to each parent for her/his own period of leave, or by reserving for each parent some portion of a family-based entitlement. (In other words, non-transferable rights disallow men from "giving" their leave allocation to their female partners). Both approaches create "use or lose" provisions that increase the incentives for fathers to make use of leave: leave time that is not taken by the father is lost to the family.

Our six model countries vary considerably in the extent to which they have actively incorporated these gender-egalitarian strategies. The strengths of gender-egalitarian policy design features are reported in Figure 1.2, in the small boxes, using a six-point scale. (See Appendix Table 2 for institutional details.) We assign policy systems one point on our "gender-equality scale" if they offer any paid paternity leave, two points if fathers have non-transferable leave rights (either "use or lose" portions of shareable leave or individual entitlements), and up to three additional points depending on wage replacement (three points if benefits are wage-related and at 80 percent or higher, two points if benefits are wage-related but at less than 80 percent, and one point if benefits are paid but only at a flat rate).

Three of the Nordic countries—Sweden, Norway, and Denmark—stand out on multiple fronts. Fathers are eligible for more benefits, and incentives were added during the 1990s to encourage them to take them up. In each of these countries, shareable family leaves are lengthened if fathers take some portion—two weeks in Denmark, four in Norway and Sweden. If these weeks are not taken by the father, they are lost to the family. Although modest in duration, these so-called "daddy quotas" send a signal that paternal leave-taking is valued and encouraged. After their introduction in Norway in 1993, fathers' take-up rose sharply (Ellingsaeter, 1999). Incentives for Norwegian and Swedish fathers to take leave are further strengthened by the high replacement rates and, for Danish fathers, by the fully individualized entitlement for the "childcare leave" that follows parental leave. Finland lags behind its Nordic counterparts with the absence of "daddy days," but grants fathers a comparatively generous eighteen days of paternity leave.[18] Belgium also incorporates elements that encourage men's leave-taking; the leave program offers some paid paternity leave (although less than a week) and some non-transferable longer-term paid leave. However, the low parental leave replacement rate is a counterbalancing disincentive to fathers' take-up. France's leave scheme (as of 2000) contained virtually no features designed to pull men into leave-taking.

Although financing mechanisms vary, all six of these countries finance these leave policies primarily through social insurance schemes. That means that benefits are funded by employee and employer contributions, often supplemented by general tax revenues. Typically, maternity leave is paid out of social insurance funds designated for sickness and/or medical payments, although in some cases, such as Belgium, it is paid out from funds that include other major social insurance programs. Parental leave, when paid, is usually financed out of the same funds as maternity benefits, although some countries finance parental leave entirely from general revenues.

A key lesson from these six countries is that none of them relies on individual families to finance leave, nor on mandating employers to provide wage replacement for their own employees. Where social insurance financing does depend heavily on firms' contributions, those contributions are independent of employees' usage rates. In all six countries, social insurance financing distributes the burden for employees and employers. The costs of caregiving are shared across employees' working years, among parents and non-parents, between leave-takers and non-leave-takers, and across enterprises as well. These financing mechanisms, especially where supplemented by substantial contributions from general tax revenues, reduce the risk for individual families and individual employers. They reduce employers' resistance and lessen incentives to discriminate against potential leave-takers.

The regulation of working time

All six of these European countries have implemented working time measures that limit work hours and increase the availability and quality of reduced-hour and part-time work. Again, the systems that shape working time vary across these countries, but they share at least three common features. First, working time measures limit weekly employment hours, setting normal working time in the range of 35 to 39 hours. Second, policies that grant paid days off assure parents at least four weeks each year of unbroken time with their families. Third, labor market measures aim to improve the quality of part-time work and to increase its availability.

In all six countries, working hours are shaped primarily through setting standards for *normal* weekly hours (above which overtime pay is usually required) as well as limits on *maximum* allowable hours (above which workers cannot be compelled to work). As of approximately 2000, normal full-time weekly hours are set at levels below 40 hours in all six countries—35 hours in France, and between 37 and 39 hours in the other five. (See Appendix Table 3 for details and Figure 1.3 for a summary.)

The incidence of very long hours—more than, say, 50 hours a week—is also limited in these countries, as each has enacted measures capping maximum weekly working time at 48 hours per week. As with parental leave, a degree of homogeneity across these countries, and throughout Europe, stems from the 1993 EU Directive on Working Time, which requires member-states to "take the measures necessary to ensure that, in keeping with the need to protect the safety and

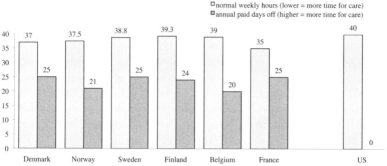

Figure 1.3
Working Time Regulations

Normal Weekly Hours (overtime threshold)
and
Annual Paid Days Off (minimum number of days)
(Approximately 2000)

Notes: Normal weekly hours are the shorter of statutory or collectively bargained standard. (See Gornick and Meyers 2003 for sources.)

health of workers . . . working time for each seven-day period, including overtime, does not exceed 48 hours." Countries are permitted to limit weekly hours "by means of laws, regulations or administrative provisions or by collective agreements or agreements between the two sides of industry." The directive stipulates that employers may not compel workers to work longer hours, nor subject them "to any detriment" for refusing longer hours.

In addition, these six countries have all adopted policies that provide extended periods of paid time off for workers. As with part-time work, the EU has influenced policy developments across Europe. The 1993 EU Directive on Working Time stipulated that employees be granted not less than four weeks of paid days off per year. All of the European countries, including these six, have codified at least that much paid time off in their laws, with about half requiring a fifth week; in some countries, collective agreements add even more time. Approximately five weeks of paid time off are now standard in Denmark, Finland, Sweden, and France, and about four weeks in Norway and Belgium. And changes continue to unfold; after 2000, collectively bargained rights to days off increased in three of these Nordic countries and in France. (See Appendix Table 4 for details on these measures, and Figure 1.3 for a summary).

A third set of working time measures complement those that influence work hours and days directly: policies that aim to raise the quality of part-time work and those that grant various rights to work part-time.

(See Appendix Table 5 for institutional details.) The primary vehicle for raising the quality of part-time work is the implementation of pay and benefit parity laws that protect part-time workers. The main strategy for increasing the availability of part-time work is the granting of some form of a right to work (or to request to work) part-time. These measures enable full-time workers who wish to reduce their hours the option to do so and, depending on the law, they create new opportunities for labor market entrants who might otherwise refrain from employment.

Policies aimed at improving part-time work are now widespread throughout Europe. A crucial force behind these measures is the 1997 EU Directive on Part-Time Work, whose official purpose was "to eliminate discrimination against part-time workers and to improve the quality of part-time work" (Europa, 2004). All six of these European countries have implemented the directive through some mix of legislation and collective agreements. The directive requires that member-states enact measures prohibiting employers from treating part-time workers less favorably than "comparable full-time workers," unless they demonstrate that this is objectively justifiable. The national measures address various combinations of pay equity, social security and occupational benefits, training and promotion opportunities, and bargaining rights.

The EU Part-Time Directive also urged, but did not require, member-states to eliminate obstacles limiting opportunities for part-time work, and instructed employers to "give consideration" to workers who request transfers between part-time and full-time work as their personal and family needs change (Europa, 2004). Long before the Part-Time Directive, Sweden had already set the gold standard on the right to part-time work. Since 1978 Swedish parents have had the right to work six hours a day (at prorated pay) until their children turn eight. In the aftermath of the directive, several European countries added new rights for workers, in most cases instituting rights to part-time or flexible schedules. In most cases employers have the right to refuse, but refusals are subject to review.[19]

Early childhood education and care

Like their paid leave and working time measures, early childhood education and care (ECEC) policies vary across these six countries, but provisions in all six of them share common features. First, publicly supported care serves a large proportion of infants and toddlers while parents are at the workplace; full-day preschool programs enroll nearly all children between about age three and the start of public school.

Second, government measures ensure that early childhood education and care is affordable. Third, government policies ensure high-quality services. And, fourth, early childhood education and care workers are well trained and well compensated.

Across our six comparison countries, two overarching systems are in place—and each provides nearly universal access to publicly supported care. The Nordic countries operate integrated "EduCare" systems, and Belgium and France have dual systems of early childcare and later preschool. (See Appendix Table 6 for details on institutional arrangements and service guarantees.)

The integrated systems in Denmark, Finland and Sweden provide the most extensive access to publicly supported care.[20] Public systems under the authority of national social welfare or educational authorities serve children from the end of parental leave periods until the start of primary school. Younger children are cared for in centers or supervised family child-minder arrangements; older children may spend all or part of their day in preschool programs. These systems are most notable for extending a nearly universal entitlement for care (with a modest parental co-payment) during the years before the start of primary school, and for the integration of care with early educational services—hence the dual focus of the term "educare." Parents have a right to a place in a public child-care setting, and the regular use of fully private care is rare. In Sweden, for example, since 1995 all children have had an entitlement to public or private (but publicly subsidized) child care from age one to the age of twelve. Child-care entitlements were initially linked to parents' employment status; they have recently been extended to children whose parents are unemployed, home on family leave, or otherwise out of the labor force. In Finland and Denmark, all children have a right to care regardless of their parents' employment status.

The Nordic countries provide higher levels of support for families. In these countries, with generous maternity and parental leave policies, children are generally cared for at home during the first months of life. Between one- and three-quarters of children in the one- to two-year age group are in publicly supported care. Among children in the three-to-five-year age group, three-quarters or more are in public care. In the last year before primary school, nearly all children are in public care (see Figure 1.4).

Outside the Nordic region, the systems in Belgium and France also stand out. Provision of early child care is moderate for younger children, as neither country provides child care as an entitlement before the start of public preschool. Spaces are available for some young children in systems under the supervision of social welfare authorities—public

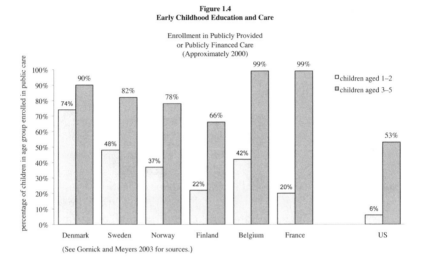

Figure 1.4
Early Childhood Education and Care

Enrollment in Publicly Provided or Publicly Financed Care (Approximately 2000)

(See Gornick and Meyers 2003 for sources.)

child-care centers or supervised child-minder arrangements—with income-adjusted parental fees. Space is limited, however, and may be targeted to families with special economic or social needs. Child-based entitlements for care commence with enrollment in preschool—the *ecole maternelle* in France and French-speaking Belgium, and *kleuterschool* in Flemish-speaking Belgium.

Overall, Belgium and France provide generous but less consistent support than the Nordic systems. Publicly supported care is available for only about 20 to 40 percent of the under-threes, and is more highly targeted on needy families. As a result, families rely more heavily on private care arrangements for younger children. On the other hand, by the age of two and a half or three, nearly every child in these countries is enrolled in a public preschool program.

Are these services affordable? These six countries have adopted various mechanisms for financing ECEC through the direct provision of public care, cost-sharing with parents through co-payments, and the use of alternative financing mechanisms such as demand-side subsidies and tax benefits. (See Appendix Table 7 for details of financing arrangements.)

In the countries providing the most affordable ECEC for families—the integrated systems of the Nordic countries—the primary mechanism is direct provision, funded by a combination of national and municipal taxes, and supplemented by parental co-payments. National tax revenues cover about one-quarter to one-third of the costs of

ECEC, and municipal governments contribute about one-half. Parent fees cover a capped share of the costs. The parental share varies between countries and with the type of care, averaging about 20 percent. Fees for individual families are calculated on a sliding scale, and often waived altogether for low-income families.

The high-provision, dual systems of care in France and Belgium also use direct provision as their primary financing mechanism. Care for younger children is financed through a combination of national, regional, and municipal funds and parental fees. Parent fees cover about 17 to 25 percent of the cost of care for children under age three (depending on care arrangements), with parental co-payments set on sliding fee scales at around 8 to 11 percent of family income. In both countries, employers also contribute a share of the costs. Care for children from about age three to the start of primary school is free to parents. Although public provisions are extensive for children beginning at age two and a half or three, parents do incur private child-care costs for younger children and for hours of care outside *ecole* and *kleuterschool*. In both countries, parents can deduct a portion of these out-of-pocket child-care expenses from income taxes.

Child-care availability and affordability are crucial for families, as is the quality of care. Quality of care is important for parents, whose ability to engage in market work depends on their trust in the care that their children are receiving while they are in the workplace. And quality of care is essential for the healthy development of children. Two key mechanisms employed by governments to assure quality are staffing structures and staff preparation; of these, staff preparation is arguably more important. Care providers who have higher levels of education, more extensive training in ECEC, and longer tenure in the field provide better-quality care for children. Compensation plays an important indirect role: higher salaries attract and retain better-qualified workers to ECEC settings. ECEC compensation is equally central to the achievement of gender equality in market opportunities and wages, because the child-care workforce is overwhelmingly female (see Appendix Table 8 for a summary of quality regulations and staff compensation levels).

The systems operating in these six countries all perform well with respect to the quality of care that they provide and in their levels of compensation for the ECEC workforce. The integrated "EduCare" systems in the Nordic countries set the highest educational requirements for workers in both child-care centers and preschool programs. All but Finland require bachelor-level university degrees of both child-care workers and preschool teachers; Finland requires a university degree for preschool teachers and a three-year vocational or polytechnic degree for child-care workers. In Sweden, 98 percent of child-care workers have specialized certification or university degrees.

In the dual and early-school-enrollment systems in France and Belgium, variation in staff preparation is more pronounced across ECEC settings. Workers in family child-care settings often have little formal training. Staff in child-care centers (who deal primarily with infants and toddlers younger than three) are typically required to complete one- or two-year post-secondary vocational programs. In contrast, teachers in preschool classrooms serving children from about age three until the start of school have the same levels of university training as teachers in the regular primary school system.

The high quality of ECEC staff is, not surprisingly, reflected in relatively high rates of compensation across these countries. To facilitate comparisons, we calculated the usual rate of pay for the equivalent of full-time ECEC workers in each country. Because usual wages vary across countries, we compared these annualized salaries to the average wage of all women workers in the same country. By this metric, the compensation for child-care providers in all six of these countries is impressive. Workers in the integrated Nordic systems earn very close to the national average for all women workers in these countries, and considerably more than the average in Denmark. Workers in the dual systems of Belgium and France are also well compensated—particularly teachers in the *ecole,* who earn substantially more than average women's wages in these countries.

VI. CONSIDERING THE OUTCOMES: WHAT DO WE KNOW?

As we have argued, working parents everywhere struggle to negotiate successful and equitable divisions of labor, and to manage competing demands from the home and the workplace. None of the industrialized countries have achieved full gender equality in divisions of labor, and none have fully resolved the time crunch for parents combining employment with the care of children. If the work–family reconciliation policies we describe above are effective, however, we would expect to see more favorable outcomes in those countries that have the highest and most gender-egalitarian provisions.

It is easy to observe and evaluate some dimensions of the outcomes of these policies. In the Nordic countries virtually all employed women have access to periods of leave with wage replacement, and couples can share as much as a full year of parenting leave at 80 percent or more of their regular wages. In these same countries a substantial share of all children aged one and two are in high-quality child-care settings, and nearly all children are in such care as they approach school age. In these countries, as in France and Belgium, care is either free or at very low cost for parents. Care in these settings is provided by professionals with high levels of education who earn wages that are comparable to or even higher than those of other workers—two of the key indicators of high-quality care.

Other outcomes of work–family reconciliation policies are more difficult to observe. We would like to know, for example, the effect of various gender-equalizing provisions on men's take-up of parenting leave, but comparable data across countries are exceedingly scarce. We do know that men's likelihood of taking leave lags behind women's everywhere in Europe, and the gender gap with respect to total amount of time taken is even larger. At the same time, although substantial gaps in leave usage persist even in the Nordic countries, fathers' use of leave in these countries is well above that of men in other European countries. De Henau (2006) reports, for example, that in Sweden, as of 2002, 78 percent of first-time fathers take some leave, compared to 90 percent of mothers. The more disappointing finding is that, while Swedish fathers account for nearly half of all leave-takers, they still take less than a fifth of the total leave days claimed by parents. (This is perhaps not surprising, given the short duration of the non-transferable leave that Swedish policy grants specifically to men.) Furthermore, the implementation of "use or lose" leave in Norway has been associated with a sharp increase in fathers' take-up, from less than 5 percent to over 70 percent following implementation (Ellingsæter, 1999; Leira, 1999). Leira (2000) concludes that the use-or-lose days—what she calls "fatherhood by gentle force"—have encouraged men to take substantial amounts of leave that they would otherwise have transferred to their partners. The introduction of so-called "daddy days" in Sweden has had less effect (Haas and Hwang, 1999), possibly because fathers' take-up was already relatively high (Leira, 1999).

Beyond evidence of coverage, benefits, and take-up, we would ideally like to know whether these policies move us closer to the Real Utopia of gender-egalitarian caregiving and employment. As a blueprint for the earner–caregiver society, we have argued that these policies have the potential to reduce three of the most difficult contemporary

Table 1.1. Key Outcomes

	gender equality		time at work			compatibility of work and family		
	mothers' earnings as a share of parents' earnings	fathers' hours in unpaid work as a share of parents' hours in unpaid work	annual hours: all workers	weekly hours, average: dual-earner couples	weekly hours, percent of couples working > 80 hours: dual-earner couples	fathers report wanting more time with family	mothers report wanting more time with family	total fertility rate
Denmark	38%	–	1504	–	–	80%	72%	1.8
Finland	37%	33%	1727	78	29%	–	–	1.7
Norway	33%	35%	1380	–	–	80%	74%	1.8
Sweden	34%	36%	1625	69	6%	83%	82%	1.6
Belgium	32%	–	1530	77	34%	–	–	1.7
France	32%	–	1500	76	32%	–	–	1.9
United States	28%	31%	1834	80	64%	95%	90%	2.0
Sources:	Gornick and Meyers, 2003	Gornick and Meyers, 2003	Mishel et al. 2000	Gornick and Meyers, 2003	Gornick and Meyers, 2003	Gornick and Meyers, 2003	Gornick and Meyers, 2003	UNDP 2005 2000-05

Notes: -- means "not available"

Total fertility rate: the number of children who would be born alive to each woman if she were to live to the end of her childbearing years and if, throughout her reproductive years, the age-specific rates for the specified year remained unchanged social problems: persistent gender inequalities in market and caregiving work, a growing time crunch for parents, and the stress of conflicting demands on parents' time and attention. Although it is difficult to observe these outcomes directly, or to establish a causal link between these outcomes and policy design, a number of indicators suggest that the countries with the most fully developed policies are making the most progress in resolving these problems.

We examine outcomes in the six countries from which we have drawn our policy designs, compared with those reported in the US, which provides one of the most dramatic comparisons in the group of OECD countries. The US is one of only five countries *in the world* that lack national maternity leave provisions. A weak national family leave law (the Family and Medical Leave Act of 1993) provides some parents with limited rights to periods of unpaid leave to take care of infants and other family members, but there is no national law requiring paid leave. The standard work week remains set at 40 hours—a level established more than six decades ago; and American working-time law is silent on maximum work hours, on equal treatment for part-time workers, on rights to part-time or flexible scheduling, and on the right to a minimum number of paid days off per year. The public child-care system in the US is among the least developed in the industrialized world, providing modest tax credits for middle-earning families and child-care subsidies for only an estimated 15 percent of eligible working poor families. In Table 1.1 we compare several indicators of each country's progress on each of the outcomes we have identified.[21]

Gender equality

While mothers (in heterosexual couples) are not commanding half of the earnings taken home by couples with children in any country, they are earning about a third of parental earnings in Norway, Sweden, Belgium and France—and as much as 37 to 38 percent in Denmark and Finland.[22] American mothers, who take home 28 percent of parental earnings, are somewhat more economically dependent on their (male) partners.

Although gender divisions in unpaid work are harder to measure and comparable data are scarce, some evidence is available from cross-national time-use data. In the three countries for which we have data—Finland, Norway, and Sweden—fathers assume a somewhat larger share of unpaid work.

Time for caregiving

Workers in these six countries log fewer hours at the workplace each year than do their counterparts in the largely unregulated American setting. Average annual hours worked in the Nordic countries, and in Belgium and France, range from 1,380 in Denmark to 1,727 in Finland; employed American workers average over 1,800 hours annually—among the longest work hours in the industrialized world.

Parents in dual-earner couples, in particular, work fewer hours for pay in these countries (at least, in the four for which we have data on weekly hours). In these families, while American couples with children spend, on average, 80 hours per week in employment, their counterparts in Finland, Belgium and France log hours in the range of 76 to 78. Swedish dual-earner couples with children work as few as 60 hours weekly—or the equivalent of a day and a half less than their American counterparts.

Perhaps more consequentially, the distribution of work hours is much narrower in these other countries. In the US, nearly two-thirds of couples jointly work for pay for more than 80 hours per week, compared to fewer than a third in these comparison countries.

Resolving work–family conflicts

The evidence also suggests that parents in these comparison countries experience strain related to time constraints, but at somewhat attenuated levels. Large shares of fathers and mothers in these six countries report that they want more time to spend with their families (72 to 83 percent), but at rates that are substantially lower than the 95 and 90 percent reported by American fathers and mothers, respectively.

What about fertility? In recent years, researchers, politicians, and journalists worldwide have paid much attention to the low and falling fertility rates seen in much of Europe, most notably in eastern and southern Europe. Low fertility raises several macro-level concerns; in some countries, future projections portend severe economic dislocations and enormous strains on the welfare state. Low fertility is also of concern at the micro-level, in a number of countries, because actual fertility lags behind preferred fertility. As Peter McDonald and other researchers have increasingly argued, fertility is falling (or has fallen) to crisis levels especially in those national settings where women experience, or perceive, the most hardship in combining parenting and employment. Faced with a stark choice between parenthood and (quality) employment, many women have only one child or forgo childbearing altogether. The key point here is that fertility rates in these six comparison countries—while all falling short of replacement level—are among the highest in Europe.

What do we make of these outcomes? Correlations between policies and outcomes cannot establish causation. Even the strongest correlation cannot rule out reverse causation (say, the possibility that high levels of female employment drive the adoption of gender-egalitarian policies) or the influence of other, unmeasured national characteristics (say, the possibility that cultural forces favoring gender equality explain both more egalitarian outcomes and the provision of supportive public policies). To establish causation we would need focused experimental designs or more sophisticated modeling approaches. And for many of the outcomes we hope to observe—such as gender symmetry in both market and caregiving work—we would also need data over a much longer period of time. Our interpretation of the outcomes in Table 1 is therefore an optimistic but cautious one: these six countries appear to be leaders not only in the provision of gender-egalitarian work–family policies, but also in progress toward the key elements of our Real Utopia: gender equality, parental time for caregiving, and reduction of work–family conflicts.

VII. UNWANTED CONSEQUENCES AND INEVITABLE TRADE-OFFS: REFLECTIONS AND CLARIFICATIONS

Public policies always have complex consequences. Many policy effects are desired, expected, and achieved, while others may be unintended, unwanted, and unanticipated. Furthermore, policy designs often involve explicit tradeoffs. Elements expected to have advantageous consequences may be knowingly bundled with features that impose costs. In this closing section, we consider three concerns linked to our policy blueprint or to the Real Utopia itself. Each involves the prospect of unwanted consequences or the possibility that desired effects may be coupled with unwanted results.

First, we raise the question: if we successfully implement policies that reduce working time across a society as a whole, will that lead to a substantial loss of income, and concomitantly a reduction in the standard of living? Second, if we implement policies that reshape the caring practices of parents, and the allocation of time between women and men, does that require that we limit the "choices" available to individual women and men and their families—and, if so, is that justifiable? Third, if we implement policies that enable parents to work at reduced hours, part-time, or intermittently, and women disproportionately take up these options, will we cement existing gender differentials into place or, even worse, create new forms of gender inequality?

The prospect of income losses

First, we consider the possibility that intentional working-time reductions would lower standards of living. Critics of European models of social protection, which often include limits on work hours, frequently observe that (all else equal) shorter work hours imply less aggregate output, and thus lower GDP per capita. That is, shorter average work hours lower standards of living. These critics often point to the US as the exemplar of an alternative model—a minimally regulated, highly productive economy. As the argument goes, Americans' long work hours may require some sacrifices by workers and their families, but, overall, their work hours enable them to enjoy a higher standard of living.

Is this a valid argument? The US does indeed rank near the top of the OECD countries in per capita income. In 2000, GDP per capita in the US—nearly US$36,000—was well higher than in any of our six comparison countries, where per capita GDP ranged from US$27,000 to $32,000.[23] And indeed, vis-à-vis the OECD as a whole, nearly half of the income advantage in the US is due to Americans' relatively long work hours. As one group of scholars note, "an important portion of the apparently higher standard of living in the US comes not from working more efficiently than other comparable economies, but simply from working longer" (Mishel et al., 2005: 428–29).

Does that mean that, on average, Americans, with their longer hours, enjoy a relatively higher standard of living? Some scholars argue—we think persuasively—that it is misleading to measure "standard of living" solely in monetary terms, without taking into account time investments. As Lars Osberg, a Canadian economist, has argued, "'Quality of life' or 'economic well-being' may be hard to define precisely, but most would agree that they depend on both an individual's income level and the discretionary time they have in which to enjoy it" (Osberg, 2005: 27).

So, American workers, on average, do take home high incomes compared to workers elsewhere; but for many American workers and their families, that economic payoff is compromised by the family time-poverty that enables it. It is also the case that Americans work such long hours that they may be on the diminishing-returns portion of the productivity curve. While the US is a leader in GDP per worker, it is ranked eighth among the OECD countries in GDP per worker-hour. And, in fact, per-hour output in the US is only average, relative to these six comparison countries with shorter work hours. It may be that American workers could shift some hours from work to family and see a rise in hourly output.

The question of "choice"

Second, we ask: given that several elements of this policy package are intended to influence the caring practices of parents, does that require that we limit the "choices" available to individual women and men, and their families—and, if so, are these restrictions justifiable?

The policies in our blueprint are designed specifically to advance two goals. The first is to give parents realistic options for combining employment and caregiving, and the second is to encourage gender equality in engagements in work and care. Promoting gender equality requires the building in of policy design elements that are intended to reshape parents' caring practices and employment behavior. That raises two questions: Do these behavior-shaping features limit or restrict parents' options? And, if so, are these restrictions justifiable?

Does this policy package, in fact, limit parents' "choices"? We can imagine alternative approaches that, at least in the short term, give parents more freedom to use government resources to support their preferred employment and caregiving arrangements. Couples might be given twelve months of shareable leave, for example, instead of separate, non-transferable rights to six months each. Rather than financing and regulating early childhood education and care programs, government could give parents cash subsidies with which to purchase private care. The entire package of support might even be "cashed out" and provided to parents as an unrestricted benefit that they could use as they wished—to replace (mothers') wages, to purchase child care, or even to save for future expenses.

We certainly agree that it is important to consider individual preferences and choices when designing policies that affect the intimate sphere of family life, especially in societies that are increasingly diverse and multicultural. While we recognize that these policies do not grant parents unrestricted options, we would argue that—on balance—the policies that we describe actually give parents considerable flexibility and room for individual choice. And they grant many parents—especially those with limited resources—"choices" that, in practice, they would not otherwise have.

Although the authorizing legislation and financing of these provisions is primarily national in the European countries, or even supranational in the case of EU Directives, program delivery is flexible enough to allow individuals and communities to tailor them to their own preferences. In the case of family leave, for example, parents in several of the Nordic countries have a nationally established and financed entitlement to a set period of leave. They have enormous flexibility, however, in scheduling their use of that leave. Parents may elect to use all their benefits within the first months after childbirth, or they may stretch their leave out over a period of several years, combining part-time employment with part-time leave. In some countries, such as Finland, they may even elect to take their benefits in the form of either leave or subsidized child care. Choice is protected in early childhood education and care as well, through the local design and delivery of program services. The educare systems in the Nordic countries, for example, set overarching objectives at the national level but tailor specific program designs at the community level.

We would also argue that, given existing economic and gender inequalities, these work–family benefits may offer many parents more realistic "choices" than less restricting forms of assistance. Parents may want to allocate substantial time to the care of their infant children but, without explicit rights to take job-protected leaves or reduce working hours, they are often unable to do so without losing their jobs or sacrificing pay and benefits. Mothers and fathers may want to share leave entitlements equally but, in the absence of high wage replacements and individual leave rights, may be unable to forfeit the income and career advancement of the higher earner, most often the father. Parents may want to enroll their children in high-quality developmentally enhancing care but, in the absence of stringent public regulation and oversight of quality, may be unable to find and purchase such care even with substantial financial resources. These and other limits on parental "choice" are not easily alleviated with other forms of assistance, such as unrestricted cash transfers.

Yet it is undeniable that some of the policy features designed to shift gender divisions of labor do limit parents' options. In perhaps the most dramatic example, allowing parents to fully transfer their leave rights and benefits to one another gives some families options that individual non-transferable rights do not. Is disallowing families from taking up those options justifiable? While we recognize that this policy design creates a very real tradeoff—in a sense, between some forms of "choice" and the promotion of gender equality—we argue that it is justifiable, especially when a longer-term view is taken. Over time, these restrictions may be even more important as a means of reducing gender inequalities, by creating incentives for both mothers and fathers to engage more fully in caregiving and waged labor. The full realization of an earner–caregiver society will require a transformation in gendered norms about both caregiving and employment. To fully transform norms about women's place in the public spheres of employment and civic life, mothers need the right and sufficient support to engage on equal terms with men in these spheres. To fully transform norms about the role of men in the private sphere of caregiving, fathers need rights and incentives to shift a greater portion of their time and labor from the market to the home. Gender-egalitarian work–family reconciliation policies—such as individual leave rights, opportunities for reduced-hour employment, and child-care entitlements—advance these rights, opportunities and incentives, thereby having the potential to advance both individual well-being and more far-reaching transformations in social and gender norms.

New forms of gender inequality

Finally, we ask: by enacting this policy package, do we run the risk of cementing gender differentials into place or, even more worrisome, catalyzing new forms of gender inequality? The strengthening of reduced-hour work and extension of family leave raise thorny questions about gender equality. If shorter full-time hours, part-time work, and family leave continue to be taken up disproportionately by women, extending these options may free up more parental caregiving time but deepen gender divisions of labor in both paid and unpaid work.

With respect to shorter-hour work and family leave, whether men will eventually take advantage of these options as often as women do is an open question. The question of whether women and men have fundamental and enduring preferences about work and care remains highly contested. British sociologist Catherine Hakim, for example (Hakim, 1997), has long argued that, while many women are career-oriented, substantial numbers are not, and that it is their preferences, not constraints or institutional factors, that explain their relatively low employment hours compared to men's, and their greater likelihood of taking leaves. In our view, it is more accurate to conclude that women's intrinsic preferences cannot be identified until gendered expectations and institutional constraints erode (Gornick and Meyers, 2003). The long-term prospect for men's take-up of these arrangements is nearly impossible to predict.

Policies aimed at raising the quality and availability of part-time work are complex, and their long-term impact on divisions of labor are, in fact, unknown. Part of the logic of improving the quality of part-time work is indeed to draw more men into it. And the evidence shows that men's engagement in part-time work increased in the 1990s in a number of European countries, including Belgium and France (European Foundation, 2004). Recent survey results indicate that a substantial majority of these male part-time workers, like their female counterparts, are voluntarily working part-time (meaning that they sought part-time hours), which suggests that new options for reduced-hour work may be a factor underlying men's increased engagement in part-time work.

Nevertheless, part-time work remains overwhelmingly feminized in most industrialized countries. A countervailing view argues that, even if part-time work remains feminized, improving its quality still has some gender-equalizing potential, in that establishing viable part-time work options draws some women into paid work who would otherwise refrain from employment altogether. It is possible that improving the availability of quality part-time work may, in some contexts, have the effect of reducing gender gaps in employment rates while increasing gender differentials in hours worked among the employed. In the end this is an empirical question, and one that calls for continuing study.

From a gender-equality perspective, it seems likely that reducing full-time weekly hours is the more promising strategy than raising the quality and availability of shorter-hour work. Mutari and Figart make this argument persuasively:

> The alternative to policies that accommodate work hours to the gendered division of labor are policies that change the male model of full-time employment. Reductions in the standard work week are a long-term solution for achieving gender equity in the labor market and the redistribution of domestic labor . . . [A] shorter work week can enable both men and women to participate in the labor market on an equal basis (Mutari and Figart, 2001: 40–1).

In fact, this view—that shortening the full-time week is a gender parity strategy—seems to be gaining ground in a number of European countries. Fagnani and Letablier observe that in France, where part-time work has always been viewed with skepticism, the French 35-hour law "had the [explicit] objective . . . of improving equality between men and women" (Fagnani and Letablier, 2004: 553). The effects of reducing normal full-time hours on gendered distributions ought to be continually monitored wherever policies with this goal are implemented.

Extending paid family leave raises parallel concerns about possibly worsening gender inequalities. Here some lessons are clear. As we have argued in this essay, family leave policies may be generous, or gender-egalitarian in design, or both. These are distinct dimensions, and hopes for increased engagement in leave-taking by men rest, to a substantial degree, on the continued incorporation of particular design elements—most notably, high wage-replacement rates, high earnings caps, and individual, non-transferable entitlements for men.

Concerns that work–family policies might in fact worsen gender gaps in employment extend to the demand side of the labor market. Some of the Nordic countries report relatively high levels of occupational segregation—a finding that has long been attributed to employers' resistance to hiring or promoting women into certain positions. Although social insurance financing can lessen the costs of leave-taking for employers, they must still manage workers' absences. Increasingly, critics of European policy models argue that generous work–family policies, in the end, both lower the "glass ceiling" for women and make it more impenetrable. According to these critics, while the absence of work–family supports may create strains for some women workers, women in settings with meager work–family provisions are more likely to reach senior positions. In economic terms, employers in policy-rich countries statistically discriminate against women, believing that they are more likely to engage in various forms of employment cutbacks than are their male counterparts—even if women and men are equally entitled. In settings with few policies operating, the incentive to statistically discriminate is much less, because women are, in effect, forced to behave like men. While there is some empirical evidence in support of these conclusions, the case has by no means been closed. What is clear is that constraints that women face, originating from the demand-side of the labor market, will be lessened if large numbers of men join them in taking up various family-oriented employment options. Whether men will do so depends on the incentives built into policy designs, and on a host of factors not yet clearly identified.

In the end, implementing the policy blueprint that we have laid out involves a gamble, and a fairly high-stakes one. If, in the long term, large numbers of women avail themselves of the options for shorter employment hours and periodic leaves while most men forgo them, then gendered divisions of labor will indeed persist, or even deepen. Clearly, we cannot predict the future, so we ask: why not implement this blueprint and see what happens? If these policies are implemented and, years later, parents' caregiving practices and gendered divisions of labor remain largely unaltered, then we will have to return to the drawing board.

NOTES

1 There are many terms in circulation that are intended to encompass these policies—including "family-friendly policies," "woman-friendly policies," and "work–life policies." We prefer the term "work–family reconciliation policies" as it is both precise and inclusive. Thus, we use that term here and in our other work, often shortened to "work–family policies."

2 There is no universally agreed-upon group of "industrialized" or "developed" countries, although these terms are widely used to refer to the highest-income countries in the world, generally captured by GDP per capita. The Organization for Economic Cooperation and Development (OECD)—an organization of countries with "democratic governments and market economies"—was founded in 1961 by eighteen European countries as well as Canada and the US. Throughout this essay, we concentrate our analyses and policy recommendations on these approximately twenty countries, and we refer to them interchangeably as the "rich," "high-income," "industrialized," or "OECD" countries. In later years, the OECD added ten more countries, including Australia, New Zealand, Japan, Korea, Mexico, and Eastern European countries. While a number of these have employment patterns and policy configurations that resemble those in the original twenty, some remain somewhat distinct. So, when we refer to "the OECD countries," we mean, for the most part, the original founding group of twenty.

3 In both the US and some southern European countries, other family members provide unpaid child-care labor, particularly for young children. Although many observers suggest that this female-dominated "kith and kin" care is a viable alternative to parental or substitute care, it is becoming less feasible with increases in women's employment rates.

4 In the European literature on the earner–caregiver society, and the associated policy packages, substitute child care often receives less attention than measures freeing up parents' time. However, it is clear that for many European feminists and welfare state scholars the state's commitment to providing or financing quality child care is taken as a given. For example, Anne Lise Ellingsaeter, writing about the "Norwegian worker–caregiver model," describes

the core policy package, which includes gender-egalitarian family leave and the right to reduced-hour work. To that, she adds: "The other main policy measure is access to high-quality public childcare. Public day care plays an important part in the everyday life of parents" (Ellingsaeter, 1999: 44).

5   The earner–caregiver model has attracted sustained attention in Europe in recent years, especially among feminist welfare state scholars (including Ruth Lister and Jane Lewis in the United Kingdom, Birgit Pfau-Effinger in Germany, Anne Lise Ellingsæter in Norway, and Diane Sainsbury in Sweden) and, to a lesser extent, in the US (see, for example, Nancy Fraser's (1994) call for men to become "like women are now"). American scholars have addressed a number of related concerns. There are large and excellent literatures on the "costs of motherhood" (Crittenden, 2001; England and Folbre, 1999a, 1999b; Waldfogel, 1998); on the determinants of gender differences in unpaid work in the home (Brines, 1994; Greenstein, 2000; Presser, 1994); and on "gendered time" (Mutari and Figart, 2001). There is also a growing literature on factors that strengthen fathers' engagement with child care–giving (see Marsiglio, 2000 for a review). Nevertheless, American scholars have not on the whole granted the earner–caregiver model the centrality in social theory or in policy analysis that European feminists have.

6   In economic language, when others can reap the benefits without paying, the public good is non-excludable; when one person's enjoyment does not diminish another's, it is characterized by non-rivalness.

7   Several countries also have leave provisions that support and remunerate time spent caring for other family members—including, for example, disabled and elderly adults—but we focus here on child-related provisions.

8   A large body of research focuses on the impact of leave on women's employment. The evidence clearly indicates that access to relatively short-term leaves has the potential to reduce labor market inequalities between men and women by facilitating continuous maternal employment, reducing women's turnover, and minimizing wage penalties associated with motherhood (Glass and Riley, 1998; Hofferth, 1996; Joesch, 1997; OECD, 2001; Smith et al., 2001). It is important to clarify, however, that while shorter-term leaves strengthen women's ties to the labor market, the effects of longer leaves, such as the two- or three-year leaves available in some European countries, are much less advantageous with respect to gender equality. Long-term leaves, paid or unpaid, are more problematic for two related reasons: they may erode human capital and, even more than shorter-term leaves, they are overwhelmingly taken up by women. OECD (2001) reviewed the small literature on these two-to-three-year leaves. They concluded that "schemes to pay parents to look after their own children at home . . . may encourage labor market detachment if they continue over a long period of time." (2001: 146) It is not yet clear at what duration leaves switch from being advantageous to

disadvantageous to women's labor market attachment; some researchers place the turn-around point at somewhere between six months and one year.

At the same time, while leave duration is a key variable, other aspects of family leave policy design, such as the extent to which employers bear the brunt of the financing, may ultimately matter more. If employers are unduly burdened, reductions in demand for female labor may set in with relatively shorter leaves.

9   The question is often raised: what about single parents, meaning parents whose children have only one caregiver? Should single parents be entitled to one "share" (six months) or two "shares" (twelve months)? There is a case to be made for either result. One share would equalize, across family types, any employment penalties associated with leave-taking. Single mothers would likely claim the same amount of leave as all other parents. Two shares would equalize the total amount of parental care that young children are likely to receive (approximately one year), regardless of their family structure. We see merit in both arguments and propose a compromise: single parents would be entitled to nine months of fully paid leave.

10   Many countries' leave provisions are already entirely non-transferable. The United States' Family and Medical Leave Act, for example, grants twelve weeks of leave to new parents; parents cannot transfer any or all of their entitlement to their children's other parent.

11   A reasonable earnings cap might be set at approximately twice the level of average annual earnings. To further ensure progressivity, a portion of high-income recipients' benefits could be taxed.

12   The new laws in Europe that codify rights to work part-time or flexible schedules have set minimum enterprise sizes at about ten or fifteen workers.

13   The term "early childhood education and care" is often used to emphasize its dual role as substitute care for parents and education for children. For convenience we sometimes shorthand this as "child care" in this essay, but we do not thereby mean to imply a different or less educationally enriching form of care.

14   Key facets of work–family policy offerings in these six countries, as of approximately 2000, are synthesized in Figures 1.2, 1.3, and 1.4. Institutional details underlying these synthetic results are presented in eight Appendix tables, and in more detail in Gornick and Meyers (2003).

15   Although we do not discuss them in this essay, due to space limitations, each of these countries also provides various kinds of "leave for family reasons." These leaves grant mothers and fathers time off throughout their children's lives to attend to short-term and unexpected needs. See Gornick and Meyers (2003) for details.

16   Figure 1.2 includes only the *earnings-related components* of family leave programs (and assumes earnings below the cap). Some of these countries supplement the benefits captured in Figure 1.2 with additional periods of leave paid at a low flat-rate—most substantially in Finland and France. We

exclude these low-paid benefits here because, in some cases (such as Finland) the benefits are not conditioned on employment, so characterizing them as wage replacement is not fully accurate. In addition, the program in France is payable only for second and subsequent children. Furthermore, take-up is much lower than in the earnings-related programs, so including them distorts the level of provision upward. Figure 1.2 also excludes the US's Temporary Disability Insurance programs because they are available in only five states.

Mothers in Finland may also collect a low flat-rate benefit (a "home care" benefit) for about two years following the end of maternity and parental leave, i.e. until the child's third birthday. The benefit is allowed only if the child is not in public child care. Parents may also choose to use that payment to purchase care from a private child-care provider. See Appendix Table 1.

17 EU Directives are binding for member countries, and Norway implements them voluntarily.

18 In Figure 1.2, we credited Finland with having a "use or lose" component. Although it is not part of parental leave (where the term is generally used), the eighteen-day paternity benefit is, in effect, "use or lose," since fathers cannot transfer those days to their partners. And its duration approaches that of the "use or lose" quotas in Norway and Sweden.

19 Three European countries that are not among our six—Germany, the Netherlands and the United Kingdom—have recently enacted laws providing some form of a right to work part-time or flexible hours. For an evaluation of their implementation and outcomes so far, see Hegewisch (2005).

20 Although Norway also provides extensive public ECEC, the costs of this care fall much more heavily on parents (due to high co-payments), and supply shortages have contributed to the growth of a "black market" in private, unregulated care arrangements.

21 See Gornick and Meyers (2003) for details on the indicators reported in Table 1.1, except annual hours and fertility. Annual hours worked are taken from Mishel et al. (2005), and total fertility rates (TFR) from UNDP (2005). The outcomes in this table pertain to the late 1990s and/or approximately 2000. An exception is the TFRs, which pertain to the period 2000–2005.

22 Mothers are earning a larger share of parental earnings in these countries, largely because the ratio of mothers' to fathers' employment rates— and of hours worked among the employed—are high in cross-national perspective. While greater wage compression may narrow the gender gap in hourly wages in these countries—relative to the US, for example—variation in wage compression is not the dominant explanation for these findings. See Gornick and Meyers (2003).

23 This comparison is adjusted for purchasing power parity. Note that GDP per capita rankings shift annually. In 2005, Norway's PPP-adjusted GDP per capita was slightly higher than that of the US.

REFERENCES

Anderson, Patricia M., and Philip Levine, 1999, "Childcare and Mother's Employment Decisions," Working Paper No. W7058, Cambridge, MA: National Bureau of Economic Research.

Bianchi, Suzanne M., 2000, "Maternal Employment and Time With Children: Dramatic Change Or Surprising Continuity?" *Demography* 37 (4): 401–14.

Blank, Rebecca, and Richard B. Freeman, 1994, "Evaluating the Connection Between Social Protection and Economic Flexibility," in Rebecca Blank, ed., *Social Protection and Economic Flexibility: Is There a Trade-Off?*, Chicago: University of Chicago Press.

Brines, Julie, 1994, "Economic Dependency, Gender, and the Division of Labor at Home," *AJS* 100 (3): 652–88.

Budig, Michelle J., and Paula England, 2001, "The Wage Penalty for Motherhood," *American Sociological Review* 66: 204–25.

Crompton, Rosemary, 1999, "Discussion and Conclusions," in Rosemary Crompton, ed., *Restructuring Gender Relations and Employment: The Decline of the Male Breadwinner*, Oxford: Oxford University Press.

De Henau, Jérôme, 2006, "Gender Role Attitudes, Work Decisions and Social Policies in Europe: A Series of Empirical Essays," unpublished doctoral dissertation, Universite Libre De Bruxelles, Faculté Des Sciences Sociales, Politiques Et Economiques/Solvay Business School.

Ellingsaeter, Anne Lise, 1999, "Dual Breadwinners Between State and Market," in Crompton, ed., *Restructuring Gender Relations and Employment*.

England, Paula, Michelle J. Budig, and Nancy Folbre, 2002, "Wages of Virtue: The Relative Pay of Care Work," *Social Problems* 49: 455–73.

England, Paula, and Nancy Folbre, 1999a, "Who Should Pay for the Kids?" *Annals of the American Academy of Political And Social Science* 563 (May): 194–207.

———1999b, "The Cost of Caring," *Annals of the American Academy of Political and Social Science* 561 (January): 39–51.

Europa, 2004, "The Part-Time Work Directive," online: http://europa.eu.int/scadplus/leg/en/cha/c10416.htm (accessed January 19, 2005).

European Foundation for the Improvement of Living and Working Conditions, 2004, "Part-Time Work in Europe," online: http://www.eurofound.eu.int/working/reports/ES0403TR01/ES0403TR01.pdf (accessed December 14, 2004).

Fagnani, Jeanne, and Marie-Thérèse Letablier, 2004, "Work and Family Life Balance: The Impact of the 35-Hour Laws in France," *Work, Employment, and Society* 10 (3): 551–72.

Folbre, Nancy, 1994, "Children as Public Goods," *American Economic Review* 84 (2): 86–90.

Förster, Michael and Marco Mira d'Ercole, 2005, *Income Distribution and Poverty in OECD Countries in the Second Half of the 1990s*, OECD Social Employment and Migration Working Papers, no. 22, Paris.

Fraser, Nancy, 1994, "After the Family Wage: Gender Equity and the Welfare State," *Political Theory* 22 (4): 591–618.

Glass, Jennifer, and Lisa Riley, 1998, "Family Responsive Policies and Employee Retention Following Childbirth," *Social Forces* 76 (4): 1,401–35.

Gornick, Janet C., 2006, "Social Expenditures on Children and the Elderly, 1980–1995: Shifting Allocations, Changing Needs," in Anne H. Gauthier, Cyrus Chu and Shripad Tuljapurkar, eds, *The Allocation of Private and Public Resources Across Generations*, New York: Springer Publishing Company.

Gornick, Janet C., and Marcia K. Meyers, 2003, *Families That Work: Policies for Reconciling Parenthood and Employment*, New York: Russell Sage Foundation.

———2004, "Welfare Regimes in Relation to Paid Work and Care," in Janet Zollinger Giele and Elke Holst, eds, *Changing Life Patterns in Western Industrial Societies*, Netherlands: Elsevier Science Press.

———2005, "Supporting a Dual-Earner/Dual-Carer Society," in Jody Heymann and Christopher Beem, eds, *Unfinished Work: Building Equality and Democracy in an Era of Working Families*, New York: New Press.

Greenstein, Theodore N., 2000, "Economic Dependence, Gender, and the Division of Labour in the Home: A Replication and Extension," *Journal of Marriage and the Family* 62 (2): 322–35.

Hakim, Catherine, 1997, "Sociological Perspectives on Part-Time Work," in Hans-Peter Blossfeld and Catherine Hakim, eds, *Between Equalization and Marginalization: Women Working Part-Time in Europe and the U.S. of America*, Oxford: Oxford University Press.

Heckman, James J., and Lance Lochner, 2000, "Rethinking Education and Training Policy: Understanding the Sources of Skill Formation in a Modern Economy," in Sheldon Danziger and Jane Waldfogel, eds, *Securing the Future: Investing in Children From Birth to College*, New York: Russell Sage Foundation.

Hegewisch, Ariane, 2005, "Employers and European Flexible Working Rights: When the Floodgates Were Opened," WorkLife Law, UC Hastings College of The Law, Issue Brief, Fall.

Hofferth, Sandra L., 1996, "Effects of Public and Private Policies on Working After Childbirth," *Work and Occupations* 23: 378–404.

Joesch, Jutta M., 1997, "Paid Leave and the Timing of Women's Employment Before and After Birth," *Journal of Marriage and the Family* 58: 1,008–21.

Knijn, Trudie, and Monique Kremer, 1997, "Gender and the Caring Dimension of Welfare States: Towards Inclusive Citizenship," *Social Politics* 4 (3): 328–62.

Leira, Arnlaug, 1999, "Cash for Childcare and Daddy Leave," in Peter Moss and Fred Deven, eds, *Parental Leave: Progress or Pitfall*, The Hague/Brussels: NIDI/CBGS Publications.

———2000, "Combining Work and Family: Nordic Policy Reforms in the 1990s," in Thomas P. Boje and Arnlaug Leira, eds, *Gender, Welfare State and the Market: Towards a New Division of Labor*, New York: Routledge.

Lindert, Peter, 2004, *Growing Public: Social Spending and Economic Growth since the Eighteenth Century, Volume I: The Story*, New York: Cambridge University Press.

Marsiglio, William, Paul Amato, Randal D. Day, and Michael E. Lamb, 2000, "Scholarship on Fatherhood in the 1990s and Beyond," *Journal of Marriage and Family* 62: 1,173–91.

Meyers, Marcia K., and Janet C. Gornick, 2005, "Policies for Reconciling Parenthood and Employment: Drawing Lessons from Europe," *Challenge: A Magazine of Economic Affairs*, September–October: 39–61.

Mishel, Lawrence, Jared Bernstein, and Sylvia Allegretto, 2005, *The State of Working America: 2004–2005*, Washington, D.C.: Economic Policy Institute.

Mutari, Ellen, and Deborah M. Figart, 2001, "Europe at a Crossroads: Harmonization, Liberalization, and the Gender of Work Time," *Social Politics* 8 (1): 36–64.

National Research Council and Institute of Medicine, 2003, "Working Families and Growing Kids: Caring for Children and Adolescents," Committee on Family and Work Policies, in Eugene Smolensky and Jennifer A. Gootman, eds, *Board on Children, Youth, and Families, Division of Behavioral and Social Sciences and Education*, Washington, DC: National Academies Press.

Nickell, Stephen, 1997, "Unemployment and Labor Market Rigidities: Europe versus North America," *Journal of Economic Perspectives* 11 (3): 55–74.

OECD, 2001, "Balancing Work and Family Life: Helping Parents Into Paid Employment," *Employment Outlook*: 129–66.

Osberg, Lars, 2005, "How Much Does Employment Matter for Inequality in Canada and Elsewhere?" unpublished manuscript, Dalhousie University.

Presser, Harriet B., 1994, "Employment Schedules Among Dual-Earner Spouses and the Division of Household Labor by Gender," *American Sociological Review* 59 (June): 348–64.

Smith, Kristen, Barbara Downs, and Martin O' Connell, 2001, "Maternity Leave and Employment Patterns: 1961–1995," *Household Economic Studies*, Washington, DC: Census Bureau: 70–9.

United Nations, 2005, "Human Development Reports: Basic Indicators for Other UN Member Countries—Total Fertility Rate," online: http://hdr.undp.org/statistics/data/indicators.cfm?x=291&y=1&z=1 (accessed February 23, 2006).

Waldfogel, Jane, 1998, "Understanding the 'Family Gap' in Pay for Women with Children," *Journal of Economic Perspective* 12 (1): 137–56.

Appendix Table 1
Family Leave: Maternity and Parental Leave Provisions
(Approximately 2000)

	Maternity Leave Benefits (paid)	Parental Leave Benefits (paid and unpaid)
DK	18 weeks. 100 percent of wages up to flat-rate ceiling of DKK2,758 (US$321) per week, equal in practice to about 60 percent prior wages. Owing to collective agreements, many employers "top up" so 80 percent of parents receive 100 percent wage replacement.	Paid leave: Parents may share 10 weeks of parental leave. Benefit level same as maternity leave. Extended to 12 weeks if father takes 2 weeks. As with maternity, 80 percent receive full wage.
FI	18 weeks (105 days). Benefit based on graduated replacement rate: approximately 70 percent at low income, 40 percent at medium income, 25 percent at high income (equal, on average, to approximately 66 percent).	Following parental leave, each parent entitled to 26 weeks of additional child-care leave (13 weeks if after first birthday). Benefit level is 60 percent of parental leave benefit level; sometimes supplemented by local authorities. Available until child's ninth birthday. Paid leave: Parents may share 26 weeks (158 days) of parental leave. Benefit level is 66 percent of earnings, flat-rate if not employed. Following parental leave, family entitled to 108 weeks home-care leave, on the condition that the child is not in public child care. Benefit paid at a low flat-rate of approximately FIM2,900 (US$475) per month. Available until child's third birthday.
NW	Paid leave: Parents may share 52 weeks of leave at 80 percent of wages, or, alternatively, 42 weeks at 100 percent of wages, up to maximum income of NOK290,261 (US$26,876) per year. Benefit can be paid while parent is employed 50–90 percent time, and leave time is extended accordingly. Available until child's third birthday.	Paid leave: 13 weeks (3 months) exclusively for the mothers, 4 (exclusively for the father). Benefits subject to maximum income of NOK290,261 (US$26,876) per year. Benefit can be paid while parent is employed 50–90 percent time, and leave time is extended accordingly. Available until child's third birthday.
SW	Paid leave: Parents may share 65 weeks (15 months) of leave. Benefit level is 80 percent of earnings for 52 weeks (12 months); flat rate for remaining 13 weeks (3 months), at approximately SEK1,800 (US$187) per month. Earnings-related benefit subject to maximum income of approximately SEK270,000 income (US$28,000) per year. Benefit can be paid while parent is employed part-time, and leave is extended accordingly. Available until child's eighth birthday.	
BE	15 weeks. 82 percent of wages for first 4 weeks (1 month), plus 75 percent of wages thereafter. Benefits during first month not subject to ceiling; thereafter, benefits subject to maximum income of approximately $95/day.	Paid leave: Each parent entitled to 13 weeks (3 months) full-time leave or up to 26 weeks (6 months) of half-time leave. Parents taking leave receive flat-rate benefit payment of BF20,400 (US$551) per month. Available until child's fourth birthday.
FR	16 weeks for first two children, 26 weeks for third and subsequent children. 100 percent of wages, up to maximum of FF387 (US$59) per day.	Paid leave: Parents may share 156 weeks (3 years) of leave. No benefit paid for first child; benefit level is flat-rate FF3,024 (US$462) per month for second and subsequent children. Benefit can be paid at reduced rate while parent is employed part-time. Available until child's third birthday.
US	No national policy of paid maternity leave. Some benefits paid under temporary disability insurance (TDI) laws in five states: California, Hawaii, New Jersey, New York, Rhode Island. Approximately 23 percent of the US population resides in these states. Maximum duration: 26–52 weeks; average duration: 5–13 weeks. Maximum weekly benefits: $170–487; average weekly benefits: $142–273.	Unpaid leave: Each parent entitled to 12 weeks' family and medical leave (if employer has 50+ employees and work history requirements fulfilled). Available until child's first birthday. Several states extend federal leave; generally, state laws broaden coverage (including smaller employers) and/or increase duration. California enacted paid parental leave in 2002. Pays approximately 55 percent wage replacement for six weeks, subject to earnings cap.

Notes:
- All durations are expressed as weeks, to help with interpretation. Where authors converted from days, years, or months, original duration is given in square brackets. All currency amounts expressed as 2000 US dollars, adjusted for purchasing power parities.
- Danish parental leave reformed March 2002. Entitlement increased to 32 weeks (to be shared between the parents) at same pay as maternity; 80 percent of employers still top up. Other changes increased the flexibility of parents' take-up options.
- Finnish parents can replace home-care leave payment with payment for private child-care provider.
- Norwegian cap equivalent to approximately 1.9 times average annual earnings among working-age mothers (part-time and full-time combined).
- Norwegian parents can use cash benefit to pay for private child care (for children aged 1 or 2) if child is not in a public slot. In addition to paid parental leave, each parent is entitled to one year of unpaid leave.
- Swedish cap equivalent to approximately 2.2 times average annual earnings among working-age mothers (part-time and full-time combined).
- French replacement rate is 100 percent of net wages (after social insurance contributions are deducted).
- French parents working 50 percent time receive 66 percent of full benefit; parents working 50–80 percent time receive 50 percent of full benefit.

(See Gornick and Meyers 2003 for details on source materials.)

Appendix Table 2
Provisions for Fathers: Paternity Leave and Incentives for Take-Up of Parental Leave (Approximately 2000)

	Paternity Leave Benefits (paid)	Incentives for Fathers' Take-Up of Parental Leave
DK	2 weeks (10 days). Benefit is same as maternity pay—equal in practice to about 60 percent prior wages. Due to collective agreements, many employers "top up" so most parents receive 100 percent wage replacement.	"Use or lose": 2 weeks of leave added to the 10 weeks of parental leave and designated for the father (for a total of 12 weeks); if he does not take them, they are lost to the family. Individual, non-transferable entitlement: the child-care leave is granted to each parent and may not be transferred.
FI	3 weeks (18 days). Benefit based on graduated replacement rate: approximately 70 percent at low income, 40 percent at medium income, 25 percent at high income (equal, on average, to approximately 66 percent).	
NW	4 weeks as part of parental leave scheme.	"Use or lose": 4 weeks of leave are designated for the father; if he does not take them, they are lost to the family.
SW	2 weeks (10 days) paternity leave, paid at 80 percent.	"Use or lose": 4 weeks of leave are designated for the father; if he does not take them, they are lost to the family.
BE	3–4 days. 100 percent of wages.	Individual, non-transferable entitlement: father has his own leave entitlement that may not be transferred. However, the low replacement rate is a disincentive to take-up.
FR	No paid paternity leave.	
US	No paid paternity leave.	Individual, non-transferable entitlement: father has his own leave entitlement that may not be transferred. However, the absence of wage replacement is a disincentive to take-up.

Notes:
- "Use or lose" days were implemented in Denmark in 1999; Norway in 1993; and in Sweden in 1995.
- Finland introduced incentives for fathers' take-up in 2003.
- As of 2002, French fathers entitled to 11 working days (2 weeks), paid at same rate as maternity benefit. (See Gornick and Meyers 2003 for details on source materials.)

Appendix Table 3

Establishment of Normal Working Hours
(Approximately 2000)

	Primary Mechanism for Regulation of Working Time	Normal Working Hours		Maximum Working Hours by Statute (hours worked above maximum may not be compulsory)
		By Statute	By Collective Agreement (Average)	
DK	Primarily collective agreements.	Legislation sets maximum hours (48) but not normal working time.	37	48
FI	Combination of collective agreements and labor law.	40 hours, with possible reduction through collective agreement.	39.3	40
NW	Combination of collective agreements and labor law.	40 hours, with possible reduction through collective agreement.	37.5	40
SW	Combination of collective agreements and labor law.	40 hours, with possible reduction through collective agreement.	38.8	40
BE	Combination of collective agreements and labor law.	39 hours, with possible reduction through collective agreement.	39	39
FR	Primarily labor law.	35 hours, since national legislation in 2000 reduced statutory work week to 35 hours (with no pay reduction). Law calls on collective bargaining "to negotiate the practicalities of actual reduction of working hours". 35-hour week applies to *all* workers, including skilled, salaried professions.	35	48
US	Primarily national labor law, with some supplementation by state laws.	Since 1938, normal working week is 40 hours. Approximately 27 percent of full-time workers are exempt.	Union coverage is low (15 percent of workers). Overall, in medium and large establishments, 86 percent of full-time employees have weekly work schedules of 40 hours or more.	No Limit

Notes:
• The 1993 EU Directive on Working Time stipulated a 48-hour maximum working week. This affects the European countries, including Norway.
• Normal working hours refers to the threshold above which an overtime premium becomes payable.
• In 2002, in Finland, the range of collectively agreed upon hours was 35–38.
• In Belgium, statutory normal hours is 38, as of 2003.
• In 2002, in Belgium, the range of collectively agreed-upon hours was 35–38.
(See Gornick and Meyers 2003 for details on source materials.)

Appendix Table 4
Regulation of Annual Days Off (Approximately 2000)

	Paid Days Off by Statute (number of days required)	Paid Days Off by Collective Agreement (number of days, average across awards)
DK	25	32
FI	24	Employees with children under age 14 receive an additional day off
NW	30 days after 1 year of service	23
SW	21	25
BE	25	25
FR	20	25
US	25	
	Not addressed in national legislation	Union coverage low (15 percent of workers) Overall, in medium and large establishments, average paid days off among full-time employees: 9.6 days after 1 year, 11.5 days after 3 years, 13.8 days after 5 years, 16.8 after 10 years.

Notes:
- The 1993 EU Directive on Working Time stipulated not less than four weeks annual paid time off. The deadline for implementation was 1996. This affects the European countries, including Norway.
- In 2002, in Finland, paid days off under collective agreements ranged from 5 to 6 weeks.
- In Norway, average number of days under collective agreements 25, as of 2003.
- In 2002, in Sweden, paid days off under collective agreement ranged from 25 to 30 days.
- Data on collective agreements in Belgium for 1993.
- In 2002, in France paid days off under collective agreements ranged from 5 to 6 weeks.
(See Gornick and Meyers 2003 for details on source materials.)

Appendix Table 5

Measures Encouraging Development of Voluntary Part-Time Employment and Improvement of the Quality of Part-Time Work (Approximately 2000)

	Measures that Improve the Quality of Part-Time Work	Measures that Grant Parents or All Workers the Right to Work Part-Time
DK	EU Directive on Part-Time Work implemented in 2001	(No information)
FI	EU Directive on Part-Time Work implemented in 2001	Employees have the right to reduce working time 40–60 percent for one year, subject to employment agreement (an unemployed person must be hired for the same position).
NW	EU Directive on Part-Time Work implemented voluntarily	Employees have the right to reduce working hours in response to "health, social or other weighty reasons of welfare" if this "can be arranged without particular inconvenience to the enterprise."
SW	EU Directive on Part-Time Work implemented in 2002	Employed parents have right to work 6-hour day instead of 8-hour day until child is 8 years old or in the first grade. Workers have right to return to full-time work with advanced notice. Law enacted in 1978.
BE	EU Directive on Part-Time Work implemented in 2000	Employees have the right to reduce their employment by one fifth (1 day or 2 half days per week) for a period up to 5 years.
FR	EU Directive on Part-Time Work implemented in 2000	Employees may request reduction of work hours for period of time for family reasons. Employees with at least a year's service may request to work part-time; request may be made during first 3 years after birth or adoption.
US	FLSA guarantees part-time workers the minimum wage. No legal protections with regard to pay equity, benefits, or job conditions.	No national law. Some unions have won the right to reduced working time on a temporary basis so that workers can take care of family needs. For example SEIU Local 715 (service employees) won a policy under which members may reduce working time by 1, 2, 5, 10, or 20 per cent for up to 6 months without loss of benefits or seniority.

Notes:
• The 1997 EU Directive on Part-Time Work calls for: (a) eliminating discrimination against part-time workers and improving the quality of part-time work; and (b) facilitating the development of part-time work on a voluntary basis.
• A number of countries (e.g. France, Norway, Sweden) also allow parents to work part-time while on parental leave. (See Gornick and Meyers 2003 for details on source materials.)

Appendix Table 6
Institutional Arrangements and Entitlements for Publicly Supported Early Childhood Education and Care (Approximately 2000)

	Primary Public ECEC Institutions	Entitlement for Children from Birth to the Age of 2	Entitlement for Children from 3 until School Age
DK	*Vuggestuer*: for children age 6–36 months; *Bornehaver*: for children age 3–6 years; *Aldersintegrerede institutioner*: for children 6 months–6 years; *Bornehaveklasser*: half-day pre-primary through school system for children age 6.	Yes, from age 1 or younger	Yes
FI	*Paivahoito* for children age 0–6; *6-votiaiden esiopetus* (preschool) for 6-year-olds.	Yes	Yes
NW	*Barnehage*: children age 0–5.	No	No
SW	*Forskola*: for children age 0–6; *Forskoleklass*: preschool through school system for children age 6.	Yes, from age 1	Yes
BE	*Kinderdagverblijf* (Flemish) and *Crèche* (French): for children age 0–36 months; *Kleuterschool* (Flemish) and *Ecole Maternelle* (French): for children age 2.5–5.	No	Yes, from 30 months
FR	*Crèche*: for children age 0–36 months; *Ecole Maternelle*: for children age 2–5 years.	No	Yes, from 30 to 36 months
US	Market-based care main option for children below age 5. Public Pre-kindergarten and Head Start: for some children age 4.	No	No

Notes:
- An estimated 87 percent of Danish municipalities guarantee places for all children between 1–5 years; national law mandates child-care slots be provided within 3 months of parent request (or shorter, following parental leave); few children are on waiting lists.
- Every Finnish child under school age has an unconditional right to day care provided by the local authority once the mother or father's period of parental allowance comes to an end, irrespective of the parents' financial status or whether or not they are in work.
- In Norway, universal access is a political priority and access varies by location.
- Swedish municipalities required to provide fee-paying spaces for all children aged 1–12 whose parents work or are in school. Spots must be made available "without unreasonable delay"—defined as 3–4 months. An estimated 95 percent of municipalities are able to meet requirement. As of 2001, children of unemployed parents also have right to services.

(See Gornick and Meyers 2003 for details on source materials.)

Appendix Table 7

Government Mechanisms for Financing Early Childhood Education and Care (Approximately 2000)

	Financing Direct Provision of ECEC	Subsidies for Purchase of Private Care	Government Incentives or Support for Employer Contributions	Tax Relief for Purchase of Private Care
DK	Direct services financed by national and municipal governments and parent fees.	Local authorities can give a cash grant to parents with a child 24 weeks–3 years; up to 70 percent of documented expenses, not to exceed 85 percent of least expensive municipal child-care spot; average grants DKK30,800–36,400 annually [US$3,586–4,327].		
FI	Direct services financed by national (27 percent) and municipal (54 percent) governments and parent fees.	Since 1997, Private Care Allowance for purchase of private day care; basic flat-rate payment of FIM700 [US$120] per child per month, with earnings supplements, paid directly to child minder or child-care center.		
NW	Direct services financed by national (36 percent) and municipal (28 percent) governments and parent fees.	Cash Benefit Scheme may be used to pay for private child care; approximately NOK3,000 [US$278] per month, roughly equivalent to state subsidy per child for pre-primary services; may also be claimed by parents providing care in home.		Documented child-care expenses may be deducted from income of lowest-earning spouse; maximum deduction (for 2 or more children) NOK23,325 [US$2,884].
SW	Direct child-care services financed by national and municipal governments (82 percent) and parent fees (18 percent); family child-care financed by municipal government (82 percent) and parent fees (18 percent).			
BE	Direct child-care services financed by regional, municipal, and federal government and parent fees; preprimary services financed by national government.		Employers provide .05 percent of wage bill for development of services for children from birth to 3.	Deduction to reduce taxable income by 80 percent of actual costs to maximum of BF450 per day [US$12].
FR	Direct child-care services financed by national (24 percent), regional (12 percent) and municipal (34 percent) government and parent fees; preprimary services financed by national (56 percent) and municipal (34 percent) governments.	Means-tested subsidies for parents using registered family day carers of up to €197 (0–3 years) and €98 (3–6 years) [US$209 and $104] per month, and for social security contribution for in-home providers up to €508 [US$539].	Employers contribute to cost of service through compulsory contributions to the Family Allowance Funds (CAFs); employer contributions cover an estimated 25 percent of cost of services in social welfare system.	Tax reductions for employed parents of up to 25 percent of child-care costs to a limit of €575 [US$610] annually per child, and 50 percent of costs up to €3,450[US$3,662] annually for in-home care.
US	Most ECEC is privately purchased. Costs of public child-care services and subsidies shared between federal and state governments and parents. Pre-primary programs financed by national government (Project Head Start) and state governments (pre-kindergarten).	Limited number of subsidies for low-income parents in welfare employment programs or employment through Child Care and Development and Temporary Assistance to Needy Families block grants; eligibility and maximum amount vary by state.	Employers can deduct portion of costs of child care from taxable payroll.	Nonrefundable tax credit for up to $2,400 (1 child) to $4,800 (2 or more children) in child-care expenses for employed parents; maximum credit of $720 for 1 to $1,440 for 2 children. Flexible spending plans allow parents to set aside up to $5,000 pre-tax earning for child-care expenses.

Notes:

• Currencies are expressed in national currency units for about 2000 (unless otherwise noted), followed, in square brackets, by the equivalent amount in 2000 US dollars adjusted for purchasing power parity.

• For Norway, goal is 50 percent national and 30 percent municipal by 2005.

(See Gornick and Meyers 2003 for details on source materials.)

Appendix Table 8
Early Childhood Education and Care, Quality Regulations and Staff Compensation (Approximately 2000)

	Quality Regulations			As a Share of All Employed Women's Annual Wages	
	Family Child-Care Staff Qualifications	Center-Based Staff Qualifications	Pre-primary Staff Qualifications	Center-Based Child-Care Worker	Pre-primary Teacher
DK	Municipal facility managers have specialized training; private child minders generally not required to have specific training.	Teachers complete 3.5-year university program.		1.35–1.69	1.35–1.69
FI	Most family child-care supervisors are qualified as pre-primary teachers; municipalities set training requirements for family child-care providers.	3.5-year training as "social educator" or 3-year secondary vocational training as pre-primary teacher.	3–4.5 years of university-level training.	0.90	0.95
NW	For every 30 children in family day care, a trained preschool teacher is available to support care workers; private child minders generally not required to have specific training.	3 years of higher education for teachers; 2-year apprenticeship for assistants.		0.88–1.20	0.88–1.20
SW	72 percent of family child minders completed certificate or municipal training program.	3 years of university training required; an estimated 60 percent of pre-school teachers have completed university-level training.		1.02	1.02
BE	Voluntary in-service training.	Flemish: one-year training in addition to professional secondary education. French: 3 years beyond diploma (at age 16).	3-year post-secondary degree.	1.12	1.45
FR	60 hours of training, with ongoing supervision and in-service training.	Teachers have 3-year college degree plus additional graduate professional degree in ECEC; assistants have secondary diploma plus additional year of vocational training in early care and education.		**	1.21–2.15; average 1.87
US	Vary from none (18 states) to pre-service plus at least 6 hours of in-service training a year (4 states).	Vary from none (30 states) to some specific ECEC training (19 states) or university degree (1 state).	Vary from some specific ECEC training (18 states) to university degree (20 states).	0.53	0.66

Notes:
- Annualized hours assume 1,920 paid hours annually (8 hours per day, 5 days per week, 48 weeks per year).
- Average wage for all women workers, full-time and part-time, calculated from Luxembourg Income Study (LIS).
- ** Not available

(See Gornick and Meyers 2003 for details on source materials.)

PART II

Principles

2

Long Leaves, Child Well-Being, and Gender Equality

Barbara R. Bergmann

Work–family programs are usually thought of as reforms of a workplace regime that gives too little allowance for the performance of home duties, particularly those traditionally done by women. The primary purpose of such programs is to allow the family to receive more services. Some versions, such as the notorious "mommy track," frankly envision limiting women's opportunities in the workplace so that they may continue to be available to provide substantial amounts of services in the home. Other versions of work–family programs may be less forthright, but most if not all have elements that produce important negative effects on gender equality.

In this volume, Janet Gornick and Marcia Meyers make the optimistic claim that, in fashioning work–family policy, "tradeoffs between gender equality, family time, and child well-being are not inevitable. The interests of men, women and children are not fundamentally at odds." They recommend that the United States adopt the kinds of policies in force in France and the Nordic countries, and claim that these policies, suitably modified, would improve things significantly for children, women, and men, and would not cause a diminution of gender equality. Would that it were so.

The policies these countries have adopted include three main features: lengthy paid leave for parents of infants, better-remunerated part-time work, and generous government subsidies for non-parental child care. The subsidies for non-parental child care would advance gender equality. However, lengthy parental leave and the encouragement of part-time work, both of which would allow parents more time at home, are destructive of it.

Most advocates of work arrangements that would allow parents more family time simply ignore the issue of gender equality, either because they don't care about it, or because they view the full-time care of infants by their own mother as surpassingly more important, or because they fail to see the connection between work arrangements and gender equality. Gornick and Meyers are unusual among such advocates in that they do pay attention to gender equality, and are concerned about it. They deserve great credit for that.

They well understand that a system that causes mothers to take long paid parental leaves, while fathers take much shorter leaves or none at all, is harmful to the cause of gender equality. They reduce the one year or more per birth offered to mothers by the European plans to six months. They increase the month or two offered on a non-transferable basis to fathers by some European plans to the same six months. This equality of treatment of mothers and fathers is the basis of Gornick and Meyers' optimistic view that gender equality would not suffer under their variant of the Nordic/Gallic model. That hope is, I believe, unrealistic.

In what follows, I describe the likely effects of the Gornick–Meyers model on gender equality, and explain why I believe adoption of that model is inimical to progress both in the home and in the workplace, and would cause retrogression. If that is indeed the case, then those of us for whom gender equality is of high importance have to consider whether we are willing to trade a retreat on that front for an increase in the time that children have with their mothers. An alternative is a high-commodification model, which would go further than we have already gone in replacing family-provided services with paid-for services, some of them provided publicly. In considering the advantages and disadvantages of high commodification, we have to examine some of the claims that non-parental child care damages children.

GENDER EQUALITY UNDER THE NORDIC/GALLIC MODEL

Gornick and Meyers' proposed solution to the work–family problem for the United States would result in an increase in the amount of time job-holders could spend at home. That, of course, is precisely the purpose of the policies they propose. The increased time at home would come mainly from paid parental leave, and from an increase in part-time work. Such a policy is designed to increase the amount of child care done by family members, and most likely would increase the amount of cleaning, cooking, and laundry they would do as well. The crucial question for gender equality is, of course, how that extra amount of housework and child care would be shared between the father and mother. (Of course, there is no father in a considerable fraction of working parents' households, and this needs to be taken account of.)

The policies Gornick and Meyers propose would incorporate features that, it is hoped, would encourage men to do more of that work. These features include a high replacement rate of salaries for those on parental leave, and an allocation of half of the family's leave time to a newborn infant's father on a use-it-or-lose-it basis. But this equality in what is offered to women and men does not necessarily translate into equality of uptake. We have to ask what men's likely response would be to the inducements designed to increase their participation in providing home services. The experience in the Scandinavian countries is not encouraging.

Sweden currently provides new fathers with two months of non-transferable leave, less than the six months that the Gornick–Meyers plan allows. Forty percent of Swedish fathers take no leave at all, and almost two-thirds take less than the two months (Ericksson, 2005). Much of what they do take merely extends their summer vacation. This is really not surprising. Doing chores such as diapering, dealing with screaming children, cleaning house, and doing laundry, all in isolation from other adults, is far from the most attractive way to spend time, at least according to the taste of most people. Men have so far been exempted from these tasks, and many if not most men are likely to resist taking them on.

In most countries at most times, there is little or no pressure on men from outside the family to do more housework. Quite the contrary: men encourage other men in shirking such work, and ridicule the ones who do take it on. In the workplace, supervisors and colleagues, who would be inconvenienced by men's time off, use threats and ridicule to minimize it. The issue is not discussed in any of the media, or in schools or churches. The only pressure on a man comes from his female partner, at the risk of strain in their relationship. Of course, the last thing the mother of a new baby needs is worry that her relationship with the baby's father will be soured, with the result that she has very little leverage. Repeated requests are ignored, and labeled as nagging. Gornick and Meyers may hope that fathers might *eventually* do fully half of the new and larger amount of housework and child care they recommend, but there is little reason to have faith that things will evolve that way. On the contrary, the early result of their program will be to send families off in the opposite direction.

So more time at home for parents means, in reality, more time at home for mother, and little if any more for father. In the short run at least, there would be an increase in the amount of child care and housework done by mothers. Furthermore, the share of such work that would be done by mothers would rise. That would more firmly cement the custom of viewing child care and household tasks as "women's work." It might undo much of the modest progress in sharing household work that has been made in the last few decades (Bergmann, 2005; Bianchi et al., 2000), and also the very modest advance in gender equality within the home that has been the result.

A US adoption of the Gornick–Meyers version of the Nordic/Gallic model would have adverse effects on gender equality in the workplace as well as the home. The availability of paid parental leave would create social pressure for mothers to make use of it—to take the leave and to stay out for the full time provided. Any woman who didn't would be branded as a bad mother.[1] Employers would have strong incentives and more excuses to resist placing women in any but routine jobs—the kind of jobs where one person can smoothly and easily fill in for another. Discrimination against women in assignment to non-routine jobs has not yet ended. Lengthy paid parental leave, as well as more part-time work, would increase discrimination and make women's chances of getting such jobs considerably lower.

A law requiring improvement in the pay and benefits of part-time workers, as recommended by Gornick and Meyers, would probably increase the number of women workers (whether currently full time or out of the labor force) interested in such jobs. Workers in such jobs are seldom given opportunities for promotion or any but routine duties.

The Swedish labor force is considerably more sex-segregated than the American (Anker, 1998; Dolado, Feigueroso and Jimeno, 2003). Women are highly concentrated in jobs performing "caring labor." While the extent of women's penetration into male-dominated occupations is obviously a result of many historical factors, it would not be surprising if the paid parental leave provisions had contributed to the continuing relatively high sex-segregation of the Swedish occupational structure.

An article in the *Chronicle of Higher Education* by Joan Williams (2006), a proponent of work–family policies, illustrates both the gender-equality problem with such policies and the blindness toward that problem on the part of such advocates. The article starts by saying, "It makes no sense for universities to hire a female professor, spend thousands of dollars setting up her lab, only to have her depart because she needs a maternity leave or a part-time schedule—

and then replace her with another woman, who, in due time, may also leave for similar reasons." What would make sense for the university, Williams argues, would be to provide such leaves and part-time schedules.

Let's face it—if women on its science faculty actually were abandoning expensive labs for such a reason, the university's most sensible strategy would be to avoid hiring a woman scientist ever again. (In fact, the publication of Williams's article in the *Chronicle* suggesting that women habitually do so may well cause a reduction in the number of young women scientists hired by universities.) Williams wants us to assume that the woman who left for such a reason would be replaced by another woman. It is more likely that her department would develop an allergy to women scientists under fifty.

In fact, universities don't face a serious danger of having to refurnish expensive labs for such a reason. Because science is so competitive, and priority of discovery is everything, few scientists of either sex will want to take long parental leaves, much less quit their jobs if they are denied such leaves. Such jobs are difficult to get, particularly for women, and are not given up easily.

The whole issue is in truth a big loser for women scientists. In fact, it is a big loser for any woman (or man) in competition for advancement in a professional or managerial role. Why did the *Chronicle* choose to run an article with such a patently unlikely storyline? They were just joining the chorus. Intoning "paid parental leave" has become as obligatory among people who want to think of themselves as good feminists as intoning "Hail Mary" is among practicing Catholics.

Is there any length of parental leave that would not constitute a detriment to gender equity? This is, of course, an empirical question, and presumably would vary by the type of job. In the absence of solid information, one might guess that one month would do minimal damage, but four months might do considerable damage. The Gornick–Meyers suggestion of six months for each parent, taken preponderantly by mothers, could be highly destructive.

In short, the parental leave and part-time features of the model of work–family policies that Gornick and Meyers favor would most likely have the effect of significantly reducing gender equality both within the home and in the workplace. It would sacrifice the interests of adult females for a perceived (but not necessarily real) benefit to children. It would benefit male adults, who would be relieved of female competitors. Female children might benefit in the short run, but would lose in the long run because of the limits to their career prospects.

This being the case, it is worth looking to see whether there are other kinds of arrangements that might bring more services to the home without the retreat from gender equality that Gornick and Meyers' model would entail. The next section presents some possibilities—though each of them has important limitations or drawbacks.

ALTERNATIVE METHODS OF INCREASING THE SUPPLY OF HOME SERVICES DELIVERED BY PARENTS

Additional time for home services by parents might be supplied in ways that do not retreat on gender equality. Ways this could be done include:

1. a cut in the standard workday for all workers, not just parents
2. half-time work for both parents for the same time period, paid at full-time rates, provided that one is at home in the morning, the other at home in the afternoon
3. requirement that, to get parental leave, both parents take successive and equal periods of time off for a baby's first few years of life
4. a recongregation of population in central cities.

A cut in the standard workday, which has not been changed in the US since the 1930s, is advocated by Gornick and Meyers as part of their package, and would be highly desirable.[2] It might even pay for itself through increased productivity. We should be watching the experience of the French in this regard. However, only a modest amount of extra home time could be provided in this way. A cut of at most one hour per day would be likely, potentially providing 10 hours more of home time per week in two-parent families. There might be some reduction in the time children spend in non-parental care, but the extent of that shift cannot be predicted. There is some evidence that people would prefer to reduce work hours, but devote the freed-up time to "self" rather than to "family" (Jacobs and Gerson, 2004). Reducing daily hours of work would not eliminate the need to put infants into non-parental care if neither parent is at home full-time.

Furthermore, a reduction in standard hours, while helpful to many, would not do much for workers in fierce competition for partnerships in law firms or for tenured professorships in universities, for those seeking to be the first to publish on some scientific subject, or seeking promotion in a corporate managerial hierarchy. Those people frequently work 60 hours or more per week. Their work/family (or work/self) problems may be beyond help.

Methods 2 and 3 assume that two parents are available—something not true in many cases. Of the children born in 2004 in the US, 34 percent were born to unmarried mothers, most of whom did not have live-in partners. A further problem with methods 2 and 3 is that forcing equal sharing of leave would go against the currently held sex-role ideology of a large part of the population. The adoption of either of these methods would be very unlikely.

Having parents work different shifts, so that one parent is always available at home, is already not an uncommon arrangement. But such a practice is frequently not conducive to a happy family life (Presser, 2003). Moreover, such an arrangement must frequently force at least one of the parents to pass up a superior job for one that fits in the appropriate time slot.

A large-scale move of population from suburbs to central cities would probably be necessary if a serious diminution of the output of gases contributing to global warming is to occur. It would also reduce the amount of time workers spent commuting, and so increase time at home. If large city apartment houses were set up with child care centers, cafeterias, dry cleaners, supermarkets, and other services, even more time could be saved (see Bergmann, 2005). Again, this is an unlikely development, at least in the near term.

FURTHER COMMODIFICATION AS A SOLUTION

We have reviewed the adverse effects on gender equity of lengthy parental leave allowances and part-time work, and the limited likely effect of measures that provide more family time but do not react badly on gender equity. An alternative course for providing more household services would be an increase in the purchase of services by the household, or the provision or subsidization of such services by government.

The commodification of household consumption—substituting paid-for goods and services for goods and services produced by family members—has been advancing ever since human beings started trading with each other. After the industrial revolution, only child care and housework remained as tasks typically performed by family members. Everything else we consume is purchased, either by ourselves or by government. (Of course, the wealthy very early commodified all household functions by hiring servants or keeping slaves.) Care for children older than five or six was largely commodified by the adoption of compulsory public schools in the late nineteenth century, although in most settings school-age children were thought to need little adult care until relatively recently. In the twentieth century there was some reversal of direction: the washer and dryer operated by the wife replaced the paid laundress, and the invention of the car induced self-chauffeuring. Since the 1960s, the entry of mothers into the workforce in large numbers has spurred further commodification, mainly in the areas of child care and the production and cleanup of meals.

Further progress in increasing men's share of housework will be achieved slowly, if it happens at all. So gender equality will be most surely approached by driving unpaid family work down toward zero—the same direction in which it has been going for the last 6,000 years. This process would be speeded up by greater government provision or subsidization of high-quality child care, as advocated by Gornick and Meyers.

THE CONSEQUENCES OF NON-MATERNAL CARE

If progress on gender equity requires that children spend long periods in non-maternal care, beginning at very young ages, then we have to ask what the consequences of that are for child development. We can then compare the benefits and costs—the benefits of progress toward women's equality versus the costs, if any, to children.

In the early 1990s the National Institute of Child Health and Human Development (NICHD) launched its Study of Early Child Care to observe the effects of various kinds and amounts of care on children's development. This study has yielded what have to be characterized as mixed results. A report that analyzed data available at the time the children were entering kindergarten (at 54 months, or four-and-a-half years) found that time spent in non-maternal care was associated to a "modest" degree with the numbers showing aggressive behavior (NICHD Early Child Care Research Network, 2003). By contrast, a report of an assessment with a different methodology, carried out when the same children were nine and had reached third grade, failed to find a connection between time in care and the number of children judged as aggressive (NICHD Early Child Care Research Network, 2004).

At 54 months, teachers and caretakers rated 9 percent of children who had averaged 0 to 9 hours per week in non-maternal child care as having a score indicating aggressive behavior that was more than one standard deviation above the mean. Of those children who had been in care between 30 and 45 hours per week on average, an extra 6 out of 100 children were judged to have this type of behavior problem. In the group experiencing over 45 hours in care, a further 4 out of 100 children (19 percent in all, as opposed to 9 percent in the lowest care group) were diagnosed as having aggressive behavior.[3]

It would be helpful in thinking about policy issues to have an idea of how bad the behavior of the children who show aggression one standard deviation or more above the average actually is. Are they merely argumentative, or are they a bit nasty at times, or are they monsters? Unfortunately, it is impossible to get that kind of understanding from these reports.

Remarkably, an analysis ostensibly by the same group of researchers, based on the same children's records as they stood in their ninth year, presents a different picture. The researchers separated the children into groups according to their history of aggressive behavior since age two. Most children were in groups that showed consistently low levels of aggression, or moderate levels that declined over time. Only 3 percent of children in the sample were characterized as having highly disruptive behavior that did not decline as the children got older.[4] At nine years of age, that group of children had lower scores on cognitive measures, lower social competence, and displayed more antisocial behavior than children in the other groups.

The differences in child-care experiences by group in the 2004 report did not support the hypothesis that long hours in child care were conducive to high aggressiveness. In fact, the group with the highest and most consistent aggressiveness had experienced on average the fewest hours in non-maternal child care. And it was the groups with the lowest level of aggression who had on average spent the longest hours in care.[5] The authors of the monograph reporting on the third-grade outcomes explain the differences between their study and the earlier one as due to "different approaches to data analysis," and the fact that the observations on aggression were made by mothers rather than caregivers and teachers.[6]

A further curiosity was an article published subsequently that went back and again rehearsed the results for the 54-month-old children. It included the following sentences:

> [O]ur results provide support for policies that reduce the amount of time children spend in childcare. These include programs that support extended welfare benefits and workplace policies that offer flexible hours and paid parental leave at any time during a child's first five years, not exclusively following the child's birth.[7]

It is not clear whether this is to be interpreted as suggesting that paid parental leave lasting five years be offered following each birth. We may speculate that differences in outlook among the twenty-six members of the committee to which authorship of all of the reports is attributed have contributed to this checkered publication history of interpretation of the results on this group of children.

Those, like the present author, who put a high value on gender equality, may remark that, even giving full credence to the finding that long hours of care may conduce to heightened aggressiveness does not necessarily require agreement with the establishment of long paid parental leaves. I would argue that the "modest" result, that an additional 10 children out of 100 may display aggressiveness at 54 months—an aggressiveness that may be temporary, and that some researchers have suggested is possibly a healthy reaction (Clarke-Stewart, 1989)—is not worth sacrificing the move toward equality for half the human race that increased use of non-parental care would allow.

CONCLUSION

I have argued that the provision for paid parental leave advocated by Gornick and Meyers would have a distinctly adverse effect on gender equality. Their advocacy of more government provision of child care would go in the opposite direction, but the net effect would probably be negative. Further commodification of household services, through family purchases and government provision, is the only promising route to gender equity now in sight.

NOTES

1   Ericksson (2005) reports that in Sweden many mothers go back to work when subsidized day care becomes available, suggesting that mothers as well as fathers prefer work to staying home with young children.

2   The Fair Labor Standards Act, passed in 1938, required overtime pay if weekly hours exceeded 40. Thus an eight-hour day, five days a week became the standard.

3   Table 8, p. 997.

4   NICHD Early Child Care Research Network, 2004: 48.

5   Ibid.: 66.

6   Ibid.: 109.

7   NICHD Early Child Care Research Network, 2006: 114.

REFERENCES

Anker, R., 1998, *Gender and Jobs: Sex Segregation and Occupations in the World*, Geneva: International Labor Office.

Bergmann, Barbara R., 2005, *The Economic Emergence of Women*, second edition, London: Palgrave Macmillan, 2005.

Bianchi, Suzanne M., Melissa A. Milkie, Liana C. Sayer and John P. Robinson, 2000, "Is Anyone Doing the Housework? Trends in the Gender Division of Household Labor," *Social Forces* 79 (1) (September): 191–228.

Clarke-Stewart, K., 1989, "Infant Day Care: Maligned or Malignant?" *American Psychologist* 44: 266–73.

Dolado, Juan J., Florentino Feigueroso, and Juan F. Jimeno, 2003, "Where Do Women Work? Analysing Patterns in Occupational Segregation by Gender," CEPR Research Network.

Eriksson, Rickard, 2005, "Parental Leave in Sweden: The Effects of the Second Daddy Month," Working Paper Series no. 9, Swedish Institute for Social Research, Stockholm University.

Jacobs, Jerry A., and Kathleen Gerson, 2004, *The Time Divide: Work, Family, and Gender Inequality*, Cambridge, MA: Harvard University Press.

NICHD Early Child Care Research Network, 2003, "Does Amount of Time Spent in Child Care Predict Socioemotional Adjustment During the Transition to Kindergarten?" *Child Development* 74: 976–1,005.

———2004, "Trajectories of Physical Aggression from Toddlerhood to Middle Childhood: Predictors, Correlates, and Outcomes," *SRCD Monographs*, 69 (4): vii –146.

———2006, "Child-Care Effect Sizes for the NICHD Study of Early Child Care and Youth Development," *American Psychologist* 61 (2): 99–116.

Presser, Harriet B., 2003, *Working in a 24/7 Economy: Challenges for American Families*, New York: Russell Sage Foundation.

Williams, Joan, 2006, "It's in Their Interest, Too," *Chronicle of Higher Education*, August 31.

3

Strong Gender Egalitarianism
Harry Brighouse and Erik Olin Wright

In this chapter we will defend a specific element in the Gornick–Meyers proposal for the design of institutions to support dual-caregiver families: the idea that such institutions should contain specific forms of incentives for men to do more child care, even if, by implication, this means constraining in certain important ways the choices of women. We will assume that these male caregiving incentive policies are joined with the full range of already existing anti-discrimination policies within the workplace and other institutions, as well as the other gender-equality policies proposed by Gornick and Meyers. Our focus, however, will only be on the caregiving problem. We will begin, in section I, by locating the Gornick–Meyers proposal within a spectrum of parental leave policies. Section II will define what we call "strong gender egalitarianism" and explain why we feel this is an appropriate goal of public policy. Section III will explain why we believe the Gornick–Meyers proposal might contribute to realizing the ideal of strong gender egalitarianism, but also why we feel a more radical form of this kind of policy might be needed.

I. THREE TYPES OF PARENTAL LEAVE POLICY

Parental leave policies can be roughly grouped into three broad categories:

Policy 1: Equality-impeding leaves. Certain kinds of parental leave policies can be seen as providing support to dual-earner families in ways which actively contribute to sustaining inequalities in the gender division of labor within the family. Caregiving leaves that are exclusively available to mothers would be the clearest example, but *unpaid* leave allocated to families should also be considered an equality-impeding policy, since such leaves will almost exclusively be taken up by mothers. Given the strains on contemporary families, both mother-only leaves and unpaid family-care leaves may improve the quality of life for the women who take advantage of them; but such policies contribute nothing to reducing inequality within the gendered division of labor in the family.

Policy 2. Equality-enabling leaves. Equality-enabling leaves provide generous paid parental leave allocated to families, thus reducing the obstacles to women being in the labor market and having children, and making it easier, if families so choose, for men also to engage in more caregiving activity. The parental leave is provided to families as units, not to the individual members of the family; in a sense it comes with the child. This policy enables egalitarian strategies within families, but it puts no particular pressures on families to adopt such strategies. The best European policies have this character.

Policy 3. Equality-promoting leaves. Equality-promoting leave policies attempt to create incentives which put some pressures on families to move toward a more egalitarian gender distribution of caregiving activities within the family. We can distinguish between moderate and radical versions of such policies. Janet Gornick and Marcia Meyers' proposal for individualized parental caregiving leaves is an example of a moderate equality-promoting policy. In their proposal, six months of parental leave allowances are provided separately to men and to women. Unused leave by either spouse cannot be transferred to the other. This "use it or lose it" feature creates active incentives for men to take more leave than they would if the same amount of time were available to the family as a unit without their participation. Even if both parents in a family would prefer the wife to take nine months and the husband only three, this is not allowed. A more radical equality-promoting policy would be one in which the amount of leave available to mothers was contingent on the amount of leave taken by fathers. This could be structured in the following way: 1) at the birth of a child, a mother gets one month of paid maternity leave to recover from childbirth;[2] 2) beyond this one month of maternity leave specifically allocated to mothers, mothers would be able to take additional paid leave equal to the amount of paid leave the father actually takes, up to a limit of six months (thus yielding a maximum of thirteen months per couple—one month of maternity leave plus six months of parental leaves each for fathers and mothers). If a father only took three months, then the mother could only take three. If a father took no months, then the mother would only get the initial one month of maternity leave. This means that fathers would have to become engaged heavily in infant childcare very early on if the family were to receive any paid parental leave.[3] This policy in effect makes the amount of paid leave for mothers dependent upon the degree to which fathers are willing to take paid leave. It also means that overall, in a society with this kind of paid parental leave system, men and women would take the same amount of paid leave, thus undermining the grounds for statistical discrimination against woman.[4] Neither the moderate nor radical equality-promoting leave policy exists anywhere.[5]

There are two fundamental reasons why we defend the third type of policy. First, we believe that, in families with children, the prospects for both men and women to flourish would in general be increased if the activities associated with caring for and rearing children were more equally shared between them, and we also believe that prospects for flourishing would be distributed more equally under those conditions. There is, in a sense, a "flourishing deficit" for women because, on average, they do too much caregiving, and also a "flourishing deficit" for men because they frequently do too little. Second, the unequal gender division of labor constitutes a serious barrier—perhaps the most important barrier—to further progress in realizing the goal of equality of opportunity between men and women. Inegalitarian gender relations thus constitute a continuing source of injustice. On the one hand, the extra burdens and responsibilities women bear within the family constrain their ability to compete in the labor market, and on the other hand, the fact that women disproportionately take on these roles reinforces stereotypes about the work commitments and priorities of "women" which hinder the opportunities even of women without such responsibilities.

If these arguments are correct, then it would be desirable to eliminate gender inequalities in the division of labor over caregiving, both because this would increase the prospects for human flourishing in general and because it would eliminate a source of injustice rooted in gender relations. We believe that policies which actively attempt to create incentives for men to increase their involvement in caregiving labor are probably necessary to move in this direction.

II. STRONG GENDER EGALITARIANISM

By "strong gender egalitarianism" we mean *a structure of social relations in which the division of labor around housework and caregiving within the family and occupational distributions within the public sphere are unaffected by gender*. By "unaffected by gender" we mean that there would be no socially constructed gender-differentiated norms around the division of labor: no specific activities would be thought of as men's work or women's work, nor would any activities be seen as more appropriate for men or for women. This does not mean that there would be no norms *about* gender; indeed, strong gender egalitarianism implies norms endorsing strong forms of gender equality in terms of power, rewards, and burdens.[6] It just means that there are no gender differentiations in roles and expectations that have normative backing. This a strong view of gender equality, for it advocates not simply a world in which men and women should have equal rights, or even equal opportunities for jobs and power—although it presupposes equal rights and equal opportunities—but a world without a socially constructed gendered division of labor. The ultimate goal of such a process would be the withering away of gender.[7]

There are two things that strong gender egalitarianism does not imply. First, it does not mean that in all households men and women would necessarily do exactly the same amount of caregiving (or housework), but simply that there would be no *economic or gendered normative constraints* on the distribution of such activities within households. There would, of course, be strong norms of equal sharing of the *burdens* associated with housework and caregiving, but equal sharing of burdens does not imply equal time spent in the tasks of child care and other forms of caregiving labor. In some households men would do more than women, in others women more than men. There would be no *socially constructed* gender division of labor, but this does not preclude differences in how individuals construct specific divisions of labor within intimate relationships.

Strong gender egalitarianism also does not imply that, in a world with a de-gendered division of labor, the average or modal amount of caregiving would be the same for men and women. It could be the case that, in a world in which there were no material incentives for women to do more than men and in which the norms of caregiving validated male caregiving as much as female caregiving, nevertheless the average amount of caregiving activity done by women might be more than that done by men. One reason for this is that, for biological reasons, it will always be easier for single women than for single men to have, and thus to raise, children; that alone means that, in the overall distributions of child-care labor in a population, the distributions for men and women will probably be different. It *could* also be the case—although on this we are more skeptical—that there would remain a biologically rooted differential in the distribution of preferences and dispositions for doing child-care labor between men and women in heterosexual families with two parents, even if

Figure 3.1

Hypothetical distributions of child-care provision by men and women living in households with children in alternative worlds

I. Existing distribution of child-care labor among men and among women with children

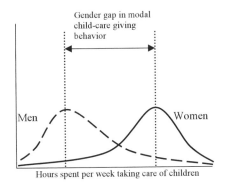

Hours spent per week taking care of children

II. Hypothetical distributions of child-care labor among men and among women with children in a world in which there were no gendered norms of appropriate child-care responsibility and no gender-specific costs to doing child care

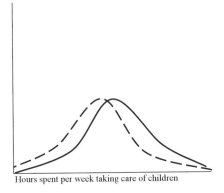

Hours spent per week taking care of children

there were no normative pressures for women to do more and no gender-differentiated material incentives around child-raising.[8] Our expectation is that the distribution of proclivities for caregiving among men and among women would greatly overlap in a world without either normative or material pressures on men and women to behave in different ways, and we are certain that it would overlap much more than in the present world; but it is pure speculation that the two distributions would actually be identical. These assumptions are represented in Figure 3.1.

The empirical claim underlying strong gender egalitarianism is that, in general, men and women would flourish to a greater extent under strong gender egalitarianism *even if they do not recognize this under existing conditions*. The strongest version of this thesis would say that this applies even to most of the *actual* men in the world today: even most men socialized in a socio-cultural regime of deeply gendered norms around child care with existing masculine identities would flourish to a greater extent if they shared equally in caregiving. We are not prepared to defend this strongest version of the empirical proposition, although we believe that many (but certainly not all) men so socialized would gain from the changes we advocate.[9] In any case, it is likely that a rapid move toward strong gender egalitarianism from the status quo will impose what could be called "flourishing costs" on at least some men, and perhaps even on some women. In what follows we shall largely ignore this cost, which we think of as transitional. What we do believe, even if we cannot provide convincing empirical evidence, is that in a world without gender inequality, in which both boys and girls were socialized to value and participate in caregiving activities, adult men would in general flourish to a greater extent than they do in the existing world of strongly gender-differentiated identities, expectations, and roles.[10] Creating such a world is the goal of strong gender egalitarianism.

III. GENDER INEQUALITY AND THE PROBLEM OF TRANSFORMING NORMS

Our analysis of the problem of transforming gender relations is embedded in an explanatory argument about the mechanisms involved in the social reproduction of gender inequality. The gendered caregiving division of labor in the household is a significant, systematic determinant of broader patterns of continuing gender inequality in the economy and politics, and these public forms of inequality in turn contribute to the reproduction of intra-family inequalities. Four clusters of causal processes interact to generate these patterns:

(1) Gender inequalities in labor markets and employment opportunities. In spite of the passage of laws against gender discrimination, women as a category continue to face disadvantages in labor markets and employment. Some of this is certainly due to direct discrimination—employers and managers treating women as a category differently from men in ways that disadvantage women. But some of this operates through more complex mechanisms, involving the way the norms of appropriate wages are attached to different kinds of jobs, and how this interacts with the occupational preferences of men and women shaped by a wide range of gendered cultural processes.

(2) Household economic incentives. Given the inequalities in (1), the careers of men in general have a bigger potential impact on household standards of living than do the careers of women. This means that the overall economic standing of the family will generally be higher if men devote more energy to work and career advancement than do their wives, and this both creates pressures on wives to devote more energy to domestic responsibilities, including child care, and reinforces the normative understanding of male careers as more important even in those households where the careers of wives are economically more important than those of their husbands. These gendered incentive structures linked to work may have weakened somewhat in recent years as earnings inequality between men and women has declined, but it is still the case that the economic trajectory of most married families depends more on the prospects of the husband's career than of the wife's. This creates economic incentives for women to take greater responsibility for non-market caregiving labor.[11]

(3) Inadequate institutional supports for caregiving activities. In much of the world it is difficult for individual families to overcome the inequalities, pressures and incentives generated by (1) and (2). In the absence of good-quality inexpensive child care, generous parental leave programs, non-punitive forms of work flexibility and other "family-friendly" policies, even if within a family husbands and wives want to move in a more egalitarian direction, it is generally difficult to do so because of a lack of external supports.

(4) Gender-regulating social norms. Prevailing social norms continue to differentiate appropriate "men's work" from "women's work," and to treat childrearing in particular as more of a responsibility for women than for men. These norms have a number of important consequences for the reproduction of gender inequality in caregiving and in the public sphere:

(a) Prevailing gender norms create widespread expectations about the likely behavior of men and women, and thus make it rational for employers to engage in statistical discrimination against women because the expected interruptions from work are greater for women in general than for men.[12] The normative backing for these expectations makes it more difficult for people to make judgments based on purely individual characteristics, and thus unmarried women, women without children, and women who declare that they do not have such caregiving responsibilities are still often treated as likely to have excessive caregiving responsibilities.
(b) These norms reinforce stereotypes about innate male and female competences, and the stereotypes in turn reinforce the norms.
(c) The norms are internalized by both men and women in identity-forming ways that influence their preferences for caregiving and career. Women are more likely than men to feel guilty in placing career demands above family, and more likely, in the "game of chicken" over the distribution of family responsibilities, to give in.
(d) To the extent that caregiving is not just a value, preference, or natural "talent," but a *skill*, and to the extent that the stereotypes about competences and the identities shaped by norms affect the acquisition of such skills, then there are likely to be differences in male and female practical competence in caregiving. This in turn reinforces the norms, stereotypes, and associated identities.

Taken as a package, these mechanisms constitute a system of relatively coherent social reproduction: discrimination reinforces behaviors that reinforce norms; norms reinforce preferences and identities that reinforce behaviors and skills that reinforce norms; the obstacles, in the form of inadequate support, increase the costs of individual defections from the cycle; and so on.

There was a time, not in the distant past, when this self-reproducing equilibrium was strongly integrated and coherent, but over the past several decades a number of dramatic social changes have disrupted some of the links within this self-reinforcing system. Of particular importance are, first, the unintended consequences of the decentralized labor-market decisions of women and the wide-reaching ramifications of those decisions for fertility choices, marriage timing, and other "private" matters; second, the struggles against discrimination which have reduced, but have not eliminated, the incentives to discriminate against women in labor markets and work; and third, the reduction of material obstacles to changes in caregiving patterns, especially in some countries, through paid parental leaves and other measures. Nevertheless, this structure of inequality-sustaining mechanisms remains sufficiently strong to seriously impede movements toward strong gender egalitarianism. In particular, the normatively backed differentiation of gender identities and expectations remains strong, and the material incentives linked to those normative processes remain sufficiently real, that much less change in the gender division of labor within the family has occurred than might have been expected given the dramatic changes in the public sphere. This in turn continues to reinforce other aspects of the gender division of labor, blocking the movement toward a de-gendered division of labor necessary for strong gender egalitarianism.

The question, then, is whether we need stronger measures for furthering gender equality, measures designed to increase the involvement of men in caregiving activities, to erode these gender-differentiated norms around those activities. Perhaps we are just too impatient—perhaps the corrosive effect of women's labor force participation and ideological struggles over gender equality will gradually erode gender-differentiated norms of appropriate behavior. But perhaps such norms are sufficiently robust and deeply entrenched to remain very sticky unless directly undermined.

To sort this out we need to think about the relationship between patterns of observed behavior and the norms which endorse or condemn that behavior. Social norms and patterns of behavior mutually affect each other: the prevalence of a norm, especially when internalized, shapes behavior; but also, patterns of behavior we observe in the world either reinforce or undermine the existing norms, depending upon the extent to which they are congruent with those norms. Our concern here is with this second kind of relation: the way changing behaviors can subvert existing norms. The more people see men in public taking care of small children—pushing baby carriages, changing diapers in airports, supervising kids at playgrounds, having them in shopping carts at grocery stores—the more such behavior will be seen as "normal" in the purely statistical sense; and the more it is seen as normal in the statistical sense, then, over time, the more it is likely be viewed as normative as well. The essential strategy of

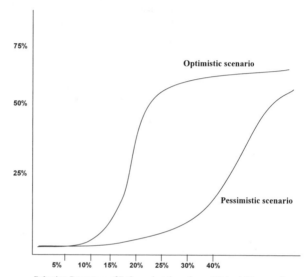

Figure 3.2

Prospects for changing norms by changing patterns of behavior: optimistic and pessimistic scenarios

Behavior: Percentage of Fathers who take active, publicly visible care of children

a public policy aimed at changing norms in ways that move toward strong gender egalitarianism, therefore, involves trying to directly change patterns of behavior in ways which, over time, will shift the prevailing norms in the society at large.

Figure 3.2 illustrates two sharply contrasting images of how this might occur. In the optimistic scenario, if the percentage of fathers actively engaged in publicly visible care of children reaches about 15 percent, small additional changes generate very large changes in public norms, so that once 20 percent of fathers are so engaged, a majority of the population will see this as normatively appropriate.[13] Furthermore, since we also know that prevailing norms affect behavior, there is likely to be a feedback process in which, as the socially prevailing norms become more accepting of fathers doing visible child care, more men are likely to behave consistently with this norm. This is likely to be particularly the case for those men for whom gender roles are less a matter of deep identities and more a question of responsiveness to social standards. Depending upon how these different processes interconnect dynamically, the process of normative change may have a real tipping point—a level of father child-care behavior which, if reached, generates a dynamic of accelerating normative change. If something like this optimistic scenario pertained, therefore, and we were currently, say, at around the 10 percent level, public policy would only have to create incentives to push this up to 15 percent or so to cross the tipping point in which the new norms stimulate new behavior, which would reinforce and extend the new norms.

The pessimistic scenario suggests that the tasks ahead are much more daunting. The gender norms around child care and caregiving are much more robust, and a strongly accelerating dynamic of change only begins when somewhere around 40 percent of fathers are visibly engaged in taking care of children. If this picture more accurately reflects the situation, then, if we were currently at the 10 percent level, public policy would have to exert a massive pressure on people to change behavior in order to set the stage for significant societal normative change. For a host of reasons, this might be very unlikely to succeed.

Data do not exist which would enable us to know what kind of curve we face in trying to move in the direction of strong gender egalitarianism. If the pessimistic scenario is in fact the accurate one, then the prospects for transforming through public policy the gender division of labor in the home—and the accompanying constraints this imposes on women—are fairly bleak. Our intuition, however, is that contemporary American and western European gender regimes are probably closer to the optimistic than to the pessimistic scenario. There has clearly been a significant softening up of gender norms already, even if behaviors have not changed as much as we would like. This at least makes it plausible that policies around caregiving could have effects on the reproduction of norms.

It is always possible that simply removing the caregiving-support obstacles currently faced by men and women when they make caregiving choices will, over time, erode the normative obstacles to strong gender egalitarianism. In Sweden a generous parental leave system and widespread availability of child-care services has, after all, had some impact on changing male behavior. While women do take much more parental leave than men, the amount men take has slowly increased. We suspect, however, that this will settle at an equilibrium below the tipping-point threshold in Figure 3.2. If this is true, and if we are serious about moving toward strong gender egalitarianism, we cannot rely on policies that simply attack discrimination or remove obstacles. It is also necessary to enact policies that actively undermine the normative systems that shape preferences by interrupting the behavior–norm reinforcement cycle. That is, it is necessary to enact equality-promoting policies that impose constraints on decisions within families in order to encourage men to do more child care. This is what the two gender equality–promoting types of policy do.

Among gender equality–promoting policies, individual-allocated leaves of the sort advocated by Gornick and Meyers are more likely to receive political support than the more radical father-linked leaves, since the latter make the options available to women contingent on the behavior of men. This flies in the face of the central ideal of feminism to enhance the autonomy of women and enlarge their range of choices independently of men. People deeply committed to gender equality are therefore likely to be very reluctant to support a policy option that seems to subordinate women's access to paid parental leaves to the choices of men. Nevertheless, if the obstacles to strong gender egalitarianism are rooted in the normative processes we have discussed, especially if these are linked to deeply internalized gendered identities, policies directly designed to get men to do more caregiving may be needed, and such policies may require imposing significant constraints on women's choices as well.

NOTES

1   Our discussion here is pegged to the problem of parental caregiving leaves for infants, but the central arguments could be extended to all forms of caregiving responsibilities, including eldercare, taking care of sick children, and so on.

2   The rationale for a *maternity* leave is distinct from the rationale for parental caregiving leaves: maternity leaves are more like medical leaves— paid time off work in recognition of the physical recovery needs after childbirth. Parental caregiving leaves are a recognition of the value of facilitating parents' involvement in the direct child-care activities of infants.

3   The proposal implies that fathers must take some leave before mothers can take any, but there is no requirement that fathers take extended initial leaves. A likely scenario for this kind of policy would be fathers and mothers taking alternating weeks or days of leave, for example. Still, in the accounting system, the father must take a leave first to create the entitlement for the mother.

4   Statistical discrimination—as opposed to pure prejudice—is grounded in the behavioral differences between groups. If mothers and fathers are more or less equally at risk in taking parental leave, then the potential for parental

leave-taking would cease to be a source of gender-specific statistical discrimination. There could, of course, still be statistical discrimination against *parents* (both men and women are "at risk" as parents in taking paid parental leave), but this is likely to be a weaker force than gender-differentiated childrearing responsibilities.

5 In Sweden a very limited form of equality-promoting policy has been introduced in the form of a one-month father-only leave that has been added to the twelve months of family-allocated paid leaves.

6 It should be noted that the norm of gender equality of power, rewards, and burdens is not derived from any distinctive feminist argument, but rather is simply a specific instance of general principles about equality of power, rewards, and burdens among people engaged in different forms of social cooperation. Cooperation within families is a particularly salient instance of social cooperation, and one within which power, rewards and burdens should be equally shared.

7 Throughout this paper we adopt the sociological convention of using the term "sex" to refer to biological difference and "gender" to refer to the socially constructed relations between men and women built around sexual difference. To speak of the withering away of gender, therefore, means the withering away of *socially constructed* differences between men and women and the socially enforced norms that sustain those differences, but it does not imply the disappearance of differences which are direct reflections of biological sex. The ultimate goal, therefore, is probably more accurately described as genderlessness rather than gender equality.

8 This possibility presupposes that our preferences and dispositions are not entirely socially constructed, but that there is a neurobiological component to the process of preference formation which interacts with these social processes. We know from work by Ernst Fehr (2004) and others that there is, for example, a significant neurobiological component to altruistic preferences. How strong this is in the case of possible sex-differences in caregiving dispositions, and what distribution of actual preferences among men and women would occur in a social context of strong gender egalitarianism, is impossible to determine from data gathered in a world of pervasive socially conditioned gender differences. Our assumption is that such biologically rooted distributions of temperaments and dispositions among men and among women would greatly overlap, but this does not mean that the distributions would be the same.

9 The claim that many men today would flourish to a greater extent if they were more involved in caregiving implies that, for many men, following conventional gender norms around caregiving is mainly a matter of conforming to social standards rather than acting on the basis of some deeply internalized identity.

10 We are not denying that there are certain privileges men have in a world of gender inequality and sharply differentiated gender norms and identities, and that they would lose these privileges in a world of strong gender egalitarianism. It is because of these privileges and advantages that come with gender inequality that moving toward gender equality is a matter of social justice, not just of enhancing the conditions for universal human flourishing. Our claim is simply that men also have something quite important to gain from strong gender equality. Because of the complexities involved and the problem of the ingrained dispositions of men as they are, we cannot say whether or not, on balance, the costs to men are greater than the gains.

11 These labor market differentials form the basis for Becker's (1981) arguments about how utility maximization within households generates a strong gender specialization in household responsibilities. This fact is also central to Goldthorpe's (1983) arguments that the location of married women in the class structure is determined by the class position of their husbands. For a discussion of these issues, see Wright (1997: chapter 10).

12 In statistical discrimination, employers substitute information about the average behavior of members of a group for information about the likely behavior of a specific individual in making hiring and promotion decisions. The standard explanation for this behavior is that the information costs of gathering reliable information on individuals are much higher than those of gathering information about the group. Of course, the cognitive practices that underlie statistical discrimination are quite vulnerable to stereotyping, which tends to exaggerate inter-group differences, and strong norms tend to reinforce such stereotypes.

13 There is no suggestion here that these shifts in prevailing norms are instantaneous. The actual process of adjustment takes time, which is not represented in the graph.

REFERENCES

Becker, Gary, 1981, *A Treatise on the Family*, Cambridge: Harvard University Press.

Fehr, Ernst, 2004, "The Neural Basis of Altruistic Punishment," *Science* 305, 27 August: 1,254–58.

Goldthorpe, John, 1983, "Women and Class Analysis: In Defence of the Conventional View," *Sociology* 17 (4): 465–88.

Wright, Erik Olin, 1997, *Class Counts*, Cambridge: Cambridge University Press.

4

Whose Utopia?

Shireen Hassim

The Real Utopias Project, and Janet Gornick and Marcia Meyers' paper on gender egalitarianism in particular, raise some unavoidable questions for those located outside the globe's wealthy countries. Who is/can be part of this utopia? Can the vision of the dual-earner/dual-caregiver model be universalized? What steps would need to be taken to make this a vision for the global poor as well as the rich? And by whom would those steps need to be taken? One could respond with weary cynicism, but I prefer to take my cue from the question posed by Erik Olin Wright: what would it take to create social institutions free of oppression? He outlines real utopias as those that are "grounded in the real potential of humanity, utopian destinations that have accessible waystations, utopian designs of institutions that can inform our practical tasks of muddling through in a world of imperfect conditions for social change." So I take as a common goal, regardless of global positioning, that the envisioning of utopias for those in the wealthier nations must, as a moral imperative, entail the possibility of universalizing institutional principles and core values. At the very least, it must be one that reshapes the structure of economy and society in the United States, as Gornick and Meyers wish, while not being built upon or reinforcing existing exclusions of huge swaths of humanity from access to global resources. In other words, our "real utopia" must be one that includes (in principle, and immediately or progressively) all of us.

Yet to imagine such an inclusive utopia raises a set of concerns that to some extent stands outside the framework of Gornick and Meyers' paper. I outline these concerns as a collective challenge to think about what institutional principles should inform movements for social change in contexts other than those with which we are most familiar, and beyond the North–South binaries. I am also convinced enough by the idea of real utopias to argue strongly that a progressive utopia must be one that is not built on the exploitation of the poor by the rich, nor one that speaks only to an elite. It must contain the seed of universalization; the way-stations must be accessible to those currently excluded. If we do not extend this discussion, we could reinforce the idea that social policy is part of the end-state of development and therefore not an appropriate or relevant debate for developing countries. The effect would be to consign poor people to the margins, as either not ready for inclusion (and the question then is, when will they "catch up"?) or as an unwelcome irritant. It seems to me inadequate to defer discussion of more inclusive models on the grounds that some states are simply not ready for them; states do not exist in isolation from each other—the poverty of poor nations is to no small extent the result of policies pursued by institutions under the control of rich countries. While some of these relationships of (particularly) crude exploitation might have their roots in more distant histories of conquest and colonization than others, contemporary states and the relationships between them bear the traces of these histories. The rules of international trade and the institutions of global control over poor economies are a prime example of current relationships of exploitation and inequality.

I argue, then, that any discussion of a real utopian transformation of institutions within the wealthy countries of the world must examine the relationship between these proposals and the conditions in the global South. There are two distinct ways in which the proposals elaborated by Gornick and Meyers might be criticized from this vantage point:

(1) *Non-universalizability.* These proposals might only be viable in the wealthy countries. The point here is not just that these policies are not *achievable* in poor countries because of a lack of political forces with sufficient power to implement them; they are not *viable* without radical changes in the economic and institutional landscape of these countries. Capitalist development has taken different forms, giving rise to different kinds of institutional arrangements in rich and poor countries. In my view, theorists of radical democracy underestimate the impact of weak and fragile institutions, assuming that the necessary institutions can be relatively easily created through political forces. If the task of strengthening and redirecting institutions is overwhelming, then the Gornick–Meyers proposals would not really be "real utopias," because they could not be universalized.

(2) *Global exploitation*. The possibility of these utopias in the wealthy countries might depend upon global inequalities and the continuing poverty of the poor countries. Here I am concerned with the possibility that the viability of the real utopia proposed is dependent upon global injustice. There are two aspects to this criticism. The first is that the viability of the Gornick–Meyers proposals depends upon the global care chain in which caregiving labor from the poor countries is imported to provide caregiving services in the rich countries. This is not simply a contingent fact; there would not be sufficient labor supply of potential child-care workers within the rich countries to provide these services. The second is that these policies are only possible because the rich countries are rich, and a significant part of this wealth is the result of imperialism in one form or another. Even apart from the labor supply problem for child-care workers, in the absence of imperialism and the global inequality it generates and perpetuates, the rich countries would not have sufficient resources to underwrite the kind of family support policies (parental leaves plus generous child-care services) required for the Gornick–Meyers proposals. For the purposes of this paper I will leave this much larger question aside, and focus on the care-chain problem.

SOCIAL PROTECTION LEGACIES: MUST DIFFERENT PATHS, DIFFERENT INSTITUTIONS AND DIFFERENT SOCIAL VALUES MEAN DIFFERENT UTOPIAS?[1]

The social organization of care work is one of the central challenges of the twenty-first century, impacting directly on the well-being of all people, and on women's ability to be full citizens. Various scenarios for addressing care needs emerged in the past century in welfare states of the North, yet it is now evident that feminist tools developed in these contexts are not easily transferred, because of the very different material and cultural conditions in which poor women in developing countries live. Nor are developing countries homogeneous; economic, institutional and cultural variations across countries and regions shape the nature of both risks faced by and forms of social protection available to women. This has led to globally skewed outcomes, with more than half the world's population excluded from any type of statutory protection. In sub-Saharan Africa and South Asia, more than 90 percent of the population are not included in any form of protection. Here I want to lay out some of these variations and spell out their implications for achieving gender equality through the central planks of an egalitarian social policy system as articulated by Gornick and Meyers.

Gornick and Meyers note that the rapid increase in women's labor force participation in the second half of the twentieth century undermined the male-breadwinner/female-caregiver model, and in Europe particularly this spurred the development of work–family reconciliation policies. However, more recent patterns of women's entry into paid labor have not produced the kinds of relationships between work and protection that were evident in earlier phases of development of northern welfare states, nor are paid jobs in developing countries anything like the "good jobs" of industrialized countries—that is, above minimum wage, unionized and benefit-carrying. Even in the advanced democracies, "good jobs" are increasingly rare. So, while in general the vision offered by Gornick and Meyers of a dual-earner/dual-caregiver society—"a society in which men and women engage symmetrically in employment and caregiving, and all parents have realistic opportunities to combine waged work with the direct provision of care for their children" (this volume: 4) is an attractive one, the issue to consider is whether such a model can be universalized. Indeed, I might provocatively go even further and ask whether such a vision can be sustained for industrialized countries only on the basis of an asymmetrical global economy in which some countries barricade themselves off from the global condition of poverty while at the same time drawing on labor from poor countries to provide care.

Gornick and Meyers provide a comprehensive account of the historical context of the Nordic and US welfare systems. The underlying pattern is that the increasing female employment rate "forced" social actors and states to develop various mechanisms for reconciling paid work and care. The gains that were made by feminists, particularly in the Nordic countries, appear to have been made in relatively closed economies in which there is a virtuous circle between progressive political mobilization and state policies: that is, with the right kinds of ideologies and strategies in place, political mobilization can create a kind of social consensus that can change policies. This raises the question of whether greater egalitarianism in the North could "trickle down" to poor countries either by particular kinds of alliances and modes of mobilization, or by setting the example of what the content of social policies should ideally be, or by changing the ways the relationships between the global rich and the global poor. Yet none of these options seem to be likely outcomes in developing countries. The rational model of policy making described by Gornick and Meyers is rarely apparent in many parts of the world, where even in democracies decision making may be opaque and driven by the "hidden hands" of donor and lending agencies and private interests, with state institutions being weak institutional partners. International financial institutions have been actively opposed to the emergence of anything like the social security systems of rich countries and have, furthermore, whittled away at state institutions and state capacities to deliver public goods. Low levels of waged labor and weak representative associations such as trade unions further undermine approaches that depend on strengthening the relationship between employment and protection as the key strategy for egalitarianism.

These patterns are particularly evident in sub-Saharan Africa, where race, gender and location have intersected in complex ways to create hierarchical societies with differentiated rights of access to state social provisioning. The indigenous population, and women in particular, have remained locked into subsistence-based rural economies, with little access to welfare. The dominance of male labor migration has intensified women's responsibility for household reproduction and care in these subsistence economies, and their concomitant marginality from the urban economy and any social benefits that have come from it. Although governments in the golden age of post-independence development prioritized the provision of important social services like health, housing and education, their efforts retained a bias toward the more developed urban areas. But even in the urban economies, a dual labor market structure has persisted that overwhelmingly privileges male workers, and leaves women with weak access to welfare and social protection mechanisms that might free them from some aspects of care work. Rearranging care work under these labor market conditions is an unviable prospect.

The small formal economy in most developing countries results in job security and work-related benefits being privileges available to a relatively thin stratum of workers—predominantly men, and especially if they were unionized. While these particular benefits could have been extended over time to other sectors of the population (as happened historically in the successful welfare states described by Gornick and Meyers, and more recently in Korea and Taiwan), since the early 1980s there has in fact been a global trend in the opposite direction: with increasing informalization of labor, even hitherto "formal" workers have lost their work-related social benefits, such as access to health insurance and pension provision. For example, in Latin America in the 1980s and 1990s eight out of every ten new jobs created were in the informal sector, while the 1999 manufacturing wage was only 3 percent higher than its 1980 counterpart (Tokman, 2002). Those who work in the informal economy are generally not covered by labor legislation for social protection, and earn less, on average, than those in the formal economy (ILO, 2002). In this context, not only work–family reconciliation but access to paid work itself has impacted on gender relations.

The surge in women's labor force participation in developing countries has produced similar tensions in social reproduction to those identified by Gornick and Meyers. For many developing countries, increasing poverty and the commodification of social services are changing the coping strategies of households and communities in a multitude of ways, causing upheavals in gender and generational patterns of work and responsibility. The commercialization of social services, including basic services such as water and health care, makes it increasingly necessary for all household members—whether female or male, young or old—to take on paid work. Increasing levels of female education, later marriages, and changing aspirations and lifestyles, are also important social forces propelling women into the workforce. Yet, as in Europe and the US, while the balance of contributions women and men make to households in the form of cash and care is changing, the changes impact more negatively on women, who have added paid work to their existing responsibilities for care, than on men, who in most countries have reduced the amount of paid work they do and increased their care work only slightly. Thus the gender division of labor is not so much disappearing as changing shape, as women enter the labor force and stay in employment for greater portions of their lives. Women's "cheap" labor in the global economy has had a noticeable impact, not least in allowing poor countries a comparative advantage in conditions of economic liberalization. Export-oriented development strategies in poor countries indeed depend on women's wage-labor for success. Yet, while they may be responsible for a significant proportion of export earnings, it has been relatively difficult for women to extend debates beyond wages and workplace-specific issues to issues of social reproduction more generally (Pearson, 2004). A more common pattern is that existing social entitlements for women workers, particularly those arising out of more communal systems of reciprocal care, are further eroded. These developments have facilitated the re-familialization of risk and social provisioning. In a context where a significant proportion of the population cannot afford its basic needs, the imposition of fees for health care has been impoverishing. These reforms seem to be based on unrealistic assumptions about poor women's ability to muster the economic resources needed to access services for themselves and their dependents, and about their unlimited time and capacity to provide unpaid care when formal care remains out of reach. The demands on women's time to provide for families' care needs are even more strenuous in countries that are experiencing an escalation of the HIV/AIDS pandemic, as home-based care and community care are expected to fill the gap caused by the erosion of health-care systems.

As Gornick and Meyers make clear, Nordic social democracies appear to have achieved relatively high levels of gender equality through female labor force participation and the redistributive mechanisms of social policy—exemplified by Sweden, which has been able to forge "participation parity" in the labor market, with nearly equal numbers of women and men in the workforce. They also recognize that this achievement masks the manner in which gender inequalities have been reinscribed in new ways, modernizing gender inequalities in much the same way as in developing countries. For example, a significant portion of women—over a third— work part-time. As Gornick and Meyers point out, significant gender inequality in the sphere of caring persists, even though parental leave schemes and "daddy leave" quotas were designed to be gender-neutral. Gender segregation in the labor market and gender divisions of care work are global phenomena, albeit with different levels of intensity. In developing countries the increasing numbers of women who work in the informal economy add new layers of exclusion to the picture. According to the ILO (2002), informal employment comprises between one half and three-quarters of non-agricultural employment in developing countries. Informal employment tends to be a larger source of employment for women than for men in all developing regions except North Africa (ILO, 2002); women are also more likely to work as own-account workers, domestic workers, and unpaid contributing workers in family enterprises than are men, while men are more likely to work as employers and wage workers (ILO, 2002; Heintz, 2005). Women informal workers tend to be overrepresented in the more precarious and less remunerative segments of informal work. A recent study based on six countries confirms that women's hourly earnings typically fall below those of men in identical employment categories, and that the gender gap in earnings is particularly pronounced among own-account workers, while it is narrowest in public wage employment (Heintz, 2005). Informal workers have the lowest levels of access to social protection and social services, including those that support care work.

Thus, despite a significant increase in women's labor force participation and the erosion of the male-breadwinner model, gender egalitarianism remains a distant goal. The emphasis in Gornick and

Meyers' proposal on the formal paid labor market cannot address conditions in which such jobs are incredibly scarce (and where workers may have little bargaining power over the conditions of such work), and where employers in the informal labor market may be distant corporations over which states, let alone individual workers, cannot exercise any form of oversight.

Let me now turn to a second aspect of the model, relating to assumptions about the institutional character of the real utopia. One important lesson of the twentieth century for feminists is the key role that can be played by the state in reducing the extent of inequalities through the provision of a range of policies and financial supports that reduce the cost of gender difference. Gornick and Meyers' proposal presupposes the existence of a capable and responsive state—a condition which is at best only unevenly present in developing countries. Yet state capacities are particularly weak in developing countries. The "activist" postcolonial nationalist governments in Africa, although initially committed to redistribution, did not expand the institutions established by colonialism (executive, civil service, police, and army) in ways that consolidated democracy, or even their long-term ability to sustain a developmental focus. In particular, institutions that would constrain executive power, such as multiparty elections, judicial independence and, outside the state, institutions that might expand the legitimacy of the state and its capacity to represent diverse interests (such as a vibrant civil society) were either severely restricted or actively repressed. By contrast, those institutions that were seen as either enhancing the capacity of elites to manage or to remain in power, such as the bureaucracy, expanded rapidly. Importantly, however, bureaucratic expansion was not tied to efficiency or to responsiveness to citizens, and for the most part the political system continues to operate in ways that do not depend on electoral responsiveness. As a result, in sub-Saharan Africa for example, many groups in society disengaged from making demands on the state, instead entrenching informal, traditionally based systems of governance and resource allocation. Citizens bypassed the state as the locus of their demands, meeting their needs through a combination of informal mechanisms and developing allegiances to local political actors rather than the state per se. These developments have a direct impact on the extent to which new models of care can be pursued. By contrast with sub-Saharan Africa, Latin American and East Asian states have demonstrated that competent public bureaucracies that are at least internally accountable can be made responsive to the needs of women. In these regions states appear to be more able to act on political agreements struck between political parties and other actors. Although there are variations in the social composition and democratic credentials of states, on the whole Latin American states have been pervasive, relatively well institutionalized, and have shown a strong history of interventionism. In these contexts, the development of gender-equitable social policies has been dependent far more on winning political support and social consensus over the direction of social policy than on the state's capacity to absorb women's demands.

By contrast with developed countries, the elaboration of social assistance and social security in developing countries has been rooted in the new global discourse of poverty, which has in turn fed into a bifurcated view of social policy. In rich countries, as Gornick and Meyers show, the core ideas of universalism remain relatively unscathed by the neoliberal turn. For poor countries, however, the idea of welfare pluralism—that is, that social needs should be met by a partnership between states, markets, families and civil society—was pushed by international donor institutions. Yet the work–family policy debates in Europe and the US, including those among feminists, remain disturbingly cut off from those governments' roles in developing-country policy prescriptions. As Ruth Pearson asks,

> given that feminists continue to defend welfare and social policies which support women workers in the north, where is the feminist resistance to the assumption that women workers in the developing countries should not or cannot earn social expenditure and welfare entitlements? (Pearson, 2004: 608)

The experiences of developed countries suggest that the most egalitarian outcomes result from universalistic programs that are financed through taxation—not employment-based contributions—and provide entitlements to benefits based on citizenship or residency criteria. These programs may have a greater potential to be socially inclusive and to contribute to human welfare and development. Yet these are not easy to argue for politically in contexts where "fiscal restraint" is the guiding principle of public policy, and where solidarity and social justice are not the underpinning values of the social policy system. To the contrary, very often the dependence on women's unpaid labor continues to be justified by recourse to ideologies of "tradition" and "good motherhood," while communitarianism (rather than solidarity) tends to devalue women's claims to personhood and support on the grounds of the needs of "the community." It is difficult to place these kinds of caring arrangements on Rosemary Crompton's continuum, as described by Gornick and Meyers: although some of the ideological aspects of the male-breadwinner/female-caregiver model are evident, women are in fact not *only* caregivers. The dual-earner/female-caregiver model may come closer to the reality, although caring is often not "part-time," as it is conducted *in parallel* with paid work (for example, in the case of homeworking). Yet, even then, care is provided by more than one person in extended family settings—social arrangements in most of the world are still far from resembling the nuclear family model; indeed, I am not sure whether we would want, as feminists, to privilege such a model. Furthermore, most poor households rely on income and survival strategies from several members (and from a variety of sources, wages being only one), rather than on a single "breadwinner." In our universalistic and egalitarian model, further elaboration of a multiple-caregiver/multiple-earner model is needed. The linearity of Crompton's continuum is slightly troubling, as it suggests that modernization will erode the overwhelming emphasis on child well-being and introduce (as a product of struggle) gender-equality concerns. Yet, as I have argued, while greater entry of women into the public sphere may facilitate an increasing concern with equality rights, such convergence is by no means guaranteed. (Nor is it merely a matter of generating a sufficiently large surplus: the oil wealth of the Middle East has been accompanied by the notorious absence of greater democracy or gender equality.)

THE IMPLICATIONS OF THE GLOBAL CARE CHAIN FOR A REAL UTOPIA

One of the striking aspects of Gornick and Meyers' paper is its focus on domestic policy models, both in the Nordic countries and in the US. Although there is careful discussion of how changes in the European Union might have affected traditional welfare system models, there is almost no consideration of the globalized nature of the economy. This is understandable; after all, the best exemplar of their model, Sweden, has insulated itself from the ill effects of neoliberal globalization relatively successfully. As I have argued in the previous section, there are a number of reasons for this: strong and relatively egalitarian formal economies, the strength and legitimacy of the state both as a set of political institutions that can act on citizen demands and as a legitimately interventionist state, and the continuing strength of the union movement. The coalition between unions and the state there has protected the labor market and lent continued support to state regulation, so that even migrant labor is drawn within the net of regulation and protection. Where migrants are employed in the care sector, they tend to be employed by the state under the same conditions as Swedish labor, and are not subject to the vagaries of individual employers who may be seeking cheap labor. This is a highly enabling set of conditions, and even within them gender segregation persists in both paid and unpaid work. It is not only developing countries that remain far from possessing these conditions. For the US, too, the picture is quite different, given its less regulated labor market, the large flows of legal and illegal migrants, and the relatively weaker union movement. Indeed, research shows that immigrant women in the US (and Canada) are most likely to be overrepresented in marginal, unregulated and/or poorly paid jobs, many of these in the care sector (Boyd and Pikkov, 2006).

Problems of low pay and poor conditions of labor in the caring sector are driving away young people with options to work elsewhere in countries such as the US and the UK (Folbre, 2006). The response of health-care sectors and individual employers in these countries has been to import care workers. Indeed, Arlie Hochschild has argued that the increasing entry of women into the labor market in the US has created a "care deficit" that is increasingly being filled by women from poor countries (who, ironically, create new care deficits in their home country as they migrate in search of better jobs—they are thus, Hochschild argues, linked in a global care chain). The global trade is estimated to involve between 1 and 1.7 million Asian women, although it is important to note that the traffic is not only between poor and rich countries of the North: Filipina maids go to Hong Kong, Japan, Jordan and Syria in large numbers. The Scandinavian countries and the US, according to the United Nations Research Institute for Social Development, have the highest percentage of migrant women employed in education and health (in Sweden, 27 percent of migrant female employment between 2001 and 2002 was in these sectors). The problem of work–family balance is thus at least to some extent negotiated between states, as well as between individuals within a household, and between households and the state.

The effect is the draining of skilled care workers away from developing countries by rich countries, so that even in countries where governments are committed to building up strong social sectors, such as South Africa, scarce tax resources are in effect being used to subsidize the training of care workers for rich countries. Ensuring that these migrant/immigrant workers access the full benefits of their labor, even if the US were to mimic the Swedish model, only solves one part of the problem. The drain on developing country resources remains a problem, and the vicious cycle of the politics of debt is reinforced. In some countries (such as Papua New Guinea) private institutes for the training of care workers have sprung up that are specifically geared to providing "qualifications" that meet Australian and New Zealand requirements for care workers (and therefore for work permits or immigration status). When they do find jobs, immigrant care workers are in what Boris and Klein call "front-line care jobs"—those dealing with bodily hygiene, cleaning and cooking. In the US, their average hourly wage is lower than that of all jobs in health care with the exception of janitors (Boris and Klein, 2006: 82). Part-time workers, and those who are paid under the counter by their employers, are also excluded from social security (Boyd and Pikkov, 2006).

Can the gender-egalitarian model be achieved in rich countries without intensifying the global inequality in care provision? This is a difficult question to address without further research. Gornick and Meyers do not quantify the labor market requirements to resource the dual-earner/dual-caregiver model, but the overall direction of their proposals would of course shift the market toward better paid, better quality child care. Whether this care can be provided within the domestically bounded model is an open question. It is presumed that shifting working hours and balancing care between parents would to some extent affect the need for more extensive paid child care, but the model is silent on the impact of the proposals for current global divisions of care work.

Balancing work and care, then, will be difficult to achieve for all of the people living in the US, let alone globally. It is perhaps in the global care chain that we see most clearly the ways in which, and institutions through which, unequal resources are distributed globally. The dual-caregiver/dual-earner model is based on assumptions that, to use Göran Therborn's phrase, are perhaps "fatally parochial in comparative perspective."

CONDITIONS FOR GLOBAL EGALITARIANISM

Clearly, the politics of egalitarianism cannot be confined to a discussion of what might work in the US, but have to extend to consider universalization on a global scale. In this section I discuss some of the conditions that need to be created in order to shift internal household relations of power—although it is by no means an exhaustive list.

Beginning with the economic level, we need to expand our model beyond the formal paid labor context. The reliance on paid employment as a key element of the Gornick–Meyers model has implications for macroeconomic policy, for it is a meaningless assumption if secure, high-quality and well-paid jobs are not available. The right to paid work needs to be recognized. In some countries (particularly in what is called the classical belt of patriarchy), women's access to the labor market is severely curtailed by ideologies of seclusion and domesticity. In these contexts women are expected to put family responsibilities above employment, and their care burdens are continually reinforced rather than shifted.

It is conceivable that the socialization of care work will open possibilities for more jobs, but great vigilance will be needed to ensure that this is not seen simply as cheap labor provided by insecure workers from developing countries. International organizing is clearly needed to improve labor conditions along all stages of the global value chain in production. Although there are debates about how best to improve working conditions—ranging from the limitations of voluntary transnational campaigns to concerns about the way international labor standards might limit investment and job creation in Third World countries—there is broad agreement that globalization is linked to new employment patterns, presenting labor unions and women's groups with new concerns about how best to improve working conditions for everyone, including those in informal and unregulated employment. In the first instance, although poverty and inequality need to be addressed within particular national contexts, the global context of care and of policy making also needs to be acknowledged more overtly. Proponents of gender egalitarianism would need to see their political terrain as including greater global redistribution guaranteeing access to the basic means of survival, as well as the power to determine the content of international regulatory frameworks. This would entail a global recognition that there should be a threshold of well-being below which no one should be allowed to fall (that is, well-being should be understood not just in terms of standards within an individual nation-state, but as a solidaristic principle that should apply universally). This means that the institutions and rules of international trade need to be addressed so that fairer conditions of trade apply for poor countries: the global double standard needs to be removed. Of course, dealing with poverty will not automatically address inequality, but it is a necessary step toward a better society.

One way to address the diminishing link between paid employment and women's quality of life would be to extend Gornick and Meyers' proposal to expand public support for care work. The small domestic tax bases in many developing countries preclude or limit local financing. To be sure, multinational companies have little interest in "caring" for their workers; but they should not be allowed to drive down the cost of labor in developing countries and, ideally, they should be taxed to provide revenue for social protection. Ruth Pearson, for example, suggests that demands for policy change should explicitly link women's work in export production to the provision of publicly supported reproductive services. She argues for a "Maria Tax," modeled on the Tobin Tax, which would

> require national governments to levy a tax on exporters reflecting the proportion of the workforce utilized to provide the commodity or service being sold to the global market. The revenue would then be reinvested to support women generally within the economy—such as childcare facilities, reproductive and occupational health facilities and education programmes. (Pearson, 2004: 610)

Not only would this contribute to women's welfare directly, it would also offer "mobilizing and advocacy" possibilities by emphasizing how the sexual division of labor still gives women overwhelming responsibility for reproductive tasks (Pearson, 2004: 618). If the kinds of proposals for employer regulation included in Gornick and Meyers' model are to be extended within the European Union, one conceivable "way-station" might be to insist that the regulations extend to the operations of European companies wherever in the world these may be. The implementation of international human rights and labor conventions is crucial, both in creating fairer trading systems and in supporting gender-equality advocates in hostile environments. As Gornick and Meyers point out, however, these normative frameworks need to understand all people as both working and caring citizens, rather than reinforcing the male-worker standard. This would seem to align well with the dual-earner/dual-caregiver model.

But this would require a prior consensus on the value of care work. Care work needs to be recognized, legitimated and valued, and the provision of care needs to be seen as a matter for public policy for developing countries. Some attempts to do this—such as the gender-responsive budgeting initiative—are opening fruitful avenues for exerting policy pressure, but they are frequently not backed up by the political commitment of governments or by political pressure from below. The addressing of gender inequality in any serious sense requires the gender division of labor to be eliminated, but this might entail the de-familialization of child-care and elder-care needs, even though this would inevitably induce tensions with patriarchal and/or communitarian ideologies. Gornick and Meyers seem reluctant to go this far, preferring to equalize responsibilities *within* households—and even, at times, normatively privileging the nuclear family as the appropriate site for such activities. Part of the rationale for retaining care within the family is the unresolved question of quality of care; high-quality care is not only expensive, it may not necessarily address the non-commodifiable aspects of care, such as affection and intimacy.

However, if care is to remain primarily a family-based (or household-based) set of activities, then more effective incentives are clearly needed to persuade (coerce?) men into sharing care work. Struggles for democratization are relevant to this process, as feminists frequently have to enlist the coercive power of the democratic state to ensure that values of equality are advanced in the face of conservative and traditionalist mobilization. Feminist struggles in developing and developed countries alike show the importance of a democratic and interventionist state. In developing countries, where procedures of representation and accountability may be weakly present, even stronger (preferably constitutional) support is needed for the recognition of women's rights to equality in order to buttress attacks from social conservatives. Rights-based arguments are frequently criticized in developing countries for supposedly promoting liberal individualism; yet it would be perfectly feasible to argue for the recognition of ethical individualism (as opposed to ontological individualism—a distinction made by the feminist economist Ingrid Robeyns): this would recognize women's personhood without unduly privileging individual freedom over solidarity. Of course, the "caring for" aspects of care are not amenable to commodification; however, cultural norms that prioritize the provision of this care by women do need to be challenged. As Gornick and Meyers show, the development of socialized systems of care has been plagued by problems related to the quality of care, and particularly by new and rising norms of "adequate" care. Concerns about the quality of care need to be addressed in their own right, not as a proxy for idealizing female caring.

I have argued extensively that states' capacity to make progressive social policy needs to be strengthened. This depends partly on the extent to which developing-country governments are allowed to respond to pressure from below (that is, to exercise a measure of economic sovereignty), rather than to the external prescriptions of donor agencies. But it also implies that there is a responsibility of advocates of egalitarianism in developed countries to advance such struggles actively in developing countries.

Finally, organized labor (in both formal and informal sectors) needs to be strengthened. In many countries, the tensions between trade unions and women workers, as well as between trade unions and informal workers, have limited the kinds of coalitions that need to be built around support for women workers (that is, workers' needs beyond wages, such as transportation and child care). Unlike Sweden, where such alliances between feminists and male union leaders were forged early in the twentieth century, in developing countries many trade unions, if they exist at all, are deeply masculinist. Women's interests tend to be taken up by NGOs instead—although new forms of unionism are emerging, such as South Africa's Self-Employed Women's Union.

Gornick and Meyers' extremely stimulating paper brings to mind an observation by South African Constitutional Court judge Albie Sachs that, in South Africa, patriarchy is the only non racial institution. In the context of this particular Real Utopias conference, I am tempted to argue that the feminization of care may well be the most globalized of institutions.

NOTES

1 This section draws substantially on arguments presented in Shireen Hassim and Shahra Razavi, "Gender and Social Policy in a Global Context: Uncovering the Gendered Structure of 'the Social'," in Razavi and Hassim, 2006. I am grateful to Shahra for her permission to use that work for this project.

REFERENCES

Boris, Eileen, and Jennifer Klein, 2006, "Organising Home Care: Low-Waged Workers in the Welfare State," *Politics and Society* 34 (1), March: 82.

Boyd, Monica and Deanna Pikkov, 2006, *Gendering Migration, Livelihood and Entitlements: Migrant Women in Canada and the United States*, Ottawa: IDRC Policy Report.

Folbre, Nancy, 2006, "Demanding Quality: Worker/consumer Coalitions and 'High Road' Strategies in the Care Sector," *Politics and Society* 34 (1).

Hassim, Shireen, and Shahra Razavi, 2006, "Gender and Social Policy in Global Conetxt: Uncovering the Gendered Structure of the 'Social'," in Razavi and Hassim, *Gender and Social Policy in Global Context: Uncovering the Gendered Structure of the "Social"*, Basingstoke: Palgrave.

Heintz, J., 2005, *The Growing Informality of Labour Markets*, paper presented at the UNRISD/CGGS Conference on Gender and Social Policy, Marstrand, Sweden, 28–29 May.

Hochschild, Arlie, 2000, "Global Care Chains and Emotional Surplus Value," in W. Hutton and A. Giddens, eds, *On the Edge: Living with Global Capitalism*, Jonathan Cape: London.

International Labour Organization (ILO), 2002, *Women and Men in the Informal Economy: A Statistical Picture*, Geneva: ILO.

Lund, Francie, 2006, "Working People and Access to Social Protection," in Razavi and Hassim, *Gender and Social Policy in Global Context*.

Molyneux, M., forthcoming, *Poverty Relief and the New Social Policy in Latin America: Mothers at the Service of the State?* Programme Paper, Geneva: UNRISD.

Pearson, Ruth, 2004, "The Social is Political: Towards the Re-politicisation of Feminist Analysis of the Global Economy," *International Feminist Journal of Politics* 6 (4).

Therborn, Goran, 2006, *Between Sex and Power: Family in the World*, London: Routledge.

Tokman, V. E., 2002, "Jobs and Solidarity: Challenges for Labour Market Policy in Latin America," in E. Huber, ed., *Models of Capitalism: Lessons for Latin America*. University Park PA: Pennsylvania State University Press.

Vivian, J., 1995, "How Safe are 'Social Safety Nets'? Adjustment and Social Sector Restructuring in Developing Countries," in J. Vivian, ed, *Adjustment and Social Sector Restructuring*, London: UNRISD/Frank Cass.

White, G., 1996, "Civil Society, Democratization and Development," in R. Luckham and G. White, eds, *Democratization in the South: The Jagged Wave*, Manchester: Manchester University Press.

===== 5 =====

Reforming Care

Nancy Folbre

Feminist theorists and activists alike have long been shifting away from an emphasis on discrimination against women toward concerns about the distribution of care responsibilities. Most policy recommendations growing out of these concerns focus on the need for more state support for child care, paid family leave, and/or more equal sharing of care responsibilities in the family. Janet Gornick and Marcia Meyers persuasively insist on the need to combine these strategies. They go beyond their predecessors by developing a comparative analysis of specific European policies and demonstrating their feasibility in the United States.

The details of their proposal deserve our concerted attention. Family policy debates remain underway even in countries, like France and Sweden, with relatively well-developed programs. Recent changes in Australia and Canada are receiving international attention.[1] In the US, a progressive family policy agenda is now moving forward rapidly on the federal as well as the state level, playing a prominent role in the Democratic Party's current electoral platform. Both Japan and Korea have implemented legislative changes designed to support and encourage parenthood (OECD 2007; Lambert 2007).

In many countries, however, efforts to provide more public support for parenting are being accompanied by efforts to reform the provision of care for other dependents, including long-term care for the elderly and home health care for the sick and disabled—services which, like child care, are often disproportionately performed by women. In this essay, I argue that family policy experts should think more broadly about the organization of and financial support for all care services. I define care services here as paid or unpaid efforts to meet the needs of dependents, including direct care work that involves personal connection and emotional attachment to care recipients. Rather than addressing the specific work–family proposals that Gornick and Meyers advance, I emphasize the need to expand and extend their analysis.

We should go wide for both theoretical and strategic reasons. Care work in general is highly gendered, reproducing inequality between men and women. Much of the work that takes place within the care sector creates personal relationships and emotional connections that can improve care quality but disempower care workers. Consideration of the specific features of care work leads toward a critique of the "market fundamentalism" that Ruth Milkman so eloquently criticizes. It also offers an explanation of the confining nature of the traditional gender roles that Barbara Bergmann so powerfully condemns. Child care does not exhaust the scope of care services. As a result, attention to the care sector may offer greater potential to build a successful cross-class, multiracial, and multi-ethnic political coalition.

The upsurge in interest in work–family policies has been accompanied by intensified concerns about the scandalously poor quality of nursing home care, the shortage of home health-care aides and nurses, the conspicuous inefficiencies of our health-care system, and the unequal opportunities for higher education in the US. At the same time, anxieties about the growing costs of children and instabilities of family commitments have intensified. The institutional complexities of the care sector are even more daunting than the details of work–family policy reform. But they invite the unrepentant utopian energies that Erik Olin Wright and his co-organizers have called for.

I believe that the social provision of a generous, equitable, sustainable, and efficient supply of care is a prerequisite of genuine gender equality. In my efforts to advance this claim, I explore four related issues: 1) the unique characteristics of care work; 2) divisions among women that make it difficult to build a coalition around work–parenting policies alone; 3) complementarities between the intrinsic merits and public benefits of care commitments; and 4) the need to consider the financial costs of caring for dependents, and their implications for government fiscal policy. I end with an emphasis on three policy priorities: greater support for caregiving outside the market, changes in the organization and quality of privately and publicly purchased care services, and the development of new systems of accounting for economic growth and government spending.

THE UNIQUE CHARACTERISTICS OF CARE WORK

Gornick and Meyers focus on childrearing with good reason. This particular activity imposes significant costs on parents, especially mothers. Increases in women's labor force participation have called attention to the changing relationship between production and reproduction, and the demographic consequences are particularly clear. Nonetheless, many of the problems they emphasize, including gender inequality, are linked to the general social organization of care—not just the organization of childrearing.

Women spend more time taking care of children than men do. They also spend more time caring for sick and disabled adults, and the elderly. Women are also disproportionately located in "caring" occupations—not just child care but also elder care, health care, and education. Children represent a specific kind of public good, but care in general also has public good aspects and spillover effects that make it vulnerable to undervaluation by the market. Children cannot exercise consumer sovereignty—neither can other dependents.

Whether provided to children or adults, care involves personal connection and emotional attachment. Care services are often "coproduced" by care providers and care recipients. Parents and teachers must elicit cooperation from children; similarly, nurses and home-care providers must elicit cooperation from patients. Care is often person- and context-specific. As a result, its quality is heterogeneous and difficult to monitor or measure. The intrinsic motivation of the care provider often affects the quantity and quality of the services provided. Indeed, the sense of "being cared for" is an important by-product that has inherent value (Himmelweit 2007).

The traditional Marxian analysis of commodification draws a bright line between goods and services produced for own use and those produced for sale in the market (Folbre and Nelson 2002). Feminist theory, however, suggests a continuum. Even some goods produced for use completely outside the market are intended for informal exchange, such as the domestic services that a homemaker provides with the expectation that a wage-earning partner will share his or her market income. Similarly, many forms of paid employment offer personal and emotional rewards—not all take the form of impersonal labor performed only for pecuniary reasons. Both unpaid and paid workers provide care services, and the similarities between their tasks often override the differences.

Debates over whether care should or should not be "commodified" often overstate the consequences of whether care work takes place inside or outside the money economy. Most forms of care for dependents—including but not limited to children—require a combination of paid and unpaid work. Substitutability between the two is limited, especially at the extremes. Few families can care for dependents entirely on their own, and few schools or hospitals can operate successfully without cooperation from family members. But most people reach for a balance among the different types of care that helps them meet their needs.

The specific characteristics of care work transcend the boundaries of the market. Recipients of care benefit from the cultural construction of caring obligation, as well as from the personal connections and emotional attachments that often grow out of the care process itself. But workers are rendered vulnerable by emotional attachment: when their work no longer takes the form of a simple exchange it is difficult to threaten to withhold it. Care workers become, in a sense, prisoners of love. Indeed, the importance of intrinsic motivation is often turned against care providers with arguments that they do a better job when they work for love rather than for money (Nelson 1999). A recent article in the *Journal of Health Economics* explicitly argues that a poorly paid nurse is a good nurse (Hayes 2005).[2]

Many of women's economic vulnerabilities are attributable to these prisoner-of-love dynamics, which are by no means limited to child care. Most women would prefer to share care responsibilities more equally. But they are seldom willing to threaten withdrawal (or noncommitment) in order to achieve this. The pattern is evident in family structure. Most mothers would prefer the active and loving cooperation of a father; but if they cannot obtain that, they do not relinquish their children, but rather assume financial as well as direct care responsibilities for them. Similarly, many women enter caring occupations despite their awareness of the lower economic security they offer. The strategic dilemma for women who feel their second-best option is to provide care for their dependents rather than not to provide it at all can be formalized, with variations, as a prisoner's dilemma or a chicken game.

This strategic dilemma applies not just to mothers, but to all those who make binding commitments to care for others. If fathers change their patterns of paid employment to more resemble those of mothers, as Gornick and Meyers propose, both mothers and children will likely enjoy many direct benefits. But fathers may suffer a reduction in earnings relative to non-fathers in paid employment, for the same reason that mothers now suffer lower earnings than non-mothers (even controlling for number of hours worked). A decline in the relative income of fathers is likely to have some negative consequences for two-parent families with children—though it is unlikely that these negative effects would offset the positive effects that Gornick and Meyers emphasize.

Similarly, even if public policy could neutralize the effects of commitments to children on family earnings, the effects of family commitments to the elderly and disabled would persist. While relatively few adults of working age spend substantial amounts of time caring for dependents other than children, those who do often find care demands unpredictable and overwhelming. Among the elderly, gender differences in care have momentous consequences. As one recent research paper puts it, married men may fail to purchase long-term care insurance because they already have it—in the form of a wife (Peters, Tennyson and Woolley 2008). In part because they are likely to outlive their older husbands, women remain far more vulnerable than men to poverty and infirmity in old age.

The historical relationship between gender and care is gradually unwinding. Women who choose neither to marry nor become mothers and move into male-dominated occupations earn approximately the same as men with the same human capital characteristics. Men as well as women pay a penalty in terms of foregone income when they assume responsibilities for the care of others. Empirical indicators include the declining male marriage premium, the lower male marriage premium for men married to women who work full-time, and lower pay for jobs that involve care.[3]

Emotional attachment has implications that cut both ways for Barbara Bergmann's critique of the paid parental leave policies that Gornick and Meyers advocate. In general, Bergmann argues that women should just break out of prison—offload caregiving responsibilities, fight their own tendencies to express caring preferences, and, more generally, try to act and feel more like men. This strategy makes sense if you think of care services as being like other exchanges. By withholding care services, women not only improve their own economic position, but also increase the explicit or implicit price that must be paid for those care services. But while the exchange metaphor may hold for "consenting adults," it does not work for care of dependents. Encouraging the withdrawal of care services may result in a reduction in the quantity or quality of care provided to them.

Bergman reasons that women should not care about this threat, because it only handicaps them. But, like it or not (and thankfully, for many of the children, sick and elderly who rely upon them), many women do care. Furthermore, many women and men are strongly disapproving of women who do not. For instance, results from the General Social Survey conducted in the US show that, regardless of gender, individuals are less supportive of nontraditional gender norms that might have adverse effects on children than those that might merely have adverse effects on adult men (Badgett, Davidson, and Folbre 2004). Would women's attitudes change more rapidly if more feminists were to endorse Bergmann's position? This seems unlikely. But, in Bergmann's defense, we don't really know how flexible or variable such gender norms may prove to be.

Bergmann correctly emphasizes that commitments to care for others reduce competitive success in other tasks. That problem will remain whether or not men and women share responsibilities for child care: fathers who choose to reduce their paid work commitments will likely face penalties in the labor market. Both mommies and daddies could get stuck on a "parent track" that shunts them away from leadership positions.

This is not an inevitable outcome, and there are, as Gornick and Meyers have emphasized, policy strategies that might minimize it. But much depends on demographic trends. If most men and women become active, engaged parents, employers will find it difficult to use active parenthood as a way to discriminate among employees. In recent years, highly paid women professionals and managers seem to have gained at least some bargaining power. As researchers have shown, women don't literally get rusty after taking time out from high-powered careers (Crittenden 2005; Hewlett 2007). On the other hand, more men and women are choosing not to become active parents, giving employers ample room to divide and conquer. Many highly educated women forgo motherhood. In a competitive global economy they may be better positioned to compete for leadership than engaged caregiving parents of either sex.

DIVISIONS AMONG WOMEN

A broader look at care services calls attention to inequalities that are not directly related to public policies regarding parenthood. Feminist theorists and strategists need to come to grips with the ways in which increased earnings inequality among women, combined with class-specific family formation patterns, has weakened the feminist mobilization that helped women advance in the 1970s and 1980s. Less-educated women are filling many service jobs in child care, home health care, and elder care that make it easier for college-educated women to devote more time to paid employment. Most jobs within these paid care occupations are poorly paid in the US, offering few benefits and few incentives to increase skills, experience or tenure. Few if any studies have explored differences in this form of the care penalty across countries.[4]

Gender inequalities have always been crosscut by inequalities based on race, ethnicity, and class; but the salience of gender inequalities was heightened by economic and demographic trends between 1960 and 1990. Women entered paid employment at a steep and steady pace, but few families could afford domestic services and the supply of low-wage care workers was limited. Women across the economic spectrum felt a similar pinch as the "forces of market production" came into conflict with the "social relations of household production." In Marxian parlance, one could speak figuratively of the "fetters" of patriarchal tradition.

These fetters still hang around most women's necks, but are sometimes cushioned by silk scarves. Since at least the 1990s, the combined effect of increasing income inequality and increases in the supply of low-wage labor has led to a small but significant redistribution of family care responsibilities.

Affluent families are able to reduce the amount of time devoted to housework and the care of family members through strategic outsourcing. The ability to buy meals away from home, or even the prepared meals in the supermarket that are more expensive than those that require time to prepare, significantly reduces the burden of domestic work. The market for domestic workers (often paid under the table) has expanded dramatically in the last few years. This phenomenon has been much remarked on in the US: in Texas, California, and most areas of the Southwest, as well as in major metropolitan areas, nannies have become a highly visible aspect of the social landscape, as well as a popular subject for best-selling fiction.[5] But it has also received much attention in southern Europe, where Romanian and other eastern European immigrant "badantes" now play a prominent role in home care for the elderly.

Immigration plays a role at both ends of the skill spectrum. Undocumented workers lower the cost of obtaining inexpensive help with housework and child care, as well as for gardening, landscaping, and construction. Recent shortages of both nurses and teachers in the US have been met by efforts to recruit from overseas—a strategy that makes it easier to restrict wage growth and to postpone investments in the state university systems that provide the bulk of training for these jobs (Folbre 2006a). The United Kingdom is increasingly dependent on nurses imported from Africa. The Philippines exports nurses as well as child-care workers to many countries around the globe.

The increased income inequality among women that is associated with globalization tends to weaken support for the kinds of policies that Gornick and Meyers propose. Highly educated women who enter professional and managerial jobs are better able than most to afford the unpaid family leave guaranteed to some workers by law, and also more likely to enjoy paid parental leave, sick leave, vacation time, and scheduling flexibility. Breastfeeding of young infants, in particular, improves health and cognitive outcomes (Smith 2005). Class differentials in breastfeeding are telling and poignant, with a steep education gradient (Kantor 2006). The paid work requirements imposed by the welfare reforms of the 1990s had a discernible negative impact on breastfeeding among low-income women (Haider, Jacknowitz, and Schoeni 2003). Further, the provision of free infant formula to low-income women through the US Department of Agriculture's Woman, Infants, and Children program—strongly supported by the agricultural lobby—heavily subsidizes an unhealthy choice (Government Accountability Office 2006).

Increased income inequality seems to be associated with changes in family structure that compound negative impacts on child outcomes (McLanahan 2004). College-educated white women are now more likely to marry, and stay married, than other women. As a result, when they have children they are much more likely to enjoy a strong claim on the earnings of a father. Nonmarital births are far more common among less-educated women; less-educated men are less likely than their college-educated counterparts to contribute either financial assistance or direct care to their children. Parents coping with the stresses of unemployment and poverty face difficult material and psychological challenges. Studies of blood chemistry focusing on levels of serotonin and cortisol suggest that the subordination associated with high levels of inequality can reduce efficacy and impair health. These problems, in turn, make it harder to establish and maintain family and community ties (Wilkinson 1996).[6]

Differences among mothers are compounded by divisions between mothers and non-mothers and, more generally, parents and non-parents. Not all adults have children. The percentage of men playing an active role with children has declined over time as the percentage of households maintained by women has risen (Akerlof 1998). The growth of childlessness among cohorts born after the Second World War is remarkably consistent across most countries for which data is available (Rowland 2007). In some countries, such as Germany and the UK, it is estimated that as many as 30 percent of all women may reach the age of forty without becoming mothers. Childlessness is lower in the US, but reached 25 percent among all women with a bachelor's degree in 2004 (US Census Bureau 2005).

Whether as cause, effect, or simple correlation, childlessness in the US goes up along with women's earnings. In a 2003 column in *Business Week*, Laura D'Andrea Tyson highlighted a finding by the consulting firm Catalyst that a third of professional women not yet in the most senior leadership don't want children because of fears of work–family conflict. She also cited the National Parenting Association's estimate that 49 percent of women earning more than $100,000 a year are childless (Tyson 2003). Whatever their earnings level, women without children sometimes feel ignored, even put-upon, by workplace policies aimed to benefit parents (Burkett 2002). As Bergmann notes, many women choose not to become mothers to pursue a passion for excellence in their field—and not necessarily to earn more money. We should never accuse them of engaging in "unfair competition" in paid employment.

More empirical research is needed on changes in the structure and composition of the care service labor force—research that treats the job of "housewife" as what it is: a job (Bergmann 1981; Folbre and Nelson 2002; Cohen 2004). Changes in occupational segregation that examine only changes in the gender composition of paid work are misleading. The process of commodification that Bergmann advocates has the effect of shifting non-market work from affluent women in the home to less-affluent women working for pay. It might simply shift gender inequality down the class ladder, further weakening the potential impact of a feminist coalition. On the other hand, it might give affluent women a greater stake in ensuring the quantity and quality of care services available for purchase, and in spreading their costs through public subsidy. This could enhance opportunities to challenge the structure of the care sector as a whole.

In short, inequalities among women do not pose an insuperable obstacle to efforts to promote equitable work–family policies. But they do suggest the need to think beyond issues of balance between paid work and family to the organization of the care sector as a whole, including improved conditions of wage employment in child care, elder care, and home health care.

INTRINSIC MERITS AND PUBLIC BENEFITS

How should we frame such a larger agenda? I believe we should emphasize both the intrinsic merits and public benefits of good care provision. Ethical and economic approaches are sometimes pitted against one another, as though invoking one somehow weakens the other. In truth, the two are complements: ethics can define our ends, and economics can help us find the means to realize them. In a world where many of our ends are difficult to reach, practical concerns deserve respect.

As feminist philosophers persuasively argue, care is a central component of an ethical society (Tronto 1993; Kittay 1999; Engster 2007). We need to articulate both the right to care and the right to be cared for in more assertive terms, moving beyond abstract definitions to the practical demands of social policy. The demands that Gornick and Meyers articulate cross the boundaries between the market and the family. They argue not just for rights to paid family leave and publicly subsidized child care but, more fundamentally, to a more equitable sharing of care responsibilities within both the family and the polity.

We should never be intimidated by accusations that improved care is too costly to consider. What's the economy for, anyway, if not to help us realize our vision of a good society? But it is also our responsibility to show that our vision can be realized. Gornick and Meyers do this by pointing to European precedents and also by offering estimates of policy cost. Efforts to develop political strategies for the care sector as a whole should build on this approach.

My recent research emphasizes the macroeconomic benefits of the time and money that parents devote to children. I argue that the children who become the workers and taxpayers of the next generation represent a public good—they provide benefits for everyone, not just for their parents and themselves. I estimate the minimal amount that society would have to pay to replace parental services if they were, hypothetically, withdrawn. I show that patterns of public investment in children are both unfair and inefficient, and could be much improved. I explain why most voters fail to understand the extent to which they benefit from the services and income transfers that their own taxes pay for (Folbre 2008).

I believe these arguments can be extended to the analysis of care for all dependents, not just children. Social insurance represents a better means of meeting care needs than private insurance. It pools risk, encourages reciprocity, and increases solidarity. Everyone in our society deserves adequate long-term care that provides support and respite for family caregivers, funding for home health-care aides to assist family caregivers, and high-quality community-based nursing homes for those who require them. Although regional and local variations make it more difficult to compare national strategies for long-term care, Sweden and Norway offer useful models here, as with child care (Folbre, Shaw, and Stark 2006; Saltman, Dubois, and Chawla 2006).

ENVISIONING A BETTER CARE ECONOMY

Much of the current progressive work–family agenda focuses on how to help parents cope with the demands of paid employment. This focus is too narrow. The increases in women's labor force participation that had such a destabilizing effect on work–family balance have leveled off (see Figure 5.1). Men's labor force participation has continued its slow decline. This somewhat puzzling trend holds across virtually all family structures and educational levels, and it is unclear whether or not it will continue. If overall levels of family labor force participation do remain flat, however, the growth of family income is likely to remain flat as well. Increases in women's paid employment will no longer offset the low, even negative growth in real wages that has often afflicted all but the top echelons of the labor force.

Figure 5.1

Labor Force Participation Rates
(Men and Women, Ages 25–54)

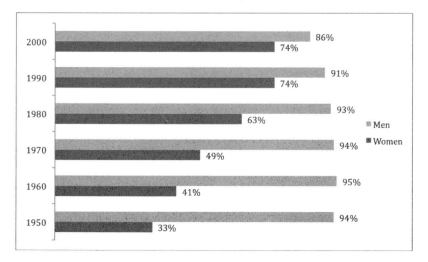

(See David A Cotter 2004.)

This potential trend may help mitigate work–family balance issues, but will highlight the economic costs of caring for family dependents and the disadvantages of entering caring occupations. These concerns about the care economy as a whole motivate the development of a more complete vision of a generous, equitable, efficient, and sustainable care economy. I offer three suggestions to help us move in that direction.

i. **Let's look beyond work–family policies such as paid parental leave and publicly provided child care to develop policies of economic support for all forms of family, friend, and neighbor care.**

Some specific policy recommendations seem obvious. Access to benefits such as health insurance and pensions should be decoupled from paid employment. Social safety nets should be improved to better protect dependents against the risk of both poverty and poor health. This will require more attention to the reform of both public assistance and tax policies. The success of the British Labour Party's efforts to reduce child poverty deserves international attention (Corak, Christine Lietz, and Holly Sutherland 2005; Levy, Lietz, and Sutherland 2005). In the US, by contrast, poverty among children and the elderly remains high by international standards.

Paid and unpaid parental leaves should be extended to cover family, friend, and neighbor care for the sick, elderly, and disabled, as well as for young children, and parental allowances should be generalized to become caregiver allowances. These policies could be modeled on those that Gornick and Meyers propose for the support of parents. However, the level of financial support for families who assume caregiving responsibilities will require more sustained attention than Gornick and Meyers provide. While wage replacement (rendered somewhat progressive by benefit caps and taxation) offers a simple principle for remunerating leaves from paid employment, the appropriate level of family allowance remains unclear. In the US a variety of tax deductions and credits, significantly boosted by changes since 2002, amount to a de facto family allowance similar in magnitude to that provided by many European countries. Even in the most generous countries, moreover, the extent of public subsidy represents only a small proportion of the total costs of rearing children (Folbre 2008).

A more general form of support for non-market care could take the form of a "participation income" or a basic income grant conditional on provision of a basic minimum amount of care to a family member, friend, or neighbor, or through a charitable care-volunteering effort. This approach could reinforce values of reciprocity and obligation while effectively fostering full employment (Goodin 1992). Some discussion of institutional details can be found in the British Labour Party's Commission on Social Justice and in descriptions of the "mutual obligation activity test" that is required for the Australian unemployment benefit (UK Labour Party 1994; Department of Family and Community Services 2000).

As with family allowances, a key question is the appropriate level of support. Excessively high levels could create disincentives to both paid and unpaid work; excessively low levels would reproduce gender inequalities. Issues of eligibility also arise—just how much care work should be required to gain access to public support? One way to address these problems might be to design programs that reward caregiving over the life cycle, but discourage individuals from specializing entirely in care provision, such as the Social Security reform described in this volume by Myra Ferree.

ii. Let's look beyond family care to the organization, cost, and quality of paid care services.

Most care services are "coproduced" by paid as well as unpaid caregivers. As a result, the organization of child-care, elder-care, and health-care services—along with the pay and working conditions of workers in care occupations—have a significant impact on family life. Market provision in some areas can be effective if combined with adequate oversight and regulation; public provision can be effective if bureaucratic tendencies are held in check by accountability and choice. The comparative perspective on work–family policies that Gornick and Meyers offer could be complemented by detailed comparative research on specific foster-care, elder-care, and home-based institutional health-care policies across countries.

Many women enter traditionally feminine jobs in the care sector—whether as workers or as managers—despite the evident economic disadvantages. Many of them understand how and why cost-cutting strategies in child care, health care, and elder care tend to backfire. So-called "high-road" strategies designed to reward intrinsic motivation, reduce turnover, and provide job ladders could benefit both care workers and care consumers (Folbre 2006b).

In the UK, concerted attention has been devoted to the "third sector" of the economy—nonprofit enterprises that fit neither the standard capitalist nor standard public enterprise model (Haugh and Kitson 2007). Emphasis on so-called "social markets" also represents a hybrid approach, one that offers local governments resources to meet care needs but encourages subcontracting to small businesses that can be held accountable for high quality. Worker-owned businesses and cooperatives offer a particularly promising model for care provision.

iii. Let's develop better accounting systems for both economic growth and welfare state spending.

As long as economists are allowed to define "output" entirely in terms of market income, proposals to ensure a higher level and quality of care will be deemed "unproductive" and inefficient. For this reason, efforts to incorporate estimates of the value of unpaid care services into alternative measures of Gross Domestic Product and household standards of living are crucial to the development of a stronger care economy. The growing availability of diary-based time-use surveys offers an important new opportunity to address this issue (Abraham and Mackie 2004; Folbre, 2009).

Current methods of accounting for public spending and taxation should also be reformed. Most individuals know what they earn, and approximately how much they pay in taxes. But few if any have a clear picture of how much public money was devoted to them before they began paying taxes on their own, or how much they will benefit in retirement. This lack of transparency makes it easy for conservatives to overstate the redistributive impact of government taxation and spending. It also makes it difficult for progressive advocates to develop a more equitable and sustainable system of social insurance and intergenerational reciprocity.

We need to redefine the welfare state in terms of contributions to family and social care that represent investment and social insurance. Gornick and Meyers reason strategically about political divisions among mothers; we should also reason strategically about conflicts of interest between the young and the old, recognizing the importance of intergenerational transfers. Better design and explanation of taxes paid and benefits received over the life cycle could help build stronger political coalitions for public support.

Women's common commitments to ideals of care—and their continuing involvement in the provision of care services—represent a force that partially offsets growing income inequality among them. Women tend to recognize that caring for children and other dependents is a productive activity—one that contributes to our collective well-being. They are less likely than men to treat these activities as forms of "consumption" or activities for which "virtue should be its own reward" (Iverson and Rosenbluth 2006). Precisely because they devote much of their efforts to the production and maintenance of human capabilities, they have a strong economic interest in the development of resilient welfare state policies.

Ironically, continued fertility decline is likely to intensify concerns about the intergenerational sustainability of the welfare state. Continued globalization—including increased immigration—is likely to intensify concerns about its economic viability. Many affluent countries depend heavily on immigrant workers to help meet their care needs, but further rapid increases in their supply will undermine incentives to solve problems in the care sector. We need to formulate policies that discourage illegal immigration while respecting immigrant rights and improving wages and working conditions for immigrant workers. Family policies have too long been compartmentalized in the feminine policy sphere. Theorizing more broadly about the distribution of costs and responsibilities for care could help bring them to the front and center of political economy.

NOTES

1   On Australia, see McDonald, this volume; on Canada, see Pachner (2007).

2   For a critique, see Nelson and Folbre (2006).

3   On the declining male marriage premium, see Hoffman and Averett (2004). On the care penalty in paid employment, see Budig, England, and Folbre (2002).

4   A first step would be to apply the kind of fixed-effects statistical analysis developed in Budig, England and Folbre (2002) to the European countries that Gornick and Meyers analyze.

5   See for example McLaughlin and Kraus (2003) and Pearson (2003).

6   On the effect of social and family relationships on health, see Sapolsky (1998).

REFERENCES

Abraham, Katherine and Christopher Mackie, 2004, *Beyond the Market*, Washington, DC: National Academies Press.

Akerlof, George A., 1998, "Men Without Children," *Economic Journal* 108: 287–309.

Badgett, Lee, Pamela Davidson, and Nancy Folbre, 2004, "Breadwinner Dad, Homemaker Mom: An Interdisciplinary Analysis of Changing Gender Norms in the United States, 1977–1998," manuscript, Department of Economics, University of Massachusetts Amherst.

Bergmann, Barbara, 1981, "The Economic Risks of Being a Housewife," *American Economic Review* 7: 8–86

Budig, Michelle, Paula England, and Nancy Folbre, 2002, "Wages of Virtue: The Relative Pay of Care Work," *Social Problems* 49 (4): 455–73

Burkett, Elinor, 2002, *The Baby Boon: How Family-Friendly America Cheats the Childless*, New York: Free Press.

Cohen, Philip N., 2004, "The Gender Division of Labor: 'Keeping House' and Occupational Segregation in the United States," *Gender and Society* 18 (2): 239–52.

Corak, Miles, Christine Lietz, and Holly Sutherland, 2005, "The Impact of Tax and Transfer Systems on Children in the European Union," Innocenti Working Paper 2005–2004.

Cotter, David A., Joan M. Hermsen, and Reeve Vanneman, 2004, "Gender Inequality at Work," Washington, DC: Population Reference Bureau, p. 3, figure 1.

Crittenden, Ann, 2005, *If You've Raised Kids, You Can Manage Anything*, New York: Gotham.

Department of Family and Community Services, 2000, *Participation Support for a More Equitable Society*, Canberra, March.

Engster, Daniel, 2007, *The Heart of Justice: A Political Theory of Caring*, New York: Oxford University Press.

Folbre, Nancy and Julie Nelson, 2002, "For Love or Money?" *Journal of Economic Perspectives* 14 (4): 123–40.

Folbre, Nancy, 2006a, "Nursebots to the Rescue? Immigration, Automation, and Care?" *Globalizations* 3 (3): 367–78.

Folbre, Nancy, 2006b, "Demanding Quality: Worker/Consumer Coalitions and 'High Road' Strategies in the Care Sector," *Politics and Society* 34 (1): 1–21.

Folbre, Nancy, 2008, *Valuing Children: Rethinking the Economics of the Family*, Cambridge, MA: Harvard University Press.

Folbre, Nancy, 2009, "Inequality and Time Use in the Household," forthcoming in Timothy Smeeding and Wiemer Salverda, eds, *Handbook of Economic Inequality*, New York: Oxford University Press.

Folbre, Nancy, Lois Shaw, and Agneta Stark, eds, 2006, *Warm Hands in a Cold Age: Gender and Aging*, New York: Routledge.

Goodin, Robert, 1992, "Toward a Minimally Presumptuous Social Welfare Policy," in Philippe van Parijs, ed., *Arguing for Basic Income*, London: Verso: 195–214.

Government Accountability Office, 2006, *Breastfeeding: Some Strategies Used to Market Infant Formula May Discourage Breastfeeding*, Washington, DC: GAO, February.

Haider, Steven, Alison Jacknowitz, and Robert Schoeni, 2003, "Welfare Work Requirements and Child Well-Being: Evidence from the Effects on Breast-Feeding," *Demography* 40 (3).

Haugh, Helen and Michael Kitson, 2007, "The Third Way and the Third Sector: New Labour's Economic Policy and the Social Economy," *Cambridge Journal of Economics* 31: 973–94.

Hewlett, Sylvia Ann, 2007, *Off-Ramps and On-Ramps: Keeping Talented Women on the Road to Success*, Cambridge, MA: Harvard Business School Press.

Heyes, Anthony, 2005, "The Economics of Vocation or 'Why is a Badly Paid Nurse a Good Nurse?'" *Journal of Health Economics* 24 (3): 561–9

Himmelweit, Susan, 2007, "The Prospects for Caring: Economic Theory and Policy Analysis," *Cambridge Journal of Economics* 31(4):581-599.

Hoffman, Saul and Susan Averett, 2004, *Women in the Economy*, New York: Addison Wesley.

Iverson, Torben and Frances Rosenbluth, 2006, "The Political Economy of Gender: Explaining Cross-National Variation in the Gender Division of Labor and the Gender Voting Gap," *American Journal of Political Science*, 50 (1): 1-19.

Kantor, Jodi, 2006, "On the Job, Nursing Mothers Find a 2-Class System," *New York Times*, September 1, online: http://www.nyt.com (accessed September 1, 2006).

Kittay, Eva, 1999, *Love's Labor: Essays on Women, Equality, and Dependency*, New York: Routledge.

Lambert, Priscilla A., 2007, "The Political Economy of Postwar Family Policy in Japan: Economic Imperatives and Electoral Incentives," *Journal of Japanese Studies* 33 (1): 1-28.

Levy, Horatio, Christine Lietz, and Holly Sutherland, 2005, "Strategies to Support Children in the European Union: Recent Tax–Benefit Reforms in Austria, Spain, and the United Kingdom," EUROMOD Working Paper EM/0/05.

McLanahan, Sara, 2004, "Diverging Destinies: How Children are Faring Under the Second Demographic Transition," *Demography* 41: 607–27.

McLaughlin, Emma and Nicola Kraus, 2003, *The Nanny Diaries*, New York: St Martins Griffin, 2003; Allison Pearson, *I Don't Know How She Does It*, New York: Anchor.

Nelson, Julie and Nancy Folbre, 2006, "Why a Well Paid Nurse Is a Better Nurse!" *Journal of Nursing Economics* 24 (3): 127–30.

Nelson, Julie, 1999, "Of Markets and Martyrs: Is it OK to Pay Well for Care?" *Feminist Economics* 5 (3): 43–59.

OECD, 2007, "Facing the Future: Korea's Family, Pension, and Health Policy Changes," online: *http://213.253.134.43/oecd/pdfs/browseit/8107061E.PDF* (accessed December 24, 2007).

Pachner, Joanna, 2007, "C-Suite Confidential," *National Post*, December 4.

Pearson, Allison, 2003, *I Don't Know How She Does It*, New York: Anchor.

Peters, H. Elizabeth, Sharon Tennyson, and Frances Woolley, 2008, "Household Bargaining and the Purchase of Long Term Care Insurance: My Wife is My Long Term Care Insurance," paper presented at the meetings of the Allied Social Science Association, New Orleans, LA, January.

Rowland, Donald T., 2007, "Historical Trends in Childlessness," *Journal of Family Issues* 28 (10): 1,311–7.

Saltman, R. B., H. F. W. Dubois, and M. Chawla, 2006, "The Impact of Aging on Long-Term Care in Europe and Some Potential Policy Responses," *International Journal of Health Care Services* 36 (4): 719–46.

Sapolsky, Robert M., 1998, *Why Zebras Don't Get Ulcers: An Updated Guide to Stress, Stress-Related Diseases, and Coping*, New York: W. H. Freeman.

Smith, Julie, 2005, "Mothers' Milk and Measurement of Economic Output," *Feminist Economics*, March: 43–64

Tronto, Joan, 1993, *Moral Boundaries: A Political Argument for an Ethic of Care*, New York: Routledge.

Tyson, Laura D'Andrea, 2003, "New Clues to the Pay and Leadership Gap," *Business Week*, October 27..

U.S. Census Bureau, 2005, *Fertility of American Women*, Current Population Reports, December.

United Kingdom Labour Party, 1994, *Social Justice: Strategies for National Renewal*, London: Vintage.

Wilkinson, Richard G., 1996, *Unhealthy Societies: The Afflictions of Inequality*, New York: Routledge.

6

Should Feminists Aim for Gender Symmetry?

*Why a Dual-Earner/Dual-Caregiver Society Is Not Every Feminist's Utopia**

Ann Shola Orloff

Janet Gornick and Marcia Meyers argue persuasively that to advance toward greater gender egalitarianism, feminists everywhere—or at least across the developed countries of the west[1]—should pursue a set of policies that will help to bring into being, and support, a utopia of "gender symmetry" in the allocation and performance of care work and paid employment (and, presumably, other kinds of participation in collective activities, such as politics). In their view, it is the gender division of labor—above all, men's greater participation in the public spheres of paid work and politics, and women's greater responsibility for unpaid care work—that underpins gender inequality. Thus, ultimately, women's emancipation demands the dissolution of that division of labor. Their main focus, however, is not on the utopia of gender symmetry and the transformations that it would entail, but on policy

* Many thanks to Julia Adams, Myra Marx Ferree, Rianne Mahon, Kimberly Morgan, Linda Zerilli and the editors of this volume, particularly Janet Gornick, for comments on earlier drafts of this essay. Thanks also, for helpful suggestions and queries, to audiences at the 2007 annual meeting of the European Social Policy research network, the colloquium at the Northwestern University Institute for Policy Research, and the workshop in Comparative and Historical Social Science at Northwestern, where I presented versions of this paper. Needless to say, I take responsibility for any remaining errors, misinterpretations or infelicitous phrasings.

institutions derived from contemporary practice in several European countries, above all Sweden, which are expected to serve as the way stations on the path toward gender symmetry. These policies include individual entitlements to paid leaves and well-developed care services available as a right, alongside a restructuring of employment to reduce work time. They argue that such policies put us on the road to gender symmetry by allowing and encouraging both men and women to work for pay and to participate in family caregiving in equal measures.

Certainly, there are many attractive features to this vision. Indeed, there is already a lot to like about the Scandinavian social-democratic model, even before its utopian extensions, including its explicit commitment to gender equality, excellent care services, and very low poverty rates among children and solo mothers (see e.g., Borchorst and Siim, 2002; Ellingsaeter and Leira, 2006)—and this is especially true when we contrast the Nordic model to current US social provision, with its yawning gaps in coverage against the everyday risks of contemporary life, and the high levels of insecurity, poverty, illiteracy and crime which have flourished in their wake. But the task here is not to contrast—yet again—existing Nordic and US welfare and gender policy models (but see Orloff, 2006; Esping-Andersen, 1999).[2] We are asked to consider a gender-egalitarian utopia and the policy institutions that might get us closer to it. But Gornick and Meyers' essay is a bit lopsided in this regard. While gender symmetry is portrayed as the opposite of the gender asymmetries that are implicated in women's oppression, the ideal is not itself subject to much probing. We are not given much of a sense of what such symmetry would look like, beyond the assumption that men's and women's time in paid work and informal care work would converge, or how we might measure progress toward symmetry. Instead, it is simply assumed that, if asymmetry is associated with inequality, symmetry should be associated with equality—a perilous assumption indeed, as I will try to demonstrate below. Gornick and Meyers lavish their attention on policy institutions that would allegedly begin to correct the asymmetries and move us along the road to their utopia. And these policy institutions do not actually look very different from what is already in place in Scandinavia—indeed, the authors see this as proof of the potential "realness" of their utopian vision.

In the following pages, I will do two things. First, I will assess Gornick and Meyers' argument for a feminist utopia based on gender symmetry, considering their proposals from the perspective of long-standing feminist debates about emancipatory projects based on "sameness" and "difference," and discuss how we can get beyond the well-known limitations of both, and perhaps find ways to overcome this very dilemma. I will attempt to unearth the assumptions about politics, culture and gender that support their contentions. And, to the question of whether feminists should pursue gender symmetry, I will answer: not as a matter of universal principle. Second, I will offer a different take on how feminists might approach political goals, which may be long- or short-term, utopian, radical or reformist. While Gornick and Meyers take an essentially structural and deductive approach, I offer a more inductive and historical approach. "Interests," or, as I prefer, goals,[3] as well as utopian visions, must be understood in specific political and historical contexts. I say this not to imply that some utopias are conceivable and desirable, but unreachable in certain countries—as some Swedophilic political realists might conclude about the political feasibility in the US of Nordic-inspired utopias featuring generous parental leave and extensive, high-quality public care services. One could agree with the ultimate goal, or utopia, of gender symmetry, and think that there might be policies other than those highlighted by Gornick and Meyers that could help deliver us there.[4] This is of course true, but hardly a startling proposition. I think we should also question the desirability of the goal itself, both in terms of its specific conceptualization of gender equality and with respect to how political goals emerge more generally.

I argue for guiding political visions that emerge inductively, from an investigation of feminist political practices and theorizing, rather than assuming that we can deduce the features of a gender-egalitarian utopia and desirable political goals from analyses of gender "interests" read from social locations and structures that seem not to vary substantially across the developed world. Thus I question Gornick and Meyers' goal—gender symmetry—from the angles of political and empirical as well as normative analysis. I contend that individuals and groups come to understand and analyze their situations and themselves as political subjects with particular sorts of "needs" and goals, and to develop strategies for stability or change, through historically specific cultural and political processes.[5] It is, I think, impossible to understand how and when any goal—or utopia—emerges and might be brought into being without considering politics; the very desirability of goals (or utopias) depends on context.

My own analysis and normative probing have led me, in the contemporary US context, to advocate political goals that would expand choice, or decisional autonomy, based in interdependence and inclusive citizenship, emerging from a consideration of diversity in modern societies and from an understanding of gender as constitutive of subjects. Further, as we fashion better policy and social arrangements, we must include mechanisms of democratic accountability and of respect for the multiplicity of gender arrangements among the diverse citizens and residents of modern states. While I am favorable to basing these entitlements on citizenship, I would also argue that this must be problematized; we need to find ways to take account of issues of immigration and integration, but I will not pursue these fully here. The policy institutions that might serve as way stations toward this utopian condition will vary, depending on context. Thus, finally, let me add that one might agree with Gornick and Meyers—as I do—that increasing support for care is desirable without supporting their vision of utopia, or believing that their preferred policy package is likely to deliver us to it.

ANALYZING GORNICK AND MEYERS' UTOPIA OF GENDER SYMMETRY: GENDER INEQUALITY, GENDER INTERESTS, AND GENDER POLITICS

Gornick and Meyers proceed from the conviction that gender difference in patterns of engaging in care work and employment is the key to gender inequality, and that "gender-symmetric" social arrangements would better suit women's—and, interestingly, also men's—interests. Their proposals have been informed by feminist thinking and long-standing Marxist theorizing about the significance of women's entry to employment in unsettling patriarchal arrangements and empowering women. In their policy proposals, they respond as well to research on children's development, and a distinctively American concern with the social problems produced by our long-hours, employment-oriented culture. The dual-earner/dual-caregiver arrangement

> is a society in which men and women engage symmetrically in employment and caregiving, and all parents have realistic opportunities to combine waged work with the direct provision of care for their children. A dual-earner/dual-caregiver society is one that supports equal opportunities for men and women in employment, equal contributions from mothers and fathers at home, and high-quality care for children provided both by parents and by well-qualified and well-compensated non-parental caregivers. (Gornick and Meyers, this volume: 4–5).[6]

Reaching the utopia of gender symmetry depends on several interrelated transformations: the dissolution of the remaining gendered division of labor in employment and in the home, a thorough transformation of workplace practices, and the establishment of state policies that would encourage and support the model of a "dual-earner/dual-caregiver" household. But Gornick and Meyers eschew any deep analysis of how gender itself might be ended—for that is the implication of "dissolving" the gender division of labor; and while they indicate the need for controls on capitalists' prerogatives, they do not examine in any detail how capitalist and masculinist employment structures could be changed, focusing instead almost exclusively on state policies that would ease conflicts between paid work and family life. They outline a package of work–family reconciliation policies that would support dual-earner/dual-caregiver arrangements: paid family leave provisions in which mothers and fathers get equal, non-transferable shares of leave; working-time regulations; and early childhood education and care services.[7] Gornick and Meyers find the inspiration for these policies in Sweden, where social-democratic policies have supported mothers' employment with less time stress than in the US, provided better care services and resources for children, and encouraged fathers' caregiving. They contend that the "realness" of their utopia rests on the existence in Sweden, and, to a somewhat lesser extent, in several other European countries, of the kind of policies that could conceivably be extended to promote more aggressively the equal sharing of care work and paid work by women and men.[8] And, indeed, while their policy proposals would dramatically change the landscape in the US were they somehow to be enacted, these proposals are already quite familiar in the Nordic countries, which are such an important source for Gornick and Meyers' policy thinking. (How—politically, culturally—and when such existing policies might be extended, in the Nordic countries or the US, is not on their agenda.) Given how close their ideal policy institutions are to already-existing practices in the Nordic countries, one might ask why these countries are not much closer to gender symmetry and women's emancipation than they are (see, for example, Bergqvist, 1999; Ahlberg et al., 2008). Although on some measures of women's relative well-being vis-à-vis men's, Swedes fare better than do Americans (e.g., gendered wage gaps, or poverty ratios), they are far from equal, and on some measures (e.g., gendered authority gaps), the US ranks higher (Wright et al., 1995; see also Estevez-Abe 2005, Orloff, 2006). Perhaps other forces—not solely the gender division of labor—are implicated in sustaining gender hierarchy? Let's take a look, then, at how Gornick and Meyers analyze gender inequality.

Underlying Gornick and Meyers' account is the assumption that gender inequality is tied to gender differences in time spent on care and family versus employment and career. As they put it,

Feminists concerned with the family have concluded that persistent gender inequality in the labor market is both cause and consequence of women's disproportionate assumption of unpaid work in the home. This conversation revolves around the ways in which men's stronger ties to the labor market carry social, political, and economic advantages that are denied to many women, especially those who spend substantial amounts of time caring for children. (This volume: 13–14)

Gornick and Meyers (this volume: 8) define contemporary problems of gender inequality as resulting from "incomplete transformations," as we have moved from full to partial gender specialization. Women have changed a great deal—taking up paid employment in addition to their work of caring (as we all know), but men have not changed enough, and still do much less care work than women. Moreover, labor market and policy institutions presuppose the traditional division of labor and fail to give adequate support to modern arrangements for caregiving. Sensibly, they do not want to focus solely on women, as some contemporary efforts at achieving better "work–family reconciliation" do (see, for example, Esping-Andersen et al., 2002, 1999; and see Stratigaki, 2004 for an astute analysis of how the radical feminist edge has been taken off "reconciliation" in contemporary European politics). Yet they do not put any of the blame on men. They claim that the interests of men, women, and children are not essentially in conflict. Rather, the "most pressing conflicts of interest arise not between men and women, nor between parents and children, but between the needs of contemporary families and current divisions of labor, workplace practices, and social policies" (this volume: 14–15) I agree with this analysis of the link between the gender division of labor and gender inequality, as far as it goes; but, as I will argue below, I think it is not fully adequate.

The gender division of labor is pivotal in shaping women's and men's gender interests, Gornick and Meyers argue. Women are all disadvantaged by the existing gender division of labor, though to varying degrees— some have the resources needed to buy private services that can help them reconcile family and employment, and can negotiate favorable bargains with their employers, while others must struggle with meager resources in unforgiving environments. Yet Gornick and Meyers stress that all women are hurt by the gendering of care burdens, either directly or indirectly—as, for example, when employers engage in statistical discrimination in the expectation that women will favor family over work commitments. Thus, without considering solutions that center on increasing direct support to women's (informal, or unpaid) care work, they assume women are in employment, and argue that all women would benefit if the current masculine model of the full-time and unencumbered worker were to be replaced by a model of an encumbered worker, who also puts in fewer hours than typical men do now. (Thus, "full-time" work hours would be revised down; on the gender politics of work time and the gendered meanings of "full-" and "part-" time, see Fagan, 1996; Mutari and Figart, 2001). Women should find attractive policies that would encourage, reward and support a more equal division of care work and paid work between men and women. Men, too, are often forced to work too hard by current social arrangements, and certainly cannot contribute more at home as long as they are held to its strictures, even if they want to. (How much they want to is another concern, but this is not pursued.) Gornick and Meyers' take on the question of gender interests thus echoes Marxist and social-democratic, more than second-wave or contemporary feminist, accounts: men and women do not have opposed gender interests; rather, it is employers and "the state" that are problematic.

Gornick and Meyers advocate policy prescriptions drawing on what is commonly understood as the second-wave feminist contention that "women's emancipation depends on reaching parity with men in the public spheres of employment and politics" (this volume: 4)—although without as much of the critical edge vis-à-vis men. Their basic commitment to women's employment is also nourished from broadly Marxist sources, which have historically linked women's emancipation to their engagement with paid work. Yet they also favor greater support for caregiving activities than was usual for either liberal feminists or orthodox Marxists. Perhaps this reflects the authors' familiarity with Scandinavian developments, which had a homegrown set of supports for caregiving linked to concerns about population, fertility, labor supply and working women's rights to be mothers (Hobson, 1993; Ellingsaeter and Leira, 2006).[9] This attention to care marks their approach as having gone beyond the assumptions of 1970s liberal feminism denounced as "sameness" feminism, or "androgyny" by more radical feminists.[10] (Nancy Fraser (1994) has argued that this type of feminism is premised on a model of women becoming breadwinners like men, which she calls "universal breadwinner" feminism.) Here, it seems clear that they have been influenced by two decades of feminist work on social policy, which has been centrally concerned with understanding the relationships between care, paid work, and welfare, the links between care and gender inequality, and many women's strong normative commitment to the value of care. This literature, however, remains invisible in this text, mirroring the neglect of feminist analysis of care work that characterizes most mainstream work on social policy.[11]

Gornick and Meyers' proposal might be positioned in the space available in the aftermath of bitter feminist conflicts in the late 1980s and early 1990s over "sameness" and "difference" in politics and policy, in which protagonists argued about whether women's interests (taking those as relatively unproblematic, at the time) would be best served by strategies assuming and promoting women's similarity to men, or by those which assumed women's difference from men. The fight was staged in many policy arenas—for example, how best to craft policy on pregnancy and employment protection (Vogel, 1993). (Is pregnancy a disability like any other, meriting inclusion in existing general disability protections? Or is it a gender- or sex-specific condition warranting a gender-specific protection?) Questions of care and the body loomed large in these discussions. While feminists (especially though not only in the US) in the 1970s seemed to gravitate toward "sameness" strategies, the 1980s had brought greater attention to the importance of "difference," especially when based on care. Since then, there have been several attempts to go beyond the problematic framing of the problem as "sameness versus difference" (see, for example, Scott, 1988).

Among feminist policy analysts, the work of Nancy Fraser has been extremely significant in seemingly offering a way out of the dilemma. Unlike poststructuralist analysts of gender discourse and performativity in the Butlerian vein, to which many social feminists find themselves allergic, Fraser works on the familiar terrain of paid work and care. I want briefly to examine Fraser's argument, because it provides insight into the analytic underpinnings of the dual-earner/dual-caregiver policy model that Gornick and Meyers have directly borrowed from Rosemary Crompton.

Nancy Fraser, in her influential 1994 article "After the Family Wage," performs a Hegelian maneuver to overcome the sameness/difference problem, which leads her to advocate a policy model analogous to the dual-earner/dual-caregiver—that of the "universal caregiver." Investigating feminist utopian visions for reforming the welfare state in gender-egalitarian directions in a period of crisis and restructuring, she identifies two approaches—dubbed "universal breadwinner" and "caregiver parity"—roughly corresponding to the respective preferences and practices of US and European feminists. The former would allow and encourage women to act as men do in the economy, as breadwinners, earning a family-supporting wage, and ceding care work to others—not the unpaid housewife of the "traditional" household, but the paid service workers of the state—thus commodifying everyone while commodifying care. While this model would lead to a number of improvements in the situation of most women, Fraser

(1994: 602) criticizes this approach as problematic on several scores. For example, while the model depends on full employment, she doubts that everyone can be employed; it also depends on care being removed from households, but she believes some care cannot be outsourced, while those who continue to perform care would be marginalized. She sums up by saying the model is androcentric and unworkable, and ultimately unhelpful to women's interest in equality, because it expects women to become like men. The "caregiver parity" model does not neglect care, or women's work as caregivers, but instead tries to compensate them for the disadvantages this work creates in a masculinist and capitalist society. So women and men continue to be different. Yet Fraser (1994: 609) also finds this model limited, because gender differences ultimately continue to create disadvantages for women that cannot be compensated—difference may "cost less," but is far from "costless"; women end up marginalized from public activities even though better protected against poverty and other hardships. Fraser's dissection of existing feminist policy approaches is extremely useful in showing the limitations of our thinking, and lays the groundwork for new perspectives—such as those championed by Gornick and Meyers, and by Rosemary Crompton before them.

The way out of the sameness/difference dilemma, says Fraser, is by a synthesis of the two earlier approaches—a political ideal she calls the "universal caregiver," in which men are made the focus of efforts at change, rather than women. In other words, the problem is that most men are unlike what "most women are now": caregivers who are also (paid) workers. This is an important analytic innovation, paralleling others working to de-center the masculine. In this way, care is valorized while not being left solely to women—we try to retain what's good about women's devotion to care while, by making it normative for men as well as women, avoiding the problems of women's marginalization and the devaluation of care. To be sure, Fraser notes, this implies that the deconstruction of gender difference is a precondition for gender equity—we must "end gender as we know it" (Fraser, 1994: 611)! This is a revolutionary demand indeed.[12] Perhaps in a more reformist vein, attempting to make men more like women— by finding ways to encourage their participation in care, such as the fully individual leave entitlements Gornick and Meyers propose— would still be a worthwhile goal. Yet it falls somewhat short of gender symmetry.

I want to probe more deeply into the analysis of gender—and of subjects and politics—that underlies the Gornick–Meyer proposal for gender symmetry. To my mind, they take too lightly the deep investments people have in gender, and the ways in which knowledge, subjectivity and agency are all constrained *and enabled* by existing gendered categories (Butler, 1990, Zerilli, 2005). Taking account of these investments matters insofar as it clarifies men's commitment to preserving the power that current social arrangements give them, but also clarifies women's concerns to preserve their power in the domain of the private, care-giving realm. Identities are formed in relation to whether men and women see themselves as caregivers or not, or to the gendered ways in which they conceive of their activities.

This can certainly be taken up from a range of different theoretical angles, but many scholars would find it hard to imagine subjects— political actors—whose "needs" or "interests" can be said to preexist culturally constituted consciousness, including gendered (self-)understandings and knowledge.[13] For example, R. W. Connell (1987) highlights political and psychic aspects of gender in an account of gender relations as shaped by three structures: labor, power, cathexis. Or take Joan Scott's (1988) germinal intervention, which defines gender first as a constitutive element of social relations based on perceived differences between the sexes and expressed in symbols, norms, institutions and politics, and subjective identities, and second as a primary way of signifying power. One might also look to political and historical accounts that allow the "primary" causes of gender relations (or, less grandly, policy and political institutions) to vary over time and across place (for example, O'Connor et al., 1999).

Scott's analysis is significant for any consideration of "sameness" and "difference" with respect to any sort of politics, utopian or pragmatic, for it points to the continuing productivity of gender. Even when we speak on behalf of gender symmetry, we speak "as women," and must refer to difference. Moreover, while Scott points to the constitutively gendered character of subjects, she makes no assumption that gendered identities necessarily lead to a politics of gender difference. *Au contraire!* Women in the democratic age have been continually attracted to universalist visions. Similarly, Denise Riley (1988) and Judith Butler (1990) point to the variability and instability of gender categories for individuals and for collectivities, and to the diverse ways gender can be mobilized politically.

Of particular concern for the prospects of a gender-symmetric utopia that will depend on men's recruitment to caregiving, men's attachment to the powers and privileges of masculinity seems to be underplayed in Gornick and Meyers' account. I am thinking here of men's attempts to maintain gendered divisions of labor by avoiding dirty work at home and in the workplace, or by excluding women from favored positions in the paid labor force through sexual and other forms of harassment, or through discrimination in hiring, pay, or occupational access. Will men be dissuaded from making these power plays simply by the offer of incentives to take up care? Women's disadvantages at work are indeed linked to the statistical discrimination practiced "rationally" by employers calculating the likely impact on employment of women's carework burdens (taking leaves, for instance). But there's plain old discrimination to deal with, too, and cultural beliefs in gender difference (see, for example, Charles and Grusky, 2004).[14] Feminists have identified a range of factors that—even if one does not accept them as principal sources of unequal gender relations—surely contribute importantly to it: sexuality, reproduction, and violence. Perhaps these factors are required to understand the continuing problem of women's oppression even in "women-friendly welfare states" like those found in the Nordic countries. Adapting Catharine MacKinnon's (1989) words, the problem for women is (at least sometimes) "domination not difference."

On the flip side, Gornick and Meyers' vision of gender symmetry and "gender-egalitarian caregiving" also seems to occlude both the body—and especially women's bodies—and women's attachment to caregiving, promoting another assumption of "sameness" with reference to men's and women's equivalence in relation to childrearing. How do the demands of pregnancy and lactation affect any shift to "gender symmetry"?[15] Many feminists have stressed bodily aspects of gender—assuming that this also implies an irreducible cultural element—and would on these grounds alone dismiss policies or utopias based on androgyny or symmetry (see, for example, Moi, 1999; and of course, de Beauvoir, 1952, who wrote eloquently about the "body as a situation").

Can we assume an unproblematic embrace of their socialist–feminist-inspired symmetric version of "egalitarianism" among women?[16] What are we to make, then, of the widespread, well-documented preferences of many women to pursue life courses that are not premised on 50/50 sharing of paid work and care work with male partners? "Traditional" women in "new orthodox" religious modes pose a particular challenge to interpretations of gender that assume all women will find egalitarian arrangements in their interests, but even less extreme versions of women's attachments to lives founded on caregiving pose problems for the symmetric scenario. The standard response to these challenges among "materialist" and structurally determinist analysts makes allusion to false consciousness, or to short-term versus long-term interests. Thus, men and women may not know it now, but surely they will be better off under egalitarian conditions defined as gender symmetry. Understanding preferences that confirm the existing division of labor as merely "adaptive" to constraining conditions may be less analytically troublesome—though such an account would be improved if cultural processes were also invoked. But it will be difficult to apply such approaches directly to the formulation of policies if we also value democratic politics and accountability in policy making.

For Gornick and Meyers, the analytic challenge of what I would call the "depth" of gender relations is matched in seriousness by a number of other challenges that might be grouped under the banner of "differences." We have just discussed the wide range of variation in men's and women's preferences relating to the gender division of labor. A separate issue concerns the multiplicity of differences among women (and men). Some analysts embracing an "intersectional" analysis contend that advantaged white women may suffer from gendered caregiving arrangements, but that they are able either to mitigate or entirely offload their problems by using services provided by disadvantaged women of color, who suffer from more severe incompatibilities between employment and care—and who in fact may be deprived of opportunities to mother at all (see Mink, 1999; Roberts, 2004; Glenn, 2002). Michael Shalev, in this volume, raises the question of class differences among women in terms of orientations about mothering and paid work, assuming that their social locations cause their interests not just to differ but to collide; Duncan and Edwards (1999) contend that such orientations (which they call "gendered moral rationalities") vary not so much by class or its proxy, educational level, as by local gender cultures. The difference between these scholars is important, but they each raise a similar problem for Gornick and Meyers' assumptions about the uniformity of women's interests. While I disagree with the social determinism of these analyses, it is clear that both the individual preferences and the political demands of different groups of women have been at odds. To take just one example, in the 1970s the National Welfare Rights Organization advocated a kind of maternalist policy of making Aid to Families with Dependent Children more generous, enabling women's full-time caregiving, while other feminist groups pursued equal employment opportunities and the extension of child-care services. And "differences among women" are not simply an American concern, arising from the vexed and racially divided history of US feminism and social justice movements. Instead, we see conflicts over gender arrangements, and disputes among feminists about how best to proceed politically, crossing the developed West, and indeed the entire globe.

"Differences among women" (and men) also indexes a key concern that is absent from Gornick and Meyers' utopian considerations: who will be entitled to these new social protections and services? Unfortunately, the authors have not paid attention to the question of exactly who would be included in these programs, although they seem to assume that nation-states would be the entities running these policies, and thus that entitlement would be based on citizenship—but the boundaries set by states, and their immigration policies, are not in question. Historical accounts of the development of systems of social provision and regulation are increasingly highlighting the link between generous programs (such as those provided in the Nordic countries, or imagined by Gornick and Meyers) and the existence of "we-feeling," or solidarity based in perceived ethnic, "racial" and/or religious homogeneity (Antonnen, 2002; Ferrera, 2006). This in turn has been linked to practices of social closure, until recently at the level of the nation-state. According to Maurizio Ferrera, who has studied the intertwined development of welfare and citizenship boundaries in Europe, despite increased transnational movement of people, capital, and ideas,

> solidarity remains a national affair... Social sharing builds on 'closure.' It presupposes the existence of a clearly demarcated and cohesive community, whose members feel they belong to the same whole and that they are linked by reciprocity ties vis-à-vis common risks and similar needs. (Ferrera, 2006: 2)

Modern welfare states of the "golden age"—the period in which Scandinavians initiated pro-gender-equality leave policies and developed public services—enjoyed an alignment of redistributive boundaries with national territorial boundaries. In countries with extensive social divisions, such as the US, not all citizens were in fact treated equally, although this was the formal premise and promise of post–Second World War national social benefits (see Glenn, 2002). Increasing immigration also tests the limits of the citizenship-based models of Europe (see Soysal, 1994; Williams, 1995; Joppke, 1998; Siim, 2008). But clearly there is a deep challenge to any nationally based utopia, such as Gornick and Meyers' seems to be, once we think globally (for which Hassim, for example, argues forcefully in her essay in this volume).

While paying too little attention to differences among women (or among men), it is not the case that Gornick and Meyers are simply stuck in an old vision of "gender difference," emphasizing "women" and "men" as unitary and essentially different categories. Rather, they have embraced an approach that promises, by shifting the burden of change to men, to overcome the problems of understanding gender inequality in terms of a masculine standard. (It is the assumption of a masculine standard that forces the framing of gender problems in terms of women's "sameness" and "difference" from men.) But their solution actually re-creates the demand of sameness in a new form: women and men will still be the same, but (allegedly) on women's terms, rather than men's. In Gornick and Meyers' gender-symmetric utopia, men must "become like what women are now," as Fraser (1994) puts it—meaning, they have to care more, while women are also working more (for pay, that is). One wonders, when women cannot become like men are now, according to many feminist critics of androcentric ideals, on account of their attachment to care (among other things), how it is that men might become like women are now?[17] How will men develop an attachment to care?[18] (And let us recall that not all women are equally attached to or attracted to care work, or undertake it in similar ways.) The vision further presupposes that all are equally capable of caregiving. Men might well be induced to care more—and I hope they are—but this is unlikely to lead to the "dissolution" of gender; rather, we are likely to see the reconfiguration of gender, perhaps in more desirable patterns. Finally, one might also fault this model for its singularity: it assumes, as Cynthia Willett (2001: 91) has said, a "single norm of a socially useful person." Is it possible that we can have greater involvement of men in care without producing anything like "symmetry" or the effacement of gender difference? Is it possible to value care more than is now the case, without assuming everyone will participate directly in giving care? As may be clear from my posing such questions, I will argue that the answer is "yes."

A CONTEXTUAL UNDERSTANDING OF FEMINISTS' POLITICAL GOALS

Let me conclude by briefly discussing an alternative approach to feminist politics and the feminist projects (some utopian, some not) that emerge from such an analysis. While I certainly share many feminist values with Gornick and Meyers and am favorable to some of their policy proposals, we differ on how to develop political goals, be they feminist "utopias" or policy "way stations." The shorthand for our analytic differences is the opposition of deductive with inductive, expert with political, singular with plural. I proceed inductively, from the historical experiences of various Western feminist and women's movements and theorists. At a very basic level, starting points for feminists in different countries vary—what kinds of social and political capacities are on hand, what women "need" versus what they already have, what kinds of conflicts characterize the polity, and so on—and these variations influence what political actors desire. Still, the culture and politics of liberal individualism of the Western countries—particularly those with a Protestant religious–political legacy—has shaped, in a foundational way, the diverse understandings of feminists and women's movements. Feminists have, of course, usually embraced a revised individualism, one that rejects masculine standards and the assumption of a rational, unconstrained subject; one that takes account of relationality and interdependence, yet it is still recognizably liberal in its assumption of the importance of personhood and decisional autonomy (Reich, 2002; O'Connor et al. 1999, chapter 2).[19] But other values are combined in distinctive ways with feminist ones, and nationally specific politics and cultures have produced a multiplicity of feminist projects and utopian visions.

Different utopias have flourished in different political contexts, and bear the marks of their parentage as well as of their adoptive context. This is not to say that specific policy legacies in any sense "dictate" corresponding utopias, or that there can be no transfer of utopian ideas—surely there is. Wollstonecraft, de Beauvoir, Wittig and Butler, to name only a few feminist utopians, have been read and appropriated globally. It is simply to say, as in any case of translation, that the receiving context shapes the reception and understanding of the transferred object.

Let us take a closer look at the contrasting situations of feminists imagining utopian futures in Scandinavia, and in the US. The Nordic welfare model of excellent support for care and mothers' employment was built on notions of class equality in the "people's home," with gender equality as a secondary theme—and one which was not constructed in opposition to ideas of gender differences (Jenson and Mahon, 1993). These systems emerged—as did all the nascent welfare states of the modern era—from a context in which support for social reproduction was infused with eugenic thinking; generous social provision was based on sharing within the nation, not outside its boundaries (Koven and Michel, 1993). Nordic feminists, especially but not only within and in alliance with social-democratic parties, have

succeeded in extending an originally gender-differentiated scheme—
a set of policies with maternalist roots, which focused on allowing
working-class, employed women to be mothers—to encourage men's
caregiving as well as allowing all women to "reconcile" motherhood
and employment (Ellingsaeter and Leira, 2006). Thus, the near-term
political goals of those who would extend this project look a lot like
Gornick and Meyers' "utopian" policy institutions of equally shared
parental leave, more extensive services, and workplace reforms.[20] But
feminists have also raised issues concerning men's greater power in
politics, the economy and personal life—problems that they do not
think can be solved simply through equalizing leave-taking (see, for
example, Bergqvist, 1999; Borchorst and Siim, 2002). Unquestionably,
some Nordic feminists are most concerned with equalizing men's and
women's time spent on care and paid work, but others have developed
utopian visions that focus more centrally on empowering women
across spheres of life, and especially in politics. And other feminists
have opposed equally divided parental leaves, responding to concerns
raised by women who do not want to give up their own leave time—
perhaps because they want to breastfeed for longer than six months,
perhaps because they fear the fathers of their children will not take
the leave (in which case total parental leave time would drop and
children would have to go to day care before the age of one or one-
and-a-half).[21]

Nordic feminists are increasingly attempting to revise their thinking
about policies, politics and ultimate goals in the face of the challenge
of diversity, dealing with the integration of ethnic minorities, especially
non-European immigrants (see, for example, Siim, 2008). They do
not yet agree on how their generous systems can change to accommodate newcomers, nor on how much such newcomers—often from
non-Western countries—should be asked to change, especially in terms
of their gender and familial practices. Here we see Scandinavian
versions of the difficult debates about the veil, sex-segregated schooling
and the like that have roiled continental Europe and Britain, and are
far from resolved. Gender and family practices have been part of what
defines the "we" of the West, especially in contrast with the Islamic,
immigrant "Other,", and yet feminists have commitments to developing
a more inclusive feminist utopia, and policy institutions to support
it. To say that this poses political difficulties is to put it mildly.

Diversity also has another face in the Nordic countries—that of
the demand for greater citizen "choice" with respect to services and
care arrangements, which has been forwarded across the developed
welfare states by "third way" and "recalibrative" projects, and connects

in complicated ways with the increasing social diversity of these societies. In combination with demands for fiscal cutbacks, these demands for wider options have helped to shift policy across the Nordic countries—even in Sweden—towards "cash for care," in which citizens can "cash out" the cost of public services (Borchorst and Siim, 2002; Berven, 2005; Ellingsaeter and Leira, 2006). It is usually mothers rather than fathers who have opted to take the cash and stay at home, and this reflects a class gradient. As is the pattern across most Western countries, well-educated women pursue life patterns that converge most with those of men of their own class (tales of "opt-out revolutions" notwithstanding), while less-educated women tend to make greater accommodation to care, and diverge more from men with similar educational levels. Feminists are divided on how to respond: Keep pushing for greater involvement of fathers in care, even if it means less time for mothers who may want it? Or support women's and men's options to decide, but attempt to make the choices about at-home care versus employment more "real" by insisting that cash-for-care policies be accompanied by guaranteed rights to spots in child-care centers?[22] Clearly, contrasting utopian visions animate these different positions—symmetry versus choice and "difference," to put it too simply. And in either case, there is a challenge to maintain and broaden solidarity while accommodating diversity in all its guises.

What about the US? First, it is important to stress that the US is not an "exemplar of limited government intervention," as Gornick and Meyers claim (this volume: 6), but that the modes of "intervention" have differed importantly from the European model, with an emphasis on regulation rather than social provision (Orloff, 2006; Weir et al., 1988). We do not confront a blank slate, or simple lack of gender policy, in the US as opposed to well-developed "women-friendly" policies in Scandinavia, but a distinctive alternative gender regime (O'Connor et al., 1999). US versions of feminism, path-breaking across many areas, have been influential in building this gender regime. The considerable influence of US feminisms, in both policy and the broader culture, is all too often forgotten when we focus on the obvious failures—like getting paid parental leave or publicly supported child-care services. One thinks of developments in our theories of sexuality and gender, the practice of queer politics, or the development of "body rights," among other things (Shaver, 1993). And the US is a leader, not a laggard, in removing discriminatory occupational barriers—getting women into many masculine blue-collar occupations and the top tiers of management and the professions, including academia (Cobble, 2004; Charles and Grusky, 2004); in developing public remedies for sexual harassment (Zippel, 2006), and, in the Family and Medical Leave Act, developing an understanding of caregiving needs that extends beyond mothers and children. The leave is not paid, and this is clearly a huge problem. Yet we should not ignore the fact that the leave is available to men and women for a very broad range of caregiving needs, and not limited by a maternalist or "reproductionist" logic.

What is inescapable, from any analytic engagement with actual feminist politics and theorizing in the US, is that political actors favoring gender equality or the abolition of "patriarchy" do not agree (and have not agreed) on questions of gender difference and "sameness" (or "symmetry"), and that they have enunciated a rather wide variety of political goals. Thus, for example, in the early twentieth century, many feminists in the US (as in Europe) imagined a maternalist utopia—one in which, based on motherhood, women might be resourced and recognized by the state with allowances and services that would empower them within still-patriarchal households and allow them, sometimes, the capacity to live independently of male relatives (Koven and Michel, 1993; Pedersen, 1993). In other words, these political actors proceeded from an assumption of gender difference, and did not aspire to symmetry in men's and women's participation in care and paid work. Rather, they sought "equality in difference."[23] Maternalist visions have remained surprisingly resilient in the contemporary period, even as they have often been revised in a de-gendering direction, from supporting motherhood to supporting care). In other words, the goal becomes sustaining caregivers generally, and not mothers specifically, although there is often an assumption that most caregivers are and will continue to be women, and that most women will be caregivers. (Again, this may or may not be combined with support to the employment of caregivers.)

Something like "gender symmetry"—a utopia premised on women's and men's similarities, and the goal of "halving it all"—has been a perennial favorite among some US feminists, to be sure. It has affinities with the broader demand for gender neutrality encouraged by the US legal–political framework. Gender neutrality has been a wedge against entrenched privilege in many occupations and educational institutions. In the judicial arena, far-reaching anti-discrimination laws, affirmative action programs, and hefty jury verdicts against employers convicted of sexual harassment have broken (or at least begun to crack) glass ceilings. American women occupy professional and managerial positions in much greater numbers than their Swedish (or other European) counterparts. But the shortcomings of this essentially liberal vision are well known. It is difficult to find ways to incentivize care by men through negative liberties, and it has been more common for feminist political actors to stress the opening of women's vocational opportunities, which can be accomplished through legal regulation and the removal of state-sanctioned barriers.[24] Moreover, as social liberals have long pointed out, one may have formal rights but lack the resources with which to enjoy them. While formal "rights to choose" are well established in the US, the resources to enable people to make choices between viable alternatives are often lacking, particularly for poor women and women of color—thus, we have rights to abortion but not to the material resources either for the medical procedure itself or for bearing and raising children (O'Connor et al., 1999). Contemporary feminists who recall the maternalist visions of early-twentieth-century women's movements have pushed in the direction of offering greater material support to disadvantaged women; for example, Dorothy Roberts (2004) calls for policies that will support "economic freedom" for such women (see also the essays in Mink, 1999, which deal with these concerns in the context of the US, following welfare reform).[25] This is especially important given that anti-natalist purposes have often motivated social policies targeted at poor women. The inequalities with which they are most concerned are those of race and class, which deny some women the option to be domestic, or to perform their own caregiving as they see fit. The proponents of this kind of feminist utopia seem relatively unconcerned with gender symmetry.

In the diversity of radical and reformist (as well as "traditional") visions that have inspired US feminists, we see the reflection of the broader culture. American society is distinctive among the developed countries for its heterogeneity and its high levels of inequality. Meanwhile, the US social policy regime is notable for the prominent role of the private provision of services, and the importance of private sources of income to citizens' and residents' well-being. These features of political life reinforce the multiplicity of life situations, not simply inequality. Understandings of the good life in the US vary widely, including with respect to ideals about family and gender relations. This is partly the result of great ethnic and religious diversity, with people from every corner of the earth among the current US population—a fact only intensified with the most recent waves of immigration. It also reflects long-standing religious, political, and ideological divisions, and the liberal–pluralist institutional compromises fashioned to accommodate them.

If there is merit to be found in the liberalism of American policy and politics—and I think there is—it is in its respect for the different visions of the good held by members of the polity, that is, in pluralism. This is not to argue, as many "political liberals" do, that policy can ever be fully neutral with respect to people's choices about how they live their lives. It cannot. Indeed, Rob Reich (2002) argues that citizens' participation in liberal and pluralist societies requires a certain level of autonomy—meaning capacities to make decisions about one's life—that undermines the authority and cohesion of groups that depend on obedience and hierarchy; he further contends that this should be understood and supported more explicitly than is typical among US political liberals. But certainly there can be greater and lesser levels of respect for all kinds of differences, and for notions of citizenship that embrace cultural multiplicity. As compared with its European counterparts, the US features greater levels of support for diversity, without having yet reached pluralist goals of toleration and respect.[26] Given the variety of religious, social, and cultural norms we expect to exist in our societies, we cannot expect a single ideal or policy model to appeal to them all. This is not an argument for relativism, but for respectful and democratic engagement among citizens with differing views of the good.

Where, then, are we US feminists left with respect to envisioning alternative futures that can animate democratic and gender-egalitarian politics? As I have been arguing, the sheer facts of diversity, of all kinds, speak against a gender-egalitarian utopia founded on gender symmetry. Gender symmetry expects and presupposes too much similarity across politically and socially significant groups in their gendered life goals and the political demands that might respond to these. It is a utopian vision deduced from an abstract analysis of gender in the rich democracies; the associated imaginings of gender interests for particular institutional way stations are comparably deracinated. Let me underline that, while I am not inspired by the utopian vision of gender symmetry, I am very much in sympathy with Gornick and Meyers' dedication to finding policy solutions to the dilemmas of combining care and paid work in ways that contribute to gender equality. But I advocate a different path toward resolving these very real dilemmas.

In this essay I have emphasized questions of "difference," but not because I think we should articulate a utopia based on valorizing, resourcing and reinforcing gender and cultural differences. Rather, I believe that feminist political projects should begin from our policy and political history; in the specific case of the contemporary US, this means that feminists must reckon with popular beliefs in, and investments in, gender differences of various kinds, and the multiplicity of their expression across cultural divides based on geographic location, "race," ethnicity, religion, and all the rest. We need to find ways to articulate egalitarian visions that can appeal to many different kinds of people, not all of whom embrace the standard feminist version of the good put forward by Gornick and Meyers. This is all to say that I do not believe it is possible, or desirable, to articulate a full-blown alternative utopia to counterpose to Gornick and Meyers' vision. Nevertheless, I can sketch out some ideas for how one might move forward in the contemporary US context.

The radical vision of opening opportunities for women—all kinds of women, and men denied access to advantaged positions in employment and elsewhere—has characterized large swaths of organized and popular feminism. It is sometimes accompanied by demands to open familial and care "opportunities" to men, to move toward something like gender symmetry; but at other times, the logic of expanding choice in the face of diverse situations and demands has prevailed, while the goal of making men's and women's lives more alike has been sidelined.[27] Given the character of gender relations, in which the category of "woman" (and gender) has varying levels of salience at both individual and collective levels (Riley, 1988), we will wait in vain for a final resolution to "sameness or difference" questions, and must be prepared to wrestle with gender forever. Thus, I suggest that our motto be "Open possibilities for men and women, remove policies and practices that impede choices," continuing the best aspects of past feminist practice in the US: removing obstacles to women's (and men's) freedom, and providing resources for a democratically selected range of options.

I hope it is clear that such a vision could inspire feminist political action around issues of care. Indeed, if I were not something of a political pragmatist, this orientation would lead me to advocate a citizen's wage, or participation income, which could cover the exigencies of care, as well as allowing people to fulfill other needs and aspirations. But (unlike many advocates of basic income, citizen's wages and the like) I would insist that such payments be coupled with strengthening efforts to develop and open "non traditional" training and employment opportunities for women, to upgrade the conditions and pay of care workers in the US and elsewhere, to encourage men's caregiving, and to develop better public and private care services. This ensemble of policies would facilitate a variety of arrangements with respect to employment, care and other important activities. Yet I believe that, in the contemporary US, gender-egalitarian policy reform starting from the premise of adult employment is far more likely to succeed—

thus, I can see political promise in all the policies I have enumerated, save a citizen's wage itself! However, this is a different discussion than the one allowed by the "real utopias" framework (although I do pursue it elsewhere: see Orloff, forthcoming).

Democracy is critical to our politics, both as means and end. The designers of polices that support social reproduction, care and employment, and that regulate these spheres, must be accountable to democratic constituencies. This is not to say that "anything goes" as long as people "freely choose" it: we must decide collectively what will be supported through public means, given legal protections to minority rights. There is no political obligation on feminists to support every possibility. Calculations of economic and political feasibility, as well as normative desirability, enter here. Within the multiplicity of political and policy possibilities, feminists can and should argue for those that empower women, that give them more freedom to define their lives and to engage in the political decisions that define and support collective ends. But we must expect agonistic political debate among ourselves and others over how this will be understood—this cannot be fixed in advance or settled for all time. The continuing, constitutive paradox of feminist politics—that we must both accept and refuse difference, as Joan Scott famously put it—precludes any ultimate decision in favor of either "symmetry" or diversity. Our present-day goals and our utopias will be created politically, and anew, as long as there are feminists and democracy.

NOTES

1 I agree with Hassim (in this volume) that the spatial, political and social limits of the proposal deserve greater scrutiny.

2 I have argued that these comparisons have been far too influenced by "Swedophilia," and that we need a more comprehensive appreciation of the advantages as well as failures of existing US gender policy (as I offer with colleagues in O'Connor et al., 1999)—but that is not the subject of our concern here.

3 Thanks to Julia Adams for illuminating conversations on this point; she convinced me that the concept of "interests" brings in its wake too much accreted semiotic baggage, especially from its Marxist past, thereby thwarting any attempt to set it free from understandings of politics as determined (in the last instance of course) by "material" forces.

4 I do believe that historically specific institutional legacies make certain policy approaches likely, possible, or impossible—this is at least partly a

matter of politics, as these legacies create, reinforce, or alter definitions of problems, understanding of patterns of coalitions and enmities, and sets of institutional capacities (Weir et al., 1988), while conditioning the way actors claim the right to name themselves (Jenson and Mahon, 1993). In short, "policy creates politics"—or, at least, helps to do so.

5   See Fraser (1990) for an influential statement of the contextualized and conflictual construction of what are understood to be "needs" or even, in some instances, "rights." Haney (2002) explores the "invention" of certain sorts of needs and subjects (for example, the "needy," or "mothers") in post-socialist Hungary, and further specifies a theory of the political and cultural construction of needs, rights and identities.

6   It is not entirely clear how one would measure progress toward gender symmetry, which is not particularly well-defined. Does it depend on 50/50 informal care and employment splits by all heterosexual couples? Most couples? What about singles or gay couples or other familial or household arrangements? Or should it be measured in the aggregate?

7   Although they mention "equal opportunities" in employment, they do not outline policies that would regulate equal treatment on hiring and wages and prevent hostile environments, sticking only with the regulation of working time. I return to this point below.

8   Gornick and Meyers claim there is widespread agreement that the Nordic countries, plus France and Belgium, constitute a "coherent cluster." I think this misreads the evidence. Yes, they all have strong elements of public provision for children's care, but that does not extend to other features of their gender policy models, nor does it reflect similarities in the political forces that brought these services into being (see, for example, Kremer, 2007; Lewis and Ostner, 1995; Pedersen, 1993; Jenson and Sineau, 2001; Mahon 1993). Specialists on the Nordic countries further insist that gender and family policies are actually becoming more distinctive within the cluster, as right or liberal parties put their stamp on policy (see, for example, Ellingsaeter and Leira, 2006). Sweden has been the principal exemplar of policies said to foster dual-earner/dual-caregiver households, yet in the most recent elections it has joined the other Nordic countries in embracing "choice" (usually meaning the right to cash out the cost of public services into an allowance to support mothers' work in the home for a year or two), and with it, continuing gender differences in care and employment patterns. Yet note that, even before the most recent policy changes, Sweden, too, has featured plenty of continuing gender differentiation in work and care patterns (Ahlberg et al., 2008).

9   Gornick and Meyers are also motivated by concerns of developmental psychology about children's well-being, mainly American in origin, but they have rebelled against a common prescription of that US literature (which is usually quite distinct from feminist analysis)—to support mothers' withdrawal

from employment. Sweden, as a source of policy inspiration, gave them a way to respond to worries about care without losing the emphasis on mothers' employment, and allowed them to fashion a credible set of policy institutions for promoting dual-earner/dual-caregiver households.

10 Perhaps this also reflects the direct influence of "difference feminism," which has characterized feminism in the developed world since the 1980s; this certainly influenced Fraser (1994).

11 This literature is vast. Key works on care in political and legal theory include Tronto, 1993; Sevenhuijsen, 1998; Kittay, 2002, Fineman, 1995, 2004; Young, 1990. Germinal scholarship linking social provision, gender, care and employment includes Land, 1978; Lewis, 1992; Williams, 2001; Jenson,1997; Koven and Michel, 1990; Gordon, 1990, 1994; Fraser and Gordon, 1994; Hobson, 1990; Knijn, 1994; Cass, 1994. Let me also note, since Gornick and Meyers do not, that I have been involved in developing this scholarship as well and I cannot here do it justice, but I have reviewed it elsewhere (see Orloff, 1996, 2005; O'Connor et al., 1999).

12 Recall that Gornick and Meyers, too, understand the "dissolution of the gender division of labor" as a prerequisite for their utopia of "gender symmetry." This strikes me as unproblematic if we are speaking of the usual understandings of utopia, but more troublesome if we are speaking of "real" utopias.

13 As Adams and Padamsee describe a similar set of analyses, these works begin from the premise that

> social position—analytically independent of and prior to consciousness— generates ideas and even identities. The latter are simply assumed to be aligned with actors' positional interests and preconceptual experiences. Further [it is assumed that] these identities apply not just to an aggregate of people with the requisite demographic characteristics, but that these actors form a natural group and that their actions can be interpreted accordingly. (Adams and Padamsee, 2001: 13)

14 I wonder about several things. Are they refraining from proposing policies targeting masculine privilege out of a political calculation that this would be counterproductive, pushing away potential allies among men, particularly in the unions and social-democratic parties that have been such important players in expanding social policy in the Scandinavian—and indeed European— context? Do we see here, then, a bit of a concern about political and practical feasibility? Or are Gornick and Meyers simply assuming that we already have policies flowing from an understanding of masculine interests in opportunity hoarding (to use the rather bloodless term favored by some theorists of inequality) or worse? They would be partially right about the US (and, to a lesser extent, other English-speaking countries); yet these sorts of policies are

rather less developed in other countries (see also Zippel's contribution to this volume). Or do they think such policies are unnecessary?

15 In Scandinavia, to date, the complete equalization of leaves between men and women has been blocked, partly because of concerns about breast-feeding (Ellingsaeter and Leira, 2006).

16 Much feminist analysis has been concerned with the power of social location to shape our political ideas, but here I do not want to make the standard "standpoint" critique of Gornick and Meyers. The problem is not that Gornick and Meyers have proposed a set of policies that somehow flow from self-interest based on their social location, and that might contradict the interests of other, "worthier" women. Rather, it is that they present their vision as something other than politically and historically contextualized. But their program—like any other—will have to contend with other visions of gender equality, or other political and social goods, that women as well as men might embrace.

17 I am grateful to Linda Zerilli for first raising this question in conversation, and continuing to discuss its implications with me.

18 Indeed, some recent research on contemporary North American men who are primary caregivers (Doucet, 2006) finds that these fathers do not see themselves as "mothering," but fathering. Perhaps we should not worry about what they call it, as long as they are engaged in providing care. Yet it seems to me that, politically, the differences in terminology and in identification will matter.

19 Certainly feminism can—and has—emerged in non-Western contexts, but as the protagonists themselves insist, it takes on context-specific forms; and it remains an open question how much any sort of feminism presupposes some kind of autonomy and individualism.

20 Iceland has recently introduced what might count as a "real-utopian" parental leave policy: each parent receives a three-month leave entitlement, and a further three months is available for couples to allocate as they wish.

21 Morgan's essay, in this volume, deals with these issues.

22 Arnlaug Leira (personal communication) has suggested that Finland comes close to assuring this choice.

23 It is important to note that some maternalist, gender-differentiated visions accepted mothers' employment, while others did not (Pedersen, 1993).

24 This has not stopped women from fantasizing about getting men to do more housework, however.

25 Gornick and Meyers, too, are concerned with expanding the resources available to women and men of all income levels, reflecting their social-democratic orientation. Indeed, they take on arguments that the policy package of leaves, services and work-time reduction will impede choice by saying that, in fact, it will allow more options as compared to the lack

of provision currently obtaining in the US. But here they are simply defending a set of policies against the status quo, not adjudicating between different visions of utopia. They do not define their utopia in terms of choice.

26 Whether respect for diversity and generous systems of social provision can coexist has not yet been demonstrated, either in the diverse but non-solidaristic US, or in solidaristic but not yet diversity-accommodating European countries.

27 Gender neutrality is a homegrown American concept, and does not mandate similarity, only that neither men nor women be given options (by the state, or regulated entities) that are not available to the other; yet "gender neutrality" seems unlikely to stir much passionate political attachment.

REFERENCES

Adams, Julia, and Tasleem Padamsee, 2001, "Signs and Regimes: Rereading Feminist Work on Welfare States," *Social Politics* 8: 1–23.

Ahlberg, Jenny, Christine Roman, and Simon Duncan, 2008, "Actualizing the 'Democratic Family'? Swedish Policy Rhetoric versus Family Practices," *Social Politics* 15: 79–100.

Antonnen, Anneli, 2002, "Universalism and Social Policy: A Nordic Feminist Revaluation," *NORA* 10: 71–80.

Beauvoir, Simone de, 1952, *The Second Sex*, New York: Knopf.

Bergqvist, Christina, ed., 1999, *Equal Democracies? Gender and Politics in the Nordic countries*, Oslo: Scandinavian University Press.

Borchorst, Anette, and Birte Siim, 2002, "The Women-friendly Welfare States Revisited," *NORA* (special issue on "Challenges to gender equality in the Nordic welfare states") 10 (2): 90–8.

Butler, Judith, 1990, *Gender Trouble: Feminism and the Subversion of Identity*, New York: Routledge.

Charles, Maria and David Grusky, 2004, *Occupational Ghettoes: The Worldwide Segregation of Women and Men*, Stanford: Stanford University Press.

Connell, R. W., 1987, *Gender and Power: Society, the Person and Sexual Politics*, Stanford: Stanford University Press.

Doucet, Andrea, 2006, *Do Men Mother? Fathering, Care, and Domestic Responsibility*, Toronto: University of Toronto Press.

Duncan, Simon, and Rosalind Edwards, 1999, *Lone Mothers, Paid Work, and Gendered Moral Rationalities*, New York: St Martin's Press.

Ellingsaeter, Anne Lise, and Arnlaug Leira, eds, 2006, *Politicising Parenthood in Scandinavia: Gender Relations in Welfare States*, Bristol, UK: Policy Press.

Esping-Andersen, Gøsta, 1999, *Social Foundations of Postindustrial Economies*, New York: Oxford University Press.

Fagan, Colette, 1996, "Gendered Time Schedules: Paid Work in Great Britain," *Social Policy* 3: 72–106.
Ferrera, Maurizio, 2006, *The Boundaries of Welfare: European Integration and the New Spatial Politics of Social Solidarity*, New York: Oxford University Press.
Fraser, Nancy, 1994, "After the Family Wage: Gender Equality and the Welfare State," *Political Theory* 22: 591–618.
Fraser, Nancy, and Linda Gordon, 1990. "Struggle over Needs: Outline of a Socialist–Feminist Critical Theory of Late-Capitalist Political Culturein Linda Gordon, ed., *Women, the State, and Welfare: Historical and Theoretical Perspectives*, Madison: University of Wisconsin Press: 205–31.
Glenn, Evelyn Nakano, 2002, *Unequal Freedom: How Race and Gender Shaped American Citizenship and Labor*, Cambridge, MA: Harvard University Press.
Gornick, Janet, and Marcia Meyers, 2008, "Institutions that Support Gender Egalitarianism in Parenthood and Employment," this volume.
Haney, Lynne, 2002, *Inventing the Needy: Gender and the Politics of Welfare in Hungary*, Berkeley: University of California Press.
Hassim, Shireen, 2008, "Whose Utopia?" this volume.
Hobson, Barbara, 1993, "Feminist Strategies and Gendered Discourses in Welfare States: Married Women's Right to Work in the US and Sweden During the 1930s," in Seth Koven and Sonya Michel, eds, *Mothers of a New World: Maternalist Politics and the Origins of Welfare States*, New York: Routledge.
Jenson, Jane, and Rianne Mahon, 1993, "Representing Solidarity: Class, Gender and the Crisis in Social-Democratic Sweden," *New Left Review*, 201: 76-100.
Koven, Seth, and Sonya Michel, 1993, *Mothers of a New World: Maternalist Politics and the Origins of Welfare States*, New York: Routledge.
Kremer, Monique, 2007, *How Welfare States Care: Culture, Gender, and Parenting in Europe*, Amsterdam: Amsterdam University Press.
Lewis, Jane, and Ilona Ostner, 1995, "Gender and the Evolution of European Social Policies," in Stephen Leibfried and Paul Pierson, eds, *European Social Policies: Between Fragmentation and Integration*, Washington, DC: Brookings Institution.
Mackinnon, Catharine, 1989, *Toward a Feminist Theory of the State*, Cambridge, Mass: Harvard University Press.
Mink, Gwendolyn, ed., 1999, *Whose Welfare?* Ithaca, NY: Cornell University Press.
Moi, Toril, 1999, *What is a Woman? And Other Essays*, New York: Oxford University Press.
Morgan, Kimberly, 2006, *Working Mothers and the Welfare State: Religion

and the Politics of Work–Family Policies in Western Europe and the United States, Stanford: Stanford University Press.

—— 2008, "The Political Path to a Dual-Earner/Dual-Carer Society: Pitfalls and Possibilities," this volume.

Mutari, Ellen, and Deborah M. Figart, 2001, "Europe at a Crossroads: Harmonization, Liberalization, and the Gender of Work Time," *Social Politics* 8: 36–64.

O'Connor, Julia S., Ann Shola Orloff, and Sheila Shaver, 1999, *States, Markets, Families: Gender, Liberalism and Social Policy in Australia, Canada, Great Britain and the United States*, Cambridge, UK: Cambridge University Press.

Orloff, Ann, 1996, "Gender in the Welfare States," *Annual Review of Sociology* 22: 51–78.

—— 2005, "Social Provision and Regulation: Theories of States, Social Policies and Modernity," in Julia Adams, Elisabeth Clemens and Ann Shola Orloff, eds, *Remaking Modernity: Politics, History and Sociology*, Durham: Duke University Press.

—— 2006, "From Maternalism to 'Employment for All': State Policies to Promote Women's Employment across the Affluent Democracies," in Jonah Levy, ed., *The State after Statism: New State Activities in the Era of Globalization and Liberalization*, Cambridge, Mass: Harvard University Press.

—— forthcoming, *Farewell to Maternalism? State Policies, Feminist Politics and Mothers' Employment in the US and Europe*, New York: Russell Sage.

Pedersen, Susan, 1993, *Family, Dependence, and the Origins of the Welfare State: Britain and France, 1914–1945*, New York: Cambridge University Press.

Reich, Rob, 2002, *Bridging Liberalism and Multiculturalism in American Education*, Chicago: University of Chicago Press.

Riley, Denise, 1988, *"Am I That Name?" Feminism and the Category of "Women" in History*, Minneapolis: University of Minnesota Press.

Roberts, Dorothy, 2004, "Welfare Reform and Economic Freedom: Low-Income Mothers' Decisions about Work at Home and in the Market," *Santa Clara Law Review* 44: 1,029–63.

Scott, Joan, 1986, "Gender: A Useful Category of Analysis," *American Historical Review* 91: 1,053–758, Gender and the Politics of History, New York: Columbia University Press.

Shalev, Michael, 2008, "Class Divisions Among Women," this volume.

Shaver, Sheila, 1993, "Body Rights, Social Rights, and the Liberal Welfare State." *Critical Social Policy* 13: 66–93.

Siim, Birte, 2008, "Dilemmas of Citizenship: Tensions between gender equality and cultural diversity in the Danish welfare state," in Kari Melby, Anna-Birte Ravn and Christina Carlsson Wetterberg, eds, *Gender Equality and Welfare Politics in Scandinavia: The Limits of Political Ambition?* Bristol, UK: Policy Press.

Stratigaki, Maria, 2004, "The Cooptation of Gender Concepts in EU Policies: The Case of 'Reconciliation of Work and Family'," *Social Politics* 11: 30–56.

Vogel, Lise, 1993, *Mothers on the Job: Maternity Policy in the US Workplace*, New Brunswick, NJ: Rutgers University Press.

Weir, Margaret, Ann Shola Orloff, and Theda Skocpol, eds, 1988, *The Politics of Social Policy in the United States*, Princeton: Princeton University Press.

Willett, Cynthia, 2001, *The Soul of Justice: Social Bonds and Racial Hubris*, Ithaca, NY: Cornell University Press.

Williams, Fiona, 1995, "Race/Ethnicity, Gender, and Class in Welfare States: A Framework for Comparative Analysis" *Social Politics* 2: 127–59.

Zerilli, Linda M. G., 2005, *Feminism and the Abyss of Freedom*, Chicago: University of Chicago Press.

Zippel, Kathrin, 2006, *The Politics of Sexual Harassment: A Comparison of the United States and the European Union*, New York: Cambridge University Press.

——"The Missing Link for Promoting Gender Equality: Work–Family and Anti-Discrimination Policies," this volume.

PART III

Designs: Modifications, Specifications, Alternatives

7

Social Policy Principles Applied to Reform of Gender Egalitarianism in Parenthood and Employment

Peter McDonald

The principal objective of Gornick and Meyers' paper is to specify a social policy regime that would support gender egalitarianism. The policy regime they propose has five main thrusts.

The first is six months' paid parental leave for each parent upon the birth of a child, with 100 percent replacement rates (with a high cap), and with benefits being non-transferable between parents. The leave can be used flexibly (taken at any time, taken as part-time on a pro-rata basis) over an eight-year period, but with substantial notification periods required for employers. The leave would be financed by a new social insurance fund with contributions by employers and/or employees. Premiums would not be experience-related at the enterprise level. The government would not contribute financially to this scheme, but would set up an employment referral agency to help employers with temporary absences. The second is a reasonable number of days each year of paid, casual leave for caring purposes, paid from the social insurance system and available to all workers, not just parents. The third relates to work hours (standard full-time work hours of between 35 and 39 per week and a standard work-year of 48 weeks).

The fourth thrust is that all employees would have the right to flexible or shorter hours, subject to the agreement of their employer. Employers could refuse on business grounds, but refusal would be subject to government review. Small businesses would be excluded. All part-time work would be subject to pro-rata benefits. Finally, the fifth thrust covers affordable, quality early childhood education and care. The amounts of care are not specified beyond "limited" amounts of infant care, "modest" amounts of toddler care (for one- and two-year-olds) and "more extensive" care for three- and four-year-olds. Eighty percent of the cost (uncapped?) would be met by government, and the remaining 20 per cent would derive from fees subject to an income test (dropping to zero cost for the poorest families). There would be a choice of the type of arrangement and of caregiver. This would be associated with the adoption and enforcement of standards of care.

In this discussion of the Gornick–Meyer proposals, I begin with a specified set of social policy principles associated with the potential policy areas affected, and discuss the proposed gender-egalitarian policies against these principles. Along the way, the relevance of other policy areas is addressed. The principles to be considered are the following: institutional versus individual-level explanations of outcomes; gender egalitarianism versus gender equity; family support policy based on horizontal equity; family support policy based on vertical equity; child development; labor market efficiency and business profitability; a lifetime perspective; simplicity and transparency; fiscal responsibility and affordability; political and cultural acceptability, including multicultural considerations; feasibility, in the sense that it is not revolutionary, but builds on or modifies existing institutional arrangements.

INSTITUTIONAL VERSUS INDIVIDUAL-LEVEL EXPLANATIONS OF OUTCOMES

The authors correctly take an institutional approach to the explanation of behavior, but might have been more explicit about this. Often, academic work in this policy area is based upon individual econometric analysis within one national policy setting. Such research usually fails to point out that, in a different policy setting, behavior might also be different. Clearly, people make their individual decisions in the shadow of the opportunities and constraints that apply in their particular context. Also, it is difficult for people to imagine a different institutional context—unless they have some experience of it. I have argued strongly that the differences in fertility rates between advanced countries are determined by institutional differences, not by differences between individuals (McDonald, 2006). Indeed, it is not uncommon to find in this area of behavior that relationships at the individual level are the opposite of those at the national level. For example, fertility tends to fall with increases in employment participation when individuals are the unit of analysis, but to rise when countries are the unit of analysis. It is likely that a similar result would apply to the relationship between fertility and gender equality.

GENDER EGALITARIANISM

A movement for gender egalitarianism must confront the argument that men and women are different, and that exact equality should not be the expected goal. This objection is inevitable when it comes from right-wing conservatives who rue the passing of the male-breadwinner model of the family and blame all of society's ills upon its passing. However, the opposition becomes more powerful when it is respectable intellectual research that argues that men and women are different (for example, Brizendine, 2006) or that motherhood is different in character to fatherhood (for example, Anne Manne, 2005).

It is useful to think of gender egalitarianism in terms of equity rather than equality. Gender equity can be defined as follows:

> In the gender equity model of the family, there is income earning work, household maintenance work and caring and nurturing work, but gender has no relationship to who does which type of work. The gender equity model does not imply exact equality between the man and the woman in any heterosexual couple, rather than that specific roles are not determined on the basis of gender. (McDonald, 2000a: 3)

Gender equity derives from an evaluation of the fairness of a society's gender system from the perspective of rights: social, political, economic and reproductive. Gender equity as the basis for reform leaves room for individual couples to make their own arrangements, so long as this takes place within a context of equal rights and equal resources in relation to the making of decisions. In contrast to gender equity, gender equality refers to symmetrical or identical outcomes between men and women, as groups. In other words, gender equity refers to equality of opportunity, whereas gender equality refers to equality of outcome.

A principle of neutrality in relation to gender and the work arrangements of the two parents does not privilege one gender or one division of labor over another (division of labor is addressed in a later section). In practical terms, neutrality can be achieved by the attaching of benefits, as far as possible, to children rather than to their parents: the existence of a child of a given age triggers the entitlement to the benefit. The Gornick–Meyers proposals are quite consistent with the neutral, gender-equity approach. In particular, the paid leave entitlement of six months for each parent represents a strong statement of gender equity, in that the same opportunity is provided to each parent but neither is forced to use it. This is more in keeping with gender equity than the approach of some Nordic countries, where couples have an entitlement of twelve months leave, but where that is reduced if the father does not use at least three months of the leave. In these Nordic countries, the rules are gender-specific.

On the other hand, there is an argument that it would be more equitable to provide the full twelve months of leave to the couple so that they can work out the sharing arrangement that best suits their personal circumstances (without the Nordic "use it, or lose it" arrangement). This may be the case particularly where there are differences in eligibility entitlements between the father and the mother. If the mother has no entitlement but the father does, maybe she should be able to use some of his entitlement. Gornick and Meyers do not discuss eligibility, and I shall return to this topic below. There is also an argument that the couple, with full bargaining strength on both sides, may decide that, at this point in time, there is value in investing in the career of one or the other. This may be the outcome of the past history of their relationship, and of their careers or intended futures. They may even take the view that full mother care (including breastfeeding) in the first year is in the best interests of the child. Should they be prevented from making these decisions by the parental leave being non-transferable? Of course, the reason that Gornick and Meyers do not propose this approach is that we do not live in a utopian world. For most couples, both sides do not have equal bargaining rights, and the effect of providing twelve months of shared leave would be that fathers would take none. In a sense, this is a question of just how utopian social reformers are willing to be. Gornick and Meyers are utopian enough to provide leave entitlements to each parent, but not to allow them to make their own decisions about how this leave might be shared between them.

FAMILY SUPPORT POLICY (HORIZONTAL EQUITY)

Gornick and Meyers do not mention the principle of horizontal equity—recognition of the additional costs for those who have children compared to those on the same level of income who do not have children. The Gornick–Meyers focus is upon comparisons between men and women, rather than between persons with and without children. Here, the horizontal equity principle could be used to justify both of the major aspects of the Gornick–Meyers policies: paid parental leave (as income replacement) and child care (as recognition of the costs of children). The horizontal equity argument is underpinned by the proposition that children have a social value. Most people without children are willing to provide some of their taxes for the support of the next generation.

Another consideration is that the provision of horizontal equity measures at the workplace level (higher benefits to parents than to non-parents) may lead to employers' discriminating between parents and non-parents in their reward systems (salary, promotion, career development). The resulting system would then provide individuals with incentives not to be parents. It is also not unusual at the workplace level for those without children to see themselves as doing more work for the same pay when those with children have more leave. Again, an emphasis upon the social value of children is the best way to promote such policies to those who do not have children.

FAMILY SUPPORT POLICY (VERTICAL EQUITY)

This is perhaps where I should address the "loose ends" of the paid parental leave scheme: who contributes to the social insurance scheme, and how much do they contribute? Gornick and Meyers say that contributions will be made by employers and/or employees. We must first settle the "and/or" question: Is it "and" or is it "or"? If the answer is "and," what are the relative contributions of employers and employees? How are the premiums set? Do employees contribute a fixed amount or a percentage of salary? What is the percentage? Is the benefit contingent upon length of contribution, or only upon current salary level? Will a parent on a low salary who has been contributing for ten years receive a smaller payment than one on a higher salary who has been contributing for one year? The answer seems to be "yes." Would this be seen as fair in the US institutional context?

Are contributions made by or on behalf of all employees, including those who will never have a(nother) child? Does a person continue to contribute after he or she has had the child? If no, there is a considerable incentive to have the baby as early as possible after contributions commence. If yes, will 55-year-old workers agree to a scheme where they can expect to receive very little from the large contributions that they would make? Or, do we start the scheme with a cohort of new entrants to the labor force? Are contributions made by or on behalf of casual employees or those employed only for short periods? How long will an employee (and/or the employer) have to contribute before he or she is eligible for the benefit?

What happens when a person has been out of the labor force and has a break from contributions before returning? What happens when the parent is no longer employed but has made contributions in the past? What happens when no contributions have ever been made in respect of a new parent? What happens if a parent returns after a first child at a part-time salary level and then has a second child? Is the leave for the second child paid at 100 percent replacement of the part-time wage only? If so, is this not a disincentive to engage in part-time work after the birth of the first child, or an incentive not to have a second child?

Can "sweetheart" deals between an employer and an employee be prevented? Because the employer does not actually pay the benefit (it is not experience-related), an employer eager to retain a high-profile employee may make a deal to increase the employee's salary in advance of the birth, so that the parental leave payment will be higher. The quid pro quo would be a solid-gold guarantee of the return of the employee to the same employer after six months. What happens to the entitlements of those who are already entitled to receive paid parental leave under existing employer-funded arrangements?

These are all annoyingly practical questions that will have to be addressed in developing the parental leave policy. Furthermore, the answers to these questions are fundamental to issues of vertical equity. If, for some of the above reasons, there are people who are ineligible to receive an entitlement or a full entitlement, then, there will be circumstances in which neither parent is eligible, or where only one parent is eligible (or receives a low payment). For second or further births, the incongruous situation could arise in which the father is eligible but the mother is not, because she has been out of the labor force caring for other children.

It seems, although this is not specifically stated, that the fund is a public fund. The actuarial risks of the fund are therefore borne by the government—that is, by the taxpayer. Many of the above problems could be ameliorated to some extent through government provision of a base level of parental payment available to any parent. The employer–employee premiums would then raise this base to 100 percent of salary level for six months. This base-level support would also tend to underwrite the viability of the scheme.

Many of the problems described above relate to the apparent

separation of benefits from contributions. The proposed scheme is a defined-benefit scheme. Issues of vertical equity can arise when a person receives a very large benefit (as high as $75,000 per couple) for very little contribution, while another person receives little or no benefit after making considerable contribution (for example, a person who has contributed for ten years but is not employed at the birth of the child). Because of inequities such as this, and because of the actuarial risks, defined-benefit schemes are now going out of favor. An alternative approach, where the government bears all risk, is an income-contingent loan system. Under this arrangement, the parental leave payment is made by the government as a loan to the parent, who then repays the loan across their lifetime through an additional percentage impost on income tax (Chapman, 2006). A subsidized interest rate applies, and incentives for early repayment can be provided. This is the way in which individuals fund their higher education costs in Australia. The advantage of this type of approach is that individuals can spread the temporary costs of the early years of childrearing across their subsequent income-earning lifetimes. Alternatively, combining the two approaches, the income-contingent loan from government could be at a fixed-base-rate paid to every parent upon the birth of a child, while, as suggested above, the employer–employee premiums would then increase this base to 100 percent of salary level. Potentially, the base payment could be tied to the twelve weeks of leave already available to new US parents through the Family and Medical Leave Act. The Australian government is now providing a payment (not a loan) in respect of all new births that is equivalent to twelve weeks of the minimum wage. This can be considered as equivalent to a nationally funded twelve-week paid maternity leave at a base rate. Despite all protestations, this payment has not led to an increase in births among the "wrong' people"—teenagers and the poor.

There are also vertical equity issues in relation to the child-care proposal. If parents are able to choose their own form of care and the government funds 80 percent of the cost, those who can afford really expensive care (a live-in, highly educated nanny) will stand to benefit enormously. Ironically, at zero cost as proposed by Gornick and Meyers, poor families could also have the expensive live-in nanny. For three- to four-year-olds, it would be much simpler to set up a free and universal early childhood education system for, say, twenty hours per week. New Zealand has recently done this, and there is considerable political pressure in Australia to achieve the same goal. Then, in relation to child care, we are talking about only the additional hours of child care for three- to four-year-olds, as well as the unspecified hours at younger ages. The current tax deductibility arrangements in the US provide some relief from these costs. Is this enough? Gornick and Meyers would say no. First, their scheme is much more generous (outside the free ECEC for three- to four-year-olds) than current tax deductibility. Also, tax deductibility does not create a quality child-care system, a goal of the Gornick–Meyers proposals. But it is clear that Gornick and Meyers need to give greater consideration to what types of child care will be supported, and to the issue of funding caps. At the 2004 Australian election, the coalition government hurriedly released a new child-care policy that would have paid 30 percent of the out-of-pocket expenses of parents for child care. Within a day of its announcement, the policy was modified to exclude nannies. After the election the policy was changed again, with the imposition of a cap of AU$4,000 per annum. The policy is still under attack for vertical equity reasons, as the AU$4,000 cap is high enough to imply expensive child care only affordable by the well-off.

In a footnote, Gornick and Meyers deal with single parents, allowing them nine months of parental leave. There are questions about why one parent should receive a longer entitlement than another. Why should a child of a single parent be entitled to three months more mother-care than a child in a two-parent family? Should non-custodial parents have a right to parental leave? Should the eligibility of a non-custodial parent be dependent upon agreement of the custodial parent (legally, the answer is almost certainly yes) and/or upon a good child-support payment record? Should a stepparent have a right to non-parental leave? If so, how long does the relationship have to exist before the stepparent is eligible? What happens with same-sex couples?

CHILD DEVELOPMENT

Policy should be designed so that that it is consistent with good child development goals. In keeping with this principle, the Gornick–Meyers parental leave policy provides access of the child to both parents in the child's early years. It would support at least six months of breast-feeding and mother care in the first six months of the child's life, provided all mothers are eligible. If a woman in casual employment had no entitlement to parental leave, she might have to return to work at a time that was detrimental to the child's development. The three days of casual leave for caring purposes would help when children were sick. In Australia, this form of leave has been extended to ten days per annum for all employees. Rights to part-time work or flexible working hours also enable parents to arrange their work lives more appropriately in relation to the needs of their children, and these are included in the Gornick–Meyers proposals.

Could child development goals be better served if parents were able to transfer their rights to parental leave between each other? There are two answers to this: yes and no. Circumstances can be envisaged where it would be in the child's best interest to be cared for by one parent rather than the other. This would be the case, for example, if one were not a particularly good parent. It might also be the case if the child had some particular chronic need for care that was better provided by one parent than the other. On the other hand, it is not a very large step from these arguments to concluding that mothers are always better parents than fathers. In passing, there is another point to be made here. In general, societal arrangements surrounding young children tend to be mother-focused. Mothers' groups, for example, are generally not at all welcoming of pioneer father-care-givers, particularly when the conversation resolves around breast-feeding and women's bodies. In moving to a greater level of father involvement in the early years of the child's life, it is not only leave provisions that need to be changed.

In relation to child care, Gornick and Meyers propose the adoption and enforcement of standards of care. The child-care system is under-specified in the proposal, and so it remains unclear exactly how standards would be raised and controlled.

LABOR MARKET EFFICIENCY AND BUSINESS PROFITABILITY

Gornick and Meyers seem to be acutely aware of potential objections to their policy proposals from employers. In the leave provisions, substantial notification must be provided to employers. The social insurance fund is not experience-rated. While this is designed to minimize (negative) discrimination, as described above, it could promote positive discrimination (sweetheart deals). The proposals could also give rise to the promotion of systems of employment (casual, short-term) or enterprise size (businesses broken into smaller entities) that rendered workers ineligible to receive benefits.

To the extent that these policies enable parents to maintain their attachment to the labor force during the early years of childrearing, they promote labor market efficiency and business profitability. It is important to argue that policies such as these are in the best interests of employers and the promotion of the nation's human capital.

However, this is not an easy task. An attempt was made recently in Australia to provide all workers with some of the entitlements that Gornick and Meyers propose (the right to part-time work, to flexible or negotiated working hours) through the Australian Industrial Relations Commission (the industrial court system). The proposals were opposed by employer organizations and the government, but were supported by the decisions of the Commission. However, before workers could take advantage of these new rights, the Australian government changed the industrial laws so that these rights did not apply, and stripped the Commission of much of its influence. Many other rights were also lost through this new legislation. The moral here is: don't underestimate the opposition. Selling these proposals to business will be a difficult task. Businesses begin with the premise that any restriction upon their employment practices will destroy their profitability. One could expect that the single most problematic Gornick–Meyers reform for employers will be the simplest: the specification of 37.5 hours as the standard full-time working week.

A LIFE-COURSE APPROACH

A reform agenda should be based on the proposition that families have lifetime strategies based on notions of their likely lifetime income streams and career objectives. Most young couples expect to have a relatively reduced income stream when they have very young children, but they also expect that their income stream will increase as the children get older. For this to happen, parents must maintain their human capital and their attachment to the labor force. The accumulation of human capital by both men and women, but especially by women, prior to the birth of the first child has been the driving force behind the delay of first births in most advanced countries. When they become mothers, women want to be assured that, during the period of more intensive care for the child, the family income will be adequate and that, after this period, they will be able to return to the labor force. This implies an intensification of government and societal support in the early years of the life of the child. The Gornick–Meyers proposals are very much in keeping with this life-course perspective. A potential exception, already discussed, is that the ability to transfer leave between parents might, in certain circumstances, have better lifetime outcomes for both parents. There may also be scope to make use of income-contingent loans that enable people to transfer income from their more affluent later years to the years when their incomes are reduced because of child-care activities.

The life-course approach is also relevant at the population level, through intergenerational accounting. In broad terms, societies fund children, and hence their parents, so that the children can become earners who can be taxed to provide support for the next generation of children and for their parents' generation at older ages.

SIMPLICITY AND TRANSPARENCY

To be understood by the electorate, policy programs need as far as possible to be simple and transparent. The principles here are that people should know their entitlements, that they should have a simple means of obtaining their entitlement, and that their entitlement should not change with every dollar change in their income, every additional hour they work, or according to a myriad of other terms or conditions. The achievement of these aims involves a tax-transfer and child/parent benefit system that has largely neutral effects as people change their incomes and workforce participation. Complexity also involves high administration costs, when that money would be better placed in the hands of parents. A transparent system enables parents to determine their entitlements with ease in advance of their decision-making.

It is too early in their development to state whether or not the Gornick–Meyers proposals pass this test. There are still many important questions to be answered regarding the operation of the parental leave and child-care policies.

THE FISCAL PRINCIPLE

Any reform must be within the capacity of the country and employers to pay. We can be certain that, ultimately, this principle will be imposed upon the reformer. Thus, cost must always be in the forefront of our considerations. Ultimately, the costing of proposals is absolutely essential. The detail of the costing exercise can also unearth problems that were not previously considered. Of course, the more complex the policy is, the more difficult it is to cost—another argument for simplicity. These policies carry a dollar cost to employers. To reveal the actual cost will have a positive impact if it is relatively small, and if it can be argued to be outweighed by the benefits. The underwriting of the leave proposals and the direct budget costs of the child-care proposals each represent a cost to government. How much will this be, and will the US government be comfortable about adding this cost to its already considerable budget deficits?

POLITICAL AND CULTURAL ACCEPTABILITY

It is also obvious that any proposed policy must be broadly acceptable in political terms. It is inevitable that governments must engage in public discussion about these issues in order to achieve political acceptance. Only about 3 percent of electors will become parents in any year, and that percentage is falling as the population ages. Of those who become parents in any year, most will have done so without these policy initiatives—that is, despite our views, many are accepting of the impacts upon them of present policies. Thus, the policy program will be immediately and directly relevant to only a very small percentage of voters. The implication from this is that, beyond its immediate beneficiaries, governments will have to convince a broad range of voters that the policy reform is warranted.

The US is a massively diverse and heterogeneous country. For example, its diversity of values is much greater than in Australia, even though, proportionally, twice as many of Australia's population were born in another country. Diversity of values makes the political acceptance of reform more difficult. Selling Swedish policies in Sweden is straightforward because of its ethnic and cultural homogeneity; selling (Swedish-style?) policy in the US, however, is a much more difficult proposition, because of its diversity of values.

PRACTICAL FEASIBILITY

Aside from cost and political acceptability, new policy is easier to implement if it is not revolutionary—that is, if it builds on or modifies existing institutional arrangements. If the new policies undermine existing administrative structures and existing benefit structures for some people, they will be opposed; if they require major new administrative infrastructure, again there may be practical difficulties; if the new policy overlaps with state and federal responsibilities, it will be much slower to implement because more political players are involved. My sense is that the paid parental leave provisions are radical, and that there is a lot more work to be done on them before they will appear to be feasible in practice.

Government-funded child care also raises the issue of which level of government will pay for it, and which level will deliver it and/or monitor its quality. If the child care is provided largely by the private sector, how are the fee levels to be controlled if the scheme provides a government refund of a percentage of the fees? Is the government component of the fees to be paid to parents or to the center?

IMPACTS OF THE GORNICK–MEYERS POLICIES UPON FERTILITY

Gornick and Meyers assert that the policy proposals they make will support US fertility at a desirable level. The emergence of very low fertility rates in many advanced countries has been attributed at least in part to the gender inequities that would be addressed by the Gornick—Meyers proposals.

The theoretical argument (McDonald, 2000a, 2000b, 2006) is that the progress of gender equity has been variable across social institutions. As individuals, women have been able to progress rapidly in the institutions of education and employment. In most advanced countries today, young women are more likely to be enrolled in higher education that young men. It is not uncommon for more than 60 percent of university students to be women. In a growing number of occupations, young women are able to compete equally with young men so long as they are willing to provide extended hours of work and to give absolute priority to the demands of their workplace. However, social institutions that are related to family life—the family itself, the tax-transfer system, and employment conditions (as distinct from employment itself)—have been slow to adapt to the changes that have affected women as individuals. The consequence has been that women have a clear understanding that their personal aspirations will be severely curtailed if they have children. Survey evidence indicates that most young women (and young men) still aspire to having children, but for many women the choice between work and family is a highly problematic one. The gender inequity consists in the fact that there is no such choice for young men.

This theoretical argument has been largely accepted in Europe, where it is evidently the case that countries with low levels of gender equity in social policy have very low levels of fertility (under 1.5 births per woman in all southern European and all German-speaking western European countries). On the other hand, those countries that have gender-equity policies of the type proposed by Gornick and Meyers have relatively high levels of fertility (between 1.7 and 2.0 births per woman in all Nordic countries, and all French-, English- and Dutch-speaking western European countries). Most European countries with very low fertility are beginning to implement gender-equity policies (McDonald, 2006).

Does very low fertility matter? In the short term, fewer births mean lower costs both for families and states. Thus, a continually falling birth rate, even to a very low level, will lead to higher living standards. The principal short-term negative effect of very low fertility is not economic, but psychosocial. It can be regarded as an unhealthy social trend if those who would otherwise have children do not do so because, in their view, society is not organized in a way that would make it easy to do so.

In the longer term—after around twenty-five years—very low fertility leads to sharp falls in the size of the labor force, at the same time that the population from the baby-boom era is reaching old age. It also means that the age of the labor force itself increases with a falling supply of younger workers. There is an argument that young workers play a key role in economic development because, with each generation of new technology, they tend to be its assimilators. In other words, very low fertility leads to a future demographic crunch.

The US fertility rate remains relatively high without the implementation of the policy regime that Gornick and Meyers propose, so it could be argued that this regime is not required in the US to support fertility. However, US fertility has been kept at a relatively high level for reasons that do not apply in other advanced countries, and may not continue in the US into the future: the continued high fertility of certain ethnic groups, especially Mexicans; the continuation of developing-country fertility levels in some US states, especially in the Southwest; the very early childbearing and inefficient use of contraception in the US. It remains the case that vast numbers of US women, especially those who are more highly educated, face the same gender-equity issues that have led to very low fertility in other advanced countries. There is a strong argument that US policy should consider the needs of these women.

It is indeed preferable to create new policy directions in a utopian way—particularly policies that are as fundamental and important as these. Gornick and Meyers have done an excellent job in this regard, and I am a strong supporter of the principles behind their policies. However, good ideas can founder on matters of detail and implementation. This is an area in which, for good reason, scholars are often less eager to deal. The next stage might be to set up a commission to examine the feasibility of implementing their menu of policies.

REFERENCES

Brizendine, L., 2006, *The Female Brain*, New York: Morgan Road Books.

Chapman, B., 2006, *Government Managing Risk: Income Contingent Loans for Social and Economic Progress*, Melbourne: Routledge.

Manne, A., 2005, *Motherhood: How We Should Care For Our Children*, Sydney: Allen & Unwin.

McDonald, P., 2000a, "Gender Equity, Social Institutions and the Future of Fertility," *Journal of Population Research* 17 (1): 1–16.

——— 2000b, "Gender Equity in Theories of Fertility Transition," *Population and Development Review* 26 (3): 427–39.

———2006, "Low Fertility and the State: The Efficacy of Policy," *Population and Development Review* 32 (3): 485–510.

8

Democratizing Care*

Johanna Brenner

As long as we are talking utopia, we might consider moving beyond the social-democratic welfare state and the family/household as the major institutions for organizing care. Given that proposals for anything like the Nordic welfare state system are already "off the charts" in the current US political climate, to envision even more radical change may appear to take us well outside the bounds of a "real utopia" project. Certainly, the reforms proposed by Gornick and Meyers are important and to be supported. However, I want to argue for going further toward socializing and democratizing the organization of care over the life cycle. At their most developed, social-democratic welfare state programs attempt to make the family/household workable by expanding public responsibilities for early childhood education and care (freeing parents from having to carry that labor entirely themselves) and subsidizing parenthood, especially in the early years of life, so that parents can withdraw temporarily from the labor force. Shorter working weeks, as Gornick and Meyer propose, provide parents more time to carry out the everyday tasks of care throughout children's growing-up years. These programs are meant to lighten the burdens on the household and redistribute those that remain, so that both men and women can be equally responsible for the work that still must be done.

Although these policies do socialize some of the responsibility for caregiving work, they leave in place the family/household as the major institution for organizing care. Relying on the family/household for

---

* I am most grateful to Janet Gornick, Marcia Meyers, and Erik Olin Wright for their very thoughtful comments on this paper. Many thanks also to Bill Resnick for helping me think through these issues.

the work of care limits possibilities for moving toward gender equity and undermines social solidarity, especially under conditions of relative scarcity. Further, although it is certainly possible for work/family policies such as paid parenting leave to gain more political support than they have now, I would wager that significant gains in this area will require broad and powerfully mobilized social movements. Under such circumstances, we ought to be ready with workable alternatives that will inspire and motivate people to join such movements and take advantage of the possibilities for radical reforms that they open up.

I offer two strategies for transcending the family/household system and the social-democratic welfare state by socializing responsibility for care and democratizing care-providing institutions. First, I explore cohousing communities—a more collective form of living that broadens and democratizes the group of people sharing the work of care. Second, I explore democratic and participatory forms of organizing public services, and consider how these might engage both care workers and those dependent on their care (for example, parents of young children, families of elders, elders themselves) in mutual governing relationships. Collective, democratic, and participatory institutions expand the possibilities for gender equity at both an individual and group level. Many studies of women's participation in democratic decision making, particularly at the local level, demonstrate their increase in confidence and leadership skills and, often, changes in their expectations about gender relations in personal life. In the practice of deliberative decision making, under supportive conditions, participants learn to present their own needs and interests in relation to those of other individuals and the larger group. Through the deliberation process, individuals are often compelled to reevaluate their own interests in light of what they learn about others, and in consideration of what will work best for the group as a whole (Fung and Wright, 2003; Mainsbridge, 2003). The deliberative decision-making process opens up an arena for questioning inequalities in life situation, providing an opportunity for both men and women to interrogate men's privileges. The culture of radically democratic institutions values equal participation and holds the group responsible for ensuring this occurs, so that it is not left up to women as individuals to fight for their place at the table. Democratic practices certainly do not in themselves challenge the gender divisions of labor which are at the heart of gender inequality. But they create a far more favorable ground on which women can press their claims for men to share more equally the burdens and pleasures of care. More indirectly, radically democratic institutions organizing care work expand the ground for gender equity because they support the deepening of social solidarity. Social solidarity, in turn, underlies political support for the kinds of programs Meyers and Gornick propose. It is true that a sense of common purpose and group connectedness within a workplace or a neighborhood is never automatically generalized to a larger collectivity. On the other hand, the highly individualized institutional relations within which the family/household carries out its responsibilities for care work, and in which family members are forced to negotiate within their workplaces and households around who is going to take up that work, tend to reinforce rather than counter individualistic striving. Collective forms of living and working at least push in the opposite direction.

COHOUSING: A REALISTIC ALTERNATIVE TO THE FAMILY HOUSEHOLD

Even two-parent families face barriers to achieving gender equity because the burdens on the household remain quite extensive. Shorter working weeks will help, but are not sufficient to manage the workload. Inevitably there is a poor fit between the demands of market work and the time needed for care work in the household. (If we were to include elder care in this discussion, the time burdens on families would be even more onerous.) For all the reasons we already understand, women take up this work much more than men do. Even in Sweden, the country where the proposed reforms are most developed, families must still provide high levels of care work; women are much more likely than men to engage in part-time work; and gender segregation in occupations and across sectors remains very high. It is true that the gender wage gap in Sweden is far narrower than in the US. But, because women are much more likely to work part-time, Swedish women's overall incomes are lower, and differences in the time that fathers and mothers spend on care work compared to wage work continue to be quite large (Thornqvist, 2006). Further, although single mothers do not sink into abject poverty in social-democratic welfare states, lone parenting is difficult enough that it cannot but have a coercive effect on mothers' choices about staying in relationships.

Cohousing offers promise, because adults share caregiving in reciprocal relationships among an extensive group of people. Cohousing combines individual living units with a central common space. Housing is designed to maximize social interaction, while also providing individual privacy. Cohousing members are expected to share responsibilities for organizing collective life, serve on committees, and participate in decision making. They are also expected to participate in community meals, although how this is organized, the frequency of the gatherings, and the intensity of expected participation varies across communities. A large, comfortable space that can accommodate the whole community for meals and social gatherings is at the heart of cohousing. The common house can include, in addition to a dining room and kitchen, a children's space, a library, recreation room, meeting rooms, a workshop, an office, shared laundry facilities, and guest accommodations (allowing individual units to remain relatively small, because visitors can stay in the common facilities.

The modern cohousing movement emerged in Denmark in the early 1970s, and is most developed there. From that beginning, cohousing has spread to the US, Canada, Australia, Sweden, New Zealand, the Netherlands, Germany, France, Belgium, Austria and elsewhere. The first cohousing community in the United States—Muir Commons in Davis, California—was completed in 1991. Currently there are 101 completed cohousing communities, and another 129 are in the planning stage or under construction.[1] They range in size from 7 to 67 residences, with the majority containing between 20 and 40 households.[2] Although in the past cohousing groups envisioned a multigenerational community, elder co-housing has recently emerged as a more collective alternative to the typical retirement community.[3]

Studies on cohousing residents find that participation in neighborhood activities and reciprocal helping are much higher than in their previous housing situation (Williams, 2005). Cohousing seems to be especially beneficial for households with children, because parents (whether single or coupled) have expanded resources for dealing with their care responsibilities—built-in child-minding, help when children or adults are ill, and so forth. Community members can easily establish relationships with the children living there if they want to, and this seems to happen—although it is generally not a requirement of membership (Wann, 2005). Single parents benefit particularly, not only because there are more adults to help care for children but also because shared tools and common facilities (such as laundry rooms) reduce individual outlays for consumer durables, and make available otherwise unaffordable resources—for example, workout space or office equipment (Williams, 2005).

At the moment, participants in the US cohousing movement are middle class, even relatively affluent. But co-housing is not inevitably a middle-class privilege. In Denmark it also began as a middle-class movement, and those who wanted to build cohousing communities faced skepticism from financial institutions and the government. Legislation passed in 1981—the Cooperative Housing Association Law—made it easier and less expensive to finance cohousing. Today, cohousing in Denmark has broad support and, most importantly, government programs have made it more affordable and available to modest-income households. By 1994 there were already ten rental co-housing communities in Denmark, financed with government-sponsored loans (Milman, 2001). In the US, recent local experiments have broadened access to cohousing. Strategies for opening cohousing to working-class people include government subsidies, sweat-equity, and internally generated loans. In Boulder a cohousing development was built using multiple resources: Habitat for Humanity built four homes, nine were financed by the city's affordable housing program, and twenty-one are market-rate (Orelans, 2004). Common Ground, in Aspen, Colorado, is exclusively comprised of permanently affordable units, and was built on land provided for free by the city and with construction costs subsidized by the county (Bader, 1998). The inclusion of rental housing along with owner-occupied units has also emerged as a strategy for incorporating people who cannot afford a home down payment into cohousing communities (Ferrante-Roseberry, 2002/03). Bank lending rules are a major obstacle to combining rental and owner-occupied units, but could be overcome through government subsidies and alternative financing sources (Wann, 2005). These initiatives demonstrate the possibilities for incorporating cohousing into nonprofit community development, and even public housing programs. Currently, single-family home ownership is promoted by federal government programs administered by local housing authorities, nonprofit local community development organizations, and national organizations. Cohousing experiments could be encouraged by these institutions through public programs and public subsidies, rather than being available only to those who have the money to make the substantial private investments necessary to create co-housing projects.

Cohousing appears to combine many of the positive aspects of earlier communes, while avoiding the forced intimacy and lack of privacy that seems to have been a principle source of destructive conflict. Cohousing communities also have their share of conflicts; however, over time the cohousing movement, drawing on the extensive experimentation in and experience with consensus process over the last decades, has developed governing structures and decisional practices that seem quite workable (Christian, 2001). Living and decision making that are more collective require people to develop various kinds of personal skills, and learning these skills has become part of the generalized culture of the cohousing movement (Daub, 2005; Renz, 2006a, 2006b; Wann, 2005).

While the suburbs continue to expand and individual American homes have become gigantic, a counter-movement within the US appeals to the desire not only for greater community but also for economic and environmental sustainability. Cohousing, eco-villages, and, in more mainstream venues, the "new urbanism," express a willingness to reduce individual living space in return for more convivial, walkable, neighborly, public space. Cohousing interests me particularly because it requires and produces levels of democratic participation, individual capacities for deliberation, and innovative structures that lay the basis for broader democratic community. Of course, left to themselves, cohousing groups can be particularistic and insular. But as part of a broader movement for social change, they offer not only a model for collective engagement in the work of caring for ourselves and others, but also the dense social networks that are the basis for grassroots political projects (see, for example, the ways in which women's extensive neighborhood ties arising from reciprocity and shared labor historically laid the ground for many different kinds of community-based movements). The communal spirit that motivates cohousing could also be mobilized in building a movement for public, universal early childhood education and care. (For an example of cohousing communities as the catalyst for a local environmental justice movement, see Wann, 2005).

The limited research on cohousing available in English has not explored gender relations in the communities or within households. However, accounts of participants' experiences in cohousing are full of comments by women, and women are often the public representatives of cohousing communities. Women seem to be completely engaged in the decision-making process, and many report satisfaction with their growing ability to negotiate contention and conflict. When difficulties over participation and the fulfillment of work obligations are discussed, neither men nor women are singled out as more problematic. In terms of work for the cohousing collective—gardening, cooking, cleaning the common house, and so on—it seems that the division of labor is not particularly gendered, though this conclusion is based on sparse and anecdotal evidence. Whether women's engagement in participatory governance has translated into a more equitable gender division of labor at this point remains an open question.

DEMOCRATIZING THE ORGANIZATION OF PUBLIC CARE

One of the challenges of advocating for publicly provided services, including caregiving, in the US is the widespread concern about "free riders" and suspicion of government. Nonetheless, these negative attitudes coexist with an appreciation (albeit sometimes sentimental) for the value of community. A potential for social solidarity exists, even if it is overwhelmed by individualistic striving within a highly competitive and insecure political economy. But does the social-democratic welfare state have a future in a period of global capitalist restructuring? Fiscal crises, and the rise of neoliberal political movements, threaten to dismantle welfare state programs. On the other hand, state programs and institutions that are universal, as they are in the Nordic welfare states, penetrate deeply into society and have the ability to mobilize constituents in their defense. The current picture seems to be fairly mixed—certainly, overall spending has not been as deeply cut as conservatives might have wished, or as welfare state supporters might have feared. Yet quality has been eroded in some areas (for example, by increasing the number of children per caregiver), and new forms of service delivery—particularly vouchers and the rise of both non-profit and private care providers contracting with the state and competing with state services for state dollars—have the potential to create a two-tier workforce, as well as two-tier services. This process, of course, is highly developed in the US, but it has even begun to work its way through the public sector in Sweden—the bastion of universal public services (Blomqvist, 2004).

The ideology of "consumer choice," embedded in paeans to the market and attacks on the rigidities of the state (and public sector unions), is a central element of the neoconservative political discourse that is fueling this process of privatization. As surveys of public opinion show, neoconservative ideology does not fully express the complicated attitudes that many people have toward the welfare state. Still, we ought to acknowledge that consumer choice, understood as an avenue for exercising control in one's life, reflects much actual experience. People's real opportunities for influencing the institutions that organize social, political and economic life are indeed restricted. This is particularly so in the US, where institutions such as unions or social movement organizations—which at one time were avenues for the exercise of some collective power—are in sharp decline. Parents are especially vulnerable to discourses that play on their fears about their children and, at least in the US, their actual experiences of (to say the least) suboptimal day-care arrangements. But even when parents are satisfied with their child care, they can feel defensive about placing their children in full-time care, especially in child-care centers. One reason for the popularity of family day care is that the informality of the arrangement offers parents the illusion that they have more influence and control over how their children are cared for, since they are dealing with only one caregiver (Wrigley and Dreby, 2005).

The idea of consumer choice also has power because it reflects the actual relationships between institutions that provide public services and the people who need them. While we can talk abstractly about public goods as those things we own in common, for the most part we experience ourselves in relation to public goods as consumers. Some philosophers and public policy analysts have captured the importance of institutional arrangements through which public goods and services are provided by making a distinction between public goods and "the commons," or commonwealth. A public good is typically what David Bollier has termed an "open-access regime"—a resource, such as a lighthouse or a park, whose benefits are accessible to everyone, but which cannot be effectively allocated by market mechanisms, and so is better provided by the state (Bollier, 2002). In contrast to an "open access regime," where users have no direct responsibility for the resource, the idea of "commons" implies an inalienable resource managed, cared for, and primarily enjoyed by a group of people cooperating with each other, committed to ensuring its availability to future generations, and capable of engaging in democratic decision making about how it will be used. It is the social relationships in the production and use of a good that make the difference between private property, open access, and a commons (Bollier, 2002; Anton, 2000). In an open access regime, although goods are not privately produced and are in that sense public, the public has no direct involvement in either administering their use or organizing their production. As users experience them, public goods delivered through bureaucratic, hierarchical, and inaccessible organizations are much closer to commodities than to a commons.

Most public service delivery constitutes the public as consumers on the one side, and workers and managers as producers on the other. Now, to a certain extent this is a necessary state of things—those of us who use services are happy to rely on the expertise and knowledge of those who organize and deliver them. However, insofar as public services are organized in traditional bureaucratic forms, they are not a common project, generating the kinds of relationships between producers and users and among users themselves that create and sustain social solidarity.

The way public services are produced, administered, and delivered can be bureaucratic or participatory, hierarchical and centralized or local and accessible, with shared governance and decision making. As Bourdieu has argued, our dispositions are developed through practice, through enactment, so that ways of imagining oneself in relation to others become deeply embedded in our identities and in our habits of being and acting. When public services are produced and administered within institutions that involve shared governance and decision making, they provide the structures and experiences within which people can develop the dispositions that are fundamental to social solidarity.

As bureaucratic and inaccessible as our contemporary public schools often are, in surveys people will generally express negative assessments of public education while nevertheless giving their own children's schools high marks. Why? Because, through their children's and their own relationship to their teachers, parents develop some sense of a shared project—they and the school have a common purpose. If this kind of feeling can be generated under the relatively alienating and alienated relations that working-class and poor parents, in particular, have with their schools, imagine what sorts of common bonds could be produced in a more collaborative institutional arrangement.

Empowered participatory governance in the state sector

What sorts of models, if any, do we have for these kinds of services? And what evidence do we have that transformations of public services toward shared governance can work? What difficulties are there, and how might they be addressed? In 2000, the Real Utopias conference engaged these issues through a discussion of empowered participatory governance. The complexities of organizing and managing empowered participatory governance within the state are many, and lie beyond the scope of this essay. They are explored well and in great depth in *Deepening Democracy*, the volume produced by the conference. Complexities notwithstanding, the book makes a strong case that empowered participatory governance can work.

In his case study of public school reform in Chicago, which devolved decision-making to the school site where parents, teachers, and administrators collaborated in making policy, Archon Fung demonstrates that localizing power has to be combined with processes for accountability and oversight managed by the central school authority. Funding for technical support and training in democratic deliberation are also fundamental. Further, as Fung and Erik Wright argue, based on a comparison of different outcomes of school reform projects, the stark differences in resources that the various players bring to the table have to be equalized. Administrators exercise managerial power through their connection to the central authority, and teachers' claims to authority based on expertise are backed up by their unions; but parents—especially working-class and poor parents—have no institutionalized base of power or authority. Fung and Wright point out that experts are generally reluctant to share power with non-experts in decisional processes, and teachers are no exception to this rule. They argue that shared governance, whereby teachers, administrators and parents truly collaborate in making school policy and solving problems, requires that parents be organized, or supported by a community-based organization—what they call a "countervailing" power to that of the insider groups (administrators and teachers)—who otherwise dominate the field. Under these conditions, they argue, schools in Chicago, Oakland, and Texas have been able to make collaborative governance work (Fung and Wright, 2003).

While parents need to be organized in order to negotiate with bureaucratic insiders, workers also need to be empowered within institutions. Although teachers can use their unions and contracts to gain some job security, they are necessarily on the defensive vis-à-vis school administration. Professionals have always relied on claims to expertise as a strategy for defending their autonomy on the job. But so long as they need to defend themselves, they are unlikely to be willing to share power with others. The more secure professional workers are, the less resistant they might be to allowing others to have a say in their work. Empowering teachers by devolving decisions to the local school is a step in this direction. From the other side, parents need time for education and training (for example, in child development and pedagogy) and for participating in the classroom, or at the day care center, if they are going to be able to collaborate effectively with teachers and administrators in democratic decision making. The reduction in working hours proposed by Gornick and Meyers would be an important background condition supporting shared governance in public child care.

Worker cooperatives in the social economy

Although we might prefer to see publicly organized and funded early childhood education and care become the norm in the US, day-care provision is dominated by for-profit and nonprofit child-care centers and family day-care providers. They will be huge contenders in any movement to expand public funding for early child care and education in the US. One way to counter their claim that they are more responsive to parental influence (through "consumer choice") is, as I argued above, to develop models of early childhood education and care within the public schools that are accessible and democratic. Another strategy for democratizing the delivery of care has emerged in what has come to be called the "social economy"—nonprofit organizations, producer cooperatives, mutual benefit societies and worker collectives—a sector of economic activity between the state and the market.

Over the past two decades, the social economy has expanded in response to needs for human services unmet by government programs. In the US, the expansion of this nonprofit sector is motivated primarily by a neoliberal restructuring of the state, which offloads public services by contracting out to nonprofits relying on non-union, low-paid, predominantly female, labor. In Sweden, Italy, and Quebec, the expansion of the social economy has also been spurred on by state retrenchment and the resulting unmet needs for caregiving services. But whereas, in the US, hierarchically managed nonprofit organizations dominate the field of government social service contractors, in other countries worker cooperatives have taken advantage of openings to create new forms of social and health service delivery. In Quebec, the expansion of worker cooperatives into the field was facilitated by a feminist social movement, with trade union support (Graefe, 2002). In Sweden, also, it appears that the trade union federations, worried about the privatization of public services, have supported public funding of worker cooperatives and other forms of non-private enterprise which contract with the state to deliver social and health services (Lorendahl, 1997). In Italy, where producer cooperatives were already well institutionalized, legislation in 1991 expanded state protection and regulation to include "social cooperatives"—worker cooperatives which are expected to provide benefits to their local community as well as to their own members. Cooperative members included, in addition to paid workers, users of the services, as well as financing entities and public institutions. The legislation also required that employment standards and benefits match those of the Italian state (Vanek, n. d.). Following the Italian model, Quebec also recognizes "solidarity cooperatives" whose membership includes those in the community using the services. Unlike in Italy, however, in Quebec the wages and benefits of workers in the social economy are not linked to those of state workers.

There is good evidence that worker cooperatives in the caregiving field offer far better wages and working conditions, including opportunities for professional development, than do private firms.[4]

In particular, the social cooperatives, combining worker ownership with a mandate to include users of services in decision making, create social relationships that have the potential to constitute publicly funded care services that are more like a "commons" than like consumer goods. On the other hand, they may also be used to facilitate a neoliberal agenda that undercuts public workers and their unions. While many of the services provided in the social economy in Quebec (such as home care) have never been delivered through public agencies, other services, such as community health care, have been moved out of the state sector into the social economy as a cost-saving strategy (Mendell, 2003). Locally based, responsive to local needs, supported by social movements and by their own regional networks, the organizations of the social economy in Quebec have resisted the worst consequences of the neoliberal restructuring and privatization that have devastated neighboring Ontario. Nonetheless, wages and benefits in the social economy lag well behind those of public workers, and enterprises in the social economy have little bargaining power in relation to the state agencies on which they depend for contracts (Graefe, 2002). Decisions about funding and levels of service are not made at the local level, where organizations of the social economy can mobilize support, but are monopolized by the traditional, highly centralized and inaccessible state bureaucracy. As Peter Graefe argues in his analysis of the Quebec social economy, "harnessing the social economy to progressive ends will at some point require democratizing the state" (Graefe, 2002: 258). The examples of empowered participatory governance in Porto Alegre, Brazil and Kerala, India outlined in *Deepening Democracy* offer hope here (Fung and Wright, 2003).

While no panacea, worker-owned and cooperatively run day-care centers have the potential to incorporate parents into decision making in ways that hierarchical and non-democratic workplaces do not. The most important aspect of a worker cooperative in this regard is that workers play guiding roles in management, and exercise greater control over work processes and policies than in typical hierarchical settings. The security enjoyed by worker–owners should facilitate shared decision making and collaboration between parents and care workers, since workers' claims to control over their conditions of work do not have to be protected from managerial intrusion. The cooperative culture that infuses the social cooperative movement and the legally mandated requirement to incorporate users in decision making encourages and enforces collaboration. Still, informal practices may undermine formal requirements for equal participation. At this point, social cooperatives are at the beginning of an exciting experiment in which, over time and no doubt through conflict as well as cooperation, the specific practices, institutional structures, and organizational scale necessary to ensure democratic participation will emerge.

Of course, democratic organizations face many of the same challenges hierarchical organizations confront: how to facilitate communication, manage conflict, motivate and engage workers, exercise authority, maintain commitment—all made more complex by the dilemmas of democratic leadership and decision making. In addition, in caregiving work, as in any work that engages expertise, differences in knowledge and skills threaten to undermine equality of participation and authority. Finally, the incorporation of those who rely on services into decision making further complicates the challenges of democratic process. Resolving such problems is no easy task—but there is a huge difference between a workplace where such inequalities are not only accepted but rewarded, and one where these inbuilt inequalities are acknowledged as a problem to be overcome (Rothschild-Whitt, 1982).

At the heart of the vastly expanded, publicly funded, and universal programs that Meyers and Gornick envision are two claims: 1) that providing care for people over the life cycle is a social responsibility, an obligation that reflects our ties to one another as a human community; and 2) that men and women ought to share equally in the work that these programs support, because we value gender equality, and because nurturing others is a basic human pleasure and skill that men should develop and enjoy. We might argue, and many have argued, for these programs in other ways: because they make workers more efficient; because without them our economy wastes women's talents; because they ensure that children grow up to be productive citizens rather than drains on the society. While these arguments may be persuasive to those who hold power and make policy decisions, they are not the ideas that inspire activism—and inspiring activism will be necessary to win these significant reforms. Since caregiving workers are overwhelmingly female and predominantly women of color, and since women are also the majority of unpaid caregivers, it will fall to women to drive this movement. Alternative models for democratically organizing care work and housing will contribute to building such a movement, because they help to counter the anxieties that women experience around their responsibilities for care—anxieties that are powerfully mobilized by both social conservative and neoliberal discourses. The people involved in these experiments, the skills they can share, and the ways of working and living they have developed, offer compelling testimony to the possibilities of social solidarity and equality.

NOTES

1 "Directory", Cohousing Association of the United States, http://www.cohousing.org/directory/ (accessed December 5, 2008).

2 See "What is Cohousing?" Cohousing Association of the United States, http://www.cohousing.org/what_is_cohousing/ (accessed December 5, 2008).

3 The Elder Cohousing Network, http://www.eldercohousing.org/ (accessed December 5, 2008).

4 Two instructive examples here are the Childspace daycare cooperative in Philadelphia and Cooperative Home Care Associates in New York City. See Sloan Work and Family Network, 1999; Inserra et al., 2002; Whitaker, n. d.; Laursen, 2006.

REFERENCES

Anton, Anatole, 2000, "Public Goods as Commonstock," in Anatole Anton, Milton Fisk, and Nancy Holmstrom, eds, *In Defense of Public Goods*, Boulder, CO: Westview Press, 2000.

Bader, Eleanor J., 1998, "Cohousing: Collective Living for the 90s," *Dollars and Sense* (January/Feburary): 22–41.

Blomqvist, Paula, 2004, "The Choice Revolution: Privatization of Swedish Welfare Services in the 1990s," *Social Policy and Administration* 38 (2), April: 139–55.

Bollier, David, 2002, *Silent Theft: The Private Plunder of our Common Wealth*, New York: Routledge.

Christian, Diana Leafe, 2001, *Creating a Life Together: Practical Tools to Grow EcoVillages and Intentional Communities*, Gabriola Island, BC: New Society Publishers.

Daub, Richard, 2005, "Cozy Living: Cohousing in Libertytown, Maryland," *Z Magazine Online,* July/August, online: http://www.zmag.org/ zmag/view Article/13724 (accessed December 5, 2005).

Ferrante-Roseberry, Lydia, 2002/03, "Living with Integrity: My Experience in Cohousing," *Social Policy*, Winter: 17–22

Fung, Archon, and Erik Olin Wright, 2003, *Deepening Democracy*, London & New York: Verso.

Graefe, Peter, 2002, "The Social Economy and the State: Linking Ambitions with Institutions in Quebec, Canada," *Policy and Politics* 30 (2): 247–62.

Horelli, L., and K. Vespa, 1994, "In Search of Supportive Structures for Everyday Life," in Irwin Altman and Arza Churchman, eds, *Women and the Environment*, New York & London: Plenum Press.

Laursen, Eric, 2006, "The Bronx, New York: Quality Job, Quality Care," *Yes!*, online: http://www.yesmagazine.org/article. asp?ID=1525 (accessed December 5, 2008).

Lorendahl, Bengt, 1997, "Integrating the Public and Cooperative/Social Economy: Towards a New Swedish Model," *Annals of Public and Cooperative Economics* 68 (3): 379–95.

Mainsbridge, Jane, 2003, "Practice-Thought-Practice," in Archon Fung and Erik Olin Wright, eds, *Deepening Democracy,* London & New York: Verso.

Mendell, Marguerite, 2003, "The Social Economy in Quebec," paper delivered at the VIII International CLAD Conference, Panama, October 28–31, available online at http://unpan1.un.org/intradoc/groups/public/documents/ CLAD/clad0047506.pdf (accessed December 5, 2008).

Milman, Danny, 2001, "Where it All Began: Cohousing in Denmark," available onlines at www.cohousing.org/cm/article/related_denmark (accessed December 5, 2008).

Orleans, Ellen, 2004, "Do We Really Value Diversity?" *Communities* (Fall): 17–20.

Renz, Mary Ann, 2006a, "The Meaning of Consensus and Blocking for Cohousing Groups," *Small Group Research* 37 (4), August: 351–76.

——2006b, "Paving Consensus: Enacting, Challenging and Revising the Consensus Process in a Cohousing Community," *Journal of Applied Communication Research* 34: 163–90.

Rothschild-Whitt, Joyce, 1982, "The Collectivist Organization: An Alternative to Bureaucratic Models," in Joyce Rothschild-Whitt and Frank Lindenfeld, eds, *Workplace Democracy and Social Change*, Boston, MA: Porter Sargent Publishers.

Sloan Work and Family Network, 1999, "Childspace: High quality childcare for working families," *The Network News*, 1 (3), Fall, online: http:// wfnetwork.bc.edu/The_Network_News/1-3/TNN1-3_Herzenberg.pdf (accessed December 5, 2008).

Thornqvist, Christer, 2006, "Family-friendly Labour Market Policies and Careers in Sweden—and the Lack of Them," *British Journal of Guidance and Counseling* 34 (3), August: 309–26.

Vanek, Wilda M., n. d., "Italian Social Cooperatives," *Grassroots Economic Organizing Newsletter*, online: http://www.geo.coop/archives/vanek.htm (accessed December 5, 2008).

Wann, David, 2005, *Reinventing Community: Stories from the Walkways of Cohousing*, Golden, CO: Fulcrum Publishing.

Whitaker, Julie, Stu Schneider, and Margaret Bau, "Home Care Cooperatives: Worker Ownership in Perspective," online: http://www.uwcc.wisc.edu /info/health/homecare.pdf (accessed December 5, 2008).

Williams, Jo, 2005, "Sun, Surf and Sustainability—Comparison of the Cohousing Experience in California and the UK," *International Planning Studies Journal* 10 (2), May: 175–77.

Wrigley, Julia, and Joanna Dreby, 2005, "Fatalities and the Organization of Child Care in the United States, 1985–2003," *American Sociological Review* 70 (5), October: 729–57.

9

Who Should Care for Under-Threes?

Lane Kenworthy

I heartily endorse much of what Janet Gornick and Marcia Meyers propose. But in my view their recommended policies may do too little to promote parental care during children's first year and too little to promote non-parental ("formal") care during their second and third years.

Gornick and Meyers recommend a focus on three aims: gender equality at work and at home; child well-being (high-quality care prior to formal schooling); more time for parents to spend with their children. In pursuit of these goals, they propose the following policies: *paid family leave*—a six-month nontransferable paid leave for each parent, to be taken at any time during a child's first eight years; *regulation of working time*—a standard working week of no more than thirty-nine hours and a standard working year of no more than forty-eight weeks, as well as a right for all employees to request a shift from full-time to part-time and equal (hourly) pay and benefits for part-time employees; *early childhood education and care*—high-quality out-of-home care and/or schooling available to all children, with parental cost adjusted to household income.

Like Gornick and Meyers, I assume that in most affluent countries public schooling (or "preschooling") for many children will begin at age three. This is already true in some countries, and even in the laggard US the momentum is in this direction (OECD, 2006). The key question, then, is how care should be provided for children under three.

THE FIRST YEAR

What paid parental ("family") leave policy would be most conducive to gender equality, child well-being, and parents' time with children?

Maximizing parents' time with children calls for a relatively lengthy leave. However, Gornick and Meyers rightly note that a long leave might conflict with the goal of gender equality at work, because beyond a certain point it is likely to discourage women's reentry into paid employment and/or hamper their opportunities for workplace advancement and high pay (OECD, 2001). We do not know what the tipping point is with respect to time out of work, but it seems likely to be somewhere between three months and fifteen months. Gornick and Meyers also want to encourage equal sharing of child care (and housework) by mothers and fathers—gender equality at home. One way to promote this is to encourage fathers to be heavily involved during a child's first year, and this is likely to be enhanced if fathers take time off from paid work. Gornick and Meyers propose a six-month nontransferable ("use-it-or-lose-it") paid leave for each parent. The expectation is that each parent would take this leave during the child's first year, though it could be used at any point during the first eight years.

Will this also be optimal for child well-being? Possibly not, if during the first year of life child well-being is best served by being with a parent. Existing research suggests that there may be adverse effects of non-parental care during the first year (Waldfogel, 2006, ch. 2). If each parent has a six-month nontransferable leave, there is a real possibility that in many two-parent families the parents will take only six, seven, or eight months of leave in total, with the mother taking her full six months but the father taking none or just a month or two. Non-use or minimal use of paid leave among fathers is common even in Sweden, despite the country's comparatively egalitarian gender norms. If this pattern turns out to be widespread, more children will end up in formal care than would be the case if, say, the parents had a twelve-month shareable leave, or if they had six shareable months and each had three nontransferable months. The Gornick–Meyers proposal is likely to achieve greater gender equality than these others, but possibly at some cost to child well-being. If such a tradeoff exists, my preference would be to prioritize child well-being over gender equality.

In a similar vein, while the ability to use the paid leave at any point during the child's first eight years enhances parents' freedom and flexibility, if child well-being is best served by parental care during the first year it may be better to encourage or require parents to use it then.

THE SECOND AND THIRD YEARS

Gornick and Meyers do not take a position on whether parental or non-parental care tends to be better for one- and two-year-olds (children aged between twelve and thirty-six months). They want to facilitate both. Their recommended policies with respect to working time and early childhood education and care would certainly help to do so.

I want to suggest some reasons why we should consider promoting formal care for this age group. (By "formal care" I mean child care provided in public or private centers and preschools, not unlicensed out-of-home care provided by a relative, friend, or neighbor.) I do not believe government should force parents to use it. In the US we currently do that for children beginning at approximately age six; they must be enrolled in formal schooling or receive permission to home-school. But we do not yet know enough about the relative merits of parental versus non-parental care for one- and two-year-olds to justify doing the same at this young age. Still, several considerations do, in my view, favor using policy to encourage (high-quality) formal care.

Child well-being

Though I am not an expert in this field, my understanding is that the best available evidence suggests that high-quality formal care after the first year tends to improve cognitive development, and that this is especially true for children from disadvantaged homes (Waldfogel, 2002, 2006; Brooks-Gunn, 2003; Carneiro and Heckman, 2003; Clarke-Stewart and Allhusen, 2005; Karoly et al., 2005; OECD, 2005, 2006). This suggests that, for one- and two-year-olds, child well-being may be best served by promoting widespread access to and use of good-quality formal care.

Gender equality

In Gornick and Meyers' view, a major drawback of the "dual-earner/substitute-caregiver" model—that is, of heavy reliance on formal child care—is that parents spend less time caring for their young children than they would like. But do parents really want this? If so, how strongly? And which parents?

Gornick and Meyers refer to survey data on mothers' and fathers' preferences regarding time with family and children:

> In surveys conducted in several OECD countries, one half or more of mothers report that they would like to have more time with their children . . . More strikingly, perhaps, fathers in these countries are even more likely to report that they feel time-poor with respect to family: 80 percent or more in most countries (this volume: 11).

I am not sure what to make of these data. One concern is that many parents may simply be offering what they believe to be the politically correct response. I am particularly suspicious of the finding that more fathers than mothers want more time with their children. The image a father may have in mind when he thinks about "time with family" or "time with the children" is not one in which he is home alone with the children, but rather one in which both he *and* the mother are home, and he is not necessarily the one in charge of supervising the kids.

In any event, when asking about what people want it is important to probe what, if anything, they would be willing to give up in exchange for it. For instance, when Americans are asked if they favor more government spending on education, the environment, crime prevention, social security, and so on, large majorities consistently say yes. But when asked if they would be willing to pay more in taxes in order to finance the expenditures, the percentages responding in the affirmative shrink, sometimes considerably. In the Gornick–Meyers proposal, after the six-month paid parental leave runs out, a parent wanting to reduce employment hours in order to care for her or his child pays for it in forgone earnings.

Jerry Jacobs and Kathleen Gerson (2004: 74–75) report some relevant findings, which I quote here at length:

> In 1998, the General Social Survey asked several questions about ideal working time, including the following: "Suppose you could change the way you spend your time, spending more time on some things and less time on others. Which of the things on the following list would you like to spend more time on, which would you like to spend less time on, and which would you like to spend the same amount of time on as now?"
>
> Of employed individuals, 32.0 percent preferred to work less, 34.7 percent wanted to work the same hours, and 20.8 percent wished to work more. (Another 12.5 percent couldn't decide or did not answer this question.). . .

The answers shift markedly, however, when the issue of wages is added, as it is in another question in this same survey: "Think of the number of hours you work and the money you earn in your main job, including any regular overtime. If you had only one of these three choices, which of the following would you prefer—work longer hours and earn more money; work the same number of hours and earn the same money; work fewer hours and earn less money?"

When the options are posed as tradeoffs between time and money, working less becomes less attractive. In this case, 28.6 percent wished to work more, 50.5 percent preferred to work the same hours, and only 8.9 percent wanted to work less. (Again, 12.0 percent could not choose or gave no answer.)

What will fathers do, given the choice between continuing to work at the same pay and reducing work hours at reduced pay to care for a one- or two-year-old child? Gornick and Meyers are agnostic: "With respect to shorter-hour work and family leave, whether men will eventually take advantage of these options as often as women do is an open question . . . The long-term prospect for men's take-up of these arrangements is nearly impossible to predict" (this volume: 47–48). Sweden may be a useful test case, as fathers have had the right since 1978 to reduce work hours by up to 25 percent (from forty hours per week to thirty) during a child's first eight years. According to a recent study by the OECD, few Swedish fathers have chosen to spend more time with their kids: "working hours for men generally remain unaffected by the presence of children" (OECD, 2005: 58).

The difficulty, then, is that policies designed to facilitate an increase in parental time with young children may not result in a "dual-earner/dual-caregiver" society. Instead, they might solidify, and perhaps accentuate, gender inequality in parental child care.

Single parents

Figure 9.1 shows that single-parent households account for nearly 20 percent of households with children in a number of countries, and nearly 30 percent in the US. It bears emphasizing that the ideal of parents shifting from full-time to part-time hours after the first year is likely to be out of reach for some, and perhaps many, single parents. Most single parents working in low-wage jobs cannot afford the loss of income.

Figure 9.1

Single-Parent Households, 2003

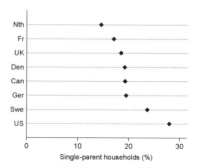

Note: Single-parent households as a share of all households with children.
(See US Census Bureau, www.census.org, Statistical Abstract, Table 1321: Single-parent households, 1980–2004.)

Figure 9.2

Adult Literacy Inequality, 1994–1998

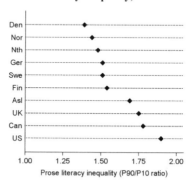

(See OECD and Statistics Canada, 2000: 176, Table 4.13.)

Formal Care, Cognitive Development, and Equality of Opportunity

Let me return to the apparent beneficial effect of high-quality formal care on young children's cognitive development. Because this effect appears to be stronger for children from disadvantaged homes, one potential impact of provision and widespread use of formal care is to reduce the inequality of cognitive ability produced by genetics, homes, and neighborhoods. Progressives have long pinned their hopes for achieving such inequality reduction on the elementary and secondary schooling system, but several decades of research have dampened this hope somewhat. It may be, however, that earlier intervention is more effective (Carneiro and Heckman, 2003).

Some useful comparative data are available from a multi-country study of adult literacy, the International Adult Literacy Survey (IALS), conducted in the mid-to-late 1990s by the OECD and Statistics Canada. Individuals were tested on three types of literacy: document, prose, and quantitative. Scores tended to correlate strongly across the three types. Figure 9.2 shows the degree of prose literacy inequality, measured as a nineteeth percentile to tenth percentile (P90/P10) ratio, in ten OECD countries. Literacy inequality was especially low in Denmark and Norway, followed by the Netherlands, Germany, Sweden, and Finland. The four English-speaking countries, and particularly the US, had the highest levels of inequality. In the US the prose literacy score at the nineteeth percentile of the literacy distribution was nearly twice as high as that at the tenth percentile.

Gøsta Esping-Andersen has suggested that the success of the Nordic countries in limiting inequality of cognitive ability is largely a product of extensive high-quality preschool care and education:

> Scandinavian day care is basically of uniform, high pedagogical standards, meaning that children from disadvantaged families will benefit disproportionately. Day care in the United States is of extremely uneven quality, and children from disadvantaged families are likely to find themselves concentrated at the low end. Additionally, it is common practice in the Nordic countries for school-age children to remain in schools after classes in organized "after-hours" activities. This implies fewer hours parked in front of the family television. The upshot is that the uneven distribution of cultural capital among families is greatly neutralized in the Nordic countries, simply because much of the cognitive stimulus has been shifted from the parents to centers that do not replicate social class differences. (Esping-Andersen, 2004: 308)

Figure 9.3

Adult Literacy Inequality by Share of Young Children in Publicly Financed Child Care

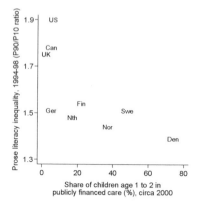

(For prose literacy inequality, see Figure 9.2. For share of children in publicly financed care, see Gornick and Meyers 2003: 204–5. Comparative data are not available prior to 2000 for use of public child care or after 1998 for literacy inequality.)

This is a plausible hypothesis. But there are two empirical problems. First, across these countries, the association between extensiveness of public child care and cognitive inequality is not terribly strong. Figure 9.3 shows the pattern for nine of the ten countries (public child care data are not available for Australia). The child-care data refer to the share of one- and two-year-old children who are in publicly financed (provided or subsidized) care. Consistent with the hypothesis, Denmark, Norway, and Sweden are at one pole, with extensive public child care and low literacy inequality among adults, while the US, Canada, and the United Kingdom are at the opposite pole, with very limited public child care and high literacy inequality. But Germany, the Netherlands, and Finland also have low literacy inequality despite having very few young children in publicly financed child care. Second, many things could account for the between-country differences in cognitive inequality. To assess the hypothesis adequately, we need longitudinal data on cognitive inequality within countries. Unfortunately, to my knowledge such data do not exist.

Even if the comparative evidence is ambiguous, the possibility that extensive use of high-quality formal child care might contribute to reduced dispersion of cognitive ability should be of considerable interest to progressives. It suggests an additional reason to consider encouraging formal care for one- and two-year-olds.

The "home care allowance" threat

Suppose momentum builds in the US in favor of a serious discussion about public funding of child care. I worry that advocating an increase in parental care for one- and two-year-olds may heighten the likelihood that government funding will end up taking the form of something like the lengthy "home care allowances" (extended paid parental leaves) that currently exist in Germany, France, Finland, and Norway. These policies provide a subsidy—some earnings-related, some flat-rate; some means-tested, some not—to help enable a parent to stay home with a child for two to three years.

This type of program has an inherent political advantage, as it can be justified on grounds of choice (Morgan, 2004). Proponents can argue that public provision or subsidization of care outside the home benefits only those who wish to use it, and is of no help to parents who prefer to stay home with their children. This argument is likely to be especially potent in the US. Many conservatives and traditionalists favor parental care for young children. If advocates of generous work–family reconciliation policies are ambivalent, that might well settle the debate in favor of a home care allowance in addition to, or more likely instead of, extensive government support for formal child care.

What consequences would a lengthy home care allowance have for gender equality? Mothers almost certainly would make far greater use of the allowance than fathers. This would reinforce, and perhaps heighten, the existing gender disparity between parents in employment and in child care. That appears to have been the result in Germany, France, Finland, and Norway. A report by the OECD in 2001 reached this conclusion (OECD, 2001), and the same is true of several recent country-specific assessments. One study finds that a three-year "baby break" has become "a virtually universal phenomenon" among employed German women who have a child (Gottschall and Bird, 2003). Among west German mothers with children under age three, the labor force participation rate fell from 28 percent to 23 percent between 1986, when the leave was first implemented, and 2000

(Morgan and Zippel, 2003: 67). And for mothers who do return to the workforce, the break appears to encourage part-time rather than full-time employment (Ondrich et al., 1999; Gottschall and Bird, 2003). France too introduced its long-term care leave in the 1980s. The eligibility criteria for the leave were eased in 1994, and in the ensuing years the rate of women's labor force participation dropped for the first time in several decades (Morgan and Zippel, 2003). Marit Rønsen and Marianne Sundstrom (2002) find that Finland's lengthy paid care leave has reduced reentry into employment after childbirth among women who had previously been employed, and Rønsen (2001) finds the same to be true in Norway.

WHAT TO DO?

Paid parental leave

Given research findings that it tends to be best for a child to be cared for by a parent throughout the first year, I would prefer a twelve-month paid leave for the family, with each parent having three nontransferable months. This would be less conducive to gender equality than the sixth-month nontransferable leave for each parent that Gornick and Meyers propose. But if we assume that, at least in the medium term, many fathers will choose to take only a month or two of leave, children will be better served by a policy that allows the mother to stay home for nine months rather than just six. It is worth emphasizing, however, that we need more research on the costs and benefits of parental versus formal care for children in the first year.

Regulation of working time

Although I have reservations about Gornick and Meyers' ambivalence with respect to parental versus non-parental care for one- and two-year-olds, I support their working-time regulation proposals.

A work week of no more than 39 hours and a work year of no more than 48 weeks strike me as desirable. A shift from a 40-hour work week to a 39-hour one seems unlikely to have much of an effect, though, and is thus perhaps not worth the political battle. If a change is to be made, perhaps 37.5 hours should be the goal.

I also favor giving employees the right to shift from full-time to

Figure 9.4

**Employment Patterns of Swedish Mothers
Before and After Introduction in 1978
of the Reduced Work-Hours Policy**

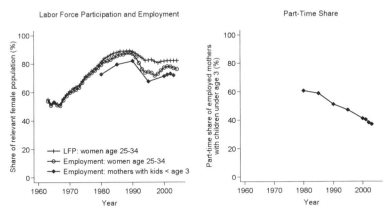

Note: LFP = labor force participation.
(For sources regarding women age 25–34, see my calculations from data in the OECD'S "Labour Force Statistics Database," available at www.oecd.org. For mothers with children under age three, see OECD 2005: 70, Table 3.5.)

part-time hours. On the plus side, this would offer parents greater choice about how to manage child care. The drawback is that this would probably increase gender inequality in parental care of one- and two-year-olds, but I suspect this effect would be fairly small. If coupled with an expansion of affordable high-quality formal care, a reduced-working-hours option might lead to relatively little reduction of employment hours among mothers with young children. If offered the choice between affordable high-quality formal care and reduced work hours at reduced pay, my guess is that most women would opt for the former.

Here, too, Sweden is the most useful test case. Since 1978 Swedish parents have had the right to reduce work hours from 40 to 30 per week. The first chart in figure 9.4 shows three time plots: one for the labor force participation rate among women aged 25 to 34, one for the employment rate among women in that age group, and one for the employment rate among mothers with children under age three. The latter figures are the ones of most direct relevance, but they are available only beginning in 1980, and only at five-year intervals. I include the labor force participation rate and employment rate for 25-to-34-year-olds because this is the age group most likely to include mothers with young children, and these data are available annually and much farther back in time. For the years of overlap the trends are virtually identical, suggesting that the 25-to-34 age group may function as a reasonable proxy for mothers with young children. The labor force participation and employment rates for 25-to-34-year-olds increased steadily in the decade before 1978, and both continued to rise in the ensuing decade. There was a slowdown in the rate of increase in the late 1980s, but that was very likely a ceiling effect, as the labor force participation rate for this age group had reached 88 percent by 1985. The trends since 1990 are not very informative, as they are dominated by Sweden's deep economic crisis of the first half of the 1990s, during which labor force participation and employment rates plummeted for both women and men and in all age groups.

Even though the employment rate for women aged 25 to 34 and for mothers with children under three continued to rise after the introduction of the reduced-hour option, the policy might have caused an increase in part-time work among these women. However, the second chart in figure 9.4 indicates that exactly the opposite occurred. The share of employed mothers with children under three working part-time—defined here as less than 35 hours per week—fell steadily in the decade after the reduced-hour policy was put in place (and has continued to do so since then).

Gornick and Meyers appear to favor allowing employees to shift from full-time to part-time work in the hope that a substantial and relatively equal number of mothers and fathers will do so in order to spend more time with their young children. I suspect that if such a policy did in fact have a sizeable impact, it would probably be bad for gender equality at work and at home, because it would be mainly mothers using it. Were that to be the case, I might oppose the policy. But while it is dangerous to generalize from a single country, the Swedish experience suggests that, provided good-quality affordable child care is available, having the option to shift from full-time to part-time work is not likely to result in a substantial decline in full-time employment among mothers with young children.

Early childhood education and care

In some countries, such as Denmark and Sweden, government centers provide much of the out-of-home child care. In the US and other English-speaking countries the private market for child care is so developed that it is difficult to imagine its being replaced by public facilities. One mechanism for subsidizing marketized formal care would be vouchers (Blau, 2001; Helburn and Bermann, 2002). How to ensure high quality? David Blau recommends that the value of the voucher vary according to the quality of the child care it is used to purchase:

> For example, a low-income family might receive a subsidy of 30 percent of the average cost of unaccredited childcare if they use unaccredited care, 60 percent of the average cost of care if they use a provider accredited as of good quality, and 100 percent of the average cost of care if they use care accredited as of excellent quality. This gives families an incentive to seek care of high quality, and it gives providers an incentive to offer high-quality care in order to attract consumers. (Blau, 2001: 219)

Earlier I suggested a variety of reasons why we might want to promote formal care for one- and two-year-olds. Given that I nevertheless support Gornick and Meyers' proposals for changes in working-time regulation, does this matter in practice? It does if there turns out to be a political tradeoff between achieving reforms in working-time regulation and in early education and care. If it is possible to get both, great; but if it is a choice between one or the other, I would strongly favor prioritizing government support for more and better formal child care.

REFERENCES

Blau, David M., 2001, *The Child Care Problem: An Economic Analysis*, New York: Russell Sage Foundation.

Brooks-Gunn, Jeanne, 2003, "Do You Believe in Magic? What We Can Expect from Early Childhood Intervention Programs," *Social Policy Report* 17.

Carneiro, Pedro, and James J. Heckman, 2003, "Human Capital Policy," in Benjamin M. Friedman, ed., *Inequality in America: What Role for Human Capital Policies?*, Cambridge, MA: MIT Press.

Clarke-Stewart, Alison, and Virginia D. Allhusen, 2005, *What We Know about Childcare*, Cambridge, MA: Harvard University Press.

Esping-Andersen, Gøsta, 2004, "Unequal Opportunities and the Mechanisms of Social Inheritance," in Miles Corak, ed., *Generational Income Mobility in North America and Europe*, Cambridge: Cambridge University Press.

Gornick, Janet C., and Marcia K. Meyers, 2003, *Families That Work: Policies for Reconciling Parenthood and Employment*, New York: Russell Sage Foundation.

——2008, "Institutions that Support Gender Egalitarianism in Parenthood and Employment," this volume.

Gottschall, Karin, and Katherine Bird, 2003, "Family Leave Policies and Labor Market Segregation in Germany: Reinvention or Reform of the Male Breadwinner Model?" *Review of Policy Research* 20: 115–34.

Helburn, Suzanne W., and Barbara R. Bergmann, 2002, *America's Child Care Problem: The Way Out*, New York: Palgrave.

Jacobs, Jerry, and Kathleen Gerson, 2004, *The Time Divide*, Cambridge, MA: Harvard University Press.

Karoly, Lynn A., M. Rebecca Kilburn, and Jill S. Cannon, 2005, *Early Childhood Interventions: Proven Results, Future Promise*, Santa Monica, CA: RAND Corporation.

Kenworthy, Lane, 2008, *Jobs with Equality*, Oxford: Oxford University Press.

Morgan, Kimberly, 2004, "Caring Time Policies in Western Europe: Trends and Implications," paper presented at the annual meeting of the Research Committee on Poverty, Social Welfare, and Social Policy (RC 19), International Sociological Association, Paris.

Morgan, Kimberly, and Kathrina Zippel, 2003, "Paid to Care: The Origins and Effects of Care Leave Policies in Western Europe," *Social Politics* 10: 49–85.

OECD (Organization for Economic Cooperation and Development), 2001, "Balancing Work and Family Life: Helping Parents Into Paid Employment," in *OECD Employment Outlook*, Paris: OECD.

——2005, *Babies and Bosses: Reconciling Work and Family Life. Volume 4: Canada, Finland, Sweden, and the United Kingdom*, Paris: OECD.

——2006, *Starting Strong II: Early Childhood Education and Care*, Paris: OECD.

OECD and Statistics Canada, 2000, *Literacy in the Information Age: Final Report of the International Adult Literacy Survey*, Paris and Ottowa: OECD and Statistics Canada.

Ondrich, Jan, C. Katherina Spiess, Qing Yang, and G. G. Wagner, 1999, "Full Time or Part Time? German Parental Leave Policy and the Return to Work After Childbirth in Germany," *Research in Labor Economics* 18: 41–74.

Rønsen, Marit, 2001, "Market Work, Child Care, and the Division of Household Labour: Adaptations of Norwegian Mothers Before and After the Cash-for-Care Reform," Report 2001/3, Statistics Norway.

Rønsen, Marit, and Marianne Sundstrom, 2002, "Family Policy and After-Birth Employment Among New Mothers: A Comparison of Finland, Norway, and Sweden," *European Journal of Population* 18: 121–52.

Waldfogel, Jane, 2002, "Child Care, Women's Employment, and Child Outcomes," *Journal of Population Economics* 15: 527–48.

——2006, *What Children Need*, Cambridge, MA: Harvard University Press.

10

The Missing Link for Promoting Gender Equality: Work–Family and Anti-Discrimination Policies

Kathrin Zippel

In their essay beginning this volume, Janet Gornick and Marcia Meyers lay out a vision of a "real" utopian future to bring us closer to the ideal of a dual-earner/dual-carer society. I agree with much of their analysis and like the main thrust of their vision. The combination of the three main policies they propose—family leave provisions, working time reduction, and child care—would be a step forward in attacking the problems for children and working parents in many countries.

Without legal and policy measures aimed at reducing gender inequality in the workplace, however, the Gornick–Meyers proposal will not be enough. It introduces policy solutions in the face of persistent forms of sex discrimination and discrimination against care workers, as well as unequal gender-division of labor in the home, but it is silent on how to achieve more gender equality at work. I am less optimistic than they are that encouraging men's leave-taking and shortening full-time working hours will in practice achieve a more equal division of labor at home. My concern is that gender inequalities at work and cultural norms of gendered work will continue to perpetuate the unequal gender-division of labor at home. In turn, the unequal division of labor at home will reinforce inequalities at work. Therefore, I suggest adding a further policy dimension to the Gornick–Meyers proposal, aimed at gender equality at work, in the form of effective affirmative action and anti-discrimination policies, supported by strong enforcement mechanisms.

A key feminist concern with policies to help parents juggle family and work responsibilities is that they risk reproducing rather than changing the unequal gender-division of labor. Gornick and Meyers state that the proposal "requires the dissolution of remaining gendered divisions of labor in employment and at home" (this volume: 17). The model certainly provides the possibility for fathers to be more involved in care work. But couples must still negotiate the division of labor in the home, and income differentials within couples play a major role in this process. Women are still more likely to take the leaves and reduce their working hours, reinforcing their primary caregiver role and risking the disadvantages associated with leaves and limiting hours. As a result, the leaves and working time reduction will most likely reproduce the persistent gender-division of labor in the home, rather than challenging it.

A second key concern is the discrimination women encounter as women and as caregivers. Workplaces are gendered organizations that still see the male worker as the norm (Acker, 1990; Martin, 2003). Despite important improvements, women are still less represented horizontally in male-dominated jobs, vertically in higher positions in organizations, and in higher-status, better-paying jobs within occupations (Charles and Grusky, 2004). Their secondary status is measurable in participation and employment rates, hours worked, pay levels, and promotional opportunities. Women in male-dominated occupations still encounter hostile environments steeped in gender and sexual harassment and discriminatory practices in hiring, training, and promotion (Zippel, 2006). Women still report not being taken seriously or given the status and respect of male colleagues. Culturally normative gendered expectations and organizational practices severely limit employment and advancement opportunities for women.

Unequal gender-division of labor in the home and lack of gender equality in the workplace are clearly intimately intertwined. Women's primary responsibility for care work in the home prevents them from full participation in the workplace. Caregivers may have to stay home to care for a sick child. They may have difficulty in jobs that demand overtime work, frequent relocation, or extensive travel (Williams, 2001). Employers have responded by creating "mommy-track" jobs that are more flexible, but have less status, pay, and advancement potential. Hence the argument that eliminating gender differences in the home results in more gender equality in the workplace.

But gendered inequalities in the workplace also reinforce gender inequalities at home. Cultural norms of gender differences and inequalities at work spill over to gender norms at home that reproduce cultural stereotypes and reinforce the unequal gendered division of labor in the home. Gendered income inequalities result in unequal earnings among couples that limit women's bargaining position. Families rely more on fathers' wages, so when families must decide between time with the children and money for the household, mothers typically stay home (or take the home care allowance). They have little power to negotiate shares of domestic work and child care, including routine activities and responsibilities. If mothers continue to contribute less household income than fathers, then couples' decisions about time spent on child care versus income will continue to be gendered.

The Gornick–Meyers policy bundle addresses specific time management needs of women and men with care responsibilities by means of flexible leave policies and reduction in working hours, but it does not challenge gender inequalities resulting from organizational discriminatory practices that use the male full-time worker without care responsibilities as the norm. Fathers who took leaves or reduced working hours might encounter similar limited hiring and promotion opportunities if employers responded by transforming male breadwinner jobs into "daddy-" or "parent-track" jobs that were less attractive, more flexible, and without opportunities. The transformation the model envisions is more likely to reinforce gendered inequalities at work, or perhaps create more gender-neutral discrimination against caregivers, than to lead to substantive gender equality in workplace arrangements.

The six "best practice" countries Gornick and Meyers analyze are useful for considering what could be done. Note, however, that Denmark, Finland, Norway, Sweden, Belgium, and France do not reflect a definitive "European model"—indeed, these five EU member-states represent less than 20 percent of the EU population. In addition, while these countries have been leaders on policies to combine work and family responsibilities, they have done less on affirmative action, anti-discrimination, and sexual harassment than the US, where affirmative action and anti-discrimination policies aim at achieving gender equality in the workplace by overcoming sex segregation, seeking to integrate women horizontally into occupations of higher status and better pay and vertically into positions with authority and responsibility. In these areas, the US has been on the forefront of policy development, with some modest successes despite uneven enforcement.

Effective affirmative action and anti-discrimination policies can eliminate "demand-side" causes of gender inequality in the workplace, which in turn can bring about changes in division of labor. Nondiscriminatory hiring can desegregate workplaces and provide access to higher-paying jobs. Enforceable pay equity laws can reduce the pay gap, and gender and sexual harassment policies can improve job

Figure 10.1

Impact of Affirmative Action and Antidiscrimination Policies

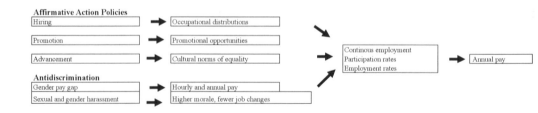

stability and seniority. Gender-equality policies can thus increase income equality between parents, which can equalize bargaining power when division of labor is negotiated in the home. Gender equality at work also reinforces cultural norms of equality, partly by breaking down barriers to men in paid and unpaid caregiving roles.

GENDER-DIVISION OF LABOR AT HOME AND GENDER INEQUALITIES AT WORK

Gender inequality at work influences equality at home in several ways. Studies of domestic work reveal that macro-level factors, including national labor force participation and gender ideologies, affect how women and men divide up the work at home. How much paid work women do and how much they earn both affect how much unpaid domestic and care work they do at home, especially in comparison to the men they live with. If mothers and fathers have different earnings and earning opportunities, then women will continue to take leaves and reduce their working hours for childrearing and domestic work.

Gender differentials of income within couples result in part from gender wage gaps and sex segregation. In addition, leave-taking and working time–reduction, even in countries with the best practices, leads to highly uneven distribution of income within parental couples. As Gornick and Meyers remind us, mothers have a larger share of parental earnings in Sweden than in many other European countries, but that share is still only one-third. (The "mommy tax" is highest in Germany and the Netherlands, where mothers' share of parental earnings is only between 18 and 19 percent; the 28 percent share they have in the US is in the middle of the field.). The lion's share of parental leave is still taken by mothers in Sweden, as elsewhere, who tend to use the maximum leave time and even space the births of children to maximize leave time (Andersson et al., 2005). The fraction of parental leave benefit days taken by Swedish fathers rose from 0.5 to 11.4 percent between 1974 and 1994. After the introduction of specific incentives for fathers, such as the "use it or lose it" feature, the fraction increased to 18.7 percent in 2004, when fathers accounted for 43.2 percent of leave users; but the average leave time taken by fathers—only thirty-two days in 2004—has not significantly increased over time; it was 32.6 days on average between 1974 and 2003 (author's calculations based on Duvander and Andersson, 2005).

GENDER AND THE BARGAINING PERSPECTIVE

In a genderless world, we might expect parents' paid work to affect their participation in unpaid work at home in a straightforward way. The basic argument from economic exchange theory is that individuals translate their economic resources into bargaining power in negotiations on household labor and child care. The more money a person makes, the less will be their involvement in unpaid labor at home. If partners contribute unequal shares, the one with the lower income will end up doing more of the unpaid care work. If partners contribute equal shares, both have an interest in investing in both careers. It will not simply be that the lower-income partner—usually the woman—automatically takes leave or cuts back time. The more equal the earnings, the more equal we would expect the division of labor to be.

Women's work indeed makes a difference to how women and men divide household labor. Jennifer Hook (2006) finds that women's working hours increase men's domestic work, and that women's earnings are a good predictor of their share of household work. But the relationship between earning differentials and division of labor in the home is nonlinear. Michael Bittman et al. (2003) find that, when wives earn less than their partners, their contribution to household income predicts their share of household labor. But women who earn more than their spouses do not decrease their housework with increasing earnings. In Australia,

> [t]he approximate magnitude of the bargaining effect was that moving from the man's providing all the money to the woman's providing an equal share decreased women's housework by about 6 hours per week, while the gender display effect was that moving from equal income

contribution to the women's providing all the income *added* about 5 to 6 hours per week to women's housework (Bittman et al. 2003: 205; my emphasis).

Hence, gender matters more than income in explaining shares of housework in the nontraditional situation where women earn more than their spouses.

Bittman et al. (2003) suspect that couples might compensate for women being more the breadwinner by increasing their share of the housework. This finding is in line with social construction arguments that economic power differentials alone are insufficient to explain the pervasiveness of the gender division of household labor. This analysis suggests that women's and men's share of housework depends on their gendered identities and the gendered expectations of their partners, family, and friends. In short, women do housework because they are expected to do it, not merely because they earn less than their partners. We need policies that both yield more income equality and challenge cultural norms supporting the unequal division of labor.

NATIONAL FACTORS

We would also expect that gender-egalitarian national environments might produce more gender equality in the home. Gender analysis predicts that policy configuration shapes gendered identities, norms, expectations, interactions, and institutions. Policies oriented toward gender equality at work would diminish the gender division of labor by setting normative expectations of equal treatment, and correspondingly diminish the salience of traditional ideologies endorsing gender difference. Egalitarian policy regimes might spill over in several ways. The more women take on male-dominated work, the less confined they might be to caregiving roles; the more men are involved in paid care work, such as child care, elementary school teaching, nursing, and working in homes for the elderly, the more we might expect them to do this work at home, too. These changes would dissolve the gender-stereotyping of occupations by changing both feminine and masculine ideals—a necessary condition for challenging the unequal division of labor in the home.

Can policy regimes make a difference? The good news is that they can. A recent line of research is testing whether national policies influence the gender-division of labor. There is much evidence for the persistence of traditional gender-divisions of labor, but men have become involved at home faster in some countries than in others. The national context of gender equality in which couples negotiate has an effect on who does household and care work, and how much they do. Hook (2006) found that, as the overall national level of women's employment increased, men's participation in household work did so, too. According to Claudia Geist (2005), couples in countries in the conservative cluster were less likely to share housework than those in social-democratic and liberal countries, pointing to macro-level differences rather than individual factors such as the couples' resources, gender ideology, or time availability. Individual women's earnings do predict the gender division of labor, but this bargaining power is stronger in more egalitarian, less traditional countries (Fuwa, 2004; Fuwa and Cohen, 2007). We would predict that economic differences within couples are less important in west Germany than in Sweden in explaining the gender-division of labor. We might also expect that in a more egalitarian country–for example, Finland—the more women experience being treated fairly and equally at work, the less they will accept being treated unfairly at home in general, and in the unequal division of labor in particular.

This research supports the point that gender equality at work is necessary but not sufficient for substantive changes in the division of labor in the home. As Richard Breen and Lynn Cooke (2005) argue, individual levels of relative economic autonomy are in themselves not sufficient to bring about an aggregate shift in the division of domestic labor. Cultural norms and ideologies about gendered work and gender equality must change.

Policies around gender equality at work, as well as women's paid work as both individual and national-level factors explain the gender-division of labor in the home. Given the persistence of gender inequalities at work, optional leave and the reduction of working hours are likely to be taken up by mothers, and to reinforce rather than ameliorate inequality in workplace and home. For the Gornick–Meyers policy bundle to avoid such unintended effects, gender equality between mothers and fathers at work is a necessary (though not sufficient) step. Parents would earn similar amounts of money, with comparable human capital. Women's expectations would include "good jobs," and be oriented toward investing in the education and qualifications for those occupations. Women would do an equal share of previously male-dominated work, and men an equal share of service-sector and helping and caring jobs. The Real Utopia bundle must include policies that set gender-equality norms and open real opportunities for all women at work that can translate into equality in the home.

AFFIRMATIVE ACTION AND ANTI-DISCRIMINATION POLICIES

I argue that policies can help challenge gender inequalities at work. Affirmative action and anti-discrimination policies can reduce the gender wage gap; reduce horizontal and vertical sex segregation, allowing women to move into jobs higher on the ladder, including leadership positions; and set normative equality standards for employment settings. Anti-discrimination policies allow employees to challenge discriminatory practices; affirmative action policies eliminate the practices in the first place.

How national policies can work is difficult to assess empirically, given that no country has consistently implemented and enforced strong affirmative action and anti-discrimination policies in the workplace over time. The US model of modest measures has developed from a range of laws, policies, and employment practices, including the 1964 Civil Rights Act and subsequent civil rights laws, "presidential executive orders, court cases, Federal implementation efforts and human resource practices voluntarily implemented by employers"(Reskin, 1998: 5), using racial segregation as a model. In 1972 the Labor Department included women as a protected group. The idea has been that these policies should challenge hiring and promotion practices that lead to racial and gender segregation and hierarchy, including discriminatory practices such as stereotyping, whether intentional or not.

Though enforcement of this bundle of policies and measures depends on the parties and presidents in power, we can evaluate its effectiveness (Reskin, 1998; Holzer and Neumark, 2000). Economists studying the impact of affirmative action and anti-discrimination policies on US employment mostly agree that they have contributed to a more equal playing field. According to Holzer and Neumark (2000: 558), "Affirmative action programs redistribute employment, university admissions, and government business from white males to minorities and women." For African Americans these effects cover the spectrum of blue- and white- collar occupations. Workplace studies show the effectiveness of gender-blind hiring. For example, Goldin and Rouse found that the percentage of female musicians in symphony orchestras rose dramatically, from less than 5 percent in 1970 to 25 percent in 1996. Changes in organizational procedures are credited: "blind auditions can explain 30 percent of the increase in the proportion female among new hires and possibly 25 percent of the increase in the percentage female in the orchestras from 1970 to 1996" (Goldin and Rouse, 2000: 738).

The overall impact of these policies has been limited (see Holzer and Neumark, 2000). Researchers face several challenges in studying this limited effectiveness, but it has been attributed partly to uneven enforcement. All employers with federal contracts have been influenced by affirmative action mandates, so some studies have compared companies with and without federal contracts. But these are only a small minority of public and private employers in the US, and other employers have over time voluntarily adopted programs similar to affirmative action. There is great variation between how these policies affect the public and private sectors, in whether affirmative action is involuntary or voluntary, and in how implementation works (Holzer and Neumark, 2000: 485). Over time, enforcement has also changed. Finally, affirmative action and anti-discrimination policies coincided with a rapid increase in women's employment; hence it is difficult to isolate the effects of policy from other factors (Reskin, 1998: 47).

Nonetheless, research has demonstrated that anti-discrimination legislation and affirmative action policies have contributed to increasing gender equality at work. Women have broken into managerial ranks, and policies and litigation have created a normative legal environment of gender equality. Workplace organizations have responded to discrimination lawsuits and threats of litigation in several ways, including embracing an ideology of diversity (Edelman et al., 2001) and implementing measures supporting it, including affirmative action plans, sexual harassment procedures, and diversity and training programs.

DO EQUALITY POLICIES REDUCE THE GENDER WAGE GAP?

The 1963 US law on equal pay for equal work made it illegal to pay different salaries to women and men for the same work. Many countries have similar laws; in fact the European Union preceded the US in prohibiting sex-based pay discrimination in the 1957 Treaties of Rome. But enforcement mechanisms are lacking in many EU states, whereas US class and individual actions based on the 1964 Civil Rights Act demonstrate that women have used litigation to hold employers accountable for wage equality.

Several factors influence the gender gap in pay—for example, overall women's employment and the distribution of human capital among women. International comparisons show how industrial systems and wage settings make a difference. Because women tend to be employed in the lower job ranks, they benefit disproportionately from mechanisms that increase overall wage equality, such as minimum wages

(Blau and Kahn, 2007; McCall, 2001). While we cannot relate the gender wage gap across countries to particular equality policies, the US gender wage gap trend demonstrates that affirmative action and anti-discrimination have helped reduce pay inequity.

The US gender pay gap has persisted, though it has decreased over time. Blau and Kahn analyzed the PSID database—a large, nationally representative sample—and found a gender wage gap of 20.3 percent in 1998; 41 percent of the differential for full-time workers was unexplained after taking into account "educational attainment, labor force experience, race, occupation, industry and union status" (Blau and Kahn, 2007: 12). Other economists have consistently found a differential of greater than 10 percent not explained by observable characteristics of the individuals concerned, other than their being women; they attribute it to gender discrimination (Holzer and Neumark, 2000: 495).

According to Blau and Kahn (2007), the gender wage gap has decreased over the past twenty-five years, though not evenly. The gap was around 60 percent until the 1970s. In the 1980s women's wages relative to men's increased rapidly; Leonard (1989, 1996) found a decline in the average wage gap of 7.6 percent in companies with federal contracts alone form 1980 to 1990. The decrease slowed during the 1990s, but picked up in the early 2000s. Over the same period, however, overall wage inequality has been increasing, and for women at the lower end of the hierarchy catching up with men has been achieved through a decline in men's wages. McCall (2001), however, finds that college-educated women have made substantive gains and decreased the pay gap in real terms.

The changes can be interpreted in several ways, including that anti-discrimination policies are working and less discrimination is occurring. The slowdown of the 1990s is difficult to explain in terms of policy impact, since the 1991 Civil Rights Act improved the situation of plaintiffs, and we would expect more litigation (Blau and Kahn, 2006: 60). Another trend, however, has been the influx of women with low education who were previously on welfare. Blau and Kahn argue that this development most likely changed the overall rate of reduction of the gap (Blau and Kahn, 2006). The persistence of the gap indicates that discrimination still exists.[1]

There is evidence that wage discrimination policies have been effective in reducing wage gaps, particularly within given occupations. Blau and Kahn (2006) argue that discriminatory practices may still be occurring in selecting employees into particular occupations, so it is important to examine the effects of US policies.

HORIZONTAL SEX SEGREGATION

Prohibiting exclusionary practices and combating racial and gender segregation in the workplace have been key to the US approach to affirmative action and anti-discrimination. Although there are several ways to measure sex segregation, researchers agree that in the US workforce it has been declining since the 1960s. Overall, segregation indices dropped by 20 percent in between 1970 and 1990 (Reskin, 1998: 53). Tomaskovic-Devey et al. (2006), who examine private employers and control by industry and occupation, find that sex segregation has been uneven since 1964. A rapid decrease during the 1970s and 1080s was followed by little change during the later 1980s, and some acceleration in the 1990s. Barbara Bergmann (1996) points out that these dynamics follow changes in the enforcement practices of the Equal Employment Opportunity Commission (EEOC) and government.

These trends vary by occupation. Women have broken into previously male-dominated occupations, men have to a lesser extent entered female-dominated occupations, and some occupations have become more feminized. Leonard (1989) shows how Black women have benefited from federal contracting, moving into occupations previously dominated by men. Charles and Grusky (2004) find that the expansion of the service sector has contributed to increased sex segregation, because the sales occupations have become feminized. By contrast, white women have done particularly well in some professional occupations.

VERTICAL SEGREGATION: WOMEN'S MOVE INTO MANAGEMENT

The proportion of women among US managers and administrators rose from 5.5 percent in 1960 to 27 percent in 1990, though there is some concern that employers reclassified clerical and sales jobs as "managerial" to create an appearance of promoting women (Reskin, 1998: 54; Charles and Grusky, 2004: 156). Analyzing EEOC data for midsize and large private sector employers, Kalev (2005: 1) found that white men held 87 percent of management positions in 1971, but only 57 percent in 2002 (white women held 28 percent, black women 3 percent, black men 3.7 percent). Black women saw the "largest relative gains," while "white women's share almost tripled."

Employers have responded to affirmative action and anti-discrimination mandates with policies, procedures, and an ideology of "diversity" (Edelman et al., 2001). These employer practices have resulted in changes in workplace composition. Kalev, Dobbin, and Kelly used federal data for 1971–2002 on 708 private sector companies to compare approaches by employers. They found that affirmative action plans, "diversity committees and taskforces, and introduced diversity managers and departments" had resulted in changes in employee composition (Kalev et al., 2006: 611). Mentoring programs enhanced Black women's access to management positions; diversity training programs were less effective. They conclude that "accountability, authority and expertise are effective means of increasing the proportions of white women, black women and black men in private sector management."

Enforcement practices influence the effectiveness of policies in helping women and minorities break through barriers to managerial job ladders: "Title VII lawsuits and affirmative action compliance reviews led to increases in women's and minorities' share of management jobs, especially in periods and juridical circuits wherein civil rights enforcement was strong" (Kalev et al., 2006: 611). There are differences in effectiveness for specific groups. For example, federal contractors under affirmative action guidelines were more likely to hire African-American women and men than white women (Leonard, 1989).

Ransom and Oaxaca (2005) show how a "regional grocery chain changed practices of hiring and promotion, and job segregation dramatically decreased after the company lost a discrimination law suit, settled the suit, and introduced affirmative action policies" (cited in Blau and Kahn, 2007: 15). Women's and men's wages were similar, but the court found that the employer had discriminated by offering different jobs to women and men. Lawsuits had important impacts on representation of women and minorities in the retail supermarket industry more generally. Skaggs (2001) showed that companies involved in lawsuits increased the percentage of both women and minority men in management; those not so involved increased the percentage of white women, but not of minorities. Kalev and Dobbin (2006) argue that compliance reviews had stronger, longer-lasting effects than lawsuits.

GENDER AND SEXUAL HARASSMENT

Women's continuing complaints demonstrate that workplace sexism and sexual harassment are still widespread, but the revolution in case law has enabled them to hold employers accountable in the courts. Employers covered by Title VII of the 1964 Civil Rights Act have adopted internal complaint procedures and some training programs to challenge sexism and abuses of power, including unwanted sexual behavior in the workplace (Zippel, 2006; Dobbin and Kelly, 2007). Like other protected groups, victims can file complaints with the EEOC, and numerous complaints and several high-profile class action lawsuits demonstrate that women no longer believe they must accept unwanted sexual behavior at work as "normal." These important changes in the awareness of women, men, and employers are crucial in challenging understandings of women as second-class employees, and contribute to gender equality in the workplace.

CRITIQUES OF AFFIRMATIVE ACTION

Changes in gender inequalities in the workplace measured by wage gaps, sex segregation, and complaints about sexual and gender harassment clearly have multiple causes. Persistent gender inequalities demonstrate that affirmative action and anti-discrimination policies have not eradicated all discriminatory practices, though they seem to have helped desegregate workplaces and reduce the pay gap, and introduced a workplace climate in which formal gender equality has replaced normative understandings of women as subordinated workers.

The US model certainly has limitations, because elimination of sex segregation is likely not to be an overall cure. Yet there is an important link between sex segregation and the US gender gap in pay. International comparisons reveal that sex segregation does not have to produce gender gaps in wages. Blau and Kahn (2006) argue that wage-setting systems explain international variation in gender pay gaps. Because of the overall lower wage inequality in Sweden, higher sex segregation of occupations does not have the same effect of increasing the pay gap as in the US. Leslie McCall (2001) points out that it is a poor standard to think about gender equality only in terms of women catching up with men, when men, especially at the lower end of the earnings scales, have seen a decline in wages. She argues forcefully that low-income women are more helped by general union bargaining and wage policies than by affirmative action policies giving them the same meager salaries as comparable men.

As O'Connor et al. (1999) argue, the US has been oriented toward gender equality as sameness—the predominant standard that has made it difficult to argue for specific measures for mothers. On the positive side, the US approach has created a legal consciousness of gender equality, in which employees are increasingly aware of their individual rights. Certainly, not everyone will challenge an employer in court, but the laws have created an expectation that women are to be treated equally and fairly.

Overall, this review of evidence of affirmative action and anti-discrimination policies shows their potential, if implemented and enforced, to increase gender equality in the workplace.

EUROPE VS. THE US

Women have not reached equality with men in the workplace in either Europe or the US. There are important national variations in pay, as well as horizontal and vertical sex segregation, but in general the unequal gender-division of labor at work and in the home is still alive and well. The EU has been at the forefront of pushing member-states to embrace laws mandating the equal treatment of women and men (since 1976) and against discrimination based on race, ethnicity, religion, or on belief, disability, age, or sexual orientation (since 2000). But many European countries struggle with bringing about policies that promote women as individuals rather than as mothers. These countries have only recently begun to tackle the difficult questions of effective anti-discrimination legislation and of implementation and enforcement in the workplace.

As we have seen, the countries that serve Gornick and Meyers for "best practice" in combining family and work are not at the forefront of these efforts. The UK and Northern Ireland, in the "liberal" cluster, have more comprehensive anti-discrimination laws. As Carol Bacchi (1996) argues, affirmative action has been sidelined in Sweden as unions, the institutional arrangements of union bargaining, and strong social-democratic parties have prioritized certain issues over others. Enhancing the individual rights of women as workers did not fit this agenda. Nor did measures to combat violence against women or sexual harassment at work (Elman, 1996). In Sweden and other mother- or parent-friendly countries, affirmative action and anti-discrimination have been depicted as unnecessary; they do not "fit" the policy logic of reducing class inequality or aiding mothers. Yet women unionists worry about problems arising from the one-way, dead-end "mommy-track" jobs for women (Morgan, 2006).

In policy areas enabling women's "access to work," as Ann Orloff (1993) puts it, or the "right to be commodified," the liberal model is not served by looking to European countries, which have lagged behind on policies that prohibit discriminatory hiring and promotion and sexual harassment. In the conservative cluster countries, policy packages, including taxation, have long been focused on the traditional male-breadwinner model, and have helped cement an unequal gender-division of labor. In many of these countries, women are seen primarily as wives and mothers (Ferree, 1995). For example, in West Germany, law until the 1970s stated that wives were responsible for the household and that husbands had to agree to wives taking a job.

Inequalities arising from the intersections of race, class, and gender have been addressed even less than in the US. EU member-states are only now introducing policies preventing discrimination on the basis of disability, age, sexual orientation, race, and ethnicity. Employers still write job advertisements for women or men, foreigners or non-foreigners. Only in 2000 did the EU adopt more comprehensive anti-discrimination tools, including the Framework Directive on equal treatment and the Directive on Equal Treatment of Race/Ethnic Minorities. In 2002 the EU revised the 1976 Directive on Equal Treatment of Women and Men. These directives now serve as a basis for member states to build legislation and enforcement mechanisms with which the US has more than forty years of history.

The EU and its member states have also lagged behind the US in how to address workplace sexual harassment by law, and how to ensure that employers take complaints seriously, and proactively create workplace cultures in which harassment does not occur. The 2002 EU Directive modified and improved some of the limits of US policies. Interestingly, workplace organizations have in practice incorporated gender-specific sexual harassment laws into broader policies on gender-neutral forms of bullying, "mobbing," and moral harassment, for which they found more support among unions and political parties than for sexual harassment policies alone (Zippel, 2006).

Because Gornick and Meyers' proposal does not mention the dimension of women experiencing discrimination at work *as women*, it seems to assume that policies in this area already exist or are doing their job. When envisioning major transformations of work based on accommodating mothers and fathers, we should not lose sight of the fact that women as women are still being discriminated against, and that measures are needed to ensure that all women, as well as men, have increasing access to good-quality jobs. As women increasingly delay childbirth and have fewer children, they usually enter the job market not as mothers but simply as women, and spend an increasing number of years in the labor market without caring for children.

The kinds of jobs and careers parents were able to achieve before having children, however, will be the foundation for the decisions couples make as to who stays home and for how long. If women tend to be concentrated in low-pay, low-status jobs, the overall gender gap in pay will continue to create strong economic differences for heterosexual couples. If women are disproportionately in dead-end jobs without expecting to increase their wages over time by promotion, couples will continue to make "economic" decisions that women, not men, should take leaves and reduce working time. If caregivers face barriers in the workplace, then choosing to take leaves and reduce working hours will likely continue to be the choice of mothers, not fathers.

US anti-discrimination legislation has certainly been limited, and still leaves much room for improvement, but European countries have lagged behind in gender equality at work. Legally enforceable US policies that prohibit discrimination in hiring and promotion based on sex, age, and race/ethnicity have, at least on paper, opened white male–dominated, better-paying jobs to white women and minority women and men. They have helped women break into male-dominated work environments and managerial ranks. Instead of jeopardizing these modest successes, the Gornick–Meyers model needs to address gender and caregiver discrimination. These policies need to be strengthened rather than eliminated to that gender equality in the workplace—a precondition for the Gornick–Meyers proposal to work without reproducing gender inequalities.

One important question is whether observed gender inequalities are a legacy of past discrimination that has disadvantaged older cohorts. In this view, if discrimination lessens over time, we would expect younger women entering the job market or coming up for promotion to be doing as well as men, and hence to see an overall increase of gender equality over time. Without effective policy interventions, this "natural" progression is questionable, however. Persistent sex segregation, especially among blue-collar workers, demonstrates that women have not achieved equal opportunities and access to better-paying male-dominated jobs. Promotion rates of female top managers, senior law partners, and senior scientists demonstrate that the "pipeline" leaks at every point, and that the metaphor itself might be deceptive, because it seems to be harder for women to enter at every career step (Xie and Shauman, 2003). Women have made inroads into US law schools, constituting half of the students for over fifteen years, but women do not represent a critical mass among senior partners: only about 16 percent of law firm equity partners have been women (National Association of Women Lawyers, 2007).

Similarly, despite the fact that pools of qualified women scientists exist in many fields, women still hold solo status in several US science and engineering departments (Committee on Maximizing the Potential of Women, 2007). There is evidence to support the view that gender inequalities stemming from discriminatory practices embedded in organizations will continue. Valian (1998) argues that the pervasive (unintentional) use of gender schemata leads to systematic devaluation of women scientists, and that these small discriminations are significant over time. In this view, discriminatory practices persist even though some women have made it through the door.

Recent challenges to Title VII of the 1964 Civil Right Act have cast doubt on whether the US will maintain its leadership in affirmative action and anti-discrimination policies without further legislative action. The 2007 Supreme Court decision weakened the pay equity law significantly. Plaintiffs now have recourse only to discrimination that occurred within 180 days before the lawsuit was filed. But wage discrimination is significant when it accumulates over the years, rather than as a one-time minor differential in a raise.

On the other side of the Atlantic, a new law on corporate gender equality demonstrates how effective legal measures with effective sanctions can be. The Norwegian parliament responded to the low numbers of women on corporate boards and in executive positions with a law that imposed quotas to close this corporate gender gap for publicly traded companies in 2003. As a result, the percentage of women on these boards increased from 7 percent in 2002 to 35 percent in 2007. The companies risked being shut down if they did not reach a certain number of women on their boards by January 1, 2008. Hence, legal regulations can make a difference in integrating women into the workplace on an equal footing with men.

The proposal Gornick and Meyers suggest is the right step toward improving the situation for working parents and their children. For a Real Utopia vision, however, the package needs to include stronger provisions and enforcement tools for gender inequality in the workplace, including anti-discrimination laws that also address the intersections of sex, pregnancy, parenthood, age, disability, race/ethnicity, sexual orientation, and citizenship. This is a necessary step in order for both the US and Europe to improve policies and implementation to assure gender equality in paid work. We cannot approach the goal of gender equality in the home if measures for gender equality in the workplace are lacking. Equality in the workplace is a necessary condition for the egalitarian dual-earner/dual-carer vision of women and men equally "sharing" child care and domestic work. Without an equal gender-division of labor, the status quo will persist; not a Real Utopia by any stretch of the imagination—at least not for mothers and children.

NOTES

1 Research shows that mothers are even more affected by the gender wage gap (Gornick and Meyers, this volume).

REFERENCES

Acker, Joan, 1990, "Hierarchies, Jobs, Bodies: A Theory of Gendered Organizations," *Gender & Society* 4 (2): 139–58.

Andersson, Gunnar, Jan Hoem, and Ann-Zofie Duvander, 2006, "Social Differentials in Speed-Premium Effects in Childbearing in Sweden," *Demographic Research* 14 (4): 51–70, online: http://www.demographic research.org/.

Bacchi, Carol, 1996, *The Politics of Affirmative Action: "Women," Equality and Category Politics*, London: Sage Publications.

Bergmann, Barbara, 1996, *In Defense of Affirmative Action*, New York: Basic Books.

Bittman, Michael, Paula England, Nancy Folbre, Liana Sayer, and George Matheson, 2003, "When Does Gender Trump Money? Bargaining and Time in Household Work," *American Journal of Sociology* 109 (1): 186–214.

Blau, Francine D., and Laurence M. Kahn, 2006, "The US Gender Pay Gap in the 1990s: Slowing Convergence," *Industrial and Labor Relations Review* 60 (1): 45–66.

———2007, "The Gender Pay Gap: Have Women Gone as far as they Can?" *Academy of Management Perspectives* 21 (1): 7–23.

Budig, Michelle J., and Paula England, 2001, "The Wage Penalty for Motherhood," *American Sociological Review* 66: 204–25.

Breen, Richard, and Lynn Prince Cooke, 2005, "The Persistence of the Gendered Division of Domestic Labour," *European Sociological Review* 21 (1): 43–57.

Charles, Maria, and David B. Grusky, 2004, *Occupational Ghettos: The Worldwide Segregation of Women and Men*, Stanford: Stanford University Press.

Committee on Maximizing the Potential of Women in Academic Science and Engineering, National Academy of Sciences, National Academy of Engineering, and Institute of Medicine, 2007, *Beyond Bias and Barriers: Fulfilling the Potential of Women in Academic Science and Engineering*, Washington, D.C.: National Academies Press.

Dobbin, Frank, and Erin Kelly, 2007, "How to Stop Harassment: The Professional Construction of Legal Compliance in Organizations," *American Journal of Sociology* 112 (4): 1,203–43.

Duvander, Ann-Zofie, and Gunnar Andersson, 2005, "Gender Equality and Fertility in Sweden: A Study on the Impact of the Father's Uptake of Parental Leave on Continued Childbearing," Max Planck Institute for Demographic Research Working Paper 2005-013, online: http:/www.demogr. mpg.de/

Edelman, Lauren B., Sally Riggs Fuller, and Iona Mara-Drita, 2001, "Diversity rhetoric and the managerialization of law," *American Journal of Sociology* 106 (6): 1,589–641.

Elman, R. Amy, 1996, *Sexual Subordination and State Intervention: Comparing Sweden and the United States*, Oxford: Berghahn Books.

Ferree, Myra Marx, 1995, "Patriarchies and Feminisms: The Two Women's Movements of Unified Germany," *Social Politics* 2 (1): 10–24.

Fuwa, Makkiko, 2004, "Macro-level Gender Inequality and the Division of Household Labor in 22 Countries," *American Sociological Review* 69 (6): 751–67.

Fuwa, Maikka, and Philip Cohen, 2007, "Housework and Social Policy," *Social Science Research* 36 (2): 512–30.

Geist, Claudia, 2005, "The Welfare State and the Home: Regime Differences in the Domestic Division of Labour," *European Sociological Review* 21 (1): 23–41.

Goldin, Claudia, and Cecilia Rouse, 2000, "Orchestrating Impartiality: The Impact of 'Blind' Auditions on Female Musicians," *American Economic Review* 90 (4): 715–41.

Gornick, Janet C., and Marcia K. Meyers, 2008, "Institutions that Support Gender Egalitarianism in Parenthood and Employment," this volume.

Holzer, Harry J., and David Neumark, 2000, "Assessing Affirmative Action," *Journal of Economic Literature* 38 (3): 483–568.

——2006, "Affirmative Action: What do we know?" *Journal of Policy Analysis and Management* 25 (2): 463–90.

Hook, Jennifer L., 2006, "Care in Context: Men's Unpaid Work in 20 Countries, 1965–2003," *American Sociological Review* 71 (3): 639–60.

Kalev, Alexandra, 2005, "Gender and Racial Inequality at Work: Changing Organizational Structures and Managerial Diversity," PhD dissertation, Department of Sociology, Princeton University, NJ.

Kalev, Alexandra, and Frank Dobbin, 2006, "Enforcement of Civil Rights Law in Private Workplaces: The Effects of Compliance Reviews and Lawsuits Over Time," *Law & Social Inquiry* 31 (4): 855–903.

Kalev, Alexandra, Frank Dobbin, and Erin Kelly, 2006, "Best Practices or Best Guesses? Assessing the Efficacy of Corporate Affirmative Action and Diversity Policies," *American Sociological Review* 71 (August): 580–617.

Leonard, Jonathan S., 1989, "Women and Affirmative Action," *Journal of Economic Perspectives* 3 (1): 61–75.

———1996, "Wage disparities and Affirmative Action in the 1980s," *American Economic Review* 86 (2): 285–9.

Martin, Patricia Y., 2003, "'Said and Done' versus 'Saying and Doing': Gendering Practices, Practicing Gender at Work," *Gender and Society* 17 (3): 342–66.

McCall, Leslie, 2001, *Complex Inequality: Gender, Class and Race in the New Economy*, New York: Routledge.

Morgan, Kimberly J., 2006, *Working Mothers and the Welfare State: Religion and the Politics of Work–Family Policies in Western Europe and the United States*, Stanford: Stanford University Press.

Morgan, Kimberly J., and Kathrin Zippel, 2003, "Paid to Care: The Origins and Effects of Care Leave Policies in Western Europe," *Social Politics: International Studies in Gender, State, and Society* 10 (1): 49–85.

National Association of Women Lawyers, 2007, "National Survey on Retention and Promotion of Women in Law Firms," online: http://www.abanet.org/nawl/docs/FINAL_survey_report_11-14-07.pdf.

Neyer, Gerda, 2006, "Family Policy and Fertility in Europe: Fertility Policies at the Intersection of Gender Policies, Employment Policies, and Care Policies," Max Planck Institute for Demographic Research Working Paper 2006-010, online: http:/www.demogr.mpg.de.

O'Connor, Julia, Ann Orloff, and Sheila Shaver, 1999, *States, Markets, Families: Gender, Liberalism and Social Policy in Australia, Canada, Great Britain and the United States*, Cambridge, UK: Cambridge University Press.

Orloff, Ann, 1993, "Gender and the Social Rights of Citizenship: The Comparative Analysis of Gender Relations and Welfare States," *American Sociological Review* 58 (3): 303–28.

Ransom, Michael R., and Ronald L. Oaxaca, 2005, "Sex Differences in Pay in a 'New Monopsony' Model of the Labor Market," IZA Discussion Papers 1870, Institute for the Study of Labor (IZA).

Reskin, Barbara F., 1998, *The Realities of Affirmative Action in Employment*, Washington, DC: American Sociological Association.

Sayer, Liana C., Suzanne M. Bianchi, and John P. Robinson, 2004, "Are Parents

Investing Less in Children? Trends in Mothers' and Fathers' Time with Children," *American Journal of Sociology* 110 (1): 1–43.

Skaggs, Sheryl, 2001, "Discrimination Litigation: Implications for Women and Minorities in Retail Supermarket Management," PhD dissertation, Department of Sociology, North Carolina State University, Raleigh, NC.

Tomaskovic-Devey, Donald, Catherine Zimmer, Kevin Stainback, Corre Robinson, Tiffany Taylor, and Tricia McTague, 2006, "Documenting Desegregation: Segregation in American Workplaces by Race, Ethnicity, and Sex, 1966–2003," *American Sociological Review* 71 (4): 565–88.

Valian, Virginia, 1998, *Why So Slow? The Advancement of Women*, Cambridge, MA: MIT Press.

Williams, Joan, 2001, *Unbending Gender: Why Work and Family Conflict and What to Do About It*, Oxford: Oxford University Press.

Xie, Yu, and Kimberlee A. Shauman, 2003, *Women in Science: Career Processes and Outcomes*, Cambridge, MA: Harvard University Press.

Zippel, Kathrin, 2006, *The Politics of Sexual Harassment: A Comparative Study of the United States, the European Union, and Germany*, Cambridge, UK: Cambridge University Press.

11

A US Model for Universal Sickness and Family Leave: Gender-Egalitarian and Cross-Class Caregiving Support for All

Heidi Hartmann and *Vicky Lovell*

The proposal of Gornick and Meyers that is the centerpiece of this volume focuses on enabling parents to provide hands-on care for children in a gender-egalitarian way. While Gornick and Meyers note that their family policy proposals could easily be extended to elder care, care for disabled adults, and so on, they justify their focus on providing care for children because of its central importance to society, since well-reared children are a public good, and because childrearing is a key factor dividing adult labor by gender. It might also be added that, since it is often done relatively early in adult life, providing care for children has a greater impact on the development of women's and men's careers than does other family care work (such as elder care), typically done at a later stage. To achieve gender equality, it is therefore especially important to address parenting and child care. In any case, it is essential for any society to raise children well and to facilitate the equitable care of children by working-age adults.

In this chapter, we seek to address an important and related social need that is critical for workers and their families but is left out of the Gornick–Meyers proposal. We seek to make the case that providing basic sick leave to all workers is required in a Real Utopia that would reduce both gender and class inequality. We see the narrow focus on parenting by Gornick and Meyers as detrimental to the development of a Real Utopia in the US, a country which is in need not only of most of the family care benefits that other industrialized nations have already begun to provide, but also of basic paid sick leave. While the US has less paid leave than many other countries, what it does have is a model, albeit of unpaid leave, that acknowledges the universal need for care and the potential for gender-egalitarian sharing of all care work, not only parenting. By embedding parenting in a universal concept of caregiving and establishing time off for caregiving—including self-care—as a right of all workers, the US takes a different tack from most European countries that typically privilege either parental or maternal care. The US model seeks to establish a new universal right of caregiving time for *all* workers, while simultaneously de-emphasizing the gendered tradition of the caregiving role.

Paid sick leave is now being pursued legislatively in the US, following the universal model used in the Family and Medical Leave Act of 1993, in which unpaid, job-protected leave is required to be provided by employers for both the worker's own illness or preventive care and for his or her care of ill or needy family members (children, spouse, and parents). We argue that this American model of universal care, while it needs to be expanded to include paid leave, has much to offer other countries that focus almost exclusively on parental care. To illustrate our argument, we discuss examples of proposed legislation in the US Congress and the growth of a nationwide movement seeking to achieve similar universal benefits at the state and local levels in the US. Before concluding the chapter with a brief summary, we analyze the potential for too much accommodation directed specifically at parenting to increase gender inequality rather than reduce it. We conclude that in the US accommodation for parenting should be subsumed in a broader program to provide caregiving rights to all, rather than being prioritized for special rights not available to others also facing caregiving demands.

THE CASE FOR BROAD AND INCLUSIVE PAID TIME OFF

Gornick and Meyers' narrow focus on parents caring for children is undesirable for several reasons. First, it would limit support for the proposed policies, as they would offer direct benefits to only a small segment of the workforce. Workers in all countries have needs to care for family members other than children, and, from the point of view of ensuring income security for workers and advancing gender equality, as well as cross-class equality, these broader care needs must be addressed. As a practical matter, as well as a moral one, the scope of the proposed policies should be broadened. Not only is this the right course of action to ensure care for all those who need it, such as the elderly, the disabled, and adults with serious health needs, but it is the right course of action to maximize support for the proposals. Second, a narrow focus on providing benefits to parents encourages employers to discriminate against parents—a group that can be readily identified. And third, from the point of view of establishing a *Real* Utopia in the US, the Gornick–Meyers proposal fails to recognize the true nature of the ground on which such a utopia would be built, a ground on which there are currently few protections for workers, and on which paid time off for self-care is unavailable to nearly half of American workers.

Paid time off when sick is crucial for all workers' health and income security, but especially for working parents and other working caregivers who support dependents. Family income needs to be stabilized when a wage-earner cannot work because of illness, and job security—the ability to return to work when well—needs to be assured. Workers without paid sick leave lose pay when they are too sick to work and, especially in low-wage sectors, even lose their jobs when they do not appear for work, regardless of the reason. Lost pay and lost jobs can spell financial ruin, particularly for those with families to support. When workers come to work sick, because they lack paid sick days and job security, productivity is reduced, coworkers can become ill, workers can become sicker and experience more serious health problems, and overall health-care costs can increase. In contrast, when workers can take time off to take care of themselves, their illnesses can be treated promptly and more effectively, contagion at work is reduced, and health-care costs are minimized. When workers can take time off to care for ill family members, children recover from illness more quickly and older people can avoid time in nursing homes, remaining at home and benefiting from care by family members.

In an earlier time, when fewer women worked and men were more likely to be sole family breadwinners, women typically provided virtually all care to ill or frail elderly family members. In most industrialized countries today, women still provide the bulk of this care, working fewer hours for pay than men in order to provide it (Gornick and Meyers, 2003). In the US it has been estimated that the typical woman will spend more years caring for elderly parents than for young children. Women also typically marry men who are several years older than they are; often this age difference results in women providing more care to their husbands than vice versa. But while women have typically done the bulk of caregiving, all workers have care needs. Workers need to care for their own health, and most have someone else for whom they must care from time to time. Parenting of minor children is only one component of the care that must be provided in human society. Including time off to provide all kinds of care as a right for all workers helps to combat the ideology that caregiving is women's work and women's work alone.

Moreover, if caregiving rights are provided only to some workers, that group can easily become subject to discrimination by employers. Because employers need to make profits, they will logically tend to discriminate against any group that they think will cost them more money or be too much trouble to employ.[1] Hence, policies that single out parents and give them new rights that others do not have should be avoided if at all possible, since such policies could easily increase discrimination against parents. (This is so even though we know that we must, as a society, socialize more of the costs of raising children, whether through providing more subsidized child care and/or more paid caregiving leaves.)

Politically, too, offering benefits that exclude others (such as the elderly or the disabled or adults who care for them) reduces the size of the coalition that will work for new legislation, and can even pit factions against each other. To provide an example of an unsuccessful, narrowly targeted policy proposal in the work–family arena from the US, the Clinton administration's decision to allow "Baby UI" (the expansion of eligibility in the federal–state unemployment insurance system to include workers with newborns) was a surprise to much of the advocacy community, who had rarely focused on parents of newborns alone. Baby UI has been singularly unsuccessful. Not a single state took advantage of the expanded federal eligibility guidelines to provide UI benefits for working parents who left work because of bearing, adopting, or caring for a new child before the administration of George W. Bush repealed the authorizing regulations.

A second US example illustrates the value of a broader approach. Long before the passage of the Family and Medical Leave Act (FMLA) in 1993—the first national law to require employers to provide any accommodation to workers' illness or family care needs—the advocacy community had worked to make any bill that would provide protection for pregnant women address broader issues than pregnancy and childbirth alone. In fact, Donna Lenhoff, widely recognized as the principal author of the FMLA, was told by members of Congress on several occasions that, if the bill were limited to pregnancy alone, Congress would probably pass even paid leave (let alone the unpaid leave specified in the FMLA). But Ms. Lenhoff, then a staff attorney at what was then known as the Women's Legal Defense Fund (now the National Partnership for Women and Families), and the coalition she led were firm in insisting that the bill include all illnesses and disabilities, as well as pregnancy, and all forms of family care—for elderly parents, spouses, and older children with serious health problems, as well as for newborns—to be available to both female and male workers (Lenhoff, 1992). In this broad form, the act's provisions (reemployment after a period of leave and continuation during the leave of any health insurance normally provided by the employer) were likely to be used by nearly as many men as women, and by workers of all ages. Given the FMLA's comprehensive coverage, employers would be hard pressed to discriminate against any one group of workers because of those workers' use of the law's provisions. To achieve this inclusive result, many compromises were made, including limiting the amount of unpaid leave that could be taken to twelve weeks per year and excluding employers with fewer than fifty workers.

In retrospect, we judge the advocacy coalition's principled stand to have been the correct one. While it perhaps delayed the passage of paid maternity leave in the US, it has set an important precedent that is now being followed in most states as well as nationally: any proposed paid maternity or family care leave must be drawn broadly. For example, when California added up to six weeks of paid family care leave to its paid temporary disability insurance (TDI) program in 2002, it covered all types of family care leave enumerated in the federal FMLA: care of ill children, spouses, elderly parents, disabled adult children, newborns, and newly adopted children. In 2008 New Jersey similarly enlarged its TDI program to include family care leave, broadly defined.[2]

While the US has led the way in ensuring that parents' rights to time off are embedded within all workers' rights, it lags behind in providing pay for time off. This outcome is perhaps not too surprising in a country whose founding ideology is based on individual rights, and whose culture views the family as a distinctly private sphere which can safely be left to take care of itself. The inevitable consequence of this laissez-faire approach is that workers with little bargaining power are offered little or nothing by way of workplace benefits to go with their low wages, while others enjoy both high wages and a generous range of benefits. A new movement is now gaining strength in the US to begin the campaign for pay for caring time with a modest proposal to require employers to provide a small number of days off with pay to all workers for both self-care and family care, informally known as "paid sick days." The need in the US is great: while many white-collar and professional workers have paid sick days, nearly half of all private-sector workers lack the right to use even a single paid sick day (Hartmann, 2007, Table 1). Even when US workers have access to paid sick days, only about three-fifths are authorized to use them for caring for ill family members or even for their own routine health needs, such as preventive care (Lovell, 2004b). In some low-wage sectors, like food service and retail, the proportion lacking paid sick days is much higher, at up to 80 percent. By providing a limited number of days for all workers, the US movement seeks to address the class inequality so evident in a country where most worker benefits are left to the voluntary action of employers. Without a universal mandate, only the higher-paid, highly skilled workers (and those relatively few lower-paid workers who benefit from collective bargaining) have access to reasonable accommodations for their self- and family-care needs.

Against this background, we are concerned that the Real Utopia proposal by Gornick and Meyers could be seen as both "pie-in-the-sky" and somewhat elitist, arguing for six months off with pay per parent when so many parents and non-parent workers in the US today lack even a single paid sick day. But, more importantly, the inclusion of such a basic need as sick leave in the Gornick–Meyers proposal would broaden its political appeal to all workers, as well as to others concerned about public health, child well-being, and the care of our growing elderly population. As an evaluation of the FMLA shows, workers are much more likely to take a leave for their own illness than for pregnancy/maternity, parenting, or to care for an ill member of their family. More than half (52 percent) of those taking an FMLA leave do so because of their own health needs, while only one-quarter use the leave for pregnancy or newborn care (26 percent) and one-third for family care (31 percent). (The sum is greater than 100 percent because some workers report more than one use of FMLA; Cantor et al., 2001.)

Indeed, we would go so far as to argue that there should be no special paid leave for parents over and above what all workers would be entitled to for any family care need. Thus, in our alternative Real Utopias model, paid time off for working parents to care for children would be a subset of paid time off to meet self- and family-care needs more generally. Both the US FMLA and the proposed Healthy Families Act's guarantee of paid sick days (see discussion below for details), and a new bipartisan proposal from Senators Dodd and Stevens for eight weeks of paid leave, known as the Family Leave Insurance Act, embody this principle.[3] In any case, in the US context we would not support generous parental leave unless all workers were first ensured a minimum standard of paid time off for illness and the care of all family members.

We are also concerned that a program focusing exclusively and intensively on parents will "overdo" it, creating serious negative consequences. Not only might such an exclusive program generate backlash—especially in the US with its prominent anti-regulation ideology—but generous parental leave might reinforce rather than reduce gender inequality. Providing parenting leaves that are overly long, for example, might encourage women to remain at home rather than return to work, or to view their employment as tangential to their central focus on domestic labor. Thus, not only do we advocate that the Gornick–Meyers model be broadened to include non-parent workers, we also urge that it be less deep. A pool of self- and family-care benefits that is broad and shallow (a wading pool) seems more desirable than a pool that is narrow and deep (a diving pool).

THE US SITUATION

Currently the US has no national or state legislation that requires employers to provide paid sick days for ordinary illness and routine health-care visits. Permanent or near-permanent disability is covered by the federal Social Security program (which also provides retirement income). The federal 1978 Pregnancy Discrimination Act requires employers who provide sick leave voluntarily for other conditions (such as heart disease) also to provide it for pregnancy and childbirth. Similarly, seven states (California, Connecticut, Hawaii, Maine, New Mexico, Washington, and Wisconsin) require both public- and private-sector employers who provide sick leave voluntarily to allow their employees to use such leave for family care purposes. As noted by Gornick and Meyers, five states (comprising 21 percent of the US population) mandate TDI programs, funded by employers and/or workers. These programs provide partial wage replacement for short-term illnesses and disabilities—usually from at least one week up to a maximum of six months or one year, although the average claim is for a much shorter period (generally less than ten weeks). Since 1978, and the passage of the Pregnancy Discrimination Act, these programs have covered pregnancy and childbirth on the same terms as other temporary disabilities, so women in states with mandatory TDI (and others covered under employers' voluntary policies) typically receive eight to ten weeks of disability benefits surrounding childbirth (US Department of Labor, Employment Standards Administration, 2007). These five states (California, Hawaii, New Jersey, New York, and Rhode Island) are the only states of the fifty that require employers to provide paid maternity leave, and it is important to note that they do so within the context of requiring partial wage replacement for all types of workers' disabilities and illnesses, not pregnancy and childbirth alone.

Public outreach and policy-maker education at the national, state, and local levels has culminated in policy proposals to provide paid sick days in several jurisdictions. A referendum requiring all employers in San Francisco to provide paid sick days (up to nine days per year for firms with ten or more workers, and up to five days for smaller employers) passed in November 2006, and went into effect in February 2007. In March 2008 the District of Columbia City Council passed a law requiring employers to provide three to seven paid "sick and safe" days (depending on firm size, with smaller employers required to provide fewer) for part-time and full-time employees who have at least one year of seniority on the job, and who have worked at least 1,000 hours in the twelve months preceding the request for leave. Paid "sick and safe" days are provided for the worker's own illness or preventive care, care of family members who need medical attention, and care needed to address domestic violence or sexual assault. Voters in Milwaukee, Wisconsin, passed a similar law by referendum in November 2008, making Milwaukee the third city in the US to require that employers of all sizes provide paid sick days. In all three cities, paid sick days follow the inclusive and universal norm that has been established in the US—all types of family care needs are included. Notably, these programs cover very small employers, including those with only one worker. State-level legislation for mandatory paid sick days has been introduced in a variety of states since 2003, including Connecticut, Florida, Maine, Maryland, Massachusetts, Minnesota, Missouri, North Carolina, Pennsylvania, Vermont and Washington

The proposed Healthy Families Act (HFA), under consideration in the US Congress, is the first national bill to require that employers provide any paid time off. Like the efforts in the states, and like the 1993 FMLA, it includes paid days off not only for workers' own illnesses or medical care, but also for addressing the health needs of workers' family members. (Unlike the FMLA, "family" is defined quite broadly in the HFA to include "any other individual related by blood or affinity whose close association with the employee is the equivalent of a family relationship."[4]) Thus, the coalition working for passage of the HFA, like that working for passage of the FMLA a dozen years earlier, includes the elderly, disability rights groups, disease groups, and medical professionals, as well as labor unions, anti-poverty groups, children's groups, religious groups, and women's and men's groups.

The federal Healthy Families Act has been introduced in each session of the US Congress since 2004. It requires all employers with fifteen or more workers to provide up to seven paid days per year that could be used for workers' own illnesses and routine health care, or for family members' health needs (including preventive care). It thus epitomizes the universal approach being used to address these issues in the US. It is important to note that the US campaign for paid sick days is also a campaign for paid family-care days, stimulating a broad base of support. National polling on paid sick/family-care days conducted by the National Partnership for Women and Families and Lake Research Partners (2007) revealed that 89 percent of likely voters favored paid sick days that could be used by a worker for self- or family care as a basic labor standard, including 94 percent of Democrats, 90 percent of independents, and 83 percent of Republicans.

DEVELOPING A NEW MINIMUM STANDARD FOR PAID SICK AND FAMILY CARE DAYS IN THE US

The proposed Healthy Families Act, developed by Senator Edward Kennedy's staff from 2000 to 2004, follows the universal approach now established as the standard in the US. It therefore provides rights to workers of all kinds for health-related absences of all kinds, including self- and family care. It helps to confront the ideology of gendered caregiving roles, and it has a large and diverse coalition behind it. When enacted it will also address class differences, in that it will disproportionately provide new paid time off to the most disadvantaged workers (who are by far the least likely to have sick leave now).

Experts from the Institute for Women's Policy Research (IWPR) were instrumental in developing the bill. In 2000, Holly Fechner, then Chief Labor Counsel for Senator Kennedy, invited IWPR staff members to a meeting with the Senator's staff members to discuss the needs of working families and brainstorm potential new legislative initiatives. At that meeting, IWPR brought to the Senate staff's attention the need for expanded availability of paid sick days. IWPR's research analyzing the Survey of Income and Program Participation (SIPP) and Jody Heymann's work using the National Longitudinal Survey of Youth were cited as evidence of the extreme need for wage replacement and time off work when ill or caring for sick family members, especially for low-income single mothers. Other empirical research had established the importance of parental involvement in improving health outcomes for sick children (Palmer, 1993).

IWPR's body of research on a nationally representative sample of low-income parents and low-wage women, using the SIPP, showed that low-income women often moved between work and welfare without collecting unemployment insurance benefits, despite often having worked considerable hours prior to their spell of unemployment (Spalter-Roth et al., 1994; Um'rani and Lovell, 2000). We suspected that, especially for single parents with marginal incomes and no personal safety nets, family needs or their own illness resulting in job loss would often push them back onto welfare. In the US, unemployment insurance (UI) is not available for those who are unable to work because of illness or family care, and the dollar value of UI benefits is often very low for those low-wage workers who are eligible. In 1995, IWPR and the National Commission for Employment Policy reported that, nationwide, "became pregnant/had child," "health reasons," and "other family or personal reasons" together accounted for 30 percent of women's job separations (compared with only 15 percent of men's job separations; Yoon et al., 1995, Table 3). Health and family care, then, are important causes of women's job separation. Family care is also an important reason why women typically accumulate fewer work hours and earnings over their lifetimes than do men (Hartmann et al., 2006). And lack of paid sick/family-care days in many low-wage jobs can disproportionately push low-earning women out of the labor market entirely, as the lack of that basic element of workplace flexibility can make employment impossible for parents of young, chronically ill, or disabled children.

Heymann's research showed that, for one cohort of young parents, poor working parents were much more likely to lack paid sick days at a given point in time or over a five-year period than non-poor parents. Some 76 percent of poor parents lacked paid sick days some or all of the time over the course of five years, while only 55 percent (still a substantial share) of non-poor parents did (Heymann, 2000, Table D.1).

The proposed Healthy Families Act that emerged after several years of Senate staff work and meetings with experts and advocates would require employers of fifteen or more workers (the 1964 Civil Rights Act employer size standard) to provide up to seven days of paid leave for a worker's own illness or medical care, and to meet the healthcare needs of family members. It encompasses all the health-related leave purposes covered by the FMLA and, as noted above, defines covered family members in a very broad way (more broadly than the FMLA). Also using a generous definition of what constitutes full-time work, the bill provides employees who regularly work thirty hours or more per week (or 1,500 hours or more per year) the full seven days. Part-timers working between twenty and thirty hours per week, or 1,000 to 1,500 hours per year, would be entitled to a prorated share of the seven HFA days.

An important context for this work was the generally raised consciousness about low-wage work in America during this period— a consciousness that resulted from the confluence of several factors. The 1996 welfare law—the Personal Responsibility and Work Opportunity Reconciliation Act—that ended the entitlement to assistance for low-income mothers, and required paid employment, raised the visibility of working mothers struggling to make ends meet on low-wage jobs whose time demands were incompatible with responsible family care. The living wage movement was proceeding apace, and increasingly recognized the need for add-on benefits. "Living wage plus," for example, came to stand for a living wage plus employer-provided health insurance. Barbara Ehrenreich's *Nickel and Dimed* became a bestseller in 2001, and numerous think tanks, columnists, and other observers frequently commented on rising income inequality in the US. The recession of 2001, as well as the 9/11 attacks, also increased public awareness of the importance of addressing economic insecurity and people's health needs. In recent years, problems of ensuring an adequate supply of the seasonal flu vaccine and worries about the bird flu and other possible pandemics have raised concerns about the importance of allowing those who are ill to avoid contact with coworkers, other children, and the general public. If ill workers could take time off with pay, they would be much less likely to go to work and infect others.

Paid sick and family-care days

In order to assess what priority should be given by policy makers and advocates to achieving paid sick/family-care days for American workers, IWPR sought to generalize Heymann's findings on one age group of workers to the entire labor force.[5]

Based on data from the US Bureau of Labor Statistics (BLS) employer survey of fringe benefits, IWPR found that in the late 1990s only 51 percent of non-federal workers had any paid sick days. The share with paid sick days was higher for state and local government than for the private sector, for union than for non-union workers, and for full-time than for part-time workers. Still, only 60 percent of all full-time workers have paid sick leave. IWPR estimated that, in 2003,

62.5 million workers lacked paid sick days, and many of those who had access to paid sick days could not use them for routine doctor visits or care of ill family members (Lovell, 2004b). Moreover, for all uses, paid sick days are much less common among those earning low wages. Among the top-earning quartile of workers, nearly 70 percent have paid sick leave and about 48 percent and 43 percent have paid leave for doctor visits or for the care of sick children, respectively. Among the bottom-earning quartile of workers, only about 23 percent have paid sick days, and only 11 percent have paid days for either doctors' appointments or for the care of sick children (Lovell, 2004b).

Because it was widely agreed that policy development would not proceed in the US without reassurance that the impact of the bill on employers would be moderate (US policy makers being so cautious about interfering with employers' behavior even in the face of workers' documented needs), IWPR calculated the costs and benefits of the proposed Healthy Families Act. Relying on its analysis of the BLS employer benefits survey, the National Health Interview Study, and other research, IWPR estimated that implementation of the Healthy Families Act would result in substantially larger benefits ($28.4 billion in 2003 dollars) than costs ($20.2 billion). The largest cost to employers would consist of paying the wages of workers who would previously have taken unpaid time off to deal with their own or their family members' illnesses, or would have stayed on the job despite their need for time off ($17.5 billion). Smaller costs would come from newly allowable uses of sick leave by workers who already had sick leave for their own illness ($2.3 billion) and from additional time taken off by workers who previously had only a few paid sick days ($35.6 million). These latter two extensions of the sick leave benefits accounted for 11.5 percent of the total cost (Lovell, 2005).

On the benefits side, the overwhelming bulk of benefits—$25.8 billion, or 91 percent of all savings—come from lower employer expenditures related to voluntary turnover. Research has documented that workers with paid sick days are less likely to move to a new employer than are workers who lack that benefit. Substantially smaller benefits would also accrue from a reduced spread of illness in the workplace (less than $1 billion) and from reduced wage payments to unproductive workers who, without paid time off, go to work sick (approximately $1.6 billion). These latter two benefits stem from a reduction in the phenomenon of "presenteeism"—the tendency to come to work when sick. A further benefit of providing paid sick days that accrues to society (in the form of taxpayers) is reduced nursing home days ($225 million), because workers would be able to tend to their ill parents rather than using nursing homes in the case of short-term illnesses and transitions home from the hospital. Many additional health benefits (other than those attributable to reduced spread of the flu and reduced use of short-term nursing-home care) cannot yet be quantified because of lack of specific evidence. For instance, it may be that having paid sick days improves overall health outcomes while reducing health-care expenditures. The use of paid sick days is also likely to reduce spending on public programs such as Temporary Assistance for Needy Families (TANF), food stamps, and unemployment insurance if workers are able to hold on to their jobs while dealing with their own or their children's health problems.

A national illness/family-care insurance program

The popularity of the universal approach to addressing workers' self- and family-care needs in the US is further demonstrated by the first substantial federal proposal designed to provide paid leave to allow workers to take care of needs lasting beyond several days. A federal initiative introduced in June 2007 would expand upon the FMLA by providing up to eight weeks of paid leave for a worker's serious health and family care needs. Modeled on the state-based Temporary Disability Insurance programs, and especially California's 2002 expansion of its TDI program to provide family-care leave, it would mandate a new social insurance system, funded by payroll taxes levied on both employers and workers. The Family Leave Insurance Act proposed by Senators Dodd and Stevens has the same coverage and restrictions on firm size as the FMLA, mandating participation by only those businesses with more than fifty employees. In an important improvement over the FMLA, businesses with fewer than fifty employees and self-employed workers may choose to opt in, with a 50 percent discount on premium payments. Like the FMLA, a worker's own serious illness is covered (which of course includes the temporary disability resulting from pregnancy and childbirth), and family-care leaves are provided for newborn or newly adopted children, children with serious illnesses, spouses with serious illnesses, and frail or medically needy elder parents. The proposed Family Leave Insurance Act is designed to pick up where the HFA coverage would end. While the HFA would require employers to provide full pay for up to seven days, the Family Leave Insurance Act would provide partial pay for longer absences and would use a social insurance mechanism to protect employers from the costs of unusually long or frequent absences. This bipartisan bill, like the proposed Healthy Families Act, has benefited from the input of advocates and experts over several years. It received substantial public exposure in the presidential candidate debates, since one of its coauthors, Senator Dodd, was a candidate for president in the 2008 election cycle.

THE US MODEL OF UNIVERSALITY

Paid sick days are a basic need of all workers. A federal law requiring employers to provide paid sick days that can also be used for one's own preventive care, and for caring for ill family members (parents and spouses as well as children) would go a long way to improve the financial security of American families as well as their health status. While paid sick days are important for everyone, and thus warrant a universal law, they are most important to the lowest earners, who include a disproportionate share of women and minorities. The Healthy Families Act, serving all workers, would also provide a better alternative than the several days per year of special paid leave that Gornick and Meyers advocate for parents only for the purpose of taking children to medical appointments and attending important school functions. Providing benefits exclusively for parents makes for poor strategy and leaves out a substantial portion of care needs. We would prefer to see attending school functions as an appropriate use of workers' vacation or personal paid time off, rather than developing a special benefit for parents only. (Indeed it is about time for the US to legislate a minimum standard for paid vacation days, which, as reported by Gornick and Meyers, is now set at twenty days in the European Union.)

The US Dodd–Stevens proposal for Family Leave Insurance essentially expands the disability insurance (TDI) model used in the states to the national level and to family care. By providing up to eight weeks of leave for both serious illness and family care, it provides both maternity leave for mothers and parental leave that can be used by fathers, but does so in a way that provides no special benefits to parents that other ill, temporarily disabled, or caregiving workers cannot also use. While many US employers already provide such plans voluntarily, many others do not; roughly 40 percent of the workforce has TDI (Lovell, 2004a) and many fewer have paid leave they can use for caregiving (US Department of Labor, Bureau of Labor Statistics, 2007). The advantage of insurance plans, of course, is that they spread the risk, so that, for example, a small employer is not hit with the cost of two or three major illness-related absences at once. Also, because the costs are shared, the individual employer's incentive to discriminate against workers most likely to use the leave is reduced. Another advantage of the Dodd–Stevens model is its relatively short length: the proposed paid leave is not long enough to encourage workers to leave the labor force permanently. By embedding parental leave in a more general form of leave, the long maternity leaves some European countries have will likely be avoided in the US.

Since the US has little mandated paid leave now, it would be relatively easy to fold new paid parental leave into a universal sickness-caregiving program. The universal provision of TDI is most likely the surest and fastest way to provide paid maternity leave to American women and paid parenting time to men, and to do so without increasing discrimination against women and men of child-bearing/rearing age. As we have noted, in the five states with TDI plans currently, pregnant women typically receive eight to ten weeks of benefits. The women who use the partial-pay TDI benefits, rather than a combination of employer-provided vacation, sick, and family care days (which are usually offered at 100 percent of pay), are undoubtedly the lower-paid workers. For these women, even partial wage replacement can be critical in preventing them from slipping into poverty, and in enabling them to meet the basic needs of their families. In addition, paid maternity leave strengthens job attachment, making it more likely the new mother will return to earning sooner. Because TDI covers all long-term illnesses and temporary disabilities (broken bones, heart disease, cancer, pneumonia, and so on), it is not generally perceived as a "women's program," though women do use it somewhat more than men (at least partly because they are more likely to be lower-wage workers who lack other coverage at a higher wage replacement rate). We note that in the US the HFA would also be necessary in addition to TDI, to ensure that workers received pay for some number of days to take care of the very short-term illnesses and medical appointments that all workers and family members must attend to.

While we would personally be pleased if state-based TDI plans also provided paid family-care leaves (such as in California and in the proposed Dodd–Stevens Family Leave Insurance Act of 2007), we do not believe paid sick days or TDI alone should be delayed until the lengthier paid family-care leaves can be included. Sick leave is a universal need whose provision has been sorely overlooked in the US. Workers of all ages and family types, both women and men, would benefit from universal wage replacement for sickness and routine medical care. We believe starting with a modest campaign for paid sick/family-care days for all workers in the US, creating a shallow and broad pool of income for leave, will be a far more successful way to achieve accommodation for parents and a reduction in gender inequality than pursuing the Gornick–Meyers model, with its focus on a deep and narrow pool for parents only.

GENDER AND CAREGIVER EQUALITY

The US, while lagging behind the other OECD countries in its lack of paid leave and subsidized child care, has led the way in proposing and implementing gender-neutral policies that do not privilege parents but rather treat all forms of caregiving—including self-care—equally. The relationship between the length of paid family-care leave and gender equality may be shaped like an inverted "U." Offering some paid leave would likely increase gender equality by strengthening women's labor-force participation and attachment to work, lengthening their job tenure, and improving their wages. At some point, however, providing more paid parental leave probably reduces gender equality by encouraging women to take extended breaks from employment. (This is particularly likely to be the case given how difficult it is to change men's leave-taking behavior and get them more involved in family-care work; long leaves for women will exacerbate existing gender gaps in caregiving time.) This hypothesized relationship is shown in Figure 11.1. The US is likely still on the upward-sloping side (in fact, near zero), while it is possible that several European countries are on the downward-sloping side. Clearly, the precise shape of the relationship and the turning point, if there is one, are empirical, though currently unanswered, questions (some early research suggests six months may be the turning point). This understanding could help to bring the views of Barbara Bergmann, a critic of maternity leaves that are too long, into closer alignment with those of Gornick and Meyers, who would certainly like to see the US adopt paid parental leave. This graph also reinforces our argument that broad and shallow (keeping leaves short and allowing them for many purposes, so as to ensure substantial leave is taken by men as well as women) is a better strategy for income replacement than deep and narrow (long leaves for parents only).

A second graph could be drawn to show a similar hypothesized relationship between the extent of provision of quality part-time jobs and gender equality. Currently in the US, because of the lack of accommodations in the workplace to family caregiving needs, many

Figure 11.1

Hypothesized Relationship Between Gender Equality and Length of Paid Family-Care Leave

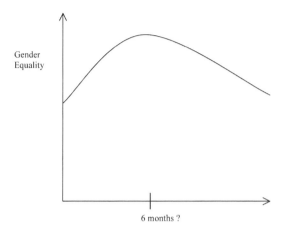

women drop out of the labor force after childbirth. If part-time jobs with decent wages and benefits were more available, it is likely that more women would participate in the labor force. US women's labor-force participation is still 20 percentage points below that of Sweden and Norway, the countries with the highest labor-force participation rates in the Gornick–Meyers study. We also believe there is substantial demand on the part of men in the US for good part-time jobs, so we do not anticipate that part-time jobs would be overwhelmingly dominated by women—if anything, as the quality of part-time jobs improves and the long-term career impacts of working a reduced schedule fade, the share held by men should increase—although currently women form the majority of part-timers (67 percent). Thus, at this stage in the evolution of women's work in the US, we would argue, with Joan Williams (2000), that the provision of good-quality part-time jobs would improve women's economic situation and increase equity with men.

As with paid family leave, however, there can be too much of a good thing. The creation of too many good (but not great) part-time jobs could lead to the development of a "golden ghetto" for women, especially if those jobs are concentrated in employment areas women currently dominate—a phenomenon that would resemble the strong occupational sex segregation in Sweden that accompanies its reduced-work-hours policies for parents. Moreover, like Gornick and Meyers, we believe good part-time jobs should not be offered as a right only to parents, both because of potentially negative political fallout and because of the increased likelihood that employers would discriminate against parents—especially mothers, who would, at least at first, be more likely to take such jobs. Providing a part-time or reduced-hours work schedule (like offering reemployment after an absence) is something only an individual employer can do, and thus there are strong incentives for employers to avoid hiring workers likely to want part-time schedules if they see those schedules as being costly and/or inconvenient. As important as we think good part-time jobs are in general, we would also like to see the standard working week shortened—preferably to thirty-five hours, as Gornick and Meyers also advocate—as well as the development of policies and practices addressing the overly long hours and mandatory overtime demanded in some occupations.

CONCLUSION

Given the strong campaign underway throughout the US, we are optimistic that short paid leaves for both workers' own illnesses and for their family-care needs will be implemented here in the coming years. We recommend the US model of universality and inclusivity to other nations as one that is better suited to advancing gender equality than the Gornick–Meyers dual-earner/dual-caregiver model, with its primary focus on parents. The US model does not privilege parents' needs to provide care above other workers' needs; nor does it privilege childbearing above other forms of temporary disability or need for medical care. Our alternative model would, then, make two universal programs available to all workers: paid leave (on which we have focused in this chapter) and flexible and reduced hours (which we have only briefly addressed). We agree with Gornick and Meyers that a substantial investment in child care is needed as the third program to complete progress toward gender equality; but we would also supplement that with increased subsidies for elder care and care for the disabled. We also endorse Zippel's call for stronger affirmative action and anti-discrimination programs in both education and employment as essential steps forward.

The US model, with its focus first on sick leave for all illnesses and conditions, and second on care for all typical family-care needs, is one that has broad cross-class appeal and universal usefulness. Rather than focusing on achieving long paid leaves for one group—parents—

the US model focuses on achieving shorter paid leaves for all. Furthermore, while parents as a group may have many different preferences regarding how to structure their lives around providing care to their children, the desire of ill workers to have time off with pay when they are too ill to work is surely universal. Embedding parental leave within a comprehensive program that provides paid sick leave, and broadening the kinds of caregiving included beyond parenting, is likely to encourage workers and voters to see parenting, too, as a universal phenomenon—something most of us go through at some point in our lives, along with all other life-cycle events, and not a unique aspect of life to be privileged over other life stages, or carried out only by women.

NOTES

1   A good example in the US is provided by a recently revealed internal Wal-Mart memo. In order to reduce health-care costs, top management instructed store managers to assign physically taxing duties to older workers, so as to discourage employment of frail workers who might be more likely to need health care. They were instructed to assign such duties to all workers so as to disguise their effort to discourage older workers especially (Greenhouse and Barbaro, 2005).

2   In contrast, Washington State enacted an as-yet-unfunded paid leave policy in 2007 that covers parents of newborns and newly adopted children only. It is a rare counterexample to the universal approach common throughout the US. The Washington program was expected to be implemented in 2009, after a specially convened commission determined a funding mechanism. The commission failed to determine a mechanism, however, and the advocacy community in the state plans work to broaden the proposal to more types of caregiving for all workers, in order to make a payroll tax a feasible method of funding the leave as well as to broaden popular support of the measure.

3   The Family Leave Insurance Act was introduced as Senate bill number 1681 in the 110th Congress.

4   The Healthy Families Act was introduced in the 110th Congress as House Bill 1542 and Senate Bill 910. Typically bills in the US are introduced in both the House of Representatives and the Senate in each new two-year session of Congress until they pass or are abandoned by their sponsors. Their provisions typically change slightly from session to session.

5   The US Bureau of Labor Statistics (BLS) provided IWPR with access to confidential data from their employer survey of benefit provision, which provides information on a sample representing 90 percent of the US labor

force (essentially the entire labor force excluding federal, military, agricultural, household, and self-employed workers).

REFERENCES

Cantor, David, Jane Waldfogel, Jeffrey Kerwin, Mareena McKinley Wright, Kerry Levin, John Rauch, Tracey Hagerty, and Martha Stapleton Kudela, 2001, *Balancing the Needs of Families and Employers: The Family and Medical Leave Surveys 2000 Update*, Washington, DC: US Department of Labor.

Employment Policy Foundation, 2002, "Employee Turnover—A Critical Human Resource Benchmark," *HR Benchmarks* (December 3): 1–5. online: http://www.epf.org (accessed January 3, 2005).

Greenhouse, Steven, and Michael Barbaro, 2005, "Wal-Mart Suggests Ways to Cut Employee Benefit Costs," *New York Times*, October 26, 2005. online: http://www.nytimes.com/2005/10/26/business/26walmart.ready.html (accessed October 2, 2007).

Gornick, Janet C., and Marcia K. Meyers, 2003, *Families That Work: Policies for Reconciling Parenthood and Employment*, New York: Russell Sage Foundation.

Hartmann, Heidi, 2007, *The Healthy Families Act: Impacts on Workers, Businesses, the Economy, and Public Health*, US Congress, Senate: Committee on Health, Education, Labor, and Pensions. 110th Congress, First session, February 13., online http://www.iwpr.org/pdf/Hartmann_HFA_testimony021307.pdf/ (accessed December 2007).

Hartmann, Heidi, Stephen J. Rose, and Vicky Lovell, 2006, "How Much Progress in Closing the Long-Term Earnings Gap?" in Francine D. Blau, Mary C. Brinton, and David B. Grusky, eds, *The Declining Significance of Gender*, New York: Russell Sage Foundation.

Healthy Families Act, 2007, online: http://www.thomas.gov/cgi-bin/query/D?c110:1:./temp/~c1109gWBK8::/ (accessed November 2008).

Heyman, Jody, 2000, *The Widening Gap: Why America's Working Families Are in Jeopardy—and What Can Be Done About It*, New York: Basic Books.

Heymann, Jody and Alison Earle, 1998, "The Work–Family Balance: What Hurdles Are Parents Leaving Welfare Likely to Confront," *Journal of Policy Analysis and Management* 17 (2), Spring: 313–21.

Heyman, Jody, Alison Earle, and Brian Egleston, 1996, "Parental Availability for the Care of Sick Children," *Pediatrics* 98 (August 2): 226–30.

Heymann, Jody, S. Toomey, and F. Furstenberg, 1999, "Working Parents: What Factors are Involved in their Ability to Take Time Off from Work When Their Children are Sick?" *Archives of Pediatrics and Adolescent Medicine* 153: 870–74.

Lenhoff, Donna, 1992, personal communication to Heidi Hartmann.
Lovell, Vicky, 2004a, "Incomplete Development of State and Voluntary Temporary Disability Insurance," in Kathleen Buto, Martha Priddy Patterson, William E. Spriggs, and Maya Rockeymoore, eds, *Strengthening Community*, Washington, DC: Brookings Institution.
––––––– 2004b, *No Time to Be Sick: Why Everyone Suffers When Workers Don't Have Paid Sick Leave*, Washington, DC: Institute for Women's Policy Research.
–––––––2005, *Valuing Good Health: An Estimate of Costs and Savings for the Healthy Families Act*, Washington, DC: Institute for Women's Policy Research.
National Partnership for Women and Families and Lake Research Partners, 2007, *Key Findings from National Polling on Paid Sick Days*, online: http://www.nationalpartnership.org/site/DocServer/Paid_Sick_Days_poll_slides.pdf?docID=2401 (accessed October 2, 2007).
Palmer, Sarah J., 1993, "Care of Sick Children by Parents: A Meaningful Role," *Journal of Advanced Nursing* 18 (February): 185–91.
Spalter-Roth, Roberta, Heidi Hartmann, and Beverly Burr, 1994, *Income Insecurity: The Failure of Unemployment Insurance to Reach Working AFDC Mothers*, Washington, DC: Institute for Women's Policy Research.
Um'rani, Annisah, and Vicky Lovell, 2000, *Unemployment Insurance and Welfare Reform: Fair Access to Economic Supports for Low-Income Working Women*, Washington, DC: Institute for Women's Policy Research.
US Department of Labor, Bureau of Labor Statistics, 2007, *National Compensation Survey: Employee Benefits in Private Industry in the United States, March 2007*, online: http://www.bls.gov/ncs/ebs/sp/ebsm 0006.pdf (accessed October 2, 2007).
US Department of Labor, Employment Standards Administration, 2007, *Federal vs State Family and Medical Leave Laws*, Washington, DC: Department of Labor, online: http://www.dol.gov/esa/programs/whd/ state/fmla/index.htm (accessed August 3, 2007).
Williams, Joan, 2000, *Unbending Gender: Why Family and Work Conflict and What to Do About It*, New York: Oxford University Press.
Yoon, Young-Hee, Roberta Spalter-Roth, and Marc Baldwin, 1995, *Unemployment Insurance: Barriers to Access for Women and Part-Time Workers*, Washington, DC: National Commission for Employment Policy.

PART IV

Transformations: Obstacles, Opportunites, the Politics of Implementation

12

Class Divisions among Women*
Michael Shalev

Women have both shared and divided interests. In the United States, this truism was forcefully brought home at the peak of second-wave feminism by African-American dissidents who criticized the movement's predominantly white and middle-class leaders and activists for imposing their own assumptions, values and interests. Since then, scholars working on gender have internalized the reality of pluralism among women, and today they often enshrine it in the concept of intersectionality between gender and other cleavages (Browne and Misra 2003; Glenn 1985; McCall 2005). As one indication of this, an online search of Google Books in April 2008 yielded over 1,200 volumes that included all three of the words "gender," "race" and "class" in their title. This paper focuses on the gender–class couplet. I argue that attending to potentially divisive class differences is essential for understanding the benefits and burdens for women of different ways of combining work and motherhood. Feminist perspectives on the intersection between class and gender have yielded important insights, but have concentrated on how gender inequality contributes to class inequality and how class subordination oppresses women. Less commonly discussed is interaction between class and gender in the sense that the consequences of gender differences are conditional on class (see Wright, 2001). Here I highlight precisely this type of interaction, by exploring how gender norms and interests vary between women in different classes.

* I gratefully acknowledge the support and suggestions of the editors. Janet Gornick has been exceptionally enthusiastic and helpful. In addition, I have benefited from comments by Hadas Mandel and by participants in the Real Utopias conference and seminars at Stockholm University and Umea University.

The context for this discussion is the political conditions for realizing Gornick and Meyers' vision of a gender-egalitarian and family-friendly society (see Gornick and Meyers, 2003). My substantive focus is on two of their most important proposals for federal government intervention: universal public child care and paid parental leave. I seek to demonstrate, with respect to these reforms, that in the US both women's normative orientations and their economic interests are divided along class lines. In relation to values, public opinion data show that the majority of women from all class backgrounds reject the male-breadwinner model of gender roles in the family. At the same time, the distribution of opinion reveals systematic differences in the ideals supported by women from different educational and occupational classes. The Gornick–Meyers proposals are most consistent with the orientations of relatively privileged women. I will go on to argue that there is an even clearer class division when it comes to the costs and benefits for women of different approaches to reconciling motherhood and paid employment. This discussion relates to both the interests of women as child-care consumers and the indirect effects of work–family policies on their labor market attainments.

When variations across classes in ideals and interests are juxtaposed, the result is ironic. Class differences in moral economy (norms) are inconsistent with class differences in political economy (the costs and benefits of policies intended to support maternal employment). While educated women in professional and managerial jobs appear to be the most favorable toward the dual-earner/dual-caregiver model, it is not in their economic interest for the state to take responsibility for making it happen. I infer that, even though relatively privileged women may strongly support the goals underlying the Gornick–Meyers program, they are unlikely to mobilize their superior political capabilities in order to push it forward. As a result, class differences and tensions between women are an unacknowledged barrier on the road to a dual-earner/dual-caregiver society.

THE MORAL ECONOMY OF GENDER

If there are significant class differences in values and orientations toward work and the family, and how best to balance these two spheres, then a "one size fits all" approach to work–family reconciliation may be inappropriate. Gornick and Meyers' ideal of a dual-earner/dual-caregiver society presumes that both caring for children and being employed outside the home are important to mothers, and that in order to reconcile conflicting demands it is preferable that fathers rather than mothers adjust by doing less paid work and taking on more domestic work. Many highly educated, career-oriented American women probably share this view. But what if lower-class women do not aspire to, and cannot realistically expect, self-fulfilling careers?[1] And what if, in addition, they (and their husbands) value women's care responsibilities at home more highly than their paid work outside? In that case, the Gornick–Meyers policy package conflicts with these women's preferences, which would be better served by "familializing" interventions aimed at raising the income of male breadwinners or subsidizing mothers who stay at home with their children.

There is a sizable survey-based literature on gender-role ideologies. This literature addresses both the rise of egalitarianism over time and its variation between countries.[2] Analyzing data from the International Social Survey Program (ISSP) for 2002, Svallfors has demonstrated the prevalence of class differences in orientations toward both family and work in diverse Western societies, including the US (Svallfors, 2006). Examining variations in an index of support for women working outside of the home, and defining classes by occupation, Svallfors finds that, in all the countries he studied, among both men and women, "the working class consistently displays more conservative attitudes than the service class."[3] Class differences were lower in the US and Britain, however, than in Europe.[4]

The General Social Survey (GSS) is a frequently utilized source for quantitative research on gender role attitudes in the US,[5] though research in this mode has not sought to identify class differences explicitly. A study by Harris and Firestone indirectly addressed this issue, finding that, net of a wide range of other determinants, education strongly affected an index of gender egalitarianism. However, no differences were detected between broad occupational groups (Harris and Firestone 1998).[6] Making different methodological choices, I do find such differences. My analysis looks directly at class effects, viewed both as the resources that individuals bring to the labor market (education) and their locations in the division of labor (occupational groups). This is preferable to the standard procedure of testing the impact of multiple and partially overlapping socioeconomic attributes in an additive, over-specified regression model. Rather than relying on statistical controls to cope with limited sample sizes, I have pooled GSS surveys for the whole of the latest available decade. This makes it possible to analyze only those respondents who represent the target audience of the Gornick–Meyers proposals: married women of prime working age living with their spouses and children.

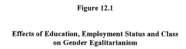

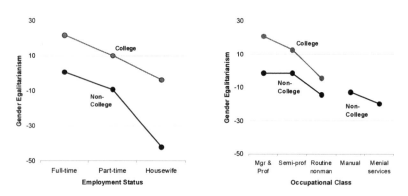

Turning now to the dependent variable, rather than potentially clouding the meaning of the attitudes analyzed by combining answers to different questions, I look at responses to a single but classic evocation of traditional gender roles: "It is much better for everyone involved if the man is the achiever outside the home and the woman takes care of the home and family." The four alternative responses offered were very unevenly distributed in my sample. Conservative choices attracted only a minority: 8 percent "strongly agree" and 20 percent "agree." Egalitarian choices dominated: "disagree" (50 percent) and "strongly disagree" (22 percent). Even when the sample was segmented in various ways, a large bloc of respondents routinely chose the "disagree" option. In order to accentuate the remaining variance, I have defined the gender egalitarianism of any group as the absolute difference between the proportion expressing *strong* disagreement, and those expressing *any* agreement (strong or not) with the traditionalist position. The results displayed in Figure 12.1 show that this simple indicator reveals substantial class differences.

The first chart shows that employment status and education have both additive and interactive effects on gender egalitarianism. Based on their activity in the week of the survey, women who work are more egalitarian than those who don't, and among working women full-timers are more egalitarian than part-timers. Among all three groups, college-educated women are more likely to choose egalitarian answers, with the difference being especially marked among housewives. The second chart examines only women in paid employment, who are grouped by broad occupational classes similar to those identified in the EGP schema (Erikson, Goldthorpe, and Portocarero, 1979). If the two working-class categories are combined, the women in this sample are distributed fairly equally between the resulting four broad classes.[7] Because of this diversity in women's class locations, it matters that their attitudes vary distinctly by class. The chart also shows the effect of educational differences among white-collar workers. A college education is associated with significantly more egalitarian values, with the size of the education effect rising as we move up the hierarchy of occupational classes.

Although evidence of class differences in the gender ideologies of married mothers is thus quite strong, we cannot be certain which way the causal arrow points. It is conceivable that, instead of their outlooks being molded by their class circumstances, women choose their education and employment trajectories in an individualistic manner on the basis of a priori preferences. This atomistic and voluntaristic view of women's aspirations has been most vigorously advocated by British sociologist Catherine Hakim. In her words, in "rich modern societies" work–family balance is "just one of the lifestyle choices open to . . . all social class and income groups." (Hakim, 2000: 73). I agree with Hakim's two main empirical claims: that women do not all have the same preferences regarding work and family, and that many of them are ambivalent and "adaptive." However, I also agree with critics who have insisted that preferences are constrained by opportunity structures and conditioned by culture.[8]

In short, both theoretical reasoning and empirical evidence oblige us to recognize class differences among women in their commitment to gender-equal work and family roles. This in turn raises questions concerning Gornick and Meyers' implicit assumption that their program is appropriate for women in general. The implications of this will be taken up in the concluding section of the chapter. At this point our empirical focus moves from orientations and values to political economy. The question now is: who gains and who loses from present arrangements for work–family reconciliation, in comparison with the arrangements that Gornick and Meyers propose?

DISTRIBUTIONAL EFFECTS OF FAMILY POLICIES

The blueprint for reform drawn up by Gornick and Meyers refers to two different types of policy. One of them is government regulation of working hours designed to facilitate more equal parental responsibility. However, I focus here on Gornick and Meyers' proposals for radical innovation in family policy: public provision of free or heavily subsidized child care and early education, made available to all parents who want it; and the right to various forms of publicly financed parental leave at high replacement rates, for fathers as well as mothers.

Any policy innovation that would alter the balance between private and public responsibility or redistribute income inevitably implies conflicts of interest between classes. Since the Gornick–Meyers program explicitly includes both of these elements, it acutely raises the question: *cui bono* (who benefits)? To answer this question it is necessary to consider two separate issues: the availability and cost of leave and care services under the present market-based system; and how the alternative state-sponsored system would be financed.

In discussing family-policy reforms, Gornick and Meyers emphasize that they would entail multiple types of redistribution, including from parents to non-parents and between families with younger and older children (Gornick and Meyers, 2003: 14). Insofar as Gornick and Meyers do discuss the possibility of vertical redistribution between classes, they frame it as a solution to problems of equity and justice. Under America's privatized system, they argue that only "the most privileged families"—those with high incomes and superior job-based parental benefits—have assured access to essential mechanisms of work–family reconciliation. Because market-based solutions have been calamitous for many American parents and children, a public system based on progressive financing is considered essential (Gornick and Meyers, 2003: 141; see also 139, 144, 232–34).

Perhaps in order to mobilize sympathy for their program, Gornick and Meyers draw attention to the burdens that current American work–family practices place on mothers and families with limited resources, rather than their beneficial consequences for advantaged women and their families, who are presented as a privileged elite. Gornick and Meyers also fail to acknowledge the radical distributional implications of the mechanisms they propose for financing new family policies. They advocate paying for child care from general revenues, possibly supplemented by co-payments, while parental leave programs would be paid for by a combination of general and social-security taxes. Clearly, then, progressive income taxes would be the major source of revenue. Under current political circumstances, this could be expected to meet resistance from middle-income families. Even stronger opposition would emanate from the rich and their allies, who so successfully led the rollback of progressive taxation in the US (Hacker and Pierson 2005).

What are the distributional implications of the work–family arrangements currently in place? Beginning with parental leave, these policies are of course a far cry from the publicly financed federal schemes and high replacement rates that Gornick and Meyers advocate. Under prevailing conditions in the US, leave is a discretionary employee benefit that is granted almost exclusively to women. Clearly, employers only have an incentive to finance leave for workers who are difficult or costly to replace. This assures built-in advantages for the privileged that Gornick and Meyers are anxious to neutralize by moving to a publicly financed system (Gornick and Meyers, 2003: 139). Supporting their and my assumption of class bias, the most recent available data from the Census Bureau indicate that, while a sizable majority (close to 60 percent) of first-time mothers with a college degree utilize some form of paid maternity leave, the proportion declines sharply at lower levels of education, reaching only 18 percent among those without a high school diploma (Johnson and Downs 2005: Table 5).

Richer quantitative evidence is available for child-care patterns. Reports by the Urban Institute, based on large-scale national surveys of families carried out in 1997 and 1999, reveal that, for children under three, care arrangements differ substantially between families with higher and lower incomes (the dividing line was twice the federal poverty line). Lower-income families and women with low education are primarily dependent on family members to look after infants and toddlers while mothers are at work, whereas the majority of higher-income households and college-educated mothers utilize paid child care (Ehrle, Adams and Tout 2001: Figures 5 and 8).[9] Among families with a child under thirteen that did purchase care, the dollar cost was about 50 percent higher for higher-income families. However, this represented only half the proportion of their household income (7 percent vs 14 percent) (Giannarelli, Adelman and Schmidt 2003: Figure 3).

Caution is needed in interpreting unqualified findings like these, since comparisons might be complicated by class differences in potentially confounding factors, including family structure (differing rates of fertility and single parenthood), the amount and quality of care received, and the effects of government aid (Meyers, Rosenbaum, Ruhm and Waldfogel: 2004). To deal with some of these issues, I have analyzed the cost of care using a carefully targeted sample drawn from a small but high-quality data set, the *National Study of the Changing Workforce*. The results presented in Figure 12.2 confirm that the burden on working mothers who are married with children and purchase preschool child care is closely related to how much they personally earn. The average cost is equivalent to a hefty one-third of the gross earnings of women in the bottom tertile, and the box plot indicates that a quarter of this group spend at least half of their income on child care. In contrast,

Figure 12.2

The Economic Burden of Paid Child Care on Working Mothers

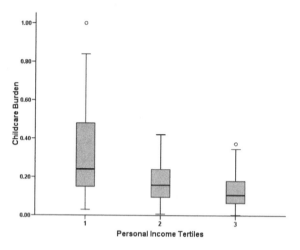

Notes: The vertical axis shows child-care expenses as a proportion of gross personal income. The horizontal axis shows tertiles (thirds) of gross personal income. The analysis refers to married working mothers (excluding immigrants) with preschool children who use paid care; n=116.
(See National Study of the Changing Workforce 2002 [interviews in 2002/03, earnings in 2001/02].)

the child care burden for women in the middle and top tertiles is only 17 percent and 13 percent, respectively.

The role of government complicates the story. Since the computations reported in Figure 12.2 are based on pretax earnings, they understate the burden on middle and upper-income women. However, some of the tax bite on these women's gross earnings is offset by credits for private child care expenses. On the other hand, the position of low-income households would be even worse if it were not for the existence of means-tested subsidies and free preschool programs. A detailed survey carried out in New York by Durfee and Meyers revealed that fully half of all families with preschool children and working mothers received one or another form of government assistance, valued at an annual average of $4,000 per recipient family (Durfee and Meyers, 2006). However, notwithstanding the fact that the role of government is apparently far more significant than studies of US family policy have previously acknowledged,[10] there is little evidence that it offsets market-based inequalities. Despite the emphasis on targeting in preschool and subsidy programs, not all of the criteria used are financial, and take-up of means-tested programs is far from complete (Shlay, Weinraub, Harmon and Tran, 2004). In addition, tax credits are by nature regressive. As a result, Durfee and Meyers conclude that the overall system is only weakly redistributive, if at all.

To summarize, from a financial perspective more advantaged families fare relatively well under the present systems of parental leave and child care. In contrast, the alternatives advocated by Gornick and Meyers would enlarge the scope of progressive taxation, which is certainly not in the economic interest of the advantaged. The evidence shows that the cost of child care is relatively modest for middle- and, especially, upper-income women.[11] Higher-class parents not only have the means to purchase high-quality substitute care, but are able to obtain this care by shouldering a smaller economic burden than lower-class parents. An important reason for this is the relatively low cost of private care, due to the ready availability in the US of low-paid, unqualified and often non-citizen female care workers. However, affordability is not the only factor with a class bias. Parents with a class advantage also have a strong interest in treating superior childhood care and early education as investments in their children's future ability to reproduce that advantage.

We turn now to the third and final substantive section of the paper, which considers the likely effects of the Gornick–Meyers policy recommendations on the wages and occupational attainments of working women, and how these can be expected to differ along class lines.

THE CLASSING OF LABOR MARKET EFFECTS

In order to promote convergence in the work and family roles of mothers and fathers, Gornick and Meyers deliberately steer clear of measures which aim only at making it easier for women to perform their traditional roles while attached to the labor market. Instead, they opt for policies designed to encourage parents to share both paid work and unpaid care responsibilities equally. While even Sweden has not implemented such a far-reaching agenda, I believe that much can be learned by treating the Swedish experience with family policy as a counterfactual guide to the likely consequences of adopting Gornick and Meyers' proposals in the US. Two different arguments may be invoked in support of this strategy. One is that Gornick and Meyers may be unduly optimistic concerning the scope for changing men's behavior through social engineering. The most radical dual-caregiver policy experiment attempted in Sweden—the introduction of earmarked paternal leave for men—has not succeeded in significantly reducing women's maternal responsibilities, and has also run into serious political limits.[12] A less controversial justification for regarding Sweden as a valid counterfactual is that, even though dual-earning/dual-caregiving is the ideal embraced by Gornick and Meyers, their work can also be read as a plea to American policymakers to emulate enlightened Nordic policies. My claim is that this would run counter to the interests of women with the highest potential labor-market attainments.

A growing literature on the effects of family policies, especially in Scandinavia, suggests that measures that facilitate women's employment also exacerbate occupational sex segregation and widen the gender wage gap.[13] However, in this respect there may be an important difference between the two policy instruments on which this paper focuses. As Estevez-Abe has pointed out,

> Statutory leaves and public childcare provision are both intended to promote women's employment. They nonetheless differ on a dimension that is critical for women's human capital development: paid leaves *increase* women's time off work, and extensive childcare provision *reduces* it. (Estevez-Abe, 2005; emphasis added)

Accordingly, provided that it is in synch with parents' work schedules, Estevez-Abe and others consider public child care to be a gender-neutral policy so far as the labor market is concerned. This is not the case for reconciliation policies that free mothers from work obligations in order to take care of newborn children and meet other family needs. Arrangements that make it easier for them to interrupt their work more frequently than men discourage employers from hiring women. In turn, this discourages women from preparing themselves for careers in which they face strong competition from men.

The purpose of the Sweden–US comparison which follows is not, however, simply to reiterate that developed work–family reconciliation policies have perverse unintended consequences for women's attainments. Instead, my argument centers once again on class differences. Specifically, I claim that state interventions considered to be mother-friendly have deleterious consequences for the labor-market attainments of relatively higher-class women, while benefiting relatively lower-class women. Consequently, the implicit class conflict between more and less advantaged women, which the previous section identified in relation to their interests as consumers of child-care services, also applies to their interests as employees. The remainder of this section seeks to make this case, first by identifying the causal mechanisms involved, and then by comparing actual outcomes in the US and Sweden to see whether they are consistent with theoretical expectations.

When the state intervenes to ease conflicts between women's roles at home and work, this makes it possible for them to avoid career tracks which strain their obligations as wives and mothers. The result is that women effectively self-select into lower-paying jobs (Hansen 1995). In contrast, when women lack the cushioning provided by reconciliation policies (including child care) they come under pressure to adjust their traditional household responsibilities to employer and career demands. In the American context, this adjustment is most readily made by purchasing private child-minding and housework services and outsourcing other domestic tasks. The critical point here is that, for both economic and cultural reasons, the likelihood of such adjustments increases as we go up the class ladder. In contrast, in the Scandinavian context women with a relatively high earnings potential have difficulty purchasing market-based services as substitutes for their unpaid work in the home.[14] The reason is that the Nordic social democracies have been leaders in social protection (decommodification) as well as family policy (defamilialization), and this has impeded the development of a low-wage private service sector (Esping-Andersen 1999). Indeed, despite a rising tide of immigration, Swedish conditions are almost the mirror image of those in the US, where a largely unregulated and non-union labor market coexists with a sizable supply of socially and politically marginal labor (immigrants and minorities).

At the same time, family policy in Sweden has mainly sought to steer a middle way between gender traditionalism and full-blown defamilialization (Lewis and Astrom, 1991; Nyberg, 2004). The limits are primarily felt by women in higher class positions. Public child care cannot meet the needs of those required to work outside standard hours. Mothers are expected and assisted to absent themselves from work when family members are sick or otherwise temporarily in need of care. Parental leave preserves new mothers' jobs and replaces their incomes, but at the cost of missed wage increases and promotions for professional women.[15]

In addition to the effects of work–family reconciliation measures on employer and employee calculations, another factor integral to the Scandinavian welfare state model is the extensive role of the welfare state as an employer (Esping-Andersen, 1990; Kolberg, 1991). In liberal political economies women are concentrated in private-sector services, while in the social-democratic regimes they specialize in providing public social services. Socialization of child care—and its cousin, unacknowledged by Gornick and Meyers: socialized elder care—adds considerably to the public-sector workforce in Scandinavia. This workforce tends to be composed mainly of women, partly as a result of the sex-typing of care occupations, but also because of the public sector's relative friendliness to mothers (Rein, 1985; Kolberg and Esping-Andersen, 1993). There is actually a double payoff for women with low earnings potential. Not only are they provided with jobs that ease work–family conflicts which might otherwise have made it uneconomic for them to work; they also suffer less severely from low pay and gender discrimination in the public than the private sector (Robson, Dex, Wilkinson and Cortes, 1999). Governments are large, law-abiding and politically sensitive employers. The public sector tends to be unionized, and its wages are usually determined in a centralized fashion and administered bureaucratically. The result is a comparatively high wage floor and compressed wage differentials, benefiting women in low-skilled care services like minding children and the elderly.

An additional implication of public-sector conditions, however, is that earnings ceilings tend to be lower than in the private sector. Consistent with this, a seven-country study by Gornick and Jacobs found that the public-sector wage premium declines as income rises (Gornick and Jacobs, 1998: Table 3). In principle this affects both men and women, but the implications depend on the extent to which the sectoral boundary is gendered. Where there is a large public social-service sector, as in Sweden, this has supply-side effects that are similar to reconciliation policies. Women—even those with high potential occupational and earnings attainments—are encouraged to opt for working conditions convenient to mothers. Consequently, extended public sectors employ the majority of women working in managerial and professional occupations. Unaffected by similar considerations, men in these occupations flock to the better-paying heights of the private sector, where it is possible to extract handsome "rents." (Hansen, 1997; Rice, 1999: 25). Once more, the very same conditions that benefit women with lesser skills and in lower-class occupations also constrain the likelihood of high-end women competing for the most powerful and lucrative positions.

Not only women workers but also their actual and potential employers are influenced by the family-policy environment. Child-care services, joint taxation, and other incentives that should be transparent to employers encourage Swedish women to return to work after giving birth. But this adjustment is also accomplished with the help of arrangements like maternal leave and part-time employment, which may be more problematic for women's careers. Employers can be expected to practice statistical discrimination against women in anticipation of their collective rights to shorter hours and discontinuous employment

(Persson and Jonung, 1998). To the extent that employer discrimination is based on a rational–economic calculus, it should be most severe in relation to jobs that require the most expertise and responsibility and offer the highest pay. Here we can expect to find the greatest reluctance to hire women, or alternatively a tendency for employers to compensate themselves by paying women less than men. Following this logic, Albrecht and her colleagues have argued that it is probably because family policy weakens the intensity of women's work activity that the gender wage gap in Sweden increases throughout the wage distribution and is widest at the top (Albrecht, Bjorklund and Vroman, 2003).

An additional approach to understanding discrimination against women by cost-conscious employers has been suggested in the literature on varieties of capitalism. Employer sensitivity is said to be greatest in "coordinated" economies, where employers rely heavily on skills and methods of training that are specific to a particular firm or industry. Women's lesser commitment to employment continuity makes them especially unattractive to firms anxious to recoup their investments in specific skills training and fearful of losing employees who are hard to replace (Estevez-Abe, Iversen and Soskice, 2001). Modifying this expectation from a class perspective, it can be argued that the risks attached to skill *specificity* should be greatest in relation to employees with the highest skill *level* (Mandel and Shalev, forthcoming). If this is true, Sweden's skills regime may compound the problem of blocked mobility for higher-class women, above and beyond the effects of its family-policy regime. In that case, part of the gap between Sweden and the US in women's attainments in private-sector employment may derive from Sweden's specific-skills regime, rather than from the unintended consequences of family policies. I do not believe this is a serious problem, however, since the skill requirements for managers and professionals (where blocked mobility is greatest) are likely to be quite similar across different economies.[16]

To sum up: the effects of both reconciliation policies and the role of the public care services as an employer of women are "classed." Due to mechanisms of self-selection by female workers and statistical discrimination by employers, policies that make it easier for women to combine household responsibilities with paid employment can be expected to have largely benign effects on the careers of lower-class women, while indirectly hampering the occupational and earnings mobility of higher-class women. In the Swedish welfare model, social rights for mothers go hand in hand with extensive public social services that are partly the result of the state's defamilialization of child and elder care. The state as an employer tends to pay lower-class workers more generously and higher-class workers less generously than private employers. It follows that Gornick and Meyers' proposal for families' care needs to be serviced by the state, and some of the reconciliation policies that they advocate, would most probably undermine the labor market attainments of higher-class women if they were introduced in the US.

I now present selected empirical data that verifies that the occupational and wage attainments of women in the US and Sweden are conditional on class position. The results are consistent with my claim that, under Swedish conditions, American women in higher classes would likely be worse off, and in lower classes better off. Rather than comparing the entire class structure, the analysis is based on two occupational classes—managers at the top, and "menial services workers" at the bottom. The latter category has been described as the postindustrial working class, encompassing unskilled and semiskilled work in sales, care work, cleaning, food services, and entertainment (Esping-Andersen, 1993). The selection of only two class categories was partly dictated by the need to ensure cross-national comparability, but it also has a theoretical rationale. These two classes represent different patterns of women's labor market integration, as well as different poles of the contemporary class structure. The first is the home ground of the glass ceiling, while the second encompasses the lower reaches of the feminized service sector.

The first thing we learn from Table 12.1 is that there is a substantial difference in class structure between the two countries. For the age group considered here (25–55), the managerial class is twice as large in the US as in Sweden. At the same time, reflecting the magnitude of the paid caregiving sector, the menial services class is considerably larger in Sweden.[17] Women have indeed been notably successful in competing with men for jobs in America's ample managerial class.[18] Not only is the proportion of managers who are women lower in Sweden, but far more of them (nearly half) owe their positions to the public sector. When the hourly earnings of managers are divided into tertiles (thirds), women in both countries are much more likely to be found at the bottom than the top—an indication of the glass ceiling effect. However, women's crowding at the bottom of the managerial wage structure and their exclusion from the top are both significantly lower in the US. These findings support my expectation that advantaged women in Sweden would have more difficulty competing with men for high-class and highly paid positions. The public sector eases this difficulty in relation to occupational attainment, but not in relation to wage attainment. Swedish women managers who work in the private

Table 12.1

Comparison of two occupational classes in Sweden and the US

	Managers		Menial service workers	
	USA	Sweden	USA	Sweden
Class as percent of all employees	10	5	10	16
% of class who are women	43	35	71	81
% of top wage tertile who are women	22	15	28	33
% of bottom wage tertile who are women	43	52	38	33
Wage differential within class (tertile ratio)	2.6	2.3	3.1	1.3
Women only:				
% in public sector	17	46	13	71
Public–private differential (in percentiles)	0	-10	+6	+7

Notes: Author's calculations from 2001 CPS (US) and 2000 LNU (Sweden). Wage-earners aged 25–55 only. Wage calculations based on gross hourly earnings. Effective sample size for US > 4,000; for Sweden, n=119 managers and 362 menials. (For further details see Mandel and Shalev 2006.)

sector earn a lot more than their public-sector counterparts (10 percentiles, in terms of the overall earnings structure).

Turning to the menial services class, as expected it is highly feminized in both countries.[19] However, judging by their wages, the economic position of working-class women in the services differs dramatically between the two countries. Whereas in Sweden they are distributed equally between the three wage tertiles of their class, in the US they are a lot more likely to be found in the bottom tertile than the top. The effects of this difference are amplified by the massive wage differential between high- and low-earning menial services workers in the US—more than 3-to-1, compared to near-equality in Sweden. Moreover, inequality is far milder not only within but also between classes in Sweden.[20] It is reasonable to infer that many of these positive outcomes for Swedish women in menial occupations are the result of their high concentration in the public sector. Table 12.1 shows that, in both countries, public employment enhances women's earnings in the menial-services class. However, because of private-sector domination, relatively few American women benefit from this sectoral effect.

Clearly, many of the advantages enjoyed by lower-class women and barriers to the attainments of higher-class women in Sweden derive from wage-setting institutions and social policies that promote class equality and earnings compression, rather than from work–family policies. However, by measuring women's representation in both the class and intra-class hierarchies, I have sought to isolate gender inequality per se from the effects of the underlying wage structure.[21] The results suggest that Swedish women have a harder time entering elite positions and are hemmed in by a lower glass ceiling, especially in the public sector. In contrast, their lower-class compatriots in the services enjoy intra-class gender equality, and most of them benefit from a sizable bonus by dint of working for local or central government. Neither of these conditions apply to American women in the menial service class. It seems plausible that these systematic differences are related to the unintended effects of family policies on the incentives facing women and private-sector employers, as well as to the role of the public sector in paying care-workers to perform work that would otherwise be the domestic responsibility of mothers.

CONCLUSIONS

In spite of continuing asymmetry in the gender division of paid labor, working women in the US now occupy diverse occupational-class positions, and they are also sharply divided by education and income. While they are largely unacknowledged by Gornick and Meyers, work–family politics are infused by these class divisions, which pose severe obstacles to the realization of a dual-earner/dual-caregiver gender order. It is unquestionably true that lower-class women would benefit enormously from free public child care, paid maternity leave and a proliferation of decent low-skilled service jobs in the public sector. Nevertheless, a significant minority of them are committed to a moral economy that favors traditional gender roles. In contrast, even though the egalitarian worldviews of economically advantaged women are well aligned with the Gornick–Meyers proposals, many of these women find the prevailing dual-earner/private-caregiver system manageable, and they are supported both by government tax subsidies and employer initiatives based on the "business case" for work–family reconciliation.

Progressive European policies that socialize child care and underwrite maternal leave would be opposed to the class interests of women who find private nannies and high-quality child care affordable.

These circumstances raise three issues that I address in this concluding section. First, assuming that there really are class differences in the moral economy of gender, why should Gornick and Meyers care? Second, Gornick and Meyers are well aware of prevailing class inequalities in child care, but if anything they interpret this as an asset rather than a liability for the political feasibility of their reforms. Why do I believe they are mistaken? Finally, it may be true that, if Swedish-type family policy and the enlarged public sector that accompanies it were imported into the US, this would dampen the mobility prospects of higher-class women. But are these women aware of the alleged danger and actively conspiring against policy change?

Class and moral economy

Gornick and Meyers seek to transcend traditional work–family reconciliation measures by packaging them with more radical policies aimed at equalizing the domestic division of labor. The findings presented in the first section of this chapter suggest that traditional policies may represent the upper limit of what many lower-class women would support. Indeed, they may well prefer even more conservative policies, such as paying mothers to care for their own children or supporting a "one-and-a-half earner" model. Consequently, it cannot be assumed that the women most in need of the proposed reforms would react with enthusiasm if they appeared on the political agenda.

Gornick and Meyers downplay this apparent contradiction. They focus instead on the injustice of current policies toward less affluent families, and strive to legitimize their reform proposals by emphasizing how much they would improve the welfare of needy mothers and their children. But do Gornick and Meyers have the right to ignore conflicts between their program and what lower-class women may actually want?[22] Their own justification seems to be that the opinions held by these women are essentially adaptations to constrained opportunity structures. Socialization along traditionalist lines, pressure from male partners, and limited career opportunities indeed make it understandable why women of humble origins may be more predisposed toward the traditional household division of labor and find little attraction in paid work. I have already suggested, however, that while moral economy and political economy are mutually selecting and reinforcing, they are also at least partly autonomous. As Sayer puts it, "normative rationales ... matter greatly to actors, as they are implicated in their commitments, identities and ways of life." (Sayer, 2004: 3) Moreover, as Uhlmann has forcefully argued, when sociologists explain away the alien (to them) norms of working-class families as responses to disadvantage, they may be guilty of imposing their own habitude and worldview (Uhlmann, 2004).

Class and child care

For Gornick and Meyers, the regressive distributional consequences of market-based child care constitute a glaring inequity that policy should address by assuring quality care for all children and spreading the costs widely. They gloss over the conflictual implication that the proposed solution would redistribute income at the expense of more affluent families, and they fail to address the possibility that advantaged parents have an interest in investing in superior child care and early education as one means of reproducing their class advantage in the next generation. Nevertheless, in muted recognition of opposing class interests Gornick and Meyers suggest emulating the universal system of Social Security for the elderly, which enjoys broad public support. In the spirit of Korpi and Palme (1998), they argue that if all classes were to benefit from a public system, solidarity would override parents' narrow calculations of whether they personally stood to lose or profit (Gornick and Meyers, 2003: 270). However, while this might be true once a universal public system is in place, it is unclear how it would motivate higher-class consent to the elimination of the present private system.

Gornick and Meyers offer two additional arguments that seemingly reinforce their expectation of a broad cross-class coalition behind socialized child care. First, following Crompton, they portray the low-paid female labor force in private child care as exacerbating the gender pay gap (Gornick and Meyers, 2003: 93). Yet not all women suffer as a result. It is logically the case that the existence of a poorly remunerated group of women has the effect of depressing women's average wage relative to men. However, if our starting point is that both women and men are differentiated by class, then the phenomenon of low-paid nannies primarily signifies unequal class relations among women (McDowell, 2006).

Gornick and Meyers also suggest that a public system of child care would benefit nearly all families because only "the most privileged" can afford private care; but it is arguable where the affordability line should be drawn. From a comparative perspective, private child care ought to be relatively inexpensive in the US. The reasons include (a) non-regulation of child-care workers' training and qualifications; (b) immigration policies that permit the inflow of caregivers from low-wage countries; (c) a conspicuous lack of direct or indirect state support for raising the wage floor; and (d) tax subsidies that partially offset private expenditure on child care (Morgan, 2005). Orloff claims that even "slightly better-off households" are able to afford private care, which is consistent with the evidence presented earlier in this paper (Orloff, 2006). Still, insofar as middle-income professional women find that high-quality private child care solutions are a serious drain on their income, they might find common cause with lower-class women in fighting for socialized child care. Equally possible, however—and in my view more likely—is that middle-class families experiencing a child-care squeeze will follow the predictions of path-dependency theorists and demand increased tax relief, rather than a radical change in the system.

Class and the labor market

Work–family reconciliation policies, and the expansion of sheltered public-sector employment which they generate, may be essential to enable "weak" women to combine motherhood with paid work. But they undermine the potential labor market attainments of "strong" women by crowding them into feminized enclaves and fueling statistical discrimination by private employers. In developing counterfactual predictions for the US based on the Swedish experience, I have already conceded that not all of the relative disadvantage of Swedish women at the higher end of the class structure can reasonably be attributed to the ripple effects of family policies. Some may be due to the different skill regimes that characterize the two countries, which may have made private sector firms in the US more amenable to recruiting women into high-level positions. Another difference between the two countries, which has arguably worked in favor of American women's entry into managerial and professional jobs, is the role of legislation and state regulation in promoting equal opportunity for women (Orloff, 2006; Zippel, this volume). Chang argues that North American states have prioritized this type of "equal access intervention" over the "substantive" interventions (reconciliation policies) favored in Scandinavia, and that this has been consequential for the rate of sex desegregation of elite occupations (Chang, 2000).

Notwithstanding these and other potentially confounding features of the US context, it is fair to conclude that adoption of the Swedish family-policy regime would be at odds with the interests of advantaged women. Inversely, the benefits of Swedish policies for disadvantaged women would clearly be amplified by the weakness of lower-class workers in America's highly commodified labor market. Public child care, rights to parental leave and other forms of paid time off for care, and the transfer of child and other care work to the public sector, would greatly curtail the current negative interplay between lower-class women's dual vulnerabilities as mothers and workers. In turn, shrinkage of the female and low-wage segment of the workforce would undermine the market-based modes of defamilialization that are currently so important for easing the work–family conflicts that face higher-class women.

Are members of the latter group aware of and concerned by these potential threats to their relatively privileged position? Perhaps not, but their class interests nevertheless form a resilient barrier to the realization of Gornick and Meyers' vision. The reason is that both higher-class women and the pressure groups which they dominate favor liberal feminism, and its sibling—liberal political economy (White, 2006).[23] They do so for good reason: both resonate well with their life experiences. It is true that, as critics point out, the status quo imposes tough choices between motherhood and career, and makes heavy demands on the time and energy of those who opt for both. Nevertheless, middle- and upper-class women are able to navigate the status quo by purchasing marketized care and housekeeping services, sometimes with government subsidies; by utilizing supports for mothers' employment offered by self-interested employers; by taking advantage of America's higher education system (where money speaks much louder than gender); and by benefiting from institutionalized state and corporate guarantees of equal opportunity at work. In short, advantaged women have good reason to preemptively forfeit social rights earmarked for mothers, and to avoid compromising on lower-paid but mother-friendly public-sector jobs. Note, however, that this probably applies more to white than to black women. College-educated African-American women are far more reliant on the public sector for opportunities to enter managerial and professional occupations, which suggests that whiteness may be an implicit condition for women to pursue the market-based route to emulating male success (Collins, 1983; Hsieh and Winslow, 2006; Newsome and Dodoo, 2002).

The interests of advantaged women will not necessarily and always prevent at least some of them from joining coalitions with women from less advantaged classes in support of family-policy reform—that depends to a great extent on politics. But comparative studies suggest that the political opportunity structure in the US is relatively unfavorable to such a scenario (Katzenstein and Mueller, 1987; Korpi, 2000; Mazur, 2003). In Scandinavia, the combination of powerful unions, governing social-democratic parties and strong states encouraged the development of cross-class coalitions of women. Solidaristic trade unions integrated their growing female membership by "adopting policies that benefited women in the same way as they benefited all low-paid workers," (Ruggie, 1987: 248) and also by acting as trailblazers, introducing gender-equality policies through collective agreements before they ever reached the legislative arena (Whitehouse, 1992). In parallel, a common interest in big government developed between social-democratic governments and women employed as social service workers (Huber and Stephens, 2000). In the US, by contrast, decentralization and fragmentation of both organized labor and the state have favored an "individualistic legalistic approach" that has yielded significant victories, but primarily "at the upper end of the occupational spectrum." (O'Connor, Orloff, and Shaver, 1999: 104)

Class interests and the character of class and gender politics stand in the way of moving the US toward a radically different set of employment and family policies. True, political economy is not everything. The current literature acknowledges a much greater role than was formerly conceded for new ideas in bringing about radical changes in policy (Blyth, 1997), and this is of course the motivation for Gornick and Meyers' tireless promotion of their utopian vision. Nevertheless, they have also taken on the challenge of infusing political plausibility into their program. *Families That Work* cogently defends this project against a variety of obstacles which are often said to prevent European-style policies being adopted in the US, including labor-market structure, political institutions and culture, demography, and diversity. The factor which is conspicuously missing from this list, although it is connected to several of those that do receive attention, is the difficulty of constructing a cross-class coalition—first and foremost of women—in favor of their proposals. I have sought to argue that this constitutes a fundamental barrier to the advent of gender-egalitarian policy activism in the US.

NOTES

1 Throughout this chapter I use the terms "higher-class" and "lower-class" in a relative fashion, not as proper names for specific classes. My concern is with broad differences in economic advantage linked to either personal resources (such as education) or positions in production (occupations). In any event, data considerations make it necessary to take an eclectic approach to defining classes for empirical purposes.

2 For a recent contribution and references, see Sjoberg (2004).

3 Svallfors (2006: 112). Svallfors's index of support for women's paid employment includes questions that tap not only whether it is seen as legitimate in terms of the division of labor with their husbands, but also whether or not it is perceived as detrimental to their families and children.

4 With age and sex controlled, class gaps were lower by roughly half in Britain and the US than in Germany and Sweden. Svallfors (2006: Table 6.2).

5 For a valuable analysis of GSS data and references to further literature, see Badgett, Davidson, and Folbre (2002).

6 Other studies have confirmed the importance of education, but without testing the effect of occupational class: Blee and Tickamyer (1995); Bolzendahl and Myers (2004).

7 Managerial and professional, 22 percent; semi-professional, 28 percent; routine non-manual, 27 percent; working class, 24 percent.

8 For example, Crompton and Fiona Harris (1998); McRae (2003).

9 The results refer to the primary care arrangement only, and the analysis of income was limited to two-parent families. Parallel findings for the care of older children (elementary-school age) reveal only small effects of income on the broad types of care utilized. See Capizzano, Tout and Adams (2000: Table 2).

10 Note, however, that Durfee and Meyers qualify their findings by pointing out that New York provides unusually extensive child-care supports.

11 On the basis of the Urban Institute surveys cited earlier, Gornick and Meyers show that for middle- and high-income families the burden of child-care costs in the US is fairly similar to France, except that a higher proportion of families have out-of-pocket expenses. However, they do not consider the effects of France's extensive public provision on taxation. Gornick and Meyers (2003: Table 7.5)

12 For a recent evaluation of the Swedish experiment, see Nyberg (2004). Indications of the political barriers to extending the current system within Sweden or exporting it to other Scandinavian countries are provided by Ferrarini (2007); Hiilamo and Kangas (2005).

13 Examples are Hakim (2000); Mandel and Semyonov (2005) and Mandel and Semyonov (2006).

14 Precisely for this reason, the center-right coalition which has held office in Sweden since 2006 favors tax rebates for families that hire private household help.

15 Online at http://www.jusek.se, cited in Nyberg (2004: 19).

16 VOC theory focuses on the overall direction favored by systems of skill formation (general vs. specific skills), but typical human capital requirements also vary between different levels of the job structure irrespective of the skills regime. In all varieties of capitalism, requirements for on-the-job training (OJT) are especially stringent in the higher (professional and managerial)

class, which comprises occupations characterized by a high degree of *task specificity*. See Polavieja (2005) Even in the US, a liberal economy in which employers are said to rely predominantly on general skills, it has been shown that women's limited participation in OJT explains much of their exclusion from highly paid jobs. See Devey and Skaggs (2002).

17 Had this analysis included workers under twenty-five, the US menial services class would have grown due to the many young people employed in the "food and fun" sector.

18 The present estimate of the difference between the two countries may be conservative. Using somewhat different procedures, including controlling at the individual level for cross-national differences in workforce composition, Mandel and Semyonov find that women's probability of having a managerial occupation compared with men's is more than 80 percent greater in the US than in Sweden. Mandel and Semyonov (2006: Figure 6).

19 Nevertheless, at 71 percent the proportion of menial service workers who are women is lower in the US than in the eleven other countries analyzed by Mandel and myself. One reason for this is the role of minority men. Non-white men are three times more likely than white men to work as menial service workers in the US. Mandel and Shalev (2006).

20 A calculation not reported in Table 12.2 indicates that, at the median, the ratio between the wages of managers and menials is 2.2 in the US and 1.6 in Sweden.

21 A similar analytical strategy, inspired by the work of Blau and Kahn, has been adopted by Gornick, Mandel and Semyonov, and by Mandel and Shalev. Needless to say, gender is to some extent endogenous to both class structure and class inequality. Blau and Kahn (1992); Gornick (1999); Mandel and Semyonov (2005); Mandel and Shalev (2006).

22 This is not the place to enter into the ethical aspects of the problem. Suffice to say that it would not be difficult for advocates of progressive family policy to argue that, for example, the importance of economic autonomy for the well-being of lower-class women justifies such policies even if the beneficiaries do not demand them.

23 From White's account it appears that major women's groups, including the National Organization for Women, have been conscious of the threat that protective labor legislation and differential treatment for women would pose to the upward mobility of more advantaged women, and have consequently opposed measures like paid maternity leave.

REFERENCES

Albrecht, J., A. Bjorklund, and S. Vroman, 2003, "Is There a Glass Ceiling in Sweden?" *Journal of Labor Economics* 21 (1): 145–77.

Badgett, M. V. Lee, Pamela Davidson, and Nancy Folbre, 2002, "Breadwinner Dad, Homemaker Mom: An Interdisciplinary Analysis of Changing Gender Norms in the United States, 1977–1998," unpublished paper, Department of Economics, University of Massachusetts Amherst.

Blau, Francine D. and Lawrence M. Kahn, 1992, "The Gender Earnings Gap—Learning from International Comparisons," *American Economic Review* 82 (2): 533–38.

Blee, K. M. and A. R. Tickamyer, 1995, "Racial Differences in Men's Attitudes About Women's Gender Roles," *Journal of Marriage and the Family* 57 (1): 21–30.

Blyth, Mark M., 1997, "'Any More Bright Ideas?' the Ideational Turn of Comparative Political Economy," *Comparative Politics* 29 (2): 229–50.

Bolzendahl, C. I. and D. J. Myers, 2004, "Feminist Attitudes and Support for Gender Equality: Opinion Change in Women and Men, 1974–1998," *Social Forces* 83 (2): 759–89.

Browne, Irene and Joya Misra, 2003, "The Intersection of Gender and Race in the Labor Market," *Annual Review of Sociology* 29: 487–513.

Capizzano, Jeffrey, Kathryn Tout, and Gina Adams, 2000, *Child Care Patterns of School-Age Children with Employed Mothers*, Washington DC: The Urban Institute.

Chang, Mariko-Lin, 2000, "The Evolution of Sex Segregation Regimes," *American Journal of Sociology* 105 (6): 1,658–701.

Collins, S. M., 1983, "The Making of the Black Middle Class," *Social Problems* 30 (4): 369–82.

Crompton, Rosemary and Fiona Harris, 1998, "A Reply to Hakim," *British Journal of Sociology* 49 (1): 144–49.

Devey, D. Tomaskovic and S. Skaggs, 2002, "Sex Segregation, Labor Process Organization, and Gender Earnings Inequality," *American Journal of Sociology* 108 (1): 102–28.

Durfee, A. and M. K. Meyers, 2006, "Who Gets What from Government? Distributional Consequences of Child-Care Assistance Policies," *Journal of Marriage and the Family* 68 (3): 733–48.

Ehrle, Jennifer, Gina Adams, and Kathryn Tout, 2001, *Who's Caring for Our Youngest Children? Child Care Patterns of Infants and Toddlers*, Washington DC: The Urban Institute.

Erikson, Robert, John H. Goldthorpe, and Lucienne Portocarero, 1979, "Intergenerational Class Mobility in Three Western European Societies: England, France and Sweden," *British Journal of Sociology* 33: 1–34.

Esping-Andersen, Gøsta, 1990, *The Three Worlds of Welfare Capitalism*, Cambridge: Polity Press.

Esping-Andersen, Gøsta, 1999, *Social Foundations of Postindustrial Economies*, Oxford: Oxford University Press.

Estevez-Abe, Margarita, 2005, "Gender Bias in Skills and Social Policies: The Varieties of Capitalism Perspective on Sex Segregation," *Social Politics* 12 (2): 180–215; emphasis added.

Estevez-Abe, Margarita, Torben Iversen, and David Soskice, 2001, "Social Protection and the Formation of Skills: A Reinterpretation of the Welfare State," in Peter A. Hall and David W. Soskice, eds, *Varieties of Capitalism: The Institutional Foundations of Comparative Advantage*, Oxford: Oxford University Press.

Ferrarini, Tommy, 2007, "Sweden Towards a New Model of Family Policy?" unpublished paper, Swedish Institute of Social Research.

Giannarelli, Linda, Sarah Adelman, and Stefanie Schmidt, 2003, *Getting Help with Child Care Expenses*, Washington DC: Urban Institute.

Glenn, Evelyn Nakano, 1985, "Racial Ethnic Women's Labor: The Intersection of Race, Gender and Class Oppression," *Review of Radical Political Economics* 17 (3): 86–108.

Gornick, Janet C. and Jerry A. Jacobs, 1998, "Gender, the Welfare State, and Public Employment: A Comparative Study of Seven Industrialized Countries," *American Sociological Review* 63 (5).

Gornick, Janet C. and Marcia K. Meyers, 2003, *Families That Work: Policies for Reconciling Parenthood and Employment*, New York: Russell Sage Foundation; and 2008, "Creating Gender Egalitarian Societies: An Agenda for Reform," *Politics & Society* 36 (3): 313–49.

Gornick, Janet C., 1999, "Gender Equality in the Labor Market," in Diane Sainsbury, ed., *Gender and Welfare State Regimes*, Oxford: Oxford University Press.

Hacker, Jacob S. and Paul Pierson, 2005, *Off Center: The Republican Revolution and the Erosion of American Democracy*, New Haven: Yale University Press.

Hakim, Catherine, 2000, *Work–Lifestyle Choices in the 21st Century: Preference Theory*, New York: Oxford University Press.

Hansen, Marianne-Nordli, 1995, "The Vicious Circle of the Welfare State? Women's Labor Market Situation in Norway and Great Britain," *Comparative Social Research* 15: 1–34.

Hansen, Marianne-Nordli, 1997, "The Scandinavian Welfare State Model: The Impact of the Public Sector on Segregation and Gender Equality," *Work, Employment and Society* 11 (1): 83–99.

Harris, R. J. and J. M. Firestone, 1998, "Changes in Predictors of Gender Role Ideologies among Women: A Multivariate Analysis," *Sex Roles* 38 (3): 239–52.

Hiilamo, Heikki and Olli Kangas, 2005, "Trap for Women or Freedom to Choose? Political Frames in the Making of Child Home Care Allowances in Finland and Sweden," paper presented at the annual conference of the Research Committee on Poverty, Social Welfare and Social Policy (RC19), Northwestern University, September 8–10.

Hsieh, C. and E. Winslow, 2006, "Gender Representation in the Federal Workforce: A Comparison among Groups," *Review of Public Personnel Administration* 26 (3): 276.

Huber, E. and J. D. Stephens, 2000, "Partisan Governance, Women's Employment, and the Social Democratic Service State," *American Sociological Review* 65 (3): 323–42.

Johnson, Julia Overturf and Barbara Downs, 2005, *Maternity Leave and Employment Patterns of First-Time Mothers: 1961–2000*, US Census Bureau, Current Population Reports.

Katzenstein, Mary Fainsod and Carol McClurg Mueller, 1987, *The Women's Movements of the United States and Western Europe: Consciousness, Political Opportunity, and Public Policy*, Women in the Political Economy, Philadelphia: Temple University Press.

Kolberg, Jon Eivend and Gøsta Esping-Andersen, 1993, "Welfare States and Employment Regimes," in Jon Eivend Kolberg, ed., *Between Work and Social Citizenship*, Armonk NY: M. E. Sharpe.

Kolberg, Jon Eivend, ed., 1991, *The Welfare State as Employer*, Armonk NY: M. E. Sharpe.

Korpi, W., and J. Palme. 1998, "The Paradox of Redistribution and Strategies of Equality: Welfare State Institutions, Inequality, and Poverty in the Western Countries," *American Sociological Review* 63 (5): 661–87.

Korpi, Walter, 2000, "Faces of Inequality: Gender, Class, and Patterns of Inequalities in Different Types of Welfare States," *Social Politics* 7 (2): 127–91.

Lewis, Jane and Gertrude Astrom, 1991, "Equality, Difference, and State Welfare: Labor Market and Family Policies in Sweden," *Feminist Studies* 18 (1): 59–87.

Mandel, Hadas and Michael Shalev, 2006, "A Class Perspective on Gender Inequality: How Welfare States Shape the Gender Pay Gap," Working Paper no. 433, Luxembourg Income Study.

Mandel, Hadas and Michael Shalev, forthcoming, "Gender, Class and the Varieties of Capitalism Perspective," *Social Politics*.

Mandel, Hadas and Moshe Semyonov, 2005, "Family Policies, Wage Structures, and Gender Gaps: Sources of Earnings Inequality in 20 Countries," *American Sociological Review* 70 (6): 949–67.

Mandel, Hadas and Moshe Semyonov, 2006, "A Welfare State Paradox: State Intervention and Women's Employment Opportunities in 22 Countries," *American Journal of Sociology* 111 (6): 1,910–49.

Mazur, Amy G., 2003, "Drawing Comparative Lessons from France and Germany," *Review of Policy Research* 20 (3): 493–523.

McCall, Leslie, 2005, "The Complexity of Intersectionality," *Signs* 30 (3): 1,771–99.

McDowell, Linda, 2006, "Reconfigurations of Gender and Class Relations: Class Differences, Class Condescension and the Changing Place of Class Relations," *Antipode* 38 (4): 825–50.

McRae, S., 2003, "Constraints and Choices in Mothers' Employment Careers: A Consideration of Hakim's Preference Theory," *British Journal of Sociology* 54 (3): 317–38.

Meyers, Marcia, Dan Rosenbaum, Christopher Ruhm, and Jane Waldfogel, 2004, "Inequality in Early Childhood Education and Care: What Do We Know?" unpublished paper, Social Inequality Program, Russell Sage Foundation.

Morgan, Kimberly J., 2005, "The 'Production' of Child Care: How Labor Markets Shape Social Policy and Vice Versa," *Social Politics* 12 (2): 243–63.

Newsome, Y. D. and F. N. A. Dodoo, 2002, "Reversal of Fortune—Explaining the Decline in Black Women's Earnings," *Gender & Society* 16 (4): 442–64.

Nyberg, Anita, 2004, *Parental Leave, Public Childcare and the Dual Earner/Dual Carer Model in Sweden*, discussion paper presented at the Swedish Peer Review of the European Employment Strategy, Stockholm, 19–20 April.

O'Connor, Julia S., Ann Shola Orloff, and Sheila Shaver, 1999, *States, Markets, Families: Gender, Liberalism, and Social Policy in Australia, Canada, Great Britain, and the United States*, Cambridge, UK: Cambridge University Press: 104.

Orloff, Ann Shola, 2006, "From Maternalism to 'Employment for All': State Policies to Promote Women's Employment across the Affluent Democracies" in Jonah D. Levy, ed., *The State after Statism: New State Activities in the Age of Liberalization*, Cambridge, Mass.: Harvard University Press: 230–70.

Persson, Inga and Christina Jonung, eds., 1998, *Women's Work and Wages*, London: Routledge.

Polavieja, J. G., 2005 "Task Specificity and the Gender Wage Gap—Theoretical Considerations and Empirical Analysis of the Spanish Survey on Wage Structure," *European Sociological Review* 21 (2): 165–81.

Rein, Martin, 1985, "The Social Welfare Labor Market," in S. N. Eisenstadt and Ora Ahimeir, eds, *The Welfare State and Its Aftermath*, London: Croom Helm.

Rice, Patricia, 1999, *Gender Earnings Differentials: The European Experience*, World Bank Policy Research Report on Gender and Development, Working Paper no. 8: 25.

Robson, P., P., S. Dex, F. Wilkinson, and O. S. Cortes, 1999, "Low Pay, Labour Market Institutions, Gender and Part-Time Work: Cross-National Comparisons," *European Journal of Industrial Relations* 5 (2): 187–207.

Ruggie, Mary, 1987, "Workers' Movements and Women's Interests: The Impact of Labor–State Relations in Britain and Sweden," in Mary Fainsod Katzenstein and Carol McClurg Mueller, eds, *The Women's Movements of the United States and Western Europe: Consciousness, Political Opportunity, and Public Policy*, Philadelphia: Temple University Press: 248.

Sayer, Andrew, 2004, "Moral Economy," unpublished paper, Department of Sociology, Lancaster University.

Shlay, Anne B., Marsha Weinraub, Michelle Harmon, and Henry Tran, 2004, "Barriers to Subsidies: Why Low-Income Families Do Not Use Child Care Subsidies," *Social Science Research* 33 (1): 134–57.

Sjoberg, Ola, 2004, "The Role of Family Policy Institutions in Explaining Gender-Role Attitudes: A Comparative Multilevel Analysis of Thirteen Industrialized Countries," *Journal of European Social Policy* 14 (2): 107–23.

Svallfors, Stefan, 2006, *The Moral Economy of Class: Class and Attitudes in Comparative Perspective*, Stanford, CA: Stanford University Press.

Uhlmann, Allon J., 2004, "The Sociology of Subjectivity, and the Subjectivity of Sociologists: A Critique of the Sociology of Gender in the Australian Family," *British Journal of Sociology* 55 (1): 79–97.

White, Linda A., 2006, "Institutions, Constitutions, Actor Strategies, and Ideas: Explaining Variation in Paid Parental Leave Policies in Canada and the United States," *International Journal of Constitutional Law* 4 (2): 319–46

Whitehouse, Gillian, 1992, "Legislation and Labour Market Gender Inequality: An Analysis of OECD Countries," *Work, Employment and Society* 6 (1): 65–86.

Wright, Erik Olin, 2001, "A Conceptual Menu for Studying the Interconnections of Class and Gender," in Janeen Baxter and Mark Western, eds, *Reconfigurations of Class and Gender*, Stanford, CA: Stanford University Press.

13

An American Road Map? Framing Feminist Goals in a Liberal Landscape*

Myra Marx Ferree

Gornick and Meyers do a fine job of describing the complex problem facing people in modern societies: achieving a balance both between caring and earning in individual and family life and between women and men in life opportunities. But their approach to finding a way to Real Utopia for American families is both familiar and improbable. Familiar because the choice to offer European models for American social policy reaches back into the early twentieth century, as the correspondence between German and US social feminists attests (Sklar et al., 1998). Thinking of gender equality in these terms has also characterized much second-wave feminist writing, with Adams and Winston (1980) being an early and influential example.[1] This framing feels convincing to American social scientists, who often see following the European social model as a sensible route to social justice.

Yet Americans in general and American policy makers in particular do not see "borrowing from Europe" as offering a useful road-map. Gornick and Meyers' approach is improbable because social policy depends on framing, and a frame that does not resonate with local

---

* My thanks to Christine Bose, Lynn Prince Cooke, Nikki Graf, Pamela Herd, Sally Kenney, Cameron Macdonald, Patricia Yancey Martin, and Sylvia Walby for their patient, astute and encouraging comments on earlier drafts of this paper. I also appreciate the thoughtful reading and helpful suggestions made by the other participants in the original Real Utopias conference, my writing group students, my long-standing Women-and-Work group colleagues, and the editors of this volume.

political values will not advance broader transformations. Frames are the "signifying processes" that give policies their meanings and connect them into an overall logic (Adams and Padamsee, 2005). Just as Gornick and Meyers seek to reframe the issues of gender equity and family support so that they are less in conflict with each other, it is important to reframe the debate to locate it within American values and institutions if it is effectively to advance American reforms. As Orloff (1996: 56) argues, Americans believe "access to cash benefits is not always an unmixed blessing," particularly if it reduces citizens to clients and enables intrusive state surveillance.

What makes Gornick and Meyers' amalgamation of policies from different European states seem attractive as a model is that these policies already exist to some degree in Sweden, France, Denmark, and other European countries. But their plausibility in Europe rests on deeply political foundations. With the widening and deepening of the EU, policies from one state are being used to leverage family and gender policy change in other EU member-states (Walby, 1999). This spread of gender-equity policy making is no accident. The European gender-equity regime that is taking shape in the EU reflects the concerted efforts of European women's policy networks, within and outside the separate member states (Walby, 2004). This political outcome, still precarious, is built on existing policy foundations through the mobilization of feminist and other women's civic organizations, academic women's expert groups, femocrats in government, and elected women representatives in the parliament of the EU and of the member states (Zippel, 2006).

This feminist network in Europe has made progress by targeting the limitations of the European social model, which has a long history of protectionist policies for women. If American feminists want to secure comparably effective policy for work–family balance, they will have to try to change a very different system—one that is notable for its lack of social protections not only for mothers but for families and citizens in general. European states have long offered maternalist policy to all families, contributing to the support of children while at the same time cementing the assumption that care for them is mother's work. Because European states still vary enormously in the degree to which work–family balance means helping women balance "their" responsibilities (as in Germany) or encouraging a better balance between women and men in care work and employment (as in Sweden), and because the EU itself has more willingly embraced the former than the latter goal (Stratigaki, 2004), European feminist networks still face significant challenges themselves in building toward Gornick and Meyers' ideal.

But the US must build policy to advance women's equality and family welfare on a very different set of political foundations. Long riven by racialized conflict, US social policy has not embraced either pro-natalist or domestic support goals, and has a low level of protection and support for families in general. This miserly welfare regime situates the US in the bottom ranks for both infant mortality and child poverty (United Nations Demographic Yearbook, 2006). American social welfare policy, never generous, has faced deepening cuts as it has expanded to cover the African-American workers and families who were once defined as ineligible for benefits (Quadagno, 1994). Racialized ethnic conflict was not part of the European welfare state regime that developed after the Second World War. European feminist networks have not yet struggled with the contradictions in using family policy as a means of disciplining and assimilating immigrants—a challenge with which American feminists are familiar (Beisel 2004). For American feminists to make progress toward gender equality in this context, they will need to consider how their own system can be expanded and deepened to help families located differently by race as well as class.

This paper reframes Gornick and Meyers' challenge, setting out to find the spots within the US system of social policy that American feminist networks could target to achieve the basic goals they endorse: more gender equality combined with, rather than at the cost of, more support for care work. A search for effective points of intervention to reach this goal leads to consideration of the Social Security system (more formally known as Old Age and Survivors Insurance or OASI). Although now regarded only as a support system for older Americans, it was originally designed to meet a wider range of family needs. It is also the largest, most universal and arguably the most effective element in the US social welfare system as a whole (Harrington-Meyer and Herd, 2007). But as families and family needs have changed, the Social Security system has become less well adapted to serve even the elderly—especially older women (Herd, 2006; Gonyea and Hooyman, 2005). Additionally, in the US, the separation of child benefits and support for unmarried mothers from the programs for old age and death of a breadwinner allowed the former to be downgraded into miserly means-tested "welfare" programs (Herd, 2005).

The end of the racial exclusivity of "welfare" in the 1960s, as a result of the Civil Rights movement, made the child-support program even more vulnerable to stigma, and the 1970 Supreme Court decision recognizing these benefits as entitlements for all eligible families created pressure to restore local discretion and reinstate moral criteria of "deservingness," which was done in the name of "welfare reform" in 1997 (Quadagno, 1994; Mayer, 2008).

These political foundations imply that American feminists who want to find a route to family-support policy should avoid targeting childbearing itself, with its historically embedded connotations of deserving and undeserving mothers. This does not mean abandoning all hope, but rather moving away from the maternalist foundations on which Europeans have built, and trying to reclaim and redevelop the more universal elements of Old Age and Survivor Insurance (OASI) instead. Rather than expanding maternalism to encompass men in families, as the more progressive elements of the European systems have done, American feminists should expand the concept of "social security" to be more truly inclusive across gender and generational lines.

The risks and opportunities for social reform are, as Gornick and Meyers suggest, particularly acute at this historical moment. Families are struggling, and American social policy seems indifferent. Rather than arguing for a model based on European experience as reformed by feminist challengers there, I suggest that the route to achieving more gender-equitable and less time-stressed families in the US should be grounded in reforming the American system as it currently exists. There are three reasons for taking this approach.

First, social policy is inherently "path-dependent"—that is, what will work in a utopian way in one context will lead in quite another direction in another. Prior policy histories continue to matter in how policy is understood and interpreted. Because the development of social policy is a path-dependent process, a simple "transplant" of policy organs developed in a different context will face rejection by its incompatible "host"—either in the form of resistance to trying the innovation, or in multiple unwanted side effects. Although the path to the goal of greater gender equality leads through the achievement of a more just and livable balance of paid work and family labor for both women and men, for all the reasons that Gornick and Meyers so eloquently lay out, the path-dependency of policy creates obstacles and opportunities that should encourage US challengers to seek a different route to this goal.

The primary obstacle in our path is that much of the infrastructure that Europeans take for granted in managing work and family—such as vacations, sick leave, and limited working weeks—has never been part of the US system, creating the need for a more universalized time-redistributive system here. The American model is family-unfriendly to a degree unimagined in Europe (Orloff, 1996). The chief opportunity offered along our path lies in the greater progress the US has made than have European countries in securing a principle of gender-neutrality and legal remedies for actions that have a disparate negative impact on one gender (Zippel, 2006). Giving up this stronger anti-discrimination regime in favor of an expanded maternalism for women, even with an "affirmative action" component for fathers, would be a step backward for US policy. The EU and its member-states today are struggling with diversity and discrimination, for the most part without the tools that US jurisprudence has developed over the past generation (Walby, 1999).

Second, implementing old as well as achieving new social policies always relies on how they are framed. How policy is interpreted cannot be abstracted from its origins and historical development, but these background factors are never simply fixed and uniform. There are always struggles over policy development; there are aspects of any policy that can be highlighted to make them seem more or less fair in relation to the broad values institutionally anchored in particular policy histories. As Adams and Padamsee (2005) argue, policies not only have material natures, but are symbolic acts that function as signs, and are adopted strategically in order to realize broader goals.

Thus the denial of benefits to poor mothers who are raising children can be framed as a legitimate effort to make them more responsible parents, or as an illegitimate move to deny that childrearing is valuable work. Each of these frames resonates with American culture, but each moves policy in a different direction. And each frame has its advocates and opponents in the contemporary political landscape. Awareness of the different symbolic content of policy in Europe and the US is essential for a feminist project to move toward gender equality and work–family balance for both men and women rather than, however unintentionally, in the opposite direction.

Third, universality is assumed in Europe but contested in the US. Because of the centrality of race to the structure of American citizenship and labor markets, the history of US policy making provides few instances of family benefits that are not means-tested. The universality of the Social Security system, as well as its role as the keystone of American social policy, therefore makes it one of few available starting places to look for paths forward to developing more support for work–family balance and gender-equality (Herd, 2006). While other social policies (relating to school systems, health and safety regulations, public transportation subsidies, and so on) can certainly also be brought into the discussion of making family-friendly policy that will also advance gender equality, I limit this paper to consideration of the Social Security system.

As a bedrock of the social policy system in the US, Social Security is at the center of debates about universal benefits. On the one hand, there is already a substantial literature that outlines reforms for Social Security that would make it more gender-equitable and reduce poverty among older Americans (Gonyea and Hooyman, 2005; Ferber et al., 2006; Favrault and Steurle, 2007; Harrington Meyer and Herd, 2007). On the other hand, Social Security is also under attack from "privatizers" who would prefer even less government protection for families at risk and even less support for workers to leave the labor force. Thus "reform" of Social Security in the next decade is already being actively contested and seems likely to occur in some form.

The shape of the reforms achieved will either be a sign of the US moving symbolically even further away from mitigating the social and economic costs of employment, or a sign that the country is willing to use government policies to respond to the modern family's needs for time and income. Unlike the introduction of a novel European-style system in the US, a reform of Social Security will move the American system on its own path, in either a progressive or regressive direction. It is therefore important to see and to seize the potential for progressive reform and to use the existing system to leverage change in a direction that would foster better work–family balance and greater gender equality, rather than the reverse. Just as European reforms reflect feminist awareness of the legacies of their own models (Stratigaki, 2004; Walby, 2004), American policy reform that is sensitive to the path-dependencies in its own system will find the opportunities to develop its own capacities.

In the next section of the paper, I provide a brief comparison between the usable opportunities in the different social-policy paths that have been followed in Europe and the US. Decommodification in Europe and anti-discrimination policy in the US are part of the institutionalized opportunity structures that shape not only the probability but the meanings of different gender-equity strategies. In the third section, I outline criteria for achieving gender equality and work–family balance in a way consistent with the premises of American social policy. Combining gender with generational equity, emphasizing formal gender neutrality and legal guarantees of non-discrimination, and expanding the universalistic elements of the system are criteria that express and build on the liberal policy foundation of this system.

In the fourth section, I consider some specifics of the Social Security system itself, arguing that reforming its current breadwinner-biased elements would be a path to greater work–family balance. In this section I first outline what Social Security now does, then describe how it could be redesigned to anchor the welfare state in a gender-equitable and family-friendly way. In the conclusion, I argue that such reforms would better meet criteria for addressing family needs across generations and promoting gender equity in the US than a transplanted European system could. But I also stress that no change in one policy sector alone could hope to correct the intersections of class, gender, race and other inequalities that permeate the US social policy system.

PATH-DEPENDENCY AND FAMILY POLICY

Not only do European policy regimes differ among themselves—with liberal, social-democratic or Christian–conservative elements dominating—they also all differ from that of the US, which is by far the most purely "liberal." American policy has remained centered on a commodified definition of citizenship, one in which social policy reflects market-based entitlements and addresses all members of the community as individual workers, albeit with gender- and race-specific identities. An American move toward gender-equitable family policy that would not backfire would take into account the particular path-dependencies of its market-centered model.

The liberal need to frame family support as fostering choice and work effort, and America's continuing struggles over race and social inclusion, have over time differentiated the US welfare state from those of Europe. The American model is far less "social" or decommodifying, and it has moved further toward incorporating women as individuals into its market-based system by extending anti-discrimination law originally formulated to address racism. Both of these developments shape the relevant criteria for family policy that promotes gender equality.

Decommodification. The classical European social model offers concrete economic benefits for both men and women. For generations, both paid and unpaid work has had benefits that US jobs lacked: paid workers of both genders had guarantees of vacations, health care and sick leaves; men's support of dependents was subsidized by the state and employers; and women's care of children brought them some income and kept most children out of poverty. This gender-segregated but generous policy regime has informed both the expectations of the public and the political critiques of feminist reformers, who have seen its logic as a major obstacle to women's autonomy. A lack of an income adequate to support a family is seen as a source of dependency and disempowerment for all women (Orloff, 1993).

In Europe, bringing men into child care by designating a share of the existing care-time benefits for them and offering women better pay for part-time work could soften the edges of this segregated regime. Assuring that families have access to affordable, high-quality care also helps women become less dependent on individual men (since they can receive state help in raising their own children and also find jobs in the state sector caring for other children), even though it does not reduce the gender division of labor. But Gornick and Meyers' route to an "earner–caregiver" model in the US would demand the introduction of maternity and early-child-care benefits as a social innovation. This would pit parents against non-parents, raise the recurrent racial issue of supporting "bad" mothering (often defined as African-American—see Roberts, 1997), and risk becoming integrated into the already demeaning local processes of "welfare" (Mayer, 2008).

The liberal policy regime has some gender-equity advantages for American women as well as costs to them and their families. As the other chapters of this volume attest, European women end up in part-time work and in gender-segregated (but paid) care work more often than American women do, even though the economic consequences of "mommy-tracking" are reduced (as they would not be in the US) by a flatter pay pyramid and a more generally progressive tax system. Part-time work in the US is also more likely than in Europe to be done by men above and below their prime working years, making these jobs more gender-integrated, even though less protected and less well paid than their equivalents in Europe.

The conflict between work and family is now experienced as a "time bind" for American women and men, but in Europe it remains a larger obstacle to women's access to better jobs. Gender discrimination is more pronounced in Europe than in the US, especially for young women aiming at demanding careers such as bench science, business management, and academic research (Holst and Schrooten, 2006). American men, though hardly doing their full share of housework and child care, are also already putting in more hours than in most western European countries, and how much they contribute also reflects state-level policy variation in the US (Cooke, 2007). This has a range of implications for gender equity.

Gender equity in the workplace. Encouraging women to replace full-time with part-time work to relieve their "time-poverty" at home would tend to reproduce the obstacles to advancement that European women are still struggling to overcome. Expanding the numbers of lower-paid care-work jobs in the public sector, where women continue to be concentrated, would fail to provide a gender-equitable wage for women. Unless the entire wage system of the US were made part of this reform plan, part-time work would be a particularly painful trap for parents to fall into. Liberal definitions of "affordability" and "skill" would make the work of caring for other people's children pay less than the median wage. Recruiting men into public child care risks feeding the moral panics about sex and sexual abuse to which the predominantly non-secular US culture is prone.

Gender equity in families. Embracing norms of gender fairness has meant a recent shift in Europe from thinking of "the worker and his family" to thinking of "the child and its parents" as the objects of social policy (Jenson, 2007). In this way, the male-centered regime of social provision to families by the state is being adapted to be more gender-equitable without losing its anti-poverty, decommodifying focus. Dismantling its "traditional family" policy regime to bring women into paid employment is the European goal, while the feminist-led reforms of this model attempt to remove some of the gender privilege in the system without endorsing neoliberal class inequalities.

But there is nothing "neo" about liberalism in the American context. In the US, the "competitive individual" remains the core object of policy, rather than either "the worker and his family" or "the child and its parents." Shifting away from the ever-available competitive individual of either gender to recognize "familied workers" and their inherent interdependencies is the American challenge. The US needs to adapt its individualist liberal regime to support familied workers of both genders without institutionalizing neo-traditional definitions of what families are and need (Fineman, 2004).

Gender equity and the state. The strength of American liberalism is connected in an organic system of policy development with its many serious weaknesses of social provision. Anti-discrimination laws, from the 1964 Civil Rights Act to the Equal Credit Act and the Pregnancy Discrimination Act, focused on how women and men could be seen as comparable individuals. Even in the absence of an Equal Rights Amendment to the US Constitution, American courts increasingly affirmed the principle of gender-neutral treatment.[2] The Supreme Court built up a body of precedent that defined direct discrimination against either women or men in gender-atypical social locations as illegal, and prohibited a range of employment practices that had a disparate impact on women and men, even if not directly targeted against either group. Introducing "affirmative action for men" in US family law risks not only a backlash against women at work, but a further skewing of divorce and custody arrangements toward fathers, even when their parenting behavior is abusive or violent.

Since the 1970s, the US Supreme Court has repeatedly affirmed a national commitment to both liberal individualism and gender-neutral language. Both of these rules would pose substantial obstacles to introducing the sorts of gender-specific policies that EU states are using to dismantle their earlier gender-segregated model of social provision. Adding a broad social insurance policy (poverty prevention through a living wage, nationalized health care, mandated paid vacation and sick leave) for all citizens, rather than desegregating a gender-centered family policy, is therefore a more prudent American path to helping women, men and children. Since any specific family-centered step can only be as helpful as its role in the wider social system allows, it is important to avoid introducing race- or gender-inequitable elements into a policy imagined in class terms. Prudence requires consideration of the criteria for a gender-equitable family policy in the US liberal context.

GENDER-FAIR CRITERIA FOR LIBERAL WORK–FAMILY POLICY

Although formulated with the feminist goal of greater empowerment for women as my central concern, the policy proposals that would meet the challenges above would not enlist the state directly into the project of making families "gender equal." In addition to reflecting my skepticism about the wisdom of even the most feminist-friendly government, my proposals actively embrace participatory democratic processes in both families and governments, and thus expect diverse outcomes from local negotiations. What democratic states *can* do is to create the conditions under which both men and women would have more investments in and resources for creating gender equality than for maintaining inequality, and thus turn the bias of state policy toward empowering women.[3]

Four key criteria would reflect the challenges for US policy described above: gender-neutrality; increased universality; benefits tied to individual effort; and equal treatment of diverse family structures. All of these are in essence liberal in that they restrict the degree to which states act directly to foster families of a particular sort, or to make equality in gender relations the direct object of policy. Instead, they work to dismantle state policies and mechanisms that still—despite gender-neutral language—support conventionally gendered roles and undervalue women and the work associated with women. All four assume that a liberal system can be reformed to be more fair to women, men and families without thereby forsaking its own philosophical heritage and policy path.

Gender-neutrality. The principle of gender neutrality is the sine qua non of US gender-equality policy. This priority reflects both a practical path-dependency and a theoretical preference among American feminists. American families and feminist policy advocates have already adapted to the liberal presumption that laws will not treat similarly situated people differently, arguing that childbirth is not so different from other temporary disabilities and that childrearing can be done by both women and men. Without specifying gender in their policies, European states assume that they could neither meet mothers' expectations of support nor offer affirmative action to men to bring them into family roles as caregivers (Morgan and Zippel, 2003). By contrast, the American path has led in the direction of insisting that every policy, no matter how historically gendered, be open equally to both women and men.

Through the 1970s, feminist organizations in the US brought lawsuits—often with male plaintiffs—to insist that educational institutions desegregate by gender, and that social policy cover both women and men in formally equal terms. For example, a male widower sued Social Security with the help of the National Organization for Women to be able to receive benefits based on his wife's earning record that would allow him to stay home and raise his two children. Anti-discrimination law is currently being extended to cover discrimination based on family responsibilities. Courts are applying existing precedents against indirect discriminatory impact; large judgments in individual cases are having a salutary impact on changing business norms; male plaintiffs are again being used to win gender-neutral rights that more frequently cover women. These are all steps down the well-worn American liberal path, and while not ideal, they are better than anything else Americans have at their disposal (Williams, 2000; Press, 2007).

As neoliberalism expands and develops globally, it spreads a more liberal interpretation of feminism and, as Berkovitch (1999) argues, the transnational tendency has been to move "from mothers to citizens" as the controlling frame for thinking about women. The EU, as a transnational political institution, has advanced this agenda in adopting proposals for anti-discrimination laws and policies that would undermine gender segregation (Walby, 1999). European feminists are slowly coming to terms with this transition from motherhood-based to gender-neutral citizenship. It would be a step backward for American feminists now to give up the liberal principle of gender neutrality that they fought earlier to secure.

Universalism. The commitment to the expansion of universalism in benefits is a necessary response to the miserliness of the American welfare state. American men will need fewer special incentives to take some sort of family leave, since many do not have a reservoir of vacation time or sick leaves to draw on in times of family need. An appropriate American social policy for work and family would "raise the floor" under the workers who currently enjoy the fewest rights to take time with their families on a daily, weekly or annual basis, as well as turn social policy away from subsidizing family time for more affluent families at the cost of those who have less.

To allow less-privileged women to share in the benefits of work–family reconciliation, the costs should be redistributed throughout the system as a whole, since otherwise poorer women become the "affordable" substitute caregivers (in or out of the home) for better-off children (whose parents can take a tax deduction) without having either a living wage or help with their own family responsibilities. A universal system is both fairer and more feasible than one that follows the path of addressing gender-, age- or class-specific needs, and universal systems carry less stigma for recipients as well.

In an American policy context, any restriction of family time to parents of young children would be counterproductive. Many Americans, of all ages and both genders, face more unrelenting demands for spending time at work than they can in all good conscience meet. In the face of such impossible demands, they feel that they are short-changing their families, and while parents of young children are among those whom the individualist, work-centered American system hurts, the absence of support for family time is a problem that cuts deeply in lives outside this group. Sandra Levitsky outlines how caring for a parent or spouse with a serious disability like Alzheimer's can throw middle-aged, middle-class Americans into bankruptcy, without lessening their belief that this is care that they owe to their families (Levitsky, 2006).

Martha Fineman, a feminist legal theorist, takes up the challenge of defining the problems of meeting family needs for care in gender-neutral and universalizing language, while also concentrating attention on the practical problems arising from women's historical position as caretakers (Fineman, 2004). Her model adds a theoretical claim to classical liberalism, arguing that there are two types of dependents that liberals should recognize: primary dependents, who are incapable of caring for themselves without help; and secondary dependents, who provide care to this former group at a cost to themselves that limits their individual freedom and autonomy. Secondary dependency—or being forced into less than self-sufficiency by the demands of care work—falls disproportionately on women, but not only on mothers.

Although more women than men have borne the costs of care for children, and have been made vulnerable to the risks of aging, the problem of dependency is an essentially gender-neutral one. Because of disability, illness and age, both women and men can become primary dependents, as are all infants and young children, regardless of whether they are boys or girls. All primary dependents need caregivers, and the age and gender of the caregiver varies with the types of need being met, even though women are the primary caregivers at all ages (Armenia and Gerstel, 2006). It is secondary dependency of all types, not motherhood alone, that is the core social challenge, especially as different ethnic and class groups have different population structures, with different fertility rates and life expectancies (thus more affluent white families may face more costs caring for the "oldest old," while Hispanic families may have more children and African-American families more single mothers and mothering grandmothers). The criteria for a fair work–family policy should be reducing the risks associated with all forms of secondary dependency—whether among grandparents or parents, husbands, wives, children or grandchildren—while also providing more adequate care to primary dependents.

This type of conceptual switch has already been made in the US Family and Medical Leave Act (FMLA) of 1993. Limited as it is in the range of workers covered (only those in larger workplaces) and in the benefits provided (time off is guaranteed, but not pay), the framing of this law embodies not only gender-neutral language but the universalizing of the dependency issue. It includes any type of immediate family medical need, ranging from keeping doctors' appointments to sitting by the bedside of a dying parent or child. Of course, a very common family and medical need is the birth or adoption of a child, but because it is not exclusive to this circumstance, the FMLA provides little reason for employers to discriminate against young women. And even though it is an unpaid benefit, poor women have taken advantage of this law to hold on to jobs that have no sick leave or vacation at all when they have children and simply must have time off. By combining this unpaid leave with short-term welfare benefits (under Temporary Assistance to Needy Families) they can manage to cover their basic necessities for six months, but at the cost of enduring the "welfare mother" stigma (Collins and Mayer, 2009). A universalized, and thus destigmatized, *paid* family and medical leave would help families at all income levels.

Market-based inequality. For better or worse, the US is a liberal-capitalist state system, and most Americans approve of this. Rewarding effort and hard work are part of this ideology, as the Clinton-era framing of "making work pay" suggests. This converts the failure of the market to provide above-poverty wages to full-time workers into an important lever for progressive challenges to the state. Allowing older individuals who have "worked hard all their lives" to fall below poverty in their old age was a scandal that not only prompted the original development of the Social Security system, but has now also been repeatedly framed as indicating a need for reform in how the system works (Burkhauser and Holden, 1982; Ferber et al., 2007; Herd, 2006).

The ways in which women and men, parents and non-parents, end up being treated differently for the combinations of paid and unpaid work they perform is also a challenge to the perceived fairness of the Social Security system as a whole (Harrington Meyer and Herd, 2007). But even more critically, this system is being framed as "in crisis" and "failing." Those who want to end the system predict that it will be unable in the future to pay the basic pensions on which most Americans depend. Although valuing Social Security for their parents' generation, many young people have been frightened into thinking that this fundamental pillar of the American welfare state will not be there for them when they retire. Paying into the system, while being unable to feel secure about the benefits it will offer, undermines long-term support for what remains the most appreciated state guarantee against unrestrained market forces. Reframing the issue not in terms of age but in relation to the principle that "people who work hard and pay taxes" as responsible citizens should be able to count on living at a level above poverty creates a common interest in continuing this program and making it more, rather than less fair for all generations and both genders.

Equal treatment of diverse families. The final criterion for work–family policy is fairness for a variety of families and needs, including both married couples and never-married women with children. This is a priority that supports women's individual freedom to form autonomous households, a concern that Gornick and Meyers share and that can be understood as quintessentially liberal (Orloff, 1993; O'Connor et al., 1999). The principle of marriage as a partnership of free and equal citizens also expresses policy resistance to the antiliberal Christian Right emphasis on "restoring traditional families." It instead emphasizes the changing real needs of American women and men in families that are often broken and reconstituted by divorce, of the third of all children who are born to unmarried parents, and of the parents who are combining multiple paid and unpaid jobs, both full and part-time.

The framing of individual choice as an essential aspect of American freedom is institutionalized in American policy language across many different issues (Stone, 1988). Framing, or the meaning conveyed in a structure of discourse, is an important part of what any specific policy can "say." The discourse institutionalized in such powerful documents as constitutions, treaties, laws, court decisions and administrative rules tilts the US toward policies that can be framed as favoring individual rights and personal choices. Taking the framing of policy seriously suggests that to be legitimate in the eyes of courts and families as well as lawmakers, US family policies should treat "neutrally" the choices about whether to marry or not, how unequal married partners' incomes should be, and whether one spouse or the other should stay home when the children are young. Policy that favors one of these choices over another can be framed as "biased" and there would be sentiment that it should be made "more fair" to all family types.

In the next section, I outline some ways in which the current Social Security system, the largest element of the American welfare state, diverges from these ideals of gender neutrality and individual choice, and is thus a prime candidate for reform. The virtual universality of benefits, and the framing of entitlements as individual accounts tied to market effort, are the two policy criteria on which Social Security already scores well. Transforming Social Security to address both primary and secondary dependency in a way that would meet not just two, but all four of the criteria above—being gender neutral, universal, related to work effort, and unbiased to particular family types—would be an American path to gender equality that would no longer come at the cost of families' ability to provide care. This policy would help workers manage both the financial and time costs of caregiving, whether provided by women or men.

RETHINKING SOCIAL SECURITY

The framing of a policy can diverge in important respects from its actual impacts, as the policy makers of the New Deal knew in framing Social Security as an "insurance" program that "paid back" to workers what they put into it. Such frames are not just "spin," but become part of what the policy itself does by creating ancillary socioeconomic demands on policy makers. For example, the "insurance" frame dictates that sound policy provide a "trust fund" specially dedicated to this purpose that must be kept "solvent" in order to pay back the workers who "invested" their earnings there. This frame allows conservatives to define the Social Security system now as "broken" and "bankrupt," and thus as an unreliable support for younger families. This makes it imperative for progressives to restore confidence in the long-term viability of the system by restructuring the system in ways that are more fair across gender and generation. Framing progressive reform as a matter of creating greater equality would not be an "add-on" to the system, but one of its essential policy elements. Only if the social security system can meet—and be seen to meet—the needs of young families, dual-earner couples, multiply divorced and remarried people and their blended families, will it be able to represent a compact between generations that will be seen as worthwhile by and for old and young, men and women, affluent and poor.

To make the Social Security system the template on which a work–family support system can be built first requires correction of the gender-specific legacies that remain embedded in it. Making Social Security more like the Family and Medical Leave Act in its gender-neutrality and support for all types of families, while making FMLA more like Social Security in its universality of coverage, progressive wage replacement and effort-based rewards, could be achieved by bringing together the strengths found in each of these existing American paths.[4]

The structure of social security

The gender logic behind the way Social Security was structured—and repeatedly restructured—from the 1930s to the 1970s was once unassailable. Since most wives did not work for pay, too many women would be left in penury if there were no survivor benefits; yet unmarried women also needed a route to a pension in their own right. Thus women were imagined as two distinct and non-overlapping groups: married mothers and unmarried "career women." Each group was offered a benefit tailored to them: a dependent's benefit for wives, an earner's benefit for career women. The benefits were alternatives, since women were expected to choose which of these two routes to economic support—marriage or a job—best fitted their lives. As increasing numbers of women in fact combined both, the "dual entitlement" category grew; but women were only able to choose the higher of the two benefits, not "stack" them for a higher benefit.

Despite arguments that the "spousal" benefit rewards women who work without pay at home, it is not tied to such work (which women with jobs also conventionally do), but is rather tied to the benefits of the higher earner (conventionally the husband), whose entitlement may be multiplied to support one or more former spouses as well as the current partner. Divorced partners can claim benefits as dependents of any former spouse to whom they have been married for ten years or more, while those who are married at the time of retirement only need the marriage to have been ten months long to qualify for the same benefit (50 percent of the higher earner's entitlement while the breadwinner is alive and 100 percent after the breadwinner's death). The Supreme Court held in 1976 that the rules had to be gender-neutral in form (speaking of earners and dependents, rather than of husbands and wives), but left the basic role-differentiated breadwinner-centered structure intact.

Although Social Security provides a higher replacement percentage for low-income workers than for higher-income ones, the size of the benefit reflects both the level of earnings and the number of years worked. Married mothers' labor force commitment has steadily risen since the 1960s, but the likelihood that they will collect on their own earnings record is still undermined by their lower earnings, their higher involvement in part-time work, and their years out of the labor force entirely. Thus, while more wives at retirement are claiming their own benefits—since they amount to more than 50 percent of their spouse's—the proportion of widows who are able to draw benefits tied to their own record is not increasing—since their own benefit is less than 100 percent of their partner's (Herd, 2006). Because the "dually entitled" can only collect one benefit or the other, women (who are nearly all of those with dual entitlements) do not receive a retirement income that would reflect their joint contributions to family care (at the cost of employment) as well as their employment histories and the substantial taxes they paid. Indeed, they combine full-time work, part-time work and full-time child care over the course of their adult lives; even well-paid workers will end up with an overall earnings record that is reduced by averaging additional years with "zero" into their work history.

The amount of Social Security tax paid does not reflect whether the earner is married or not. Thus a spouse (usually a wife) who earns less than his or her partner will still pay the same 6.2 percent of his or her paycheck in Social Security taxes as a "serial monogamist" (usually a husband), even though "her" taxes will very likely not increase her retirement benefit much, if at all, while "his" 6.2 percent could generate two or even three dependent benefits. This fails both the disparate-impact test for gender neutrality and the principle that higher effort should relate to higher reward. While this benefit for divorced spouses was introduced in the 1970s to protect "displaced homemakers" who were "traded in" for a younger wife, and who therefore carried a disproportionate share of the costs of divorce, it amplified the gender effect by which the dollars paid into Social Security translated into different rates of return for average women and average men (Burkhauser and Holden, 1982). Although the "displaced homemakers" of the 1970s and 1980s were typically upper-middle-class women with no post-marriage earnings, the divorced mothers of today typically spend many years in the labor force before, during and after they have children. Giving a woman a "choice" between a record based on an ex-husband's earnings, a current husband's earnings, or her own earnings is thus asking her to choose between benefits all of which are merely partial reflections of the paid and unpaid work life she has had.

Because the "flat tax" of Social Security works through the pattern of gender relations in marriage, it becomes a "gender tax" that makes women pay more per dollar of expected benefit, and yet leaves them disproportionately poor in old age. The worst effects of this are cushioned by the design of the system to replace a higher percentage of a worker's earnings at the low end of the income distribution, where women are clustered, than at the higher end. But the flat Social Security tax weighs far more heavily on low-income workers than on higher-income workers, not least because most of the taxes low-income workers now pay are designated as going to the Social Security trust fund (although in reality used to offset current deficits). Moreover, the cap on income subject to Social Security tax (currently set at $97,500) means both that more men than women are seeing some of their income sheltered from this tax (20 percent of all earners are above this ceiling, overwhelmingly men) and that couples with a conventional breadwinner–housewife structure and a combined income of $100,000 pay less in taxes but can receive more in benefits than a couple with the same income equally earned by both partners.[5] Eliminating this large state subsidy for gender inequality is a means of shifting toward a more gender-equal division of work, both in and outside the home.

The individualized "insurance" framing has facilitated arguments from neoliberal privatizers that people with good earnings could get a higher rate of return if they invested their retirement income outside the system. This might even be true (albeit with greater market risk) for upper-middle-income dual-earner families, which helps to erode an important political constituency for Social Security. Moreover, it is hard to convince families who are calculating whether it is "worth" a mother's time to work for pay and also pay for child care that the relatively large proportion of her (low) income taken by Social Security taxes is worthwhile, when the odds of its increasing her pension are so poor. This undermines the credibility of Social Security as a system for young families—a weakness that the political right is happy to exploit. It also creates a perverse incentive for married women to work "off the books" so that their taxes will not eat up the family's current income with what is perceived to be (and may in fact be) little chance that the taxes paid on her work will improve her standard of living in retirement.[6] Given this "gender tax," which applies to all dual-earner couples, it is no surprise that most of the workers who are left in poverty at retirement are women, including women whose own earnings brought their families up to middle-class status.

In addition, Social Security once formally excluded agricultural, domestic and government workers from coverage, which particularly marginalized African Americans. Urbanization changed the African-American employment structure, and the legal reforms that prohibited racial discrimination in schooling and employment brought more African-American women and men into the system, but semi-legal employment (involving under-the-table payment) still marginalizes agricultural, construction, and domestic workers in particular. African Americans and all Hispanics, as well as first-generation Asian legal immigrants, remain more likely to be paid off the books and thus not accrue any pension entitlement (Kijakazi, 2006). As in school desegregation, much of the change in Social Security has been from de jure to de facto exclusion.

Re-imagining social security

Reforming Social Security in ways that would make it more supportive of gender equity and more reflective of current family needs is certainly imaginable. Various reforms and amendments to the Social Security Act were made in the 1960s and 1970s to modernize it. There is also pressure for change. Social Security taxes fall hardest on lower-middle-class and working-class families, feeding the anti-tax anger in the middle class that the political right has mobilized to cut income taxes on the upper ends of the distribution. Yet Social Security remains the one popular American redistributive policy because of its apparent link to one's own efforts and its actual effectiveness in reducing unwelcome family dependence among the elderly. Even in the rightward-leaning political climate of 2000 to 2007, moves to "privatize" Social Security were blocked.

But in the absence of reform, the inviolability of Social Security can instead become a force against making work–family balance easier, since it will pit the needs of older Americans against those of children. The current tax falls hardest on young, dual-earner families, and yet cutting these taxes directly would withdraw essential income from their grandparents and parents. Rather than merely "defending" Social Security as it now is, the challenge is to "modernize" it far more thoroughly. Like past adjustments to "fix problems" such as excluded occupations and displaced homemakers, this modernization should address specific problems in universalizing ways.

Although other ways of reconfiguring the Social Security system could also meet the four general criteria outlined above, it is useful to make the abstract shift in policy thinking called for above into a concrete proposal. There are three elements to this sample proposal: shifting from an individual record to continuous income-sharing among those who enter into partnerships; raising the ceiling on taxable incomes while providing a minimum benefit to low-income workers; and, most innovatively, opening up eligibility for benefits to younger workers who leave the labor force temporarily to meet family and medical care needs.

Income-sharing. My variation on this frequently offered proposal would not touch the earnings records already accumulated under the old rules, but from this point on would create an earnings record for every worker every year.[7] Americans believe in individualism but also in partner marriages (two spouses who share the load of work and family life), even if they achieve neither. In this variant of an income-sharing proposal, any two persons could enter into a "tax partnership." Legal marriages, with or without children, would be treated as tax partnerships for pooling incomes and dividing the record in two each year for Social Security purposes. Past marriages or partnerships would be taken into account in a continuous rather than an all-or-nothing way at the time of retirement, because in each year or quarter in which a person was in a "registered tax partnership,"[8] each person's earnings record would equate to both partners' earnings added together, divided in half and credited to the account of each individual. A person who did not want to share a pension entitlement would be required not to enter a tax partnership.[9] Sharing (or not sharing) in any given year or quarter would not change either the past record accumulated or the record that would be calculated in future year or quarters. As a result, one high-earning person married to three different spouses for ten years each would no longer be entitled to have these tax contributions result in four benefits (three dependents' benefits plus one primary one), and one low-earning person married to three different spouses for ten years each would not have to choose only one pension from among four possibilities (one based on personal earnings and three half-pensions reflecting the different earnings of three ex-spouses).

More significantly for more parents, child-care time taken out of the labor force, which now leads to "zero" years or quarters in the caregiver's individual earning record, would be replaced with a half-entitlement to the wage-earner's earning record.[10] The earnings-sharing model would thus realize the marital ideal that families today say they embrace: that it is a joint decision which partner, if any, reduces his or her hours of work, and that the costs of child care are to be borne equally—even if not in precisely the same way—by both partners. Then the high-earner and the low-earner in a partnership are facing the same long-term costs and rewards for their avowedly joint choices, and intermittency—whether of marriage or employment—can be smoothed over by combining different types of entitlement on a year-by-year basis, regardless of the gender of the person who takes time off, and whether or not the marriage itself endures.

The downside of this model would be the reduction of total benefit levels that would arise if married couples no longer had the one-and-a-half benefit that the current system offers (an earner and a dependent benefit). This could be fixed most smoothly by increasing the amount of entitlement created by each year of credited employment in the new system, and there is nothing in this plan that would be inconsistent with also adding a "care-credit" to any individual or shared record based on physical custody of a primary dependent, though this might well open a huge debate about retroactivity. Instead, if calculated in the progressive way that Social Security benefits currently are, simply raising the value of each year of *future* employment credited would have the advantage of giving a greater increase in benefits to non-partnered people (such as single mothers) and to low-wage workers. This would still allow the years of credit for shared benefits at the new rate to be combined with years of credit accumulated at the old rate in the old system, thus reducing transition costs not only for individual workers but for the system as a whole.

Because combining a shared earnings record in partnership periods with a separate earnings record in non-partnered periods allows for sequential combinations, the "dual-entitlement" problem is finally completely removed. Part-time, intermittent and low-wage work—so typical of mothers—would still increase the total entitlement of a partnership; crediting of half a partner's higher wages would create more entitlement for those whose earnings were compromised by caregiving (whether for children, elderly parents, or disabled siblings); and allowing a combination of partnered and unpartnered years across the life course would more realistically reflect the multiple changes in work and family status through which people pass.

Raising the floor on benefit payments per credited year would also help low-earning men as well as women in retirement. Earnings sharing (with higher benefits per entitlement year) would reduce the incentive that partnered low-wage workers have to work off the books. Any earnings, even low ones, would increase the total benefits paid at retirement to that individual, and their benefit would be able to be combined in any way with those of other retirees, whether in or out of a registered partnership at that time. This would spur a more equal gender division of labor at home as well, as the middle-class women who now are willing to hire other women as maids and nannies rather than demand their husbands share housework and child care would face a shift in costs: hiring another woman would become more expensive (since she would want her Social Security taxes paid), and a husband reducing his paid work time to do domestic work would be cheaper (since his entitlement record would be less dominant in determining the couple's benefits).

Raising the income ceiling. Because the income of a single earner is now untaxed over $97,500, a couple today with $150,000 of annual income from a single earner pays *less* in taxes than a couple with $150,000 earned by two partners, even though the latter couple's expenses for child care are likely to be greater. In an earnings-sharing system, all couples whose earnings were $150,000 would be treated the same (as if $75,000 were earned by each). If this were combined with raising the earnings ceiling, the earnings from a high earner would be less sheltered, removing the incentive for both partners to support specialization in income-earning by just one of them.

Raising the income ceiling to a more realistic, modern level (such as $300,000) would both fix the "broken" and "bankrupt" aspects of the current system and also redirect the anti-tax anger of the middle class to a more appropriate target, by focusing on the exemption from taxes enjoyed by the individual earning over $97,000 a year contrasted with the dual-earner couple who juggle their work together to make this level of income in a year. Raising or removing the income ceiling would also generate additional income that the Social Security system could use immediately to cushion the impact of baby-boom retirements. Better still, using general revenue to "tide over" the system as it deals with this one generation would allow the increased income generated by Social Security (in taxes paid on incomes previously kept off the books or over the ceiling) to provide benefits now to younger families that would increase their sense of investment in the system.

Merging FMLA with Social Security. The basic premise of this approach is that the earnings record that creates an entitlement to Social Security benefits should be partially decoupled from an age specification. Any person—of any age or gender—who has accumulated at least five years of covered employment should be entitled to draw down their Social Security account by a quarter-year for family and medical leave. The idea of drawing down an account preserves the fundamental framing of an individual insurance system on which American support for Social Security rests, but opens up the range of choices available to people about when they need to use the entitlement to paid leave that their taxes create, rather than insisting that this is only for "retirement" at a specified age (or even adding just an option for birth or the adoption of a child).

Hypothetically, the extent of draw down could be limited to one quarter-year for each five years of earnings record accumulated (based on individual or partnered records). The rate of benefits for what I am calling Family and Medical Leave Allowances (FMLAs, paid extensions of the current Family and Medical Leave Act) could be fixed to be equal to the Social Security benefit currently paid at retirement for the median worker. This would make wage replacement less gendered and more helpful for lower-wage workers who are less able to call on private benefits. However, it should be permissible to combine this base rate of FMLA benefit with private benefits such as sick leave, vacation time, disability benefits, or state-level FMLA benefits (as in California), as is now the case with private pensions for the elderly, thus encouraging multiple provision to replace earnings for more advantaged workers.

The registered tax partnership rule would also apply to the draw-down of benefits, so that each partner's record would be reduced by one-eighth of a year if the minimum draw-down of a quarter was taken by only one partner. The eligibility, however, would extend across the partnership, so that both partners' entitlements could be reduced by a quarter to pay only one partner to take a half-year of paid leave, or to allow each partner to take "their own" quarter. The draw-down in any case would always be equal across the partners' accounts, regardless of which partner took it, since the earnings record would be shared. A partner with a ten-year earnings record and one with five years would be eligible for a draw down of nine months (three quarters) in total, regardless of which partner took it.

The maximum draw-down might be limited before age sixty-five to two years in an individual's record (which for registered partners could mean one partner taking four years off work to care for an aging parent, or for an ailing spouse whose record is part of what is drawn upon to cover the leave). But it should be limited by the number of years already worked that are being banked to draw upon, because this is another aspect of the system that would increase the incentive for low-wage workers to insist on being paid on the books, as well encouraging low-wage workers to defer childbearing (as schooling now does for middle- and upper-class young people), but with a "carrot" rather than the "stick" now applied in the welfare (TANF) system. The connection of paid leave to an earnings record would also be a way to "make work pay," while also ensuring paid time for child care, even for low-wage workers, and returning family care to the status of an entitlement.

The reduction in pension entitlement foreseen here could be taken either as a reduction of income at retirement (indirectly, by averaging in these quarters as zero earning quarters, as is now done in individual records) or as an extension of age to retirement (to reach the 160 quarters at which calculation of benefits would be capped). The use of quarters as the basis for calculation accommodates the in-and-out quality of caregivers' employment. Taking the shortest leave one personally (or, in a partnership, jointly) decides is needed for good child development is encouraged, because leave that is not used at that paid time is still "in the bank" to be drawn on for other family and medical needs—children's or partners' illnesses, parental decline, injury, or accidents.

Thus there is no need for "the government" (that bogeyman of American policy) to decide that it is best for women (or men) to spend some specific amount of time out of work providing at-home child care, but the financial door is opened to supporting that choice to stay home for parents of either gender and at all income levels. By limiting the total amount of time to two years per earnings record, the cost at retirement would not be too large (especially given longer modern life expectancies), and an earlier retirement (for those partnerships or individuals who have not borrowed against it) could also be allowed as an option. Thus, simply raising the age of retirement for everyone, as has been done in the past to reduce costs and increase income for the system, would be replaced by a more discretionary time system (within two-year limits).

The definition of this FMLA leave as being available at any point in life to any person who has accumulated the appropriate earnings record creates a community of interest between older and younger generations, as well as those with and without children, since the five-year/twenty-quarter rule would mean that even fifty-year-olds could see a personal interest in having such a leave option begin to accrue in their account to cover the demand for caring for an aging parent, disabled spouse, or grandchild. Pegging the benefit levels of leave-takers and average retirees to be equal would create a community of interest rather than a conflict between generations, and would keep both groups politically engaged in making sure that the value of those benefits was not eroded by inflation.

Modern benefits for modern families?

Taking all three proposed changes together highlights the benefits in this plan that would allow it to be framed as a "modernization" of the American system that would appeal to many different constituencies. There would be a positive incentive for low-wage workers to be in the system and accumulate the equivalent of five years of work experience (even if discontinuous) before having a child. Single parents and married parents would be treated as equally entitled to leave with pay, and brought up to a standard of income that reflected the median considered decent for an elderly retiree, thus relinking the welfare of the elderly and children into a single system.

The reform is also easy to frame as good in American terms: it is gender-neutral (even though we would expect more women than men to benefit, at least initially); it is universal, both by gender and by generation; it is liberal, in allowing a high level of individual choice about how to make a family and in rewarding work effort; it is fair, in that it treats families equally regardless of their allocation of work roles; and it remains market-dependent, treating people differently depending on how much they earn, but without tying their ability to take leave to a particular employer or to a full-time work relationship.

This reform model does not conjure up the notion of a new tax and a new state bureaucracy, or of a "European welfare system" that ties benefits to citizenship rather than to work—ideas that have made Americans resistant to paying for such leaves. It would also give young families more of a stake in the Social Security system as a whole—not only in protecting it from attacks by privatizers, but potentially raising the level of voting participation among such families (as Social Security does for older Americans and Head Start does for families in this program—see Bruch et al., n.d.).

It is important to note that this plan is not a "European-style" child-care leave. It does not single out women as especially likely to be the users of it, nor restrict it to a certain age group. It therefore diminishes the discriminatory effects on women's employment that are still the bane of European systems. It does not allow the state to prescribe how much family labor should go into child care, nor how family labor should be allocated by gender, nor for how long or at what ages children are going to be most in need of parental care; and it encourages saving one's leave time for when it is needed most (or cashing it in for an earlier retirement age if one is able and willing to wait). It is nonetheless a feminist proposal that would reduce significant obstacles to gender equality currently in the system. It is also a work–family system that would allow families real choices in how and when paid work should take second place to caregiving for both women and men. It does not assume the luxury of modifying an already strong welfare state, as Gornick and Meyers do, but begins to move the US in the direction of greater social justice for women and men, families and singles, young and old.

Although achieving greater gender equality in the US demands a better work–family balance for both women and men, looking to a European road map for guidance will not take us there. Instead, following a European policy map risks crashing into the obstacles of means testing and social exclusion that the long history of American policy development has left in our long liberal path. While some would accept the risks of relegitimizing gender-differentiated social policies in order to help families cope with their lack of income and/or time, this appears to be an unnecessary tradeoff. American liberal democracy offers different, but potentially effective routes to gender equality that will also increase family welfare.

Accepting the path dependency of the American system as a real constraint, but thinking in utopian terms about reframing and reforming it, suggests some theoretical and practical routes toward making it more gender-neutral and family-fair in practice. Using Social Security as a base for such speculation, this essay has imagined reforms to existing systems that would make them more adequate and universal in their coverage without abandoning the core American commitment to paid work as a basis for entitlements, or imposing costs on one generation alone.

American children are now disproportionately bearing the costs of the miserly social welfare system of the US. But the appropriate response to their needs, as well as those of their parents, is neither to offer targeted benefits to them as a special group nor to "privatize" Social Security so that the older generation is returned to the same level of risk and poverty that children are facing today. An approach to the need for social provision for families in a US context calls for more universal measures. Of course, helping children by making sure they are covered by state-funded health insurance (the so-called "S-CHIP") is a good thing, but universal health-care coverage is better—and the pressure to bring it about is lessened whenever groups that are framed as deserving (like children) are addressed one by one. Gornick and Meyers' range of targeted benefits is also good, but a truly universal system would be better.

The gender-neutral language and individualistic system of entitlements that are characteristic of liberalism create opportunities to build a framework that allows both single people and families to make more truly free choices about how they want to organize both care work and paid employment. Framing this as a "market failure" to provide time to care and a "state failure" to provide equal treatment to all people and families allows progressive reformers to frame the need for reform as urgent, lest these continue to contribute to "family failure" to meet members' obligations to care for each other in times of need. We are all, at various times in our life course, primary dependents, and we all therefore need a system that will insure that others can afford to care for us. By reframing the need for Social Security reform in terms of the demand to modernize the system and to respond to the needs for caregiving that all people face at some point in their life course, a path can be found toward gender equality in the American liberal landscape that will help create a broad, progressive coalition for social welfare reform.

Its task would by no means end with this reform, no matter how utopian. Unlike Europeans, Americans are still being challenged to design a welfare state that will address the massive social inequalities of its history, as well as the new dislocations of a changing economy. Facing decaying public schools and declining state investment in social infrastructure of all sorts, a political response has to be far more comprehensive if Americans are actually going to be supported in their caregiving work. State support for public transportation, subsidized housing that would bring workplaces and affordable homes closer together and reduce commuting times, universal health care provision, and actual desegregation of towns and cities would all support a richer and more gender-equitable family life. These are the policies that get left out when "family policy" is thought of narrowly as pertaining only to that one, supposedly separate, sphere.

Of course, conventional policies such as state subsidies for care outside the home and state mandates for vacation time and sick days that would facilitate care at home are needed to enable both women and men to be better fathers and mothers (and care for their own mothers and fathers). Other reforms, from extended school hours to better transportation, would help both custodial and non-custodial parents to be connected with and care for children. But "family policy" is really all of social policy, and no one thread can be pulled entirely out of the fabric.

The fabric of American liberalism, despite its ungenerous welfare state, can support other paths toward greater support for children, mothers, families and care work. For example, laws that prohibit discrimination "against pregnant people" should include prohibitions of discrimination against "lactating people" and "people with family responsibilities." These forms of discrimination can easily be shown to exist (Correll et al., 2007; Williams, 2000). The treatment of what is newly being framed as illegal family responsibility discrimination as posing a serious problem throughout the life course should ensure that young women are not singled out as being special motherhood risks to employers. A few high-profile class action suits would be helpful in institutionalizing a culture of parental protection in corporate America.

For over twenty-five years, American feminists have used Sweden as their image of utopia, much to the dismay of Swedish feminists (see Morgan, this volume). Gornick and Meyers' proposals are just the most recent in a long tradition of disregarded entreaties to make the US more "European." But I have argued not only that American middle-class women and families, in looking to European family-leave policies, will never be made to feel enough policy envy to trump their other political concerns, but also that their liberal concerns are valid in the policy context in which they live. Special benefits for families, mothers, or children work against the development of the universal benefits that Europeans can take for granted, and that Americans must still try to create. Rather than moving backwards in thinking about women, by starting with assumptions about policy revolving around families and motherhood rather than around citizens and equality, imaginative social policy in a liberal landscape can move gender neutrality from its status as a legal principle toward becoming a social reality.

NOTES

1   The typical model advanced is Sweden. As analysis of the gender content of US introductory sociology textbooks documented, Sweden was the one country repeatedly cited in the 1980s as offering a policy model for gender equality (Ferree and Hall, 1996).

2   Its adoption was blocked from the 1920s through the 1960s by social-democratic forces in the US, from unions to feminists, as antithetical to protective legislation. After a brief moment of opportunity in the 1970s, when it was reintroduced in the context of liberal opposition to gender-specific treatment, it failed to be ratified in the states as a result of Christian conservative mobilization that stressed its potential to "de-segregate" restrooms, bring women into the military, and secure abortion rights. The path-dependency of the interpretation of policy, not just its feasibility, is underlined by this history, as European countries that adopted similarly worded equal rights provisions in their constitutions found their courts accepting protective legislation as consistent with, rather than antithetical to, this guarantee (see Moeller, 1993, for the German case; and Mansbridge, 1986, for the US).

3   This also reflects my understanding of feminism as a goal that can be reached by diverse routes, rather than as an ideology, such as socialism, that prescribes both the means and the ends of social change (see Ferree and Mueller, 2004).

4   As ever, the devil is in the details, and there are many excellent studies that attempt to assess just how certain detailed assumptions about program configuration will work out. However, one such simulation study does show that an earnings-sharing model similar but not identical to this one would both reduce women's poverty in old age and increase equality in women's and men's rate of

return, both of which are important feminist goals (Favrault and Steuerle, 2007). The dynamic Urban Institute model used for testing this and other models could easily be applied to a more specific version of this proposal as well.

5   In the single-earner household some income is sheltered from taxation; but the couple will receive 150 percent of the primary earner's benefits at retirement, while the dual-earner couple will each get only their own benefits, since the lower earner's benefit as a dependent will be less than the entitlement gained from employment. When widowed, the non-employed wife gets 100 percent of her spouse's benefit (or a 33 percent drop in income), while the co-earner has to choose between her benefit or his (or a 50 percent drop in their already lower income).

6   For lower-income families in particular, off-the-books work for one or the other partner (regardless of gender) makes considerable sense, since the reporting worker will earn benefits for both that are calculated to replace a greater percentage of income, and the non-reporting worker avoids paying taxes that would fail to increase that benefit. This incentive to keep one partner off the books combines with the earnings-ceiling effect on sheltering income to reduce the actual taxes paid into the system from both ends.

7   Many variants of income-sharing proposals have been advanced over the years, and the most typical type has been evaluated as potentially affordable within the current allocations for Social Security, even though it would be retroactive and thus more expensive than the model I am advancing here (see Faverault and Steuerle, 2007).

8   This option is not only a way to avoid the current controversy over "gay marriage" in a way that would not leave the system again old-fashioned, but also to offer a gender-neutral way to acknowledge the variety of modern family forms: grandparent and daughter raising the latter's children; cohabitation, with or without children; nonsexual co-residence with shared household finances, as with adult siblings with and without disabilities, and so on. Entering or leaving a registered tax partnership could follow various state rules, but would demand that state-registered partnerships be recognized federally for the purpose of federal taxation. A person could change partners as often as they would want to go through the paperwork, but only one partner would be recognized in any given tax year.

9   There may be reason to allow even married couples to choose not to enter a tax partnership, but like any other prenuptial agreement, both parties would have to sign off on this before marriage. Unlike a prenuptial agreement of other sorts, the choice could be made later to enter into a registered tax partnership as any other two people can do, regardless of marital status. High-earning and low-earning couples especially would both have some financial incentive to keep their records separate despite marriage.

REFERENCES

Adams, Carolyn Teich, and Kathryn Teich Winston, 1980, *Mothers at Work: Public Policies in the United States, Sweden, and China*, New York: Longman.

Adams, Julia, and T. Padamsee, 2001, "Signs and Regimes: Rereading Feminist Work on Welfare States," *Social Politics* 8 (1): 1–23.

Armenia, A, and Naomi Gerstel, 2006, "Family Leaves, the FMLA and Gender Neutrality: The Intersection of Race and Gender," *Social Science Research* 35: 871–91.

Beisel, Nicola, 2004, "Abortion, Race and Gender in Nineteenth-Century America," *American Sociological Review* 69 (4): 498–518.

Berkovitch, Nitza, 1999, *From Motherhood to Citizenship: Women's Rights and International Organizations*, Baltimore, MD: Johns Hopkins University Press.

Bruch, Sarah, Myra Marx Ferree, and Joe Soss, forthcoming, "From Policy to Polity: Democracy, Paternalism, and the Incorporation of Disadvantaged Citizens," *American Sociological Review*.

Burkhauser, Richard, and Karen Holden, 1982, *A Challenge to Social Security: The Changing Roles of Women and Men in American Society*, New York: Academic Press.

Collins, Jane, and Victoria Mayer, forthcoming, *Both Hands Tied: Welfare Reform and the Race to the Bottom in the Low Wage Labor Market*, Chicago: University of Chicago Press.

Cooke, Lynne Prince, 2007, "Policy Pathways to Gender Power: State-Level Effects on the US Division of Housework, *Journal of Social Policy* 36 (2): 239–60.

Correll, Shelley J., Stephen Benard, and In Paik, 2007, "Getting a Job: Is there a Motherhood Penalty?" *American Journal of Sociology* 112 (5): 1,297–338.

Favreault, Melissa M., and C. Eugene Steuerle, 2007, "Social Security Spouse and Survivor Benefits for the Modern Family," Urban Institute Retirement Project, Discussion Paper 1, Washington DC: Urban Institute.

Ferber, Marianne, Patricia Simpson and Vanessa Rouillon, 2006, "Aging and Social Security: Women as the Problem and the Solution," *Challenge* 49 (3): 105–19.

Ferree, Myra Marx, and Elaine J. Hall, 1996, "Rethinking Stratification from a Feminist Perspective: Gender, Race and Class in Mainstream Textbooks," *American Sociological Review* 61 (6): 1–22.

Ferree, Myra Marx, and Carol McClurg Mueller, 2004, "Feminism and the Women's Movement: A Global Perspective," in David A. Snow, Sarah A. Soule, and Hanspeter Kriesi, eds, *The Blackwell Companion to Social Movements*, New York: Blackwell.

Fineman, Martha Albertson, 2004, *The Autonomy Myth: A Theory of Dependency*, New York: Norton.

Gonyea, Judith, and Nancy Hooyman, 2005, "Reducing Poverty among Older Women: Social Security Reform and Gender Equity," *Families in Society* 86 (3): 338–46.

Harrington Meyer, Madonna, 1996, "Making Claims as Workers or Wives: The Distribution of Social Security Benefits," *American Sociological Review* 61 (3): 449–65.

Harrington Meyer, Madonna, and Pamela Herd, 2007, "Market-friendly or Family-friendly? The State and Gender Inequality in Old Age," Rose Monograph Series, New York: Russell Sage.

Herd, Pamela, 2005, "Reforming a Breadwinner Welfare State: Gender, Race, Class, and Social Security Reform," *Social Forces* 83(4): 1,365–94.

——— "Crediting Care or Marriage? Reforming Social Security Family Benefits," *Journals of Gerontology* 61 (1): 24–34.

Holst, Elke and Mechtild Schrooten, 2006, "Führungspositionen: Frauen geringer entlohnt und nach wie vor seltener vertreten," *DIW Wochenbericht* 73 (25): 365–77.

Jenson, Jane, 2007, "Building with Lego," paper presented at European Union Center of Excellence conference, UW-Madison (March).

Levitsky, Sandra, 2006, "Private Dilemmas of Public Provision: Political Consciousness and the Contemporary American Welfare State," PhD dissertation in the Department of Sociology, UW-Madison.

Kijakazi, Kilolo, 2006, "Impact of Unreported Social Security Earnings on People of Color and Women," *Public Policy and Aging Report* 12 (3): 8–12.

Mansbridge, Jane J., 1986, *Why We Lost the ERA*, Chicago: University of Chicago Press.

Mayer, Victoria, 2008, "Crafting a New Conservative Consensus on Welfare Reform: Redefining Citizenship, Social Provision, and the Public/Private Divide," *Social Politics* 15 (2): 154–81.

Moeller, Robert G., 1993, *Protecting Motherhood: Women and the Family in the Politics of Postwar West Germany*, Berkeley: University of California Press.

Morgan, Kimberly, and Kathrin S. Zippel, 2003, "Paid to Care: The Origins and Effects of Care Leave Policies in Western Europe," *Social Politics* 10 (1): 49–85.

O'Connor, Julia S., Ann Shola Orloff, and Sheila Shaver, 1999, *States, Markets, Families: Gender, Liberalism, and Social Policy in Australia, Canada, Great Britain, and the United States*, NY: Cambridge University Press.

Orloff, Ann Shola, 1993, "Gender and the Social Rights of Citizenship: The Comparative Analysis of Gender Relations and Welfare States," *American Sociological Review* 58 (3): 303–28.

―――― 1996, "Gender and the Welfare State," *Annual Review of Sociology* 22: 51–78.
Press, Eyal, 2007, "Family Leave Values," *New York Times Magazine*, July 29: 36ff.
Quadagno, Jill, 1994, *The Color of Welfare: How Racism Undermined the War on Poverty*, New York: Oxford University Press.
Roberts, Dorothy E., 1997, *Killing the Black Body: Race, Reproduction, and the Meaning of Liberty*, New York: Pantheon Books.
Sklar, Kathryn Kish, Anja Schuler, and Susan Strasser, 1998, *Social Justice Feminists in the United States and Germany: A Dialogue in Documents, 1885–1933*, Ithaca, NY: Cornell University Press.
Stone, Deborah A., 1988 (rev. edn. 2002), *Policy Paradox and Political Reason*, New York: Norton.
Stratigaki, Maria, 2004, "The Cooptation of Gender Concepts in EU Policies: The Case of 'Reconciliation of Work and Family'," *Social Politics* 11 (1): 30–56.
United Nations Demographic Yearbook, 2006, online: http://unstats.un.org/unsd/demographic/default.htm.
Walby, Sylvia, 1999, "The European Union and Equal Opportunities Policies," *European Societies* 1 (1): 59–80.
―――― 2004, "The European Union and Gender Equality: Emergent Varieties of Gender Regime," *Social Politics* 11 (1): 4–29.
Williams, Joan, 2000, *Unbending Gender: Why Family and Work Conflict and What to Do about It*, New York: Oxford University Press.
Zippel, Kathrin S., 2006, *The Politics of Sexual Harassment: A Comparative Study of the United States, the European Union, and Germany*, New York: Cambridge University Press.

14

The Political Path to a Dual-Earner/Dual-Caregiver Society: Pitfalls and Possibilities

Kimberly J. Morgan

Janet Gornick and Marcia Meyers highlight real-world examples of policies that have brought several countries closer to the dual-earner/dual-caregiver model. Doing so offers some hope for reformers, showing that gender-egalitarian policy change is possible in the world today. Yet, as they also note, public policies are not enough to achieve the dual-earner/dual-caregiver model in practice: social and economic changes must follow, some of which are beyond the realm of public policy. They also observe that no country has yet fully adopted the necessary policies that would make the dual-earner/dual-caregiver model possible. These facts raise several questions: What are the barriers to the full adoption of this model of public policy? Are there risks in what we are more likely to see—partial transformation of policies and societies, rather than a full embracing of the dual-earner/dual-caregiver model?

This chapter addresses these questions as a way to explore the politics of the work–family issue as it is now playing out in western Europe. Governments in many European countries now embrace the goal of improving the lives of working parents, and the Scandinavian model is ever-present in the minds of these policy makers. Yet the political context in most countries frustrates efforts to enact a unified, comprehensive vision like the dual-earner/dual-caregiver model. More commonly, countries have adopted partial measures without a coherent, overarching framework that unites them. These partial reforms can be extremely helpful to parents, and may ultimately cumulate into something close to the model described by Gornick and Meyers. However, some of these policies risk undercutting larger reform efforts and reinforcing the traditional division of labor. Rather than arriving at a set of gender-egalitarian arrangements for work and care, countries may stall halfway there in a modified male-breadwinner model.

Even the Nordic countries have not yet attained the dual-earner/dual-caregiver model either in public policy or in practice. Although men's role in caregiving has increased in many of these countries, women still take the vast majority of parental leave days, and often reduce their working hours while their children are young. This preserves women's attachment to paid work and enables the balancing of paid work and family, but equality in the domestic division of labor is far from being achieved. One of the most important policy measures that could further this goal—mandating the equal sharing of parental leave time—has not been enacted, other than in a measure adopted in Iceland that reserves one-third of parental leave time for men. In Sweden, recent debates about such a reform came to naught, as both public opinion and the leadership of the major political parties were against the idea.

These realities should not lead to pessimism about the likelihood of any country ever reaching the dual-earner/dual-caregiver model. Several countries have gone a long way toward this model, and one can envision future policy and societal changes that might enable these countries to achieve a more egalitarian division of labor. What current work–family politics in western Europe do reveal are some lessons about the pathways to this model, and potential pitfalls along the way. Advocates should be careful in what they ask for, as seemingly "family-friendly" policies such as extended parental leaves are likely to undermine gender equality, particularly if there are few incentives (or requirements) that men take these leaves. More generally, one of the greatest challenges that advocates will face is to keep gender-egalitarian goals at the center of a policy making process over which they will not have full control. Governments in western Europe appear increasingly inclined to promote women's employment, yet they are often driven by other aims, such as increasing fertility rates or improving economic efficiency. Although the new climate offers opportunities for policy change, advocates will have to work to make sure that gender-equality objectives shape the design of work–family policies.

POLITICAL LESSONS FROM THE NORDIC COUNTRIES

The Nordic countries provide the best-case scenarios for dual-earner/dual-caregiver policies, with their extensive public child-care systems, generous parental leave rights for both parents, and rights for parents to work reduced hours. Even in these countries, however, advocates have struggled to keep gender-egalitarian motivations at the center of the policy-making process, and certain policies, like a mandated sharing of parental leave, have yet to be enacted. Although it may only be a matter of time and further societal change before these countries attain the dual-earner/dual-caregiver model, some scholars worry that they may be stalling partway, due partly to some unintended consequences of family-friendly policies.

The development of work–family policies in the Nordic countries has been shaped by unusual political circumstances that are not likely to be replicated in other countries. Three of the four (Denmark, Norway, Sweden) have frequently been governed by social-democratic parties allied with a powerful union movement, both of which are committed to a generous and universal welfare state (Esping-Andersen, 1990). These are also centralized political systems in which corporatist bargaining arrangements are often employed to build agreement around a particular course of action. This makes possible more unified action on policy than can be found in many other nations (Ruggie, 1984). In addition, Nordic societies are homogeneous, albeit with increased diversity in recent years owing to immigration, and are highly secular. The latter fact has been important in dampening traditional attitudes toward gender roles and matters of sexuality, and these countries were pioneers in the liberalization of laws on divorce, abortion, and homosexuality, and in the treatment of women as individuals under the law, not as subservient to husbands and fathers (Melby 2000).

All of these factors enabled the transition from a male-breadwinner model of social policy, which had been dominant in the post–Second World War period, to a model that assumed all women would, and should, be in paid work. The transition began in the late 1960s and 1970s, when both labor shortages and a wide-ranging societal debate about sex roles spurred a shift in social-democratic ideology about women's employment (Dahlström, 1971). Women's groups, often acting within unions and the political parties, played a critical role in putting this issue on the agenda and demanding egalitarian policies (Mahon, 1997; Bergqvist, et.al, 1999). The shift in policy was facilitated by the weakness of conservative political forces, although opposition was stronger in Norway and Finland (Leira, 2002). It was also facilitated by bargains reached within corporatist institutions, which insulated policymakers from the larger political environment (Ruggie, 1984).

The Nordic countries also benefited from the fact that educational programs for preschoolers were weakly developed at the time they began debating the need for public child care. For instance, in the early 1970s, Sweden and Norway had the lowest availability of preschool programs of nearly any country in the western world, with a mere 2 percent of four-year-old children attending preschool in Sweden, compared to over 80 percent in France and the Netherlands (Morgan, 2006). Preschool programs are often structured around purely educational objectives, rather than seeking both to provide pedagogic stimulation and to help working parents. Once institutionalized, these programs can be difficult to change later on, due to resistance from teachers and education ministries. Thus the weak development of these programs in the Nordic countries left a void that could then be filled by a unified set of programs that fused caregiving and educational motivations—the "educare" model (Morgan, 2006). In this way, the initially slow expansion of the Nordic early childhood education system actually enabled more coherent policy making.

Even under these auspicious circumstances, it has at times been challenging to keep gender-equality goals at the forefront of work–family policy. The dual-earner/dual-caregiver ideal has been strongest in Sweden, but weaker elsewhere.[1] The earliest Swedish policies reflected these aims: in 1974 Sweden was the first country to abolish maternity leave and replace it with a parental leave to which both parents were entitled, the explicit purpose being that men and women should share this leave. In 1979, parents of small children gained the right to work a six-hour day. Not content simply to enable men to spend more time at home, the government also began vigorous public campaigns to try to turn "men into fathers." Public officials created a series of posters showing famous weightlifter Hoa-Hoa Dahlgren and other men holding babies (Bergman and Hobson, 2002). The government also began massive investments in public child care.

The other Nordic countries have been less fully committed to the dual-earner/dual-caregiver model. In the case of Denmark, Anette Borchorst argues that gender-equality goals have never been the main objective of work–family policies, which were instead driven by labor shortages and the increase in women's workforce participation (Borchorst, 2006). Concern about changing men's roles entered less into the debate or into public policy. Thus, although Denmark has long had the greatest availability of public child care in the region, parental leave was instituted only in 1984, and a quota of "daddy days" was created in 1998 but eliminated in 2002.

In Finland and Norway there has been stronger conservative resistance to mothers working while their children are young. Norway has the most significant Christian Democratic party in the region, and this party has helped unify conservative opposition to public child care (Morgan, 2006). In Finland, social democrats have never been hegemonic, but have frequently shared or alternated power with a center-right agrarian party whose rural constituency is less interested in public child care. In both countries, there was a strong push from center-right parties to institute home care allowances that parents could use either to stay home for several years or to help pay for informal or private forms of care (Morgan and Zippel 2003). Finland first instituted a home care allowance in the mid-1980s, and later expanded it. Norway created a similar allowance in the 1990s (Leira 1998). Even Sweden briefly had such a measure: in 1994, a Conservative government created a cash-for-care allowance, although it was immediately revoked when the Social Democrats came back to power later that year.

Home care allowances contravene the goals of the dual-earner/dual-caregiver model. As these are flat-rate payments rather than income-related benefits, men have virtually no incentives to take these leaves and rarely do. And because the leave period usually lasts until the child is three, mothers are encouraged to leave the labor market for up to three years. In Finland, the effects of this on women's employment have been somewhat counterbalanced by the requirement that all municipalities offer all children whose parents desire it a place in child care. Social democrats pushed hard for this requirement so that the care allowance would not undermine the public child-care system or constrain parental choices. In Norway, the development of the child-care system has been slower, and so parents lack real choices between work and care in some parts of the country (Leira 2006).

More problematic for the dual-earner/dual-caregiver model has been the failure to mandate equal sharing of the lengthy parental leave. On the one hand, the Nordic countries pioneered the use of father-only days to increase men's use of parental leave. The number of weeks in the father quota has expanded in both Sweden and Norway, and is now six weeks in Norway and two months in Sweden. There is no doubt that these measures have increased men's use of leave days. Men in Sweden take the highest percentage of parental leave days—a little under 19 percent in 2004, which represents a significant increase from the past. When the gender-neutral parental leave was created in the 1970s, men took only about 2 percent of leave days, on average, and that rose to over 6 percent in the 1980s. Thus, the combination of father-only quotas and moral suasion on the part of Swedish authorities has made a difference in promoting a more equal distribution of the leave.

On the other hand, the dual-earner/dual-caregiver model requires that the leave be equally split between men and women, and this is unlikely to be achieved without a policy mandate. This is extremely important: long and generous parental leaves are a great help to many parents, but if women alone take them, they risk being stereotyped as less committed to the workforce, and could suffer job discrimination as a result. Although Swedish men take a relatively high proportion of parental leave days, women still take over 80 percent of the leave days, and the proportion is higher in the other Nordic countries: in 2003, nearly 95 percent of the days were taken by women, as opposed to men, in Denmark and Finland, and 91 percent in Norway (Leira 2006: 23). For this reason, feminists and fatherhood activists have advocated mandating either an equal split of the entitlement, or else the Icelandic 3–3–3 model, in which each parent is entitled to one-third of the leave and the last third is to be shared.

Thus far, these ideas have gained little political traction. In Sweden, a government commission declared in 2005 that the country should augment the length of its well-paid leave to fifteen months (from thirteen), and entitle men and women to five months each, and allow the rest to be shared. None of the major political parties endorsed the idea, however, other than the recently created, and politically unsuccessful, Feminist Party. The Social Democratic Party leadership was also skeptical while in power, instead favoring bonus payments for fathers who take more months of leave.

One obstacle to mandating the equal sharing of leave is the fact that, if men did not take up their share, children would have to go to child care much earlier, and the state would have to build more child-care centers and outfit them for infant care. Infant care is expensive, particularly as it requires higher staff–child ratios. Currently, most Swedish children do not start in child care until they are sixteen months of age. In 2005, for example, a total of thirty children under the age of one were in publicly funded child care, of which eight were in center-based care and twenty-two were in family child care (National Agency for Education, 2007: 19). Thus, the current system of lengthy parental leaves serves the interests of state officials eager to keep down the costs of child care.

In addition, public opinion appears unfavorably disposed toward mandating an equal sharing of leave time. Some fear that, if such a policy were instituted, many men would simply not take the leave, and these months would be lost to the family. Women would have to go back to work earlier, and babies would have to go to child care, neither of which are popular ideas. Such an outcome would also run counter to powerful "expert" signals sent to Swedish parents about the importance of parental care during the first year of life, and of mothers breastfeeding their babies for a lengthy period of time (Brachet, 2001). Since the 1980s, the Swedish government has led a campaign to encourage breastfeeding and help mothers with it, and currently more than 75 percent of children are breastfed (exclusively or partially) at the age of six months—a very high proportion (Brachet, 2001). Similar concerns have been raised in other Nordic countries about proposals to split the leave equally. In Norway, for example, the issue of breastfeeding has been used as a strong argument against adoption of the Icelandic model (Ellingsæter, 2006: 126).

More generally, there is evidence from several of these countries that parents prefer to divide the parental leave largely as they have done so far, with mothers taking most of it (Lammi-Taskula, 2006: 87–8). It is hard to know how much this is a result of various constraints that people face, such as the actions of private employers, the lack of infant child care, and a strong normative presumption against using such services for very young children. Clearly, different societal standards and expectations are applied to men and women when it comes to parental leave. When fathers take ten weeks of leave this is considered "long," and something for which to reward them, whereas a ten-week period of leave for mothers is seen as too short (Leira 2006: 45). As one Swedish mother said to an interviewer, "It would have been seen as quite weird, had I not stayed at home when the child was young."[2] Given these views, some scholars argue that the lengthy parental leave has reinforced the norm that mothers should be at home with their children for at least the first year of their lives (Brachet, 2001).

The generalization of part-time work poses some similar risks, as women are more likely to reduce their working hours than men. Reduced work time may be popular with parents who wish to shorten the length of time children spend in child care. One problem, however, is that as part-time work becomes widespread for women working in particular sectors of the economy, these sectors become organized around the assumption that many of their employees will work part-time. This became a great concern to the main Swedish trade union confederation, the Landsorganisationen i Sverige, as the problem of involuntary part-time work (or "part-time unemployment") became apparent. For example, a study of Swedish nurses found that over half had been forced into part-time work during the past five years (Kapborg, 2000). Thus, as with parental leave, the creation of a gender-neutral right to part-time work has created or reinforced gender inequality in labor markets—reflecting both economic realities and societal beliefs about gender roles in work and care.

Yet these norms need not be irreversible; the power of public policy to shape social behavior can be seen in the effects on men's use of leave time of the Icelandic parental leave reform. In 2000, Iceland lengthened its parental leave from six to nine months, with three months reserved only for the father, three for the mother, and three that could be shared between the two however they wished. The reform was phased in over three years, with an additional month available to men in 2001, 2002, and 2003. The reform also replaced the flat-rate parental leave benefit with a benefit that replaces 80 percent of earnings (Eydal and Olafsson, 2003). As Figure 14.1 shows, these changes had a dramatic effect on men's use of parental leave, which increased each year as the entitlement was expanded. While women usually take the remaining six months of leave, this is considerably shorter than the leave period taken by women in Sweden, Denmark, Finland, and Norway.

Why was Iceland able to adopt this change when other countries have not? One answer may lie in the relatively late development of Iceland's parental leave system. Iceland created a three-month paid leave in 1980, and expanded it to six months in the 1990s—still relatively short compared to the other Nordic countries. Although women pushed for extending the overall length of the leave, the Icelandic government decided only to expand the entitlement of men, adding three months of father-only time onto the existing six months of leave (Mósesdóttir, 2005). While this lengthened the leave, it did not require taking anything away from what women already had—their own leave time was not shortened unless they chose to split some of the three months that either partner could take. By contrast, the other Nordic countries already have long leaves that women are accustomed to, and so creating a father-only quota within the existing leave would subtract from women's leave time. Attempting to appease this view by adding on more months to the existing leave would make the entire parental leave system very time-consuming and expensive. Thus, Iceland may have benefited by being

Figure 14.1

Percentage of Parental Days Taken by Fathers, 1994–2003/4

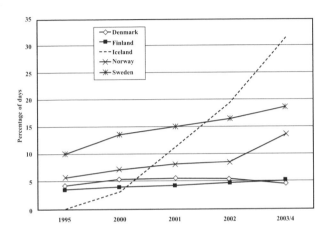

(See Datta Gupta, et al. 2006 for sources.)

a relative laggard; once it decided to expand the parental leave, it was able to do so in a gender-egalitarian way.

What lessons can be learned about the political path to a dual-earner/dual-caregiver model in the Nordic countries? These countries represent the best-case scenario for the adoption of this model. As many analysts have pointed out, however, the low take-up rates of parental leave and part-time work by men impede the realization of this ideal. It appears that the only way to achieve fundamental change is by mandating the equal sharing of parental leave time, yet currently this idea lacks sufficient support among political elites and the public. That hardly means these countries have reached the endpoint of their work–family policies; the degree of social change over the past three to four decades is remarkable, as women's workforce participation rapidly increased and men began taking on a greater role in caring for children. If social norms and practices continue to change, one can imagine openings for truly egalitarian parental leave policies that achieve the dual-earner/dual-caregiver model.

WORK–FAMILY POLICIES IN CONTINENTAL EUROPE

Governments in continental Europe are less likely to engage in the kind of unified, coherent policy making found in the Nordic states, and thus more likely to introduce only pieces of the dual-earner/dual-caregiver model. In many of these countries, partial reforms have made a difference in helping parents reconcile work and family, but there are risks attached to some of these measures. More than in Scandinavia, public policies in much of continental Europe often focus on restructuring mothers' work and caring time than on either changing men's behavior or improving access to care services. Thus, these policies may "solve" the difficulties parents face in a way that undermines the push for more gender-egalitarian reforms.

Outside of Scandinavia, most European countries have long been exemplars of the male-breadwinner model of social policy that provided few supports to working mothers. Many were dominated by conservative or Christian Democratic parties that hewed to a traditional vision of gender roles and family life (van Kersbergen, 1995). Child care was seen as a purely family responsibility, not one deserving of state intervention. Thus, short maternity leaves and the low provision of child-care services made it difficult, if not impossible, for mothers to combine paid work and family (Bussemaker, 1998; Ostner, 1994; Saraceno, 1994).

Policy change has come slowly, but intensified in recent years. France and Belgium started expanding their public child-care services and subsidies in the 1970s and 1980s. Other European countries have begun embracing the goal of helping parents balance paid work and family since the 1990s, spurred in part by economic and demographic conditions. Increasingly, policy makers fear the prospect of labor shortages and a declining population in sustaining expensive pension commitments to the baby boomer generation. International and supranational organizations have also put work–family reconciliation on the agenda, with the EU setting targets for mothers' employment and child-care provision and the Organization for Economic Cooperation and Development (OECD) chiding states that lack adequate early childhood care and education programs (Mahon, 2008; Morgan, 2008).

These and other imperatives have impelled changes in some of the most conservative welfare regimes. Since the 1990s, the Netherlands has adopted a strategy of encouraging part-time work for all parents and expanding child-care subsidies. This has produced a dramatic increase in women's employment, albeit largely in part-time work. In

Germany, both demographic decline and the so-called "PISA shock" (an OECD-PISA study showing the academic weaknesses of German children compared to those in other nations) have spurred the current grand coalition government to create a well-paid parental leave, and to encourage municipalities to develop more child-care centers (Evers, Lewis and Riedel, 2005: 199; Hege, 2006). The British Labour government has also expanded the maternity leave system and increased the resources devoted to public child care, although much of the latter has been in part-time services (Lewis, 2003).[3]

One challenge to coherent work–family policies in these countries is that most maintain a sharp division between education and care programs. For example, in France and Belgium—two countries often held up as exemplars of good policy in western Europe—there is an institutionalized divide between preschools and child care. Preschools form the backbone of their early childhood care and education system, offering universal services for all children between the ages of three and six.[4] These are largely free to parents, and are open during a long school day (usually 8:30–3:30 or 8:30–4:30), with programs often closed one afternoon a week.[5] For children below the age of three, the situation is more heterogeneous: there are crèches run by local governments that are publicly funded, yet access to these programs is fairly limited (to about 10 percent of children under the age of three in France). There also are subsidized and regulated networks of family child care, which are more widely available than the crèches in both countries.

Different institutional actors have responsibility for these two areas of policy, making coherent planning difficult. Family policy or child welfare institutions generally oversee child care for the under-threes (and after-school care), whereas educational ministries control the preschools and tend to view them as educational programs without a caregiving vocation.[6] These understandings, combined with the institutional division, make it difficult, if not impossible, to forge a coherent "educare" policy of the kind found in the Nordic countries. It also impedes changes to the opening hours of the schools to make them compatible with parents' work schedules.[7] In many countries, preschool programs and the regular school system offer short-day programs and lack lunch facilities at school. Changes to these practices usually run up against powerful interests for the status quo, among both teachers' unions and education ministry officials. Further complicating matters is the fact that child-care policy has been substantially decentralized to local governments since the 1980s in France, and to regional governments in Belgium.

Such difficulties of coordinating care and education are common outside the Nordic countries, as responsibility is usually divided between social services or family ministries and educational ones (OECD, 2006: 46–7). Federal systems exacerbate this bureaucratic fragmentation. In Germany, the federal system assigns responsibility for child care and preschool education policies to the *Länder*, municipality, and district, and reserves a large role for the voluntary sector (Hege, 2006: 197–8). It is therefore challenging for the federal government to achieve changes in school schedules or the availability of public child care.

Another source of fragmentation in the policy-making process is that work–family policies are often driven by multiple and at times competing goals. France, for example, has lurched between various policy objectives since the 1970s. Initially, the goal was to assist working mothers, but as unemployment rates rose by the end of that decade, governments created a three-year unpaid leave to encourage mothers to stay at home. Then a socialist government came to power and child care was again a priority, but this quickly lost ground to anti-unemployment and fiscal concerns. A benefit was created for mothers who stay home for several years, and subsidies were created for cheaper, less-regulated forms of care (family child care, nannies) (Jenson and Sineau 2001). Notably, gender equality was *never* one of the dominant motivations: helping out working mothers has been one objective, but French policy makers have never seriously sought to tackle the gendered division of labor and unequal take-up of parental leave time in the way that Sweden and Iceland have tried to do.

The shifting motivations of French policy makers are echoed in many other European countries, as gender equality aims sometimes compete with economic, demographic, or educational objectives. For decades, the fight against unemployment has been preeminent, and this has produced policies that reduce the supply of women in paid work, such as lengthy care leaves (Morgan and Zippel, 2003). Somewhat paradoxically, the concern in the past ten to fifteen years has shifted to activating more of the labor supply rather than reducing it, particularly with an eye to future labor shortages and concerns about demographic decline. These concerns have dovetailed with debates about the need to help single mothers attain self-sufficiency. Thus, governments increasingly privilege activation, including of women with children.

While this may open up a window of opportunity for policy change, the challenge for advocates of a dual-earner/dual-caregiver model is to keep gender-egalitarian goals front and center. In recent years, many European countries have reformed and expanded their parental leave systems and augmented the rights of parents to work part-time (Fagan, 2003). The expansion of affordable, public child care has been slower, and in fact the increase in subsidized caring time at home may reduce pressure for the continued development of child-care services. Indeed, one reason that governments have created such leaves or reduced work time possibilities has been to reduce their own responsibility for such programs. In this they are often successful. In France, the expansion of the home care allowance in the mid-1990s produced a sharp drop in the employment of mothers with two children.[8] This took some pressure off public officials to improve access to the public crèches, and the proportion of children in these programs has been constant since the early 1990s.

Even where gender-egalitarian goals are officially present, societal outcomes may defy policy makers' expectations. The Netherlands adopted a law that, since 2000, gives all employees the right to request reduced work hours from their employers. One of the stated aims of allowing all people to request part-time work was to give parents the ability to be in paid work while still having time to care for their children. One hope was that, with all people having the right to work part-time, both fathers and mothers would reduce their working hours and divide up work and caring time more equally—the *combinatie scenario* (Knijn, 2001). With each parent working three or four days a week, the child would attend child care for two or three days each week, and be home for the rest.

Despite these gender-egalitarian intentions, in practice very few couples actually follow this model. In 2005, for example, in only 8 percent of couples with young children were women working full-time (over 35 hours per week), whereas in 52 percent of couples women worked part-time, and in 40 percent women did not work at all (Portegijs, et al., 2006). If anything, fathers' time in paid work has increased over the past decade, and while their time in unpaid work has increased somewhat, it is still considerably less than the time women spend in unpaid work. In 2005, in couples with at least one child under age five, men performed on average a little over 23 hours of unpaid work each week, compared to over 47 hours of unpaid work done by women. Men were in paid work an average of 41.5 hours per week, whereas women spent on average 14 hours per week in paid work (Portegijs, et al., 2006: 106).

Do policies allowing extended leaves and part-time work reinforce traditional gender roles? Or are they promoting some slow changes in social practices and beliefs? There is little data that can satisfactorily

Figure 14.2

Percentage of Respondents Who Believe Mothers of Preschool Children Should Stay Home Full-Time, 1994 and 2002

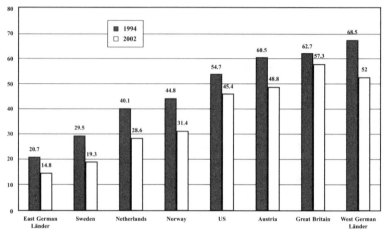

(See International Social Survey Program)

address this question, but we can at least note that there has been some shift in beliefs about mothers working while their children are young. Comparative public opinion data shows declining support for the traditional male-breadwinner model in the last decade (see Fig. 14.2). Particularly in countries like Austria, Germany, the UK, and the Netherlands, the previously high support for the idea that mothers should be at home full-time while their children are young has declined. Even though mothers work far fewer hours than men in a country such as the Netherlands, they have a much stronger attachment to the labor force than in the past, when the Dutch had some of the lowest rates of female workforce participation in Europe.

At the same time, however, the percentage of people who believe mothers should work full-time is not very high, even though it has increased somewhat (Fig. 14.3). Increasingly, the public in many of these countries—including the Nordic countries—favor the idea of a reduced work schedule for mothers. There are multiple ways to interpret these figures: it may be that, if it were truly possible for mothers to work full-time while they had young children, more people would embrace the idea of them doing so. On the other hand, even in Sweden where mothers'

Figure 14.3

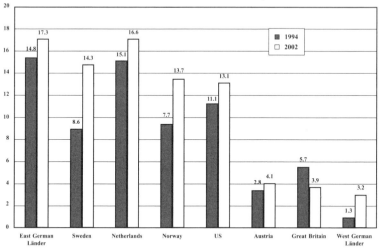

Percentage of Respondents Who Believe Mothers of Preschool Children Should Work Full-Time, 1994 and 2002

full-time work is possible, support for the idea is fairly low. One might therefore conclude that the public is fairly comfortable with policies that restructure mothers' time so that they can spend time with their children while they are young, yet still preserve their place in employment.

POLITICAL LESSONS FROM WESTERN EUROPE

What are some of the lessons we can draw from the European experience with work and family policies? One is that advocates of the dual-earner/dual-caregiver model of public policy should proceed cautiously. As the experiences of both the Nordic and continental European countries show, advocates are likely to see only part of their package of reforms implemented, and countries could stall halfway along the path to this model. Part-time work for women can undercut the drive for other kinds of reforms, and become entrenched as a pattern of behavior and a set of economic structures that are difficult to alter. Long parental leaves have similar effects, particularly if they dampen pressures for expanded child-care spending by allowing parents more paid leave time at home.

One way to deal with this is to keep the emphasis on care services while slowly expanding parental leave. In Finland, for example, social democrats pushed to create a right for parents to have access to care services, ensuring that no one is forced to take a lengthy leave against their will. Both Finland and Sweden now mandate that all children have access to a child-care place by a certain age (OECD, 2006: 80–81). Still, the lack of services for children below the age of one, coupled with powerful societal expectations about the acceptable age for infants to go to child care, ensures that there is little choice for mothers during the first year of their child's life. The lack of real choices is more evident in other parts of Europe, where child-care services for under-threes are insufficient and, in countries like Britain or the Netherlands, often quite expensive. Taking a lengthy parental leave or part-time work may thus be the only option, and usually mothers are the ones to reduce their working time. This may correspond with their preference, but as long as adequate care services are lacking it is hard to know whether or not mothers are truly exerting their "free choice" in the matter.

Another lesson is that gender-equality advocates should work to make sure that expansions of parental leave time come largely through increased rights for fathers. Once lengthy and generous leave entitlements are in place and being taken by mothers, it may be difficult to reverse these entitlements. Iceland resisted calls for expanding parental leave in general, and instead added only additional months for fathers, and the result was a significant increase in the percentage of days taken by men. This might be a good model for other countries looking to expand their parental leaves. The 2006 parental leave reform in Germany created a twelve-month, well-paid leave open to both parents, but added two additional months that could only be taken by the partner who had not taken the bulk of the leave. Notably, the original proposal was for a ten-month leave, with two additional months for the father, but this ran into opposition on the grounds that the leave mothers would likely take would be too short. Even though reformers had to compromise and add more months to what would likely be mothers' time off, including mandates for the other partner to take leave was an important way to implant gender-equality objectives when the leave was being created.

A third lesson is about the multidimensional nature of work–family policies, which offers both opportunities and pitfalls for reformers. State investment in this area can be justified on a number of grounds, such as aims of pedagogy, of fostering gender equality, of improving economic efficiency, and of combating demographic decline, among others. In some political climates, some of these rationales may be more effective than others, yet each could produce policies that would be helpful to parents or good for children, while hardly advancing the gender-egalitarian aims of the dual-earner/dual-caregiver model. Early childhood education programs offer an apt example: the expansion of these programs has been justified largely on pedagogic grounds, and there is now wide agreement across western Europe that young children benefit from access to them. Yet reforms based on these aims often produce part-time programs that are ill-adapted to the needs of working parents. Once in place, such programs can be difficult to change; German reformers are now grappling with how to transform their largely part-day programs with often irregular schedules (particularly in the western *Länder*) into longer-day programs.

At the same time, the multiple dimensions of work–family policies may provide a resource for coalition-building, enabling groups with divergent perspectives to agree on reforms that meet multiple objectives. A system of universal early childhood education, as was developed in France, could be popular in other countries as both a form of educational enrichment, and as an aid to working parents. Although they are not perfectly adapted to parents' work schedules, some municipalities have added on after-school services that round out the already lengthy day spent in these programs, and parents can otherwise use subsidies to help purchase child care for the hours after school. The French approach thus preserves the educational goals at the heart of the preschool system and enjoys wide support among parents, all of whom send their children to preschool for its educational benefits whether they are in paid work or not. The French approach also does not attempt to make teachers extend their hours at school, which they would likely resist, but pragmatically builds upon existing services to help meet working parents' needs. The result is not the unified educare model found in the Nordic countries, but a heterogeneous mix of services and subsidies that address a wide range of parental preferences.

The challenge for gender-equality advocates will be to make sure that their aims are taken seriously by those in power who might be driven by other goals. A window of opportunity for policy change has been opening in many European countries, with concerns about demographic decline, future labor shortages, welfare dependency, and educational readiness sparking reform efforts in countries that previously did little to help parents balance work and family. Yet governments may adopt policies that fail to advance their societies very far along the pathway to the dual-earner/dual-caregiver model, such as lengthy parental leaves largely taken by women, or rights to part-time work that few men take up. Equality advocates will thus have to fight to make sure that public policy not only seeks to ease the burden on women of work and care responsibilities, but also to shift some of that burden onto the shoulders of men.

NOTES

1   A Swedish scholar, Rita Liljeström, provided one of the earliest academic formulations of this model. See Leira (2006: 29).

2   Cited in Lammi-Taskula (2006: 93).

3   The government's 2001 Employment Bill created a right for fathers to take two weeks' paternity leave, a right to twenty-six weeks paid adoption leave and twenty-six more weeks of unpaid leave, and extended the maternity leave to twenty-six weeks of paid leave and twenty-six more unpaid weeks.

4   The age of entry into the preschool is two-and-a-half in both Belgium and France.

5   Closing preschool and elementary school for one afternoon per week was instituted to allow time for parents to arrange for religious education. Although few parents arrange for such education any more, the continuation of this is an excellent example of the path-dependence of now-obsolete structures.

6   In Belgium, this is complicated by the devolution of responsibility to the French- and Flemish-speaking areas. In French-speaking Belgium, a Ministry of Childhood oversees all early childhood care and education, but there is still an administrative separation between education and care. In the Flemish areas, the Ministry of Education oversees the preschool system and the Ministry for Welfare, Family, and Equal Opportunities has responsibility for child care. OECD (2006: 283, 289).

7   Some municipalities add on after-school care services for children attending these preschools as a cheaper way to provide child care: the facilities are paid for by the national Education Ministry, but the local government pays the costs of the care staff who work after official school hours. For some working parents, this rounds out the full work day, while others will hire a babysitter to pick up their child(ren) after preschool is over.

8   Eligibility was increased, as was the value of the benefit. Parents also gained the right to take it part-time. Bonnet and Labbé (1999).

REFERENCES

Bergman, Helena and Barbara Hobson, 2002, "Compulsory Fatherhood: The Coding of Fatherhood in the Swedish Welfare State," in B. Hobson, ed., *Making Men into Fathers: Men, Masculinities and the Social Politics of Fatherhood*, Cambridge: Cambridge University Press.

Bergqvist, Christina, Jaana Kuusipalo and Auður Styrkarsdóttir, 1999, "The Debate on Childcare Policies," in Ann-Dorte Christensen, Christina Bergqvist, Anette Borchorst, Nina C. Raaum, and Auður Styrkársdóttir, eds, *Nordic Democracies: Gender and Politics in the Nordic Countries*, Oslo: Scandinavian University Press.

Bonnet, Carole and Morgane Labbé, 1999, "L'activité professionnelle des femmes après la naissance de leurs deux premiers enfants: l'impact de l'allocation parentale d'éducation," *Etudes et Résultats* 37.

Borchorst, Anette, 2006, "The Public–Private Split Rearticulated: Abolishment of the Danish Parental Leave," in A. L. Ellingsæter and A. Leira, eds., *Politicising Parenthood in Scandinavia*.

Brachet, Sara, 2001, *Politiques familiales et assurance parentale en Suède*, Paris: CAF Dossier d'Etudes no. 21.

Bussemaker, Jet, 1998, "Rationales of Care in Contemporary Welfare States: The Case of Childcare in the Netherlands," *Social Politics: International Studies in Gender, State & Society* 5 (1): 70–96.

Edmund Dahlström, ed., 1971, *The Changing Roles of Men and Women*, Boston: Beacon Press.

Ellingsæter, Anne Lise, 2006, "The Norwegian Childcare Regime and Its Paradoxes," in Ellingsæter and Leira, eds., *Politicising Parenthood in Scandinavia*.

Esping-Andersen, Gøsta, 1990, *The Three Worlds of Welfare Capitalism*, Princeton: Princeton University Press.

Evers, Adelbert, Jane Lewis, and Birgit Riedel, 2005, "Developing Child-Care Provision in England and Germany: Problems of Governance," *Journal of European Social Policy* 15 (3): 195-209.

Eydal, Gudny Bjork and Stefan Olafsson, 2003, *Social and Family Policy: The Case of Iceland*, third report for the project "Welfare Policy and Employment in the Context of Family Change," online: http://www.york.ac.uk/inst/spru/research/nordic/icelandpoli.pdf (accessed May 21, 2007).

Fagan, Colette, 2003, *Working-Time Preferences and Work–Life Balance in the EU: Some Policy Considerations for Enhancing the Quality of Life*, Dublin: European Foundation for the Improvement of Living and Working Conditions.

Hege, Adelheid, 2006, "Pères, femmes, enfants, migrants: changement de paradigme et résistances," *Chronique internationale de l'IRES* 101, July: 11–21.

Jenson, Jane and Mariette Sineau, 2001, "France: Reconciling Republican Equality with 'Freedom of Choice'," in Jenson and Sineau, eds, *Who Cares? Women's Work, Childcare, and Welfare State Redesign*, Toronto: University of Toronto Press.

Kapborg, Inez, 2000, "Swedish Nurses' Experiences of Being Forced into Part-Time Employment," *Nursing and Health Sciences* 2: 173–77.

Knijn, Trudie, 2001 "Care Work: Innovations in the Netherlands," in Mary Daly, ed., *Care Work: The Quest for Security*, Geneva: ILO.

Lammi-Taskula, Johanna, 2006, "Nordic Men on Parental Leave: Can the Welfare State Change Gender Relations?" in A. L. Ellingsæter and A. Leira, eds, *Politicising Parenthood in Scandinavia: Gender Relations in Welfare States*, Bristol: Policy Press.

Leira, Arnlaug, 2002, *Working Parents and the Welfare State: Family Change and Policy Reform in Scandinavia*, Cambridge: Cambridge University Press.

Leira, Arnlaug, 2006, "Parenthood Change and Policy Reform in Scandinavia, 1970s-2000," in A. L. Ellingsæter and A. Leira, eds, *Politicising Parenthood in Scandinavia: Gender Relations in Welfare States*, Bristol: Policy Press.

Leira, Arnlaung, 1998, "Caring as Social Right: Cash for Child Care and Daddy Leave," *Social Politics: International Studies in Gender, State & Society* 5 (3): 362–78.

Lewis, Jane, 2003, "Family Change and Family Policies in the UK," *Journal for the Study of British Cultures* 9 (2): 209–22.

Mahon, Rianne, 1997, "Child Care in Canada and Sweden: Policy and Politics," *Social Politics* 4 (3): 382–418.

Mahon, Rianne, 2008, "Babies and Bosses: Gendering the OECD's Social Policy Discourse," in Rianne Mahon and Stephen McBride, eds, *The OECD and Transnational Governance*, Vancouver: University of British Columbia Press.

Melby, Kari, Anu Pylkkanen, Bente Rosenbeck, and Christina Carlsson Wetterberg, eds, 2000, *The Nordic Model of Marriage and the Welfare State*, Copenhagen: Nordic Council of Ministers.

Morgan, Kimberly J. and Kathrin Zippel, 2003, "Paid to Care: The Origins and Effects of Care Leave Policies in Western Europe," *Social Politics: International Studies in Gender, State & Society* 10 (1): 49–85.

Morgan, Kimberly J., 2006, *Working Mothers and the Welfare State: Religion and the Politics of Work–Family Policies in Western Europe and the United States*, Palo Alto: Stanford University Press.

Morgan, Kimberly J., 2008, "Towards the Europeanization of Work–Family Policies? The Impact of the EU on Policies for Working Parents," in S. Roth, ed., *Gender Politics in the Expanding European Union*, Oxford/New York: Berghahn Books.

Mósesdóttir, Lilja, 2005, *Reconciliation of Work and Private Life in Iceland*, report written for the European Commission, Gender and Employment Network, Group of Scientific Experts on Gender, Social Inclusion and Employment: 13; online: http://www.bifrost.is/Files/Skra_0012275.pdf (accessed May 21, 2007).

National Agency for Education, 2007, *Descriptive Data on Childcare, Schools, and Adult Education in Sweden 2006*, Stockholm: National Agency for Education.

OECD, 2006, *Starting Strong II: Early Childhood Care and Education*, Paris: OECD.

Ostner, Ilona, 1994, "Back to the Fifties: Gender and Welfare in Unified Germany," *Social Politics: International Studies in Gender, State & Society* 1 (1), Spring: 32–59.

Portegijs, Wil, Brigitte Hermans, and Vinodh Lalta, 2006, *Emancipatiemonitor 2006*, The Hague: Sociaal en Cultureel Planbureau.

Ruggie, Mary, 1984, *The State and Working Women: A Comparative Study of Britain and Sweden*, Princeton: Princeton University Press.

Saraceno, Chiara, 1994, "The Ambivalent Familism of the Italian Welfare State," *Social Politics: International Studies in Gender, State & Society* 1 (1) Spring: 60–82.

van Kersbergen, Kees, 1995, *Social Capitalism: A Study of Christian Democracy and the Welfare State*, London: Routledge.

15

Class Disparities, Market Fundamentalism and Work–Family Policy: Lessons from California

Ruth Milkman

The problem of reconciling work and family commitments is not new; indeed, it has been a central concern for feminists since the birth of industrial capitalism. Recently the issue has entered the mainstream of public debate, as maternal labor-force participation rates have climbed to unprecedented levels and the "male-breadwinner/female-homemaker" family has declined throughout the global North. In wealthy nations on both sides of the Atlantic, despite the fact that the vast majority of wives and mothers today are employed outside the home, gendered expectations (and behavior!) regarding housework and family care have been altered relatively little. What Gornick and Meyers call "partial gender specialization," with women continuing to shoulder the vast bulk of caregiving labor alongside their paid work, is now the norm. The resulting time pressures on mothers and other women with significant care-work commitments, as well as on those men with such commitments, have sparked increased concern about work–family "balance."

The US has long been on the leading edge of these transformations. Second-wave American feminists succeeded in opening up professional opportunities for women as early as the 1960s and early 1970s, even as ongoing economic restructuring (especially the growth of the tertiary sector) increased demand for women workers in the labor market as a whole. On the supply side, meanwhile, sharply declining real incomes among non-college-educated men since the 1970s led growing numbers of married women and mothers to join the labor force to keep their families afloat.

Over the years since then, although outright gender discrimination in the labor market and job segregation by gender have by no means disappeared, young women's career aspirations have risen substantially, and gender-based wage disparities in entry-level jobs have narrowed considerably. The current pattern is one of accumulating disadvantage for women, so that the gender gap in pay widens over the life course, particularly for mothers (Valian, 1998; Glass, 2004). Mothers' greater labor market disadvantage partly reflects the persistently asymmetric gender division of housework and family care, but there is also accumulating evidence of an employer-driven "motherhood penalty" in the managerial and professional ranks, while fathers in these occupational categories enjoy a wage premium (Correll et al., 2007).

By the twentieth century's end, as working hours grew longer and time demands intensified in the "new economy," both genders expressed the desire for relief with ever-growing urgency. The "time bind," as Arlie Hochschild (1997) memorably labeled it a decade ago, is especially acute in the US. Survey after survey has found work–family balance to be high on the wish list for working Americans (even as feminism itself remains, for many, anathema). And public support has burgeoned for policy measures to ease the burden on employed parents. In a 2003 survey of adult Californians, for example, 85 percent of respondents expressed support for the idea of paid family leave, with extensive majorities in every demographic category and across the political spectrum (Milkman and Appelbaum, 2004). In a rare exception to the ongoing rollback of state regulation of the labor market, political momentum for positive governmental intervention on this front is growing rapidly. Yet most employed women in the US must still find private, individual "solutions" to "their" problems with work–family balance. Feminists and labor activists have long promoted more collective approaches, but their success so far remains limited.

Indeed, the nation's famously minimalist welfare state, along with an exceptionally strong tilt toward gender-neutrality in those laws and policies that do exist, has produced what is incontestably the industrialized world's most meager public provision for work–family support. In this respect, the US could hardly be more different from Europe, where a long and deeply entrenched family policy tradition, historically rooted in demographic concerns as well as in social-democratic efforts to use the state as a social leveler, has generated a vast state-sponsored apparatus of support for women (and sometimes men) who are actively involved in both caregiving and paid work. On the other hand, feminist influence on this policy arena developed later in Europe than in the US, and was (at least initially) weaker.

Gornick and Meyers do a superb job of excavating these developments and the complex social, political and economic dynamics underlying them. Their "dual-earner/dual-caregiver" model is a compelling approach that neatly combines the insights of second-wave feminism with the legacy of social-democratic family policies. For researchers who focus on the US, their comparative perspective is especially welcome. By carefully conceptualizing gender-egalitarian policy proposals that improve on existing European work–family policies, Gornick and Meyers make an especially valuable contribution. Yet, advancing this policy agenda in the US context involves some special challenges.

This chapter focuses on two distinctive dimensions of the US case that Gornick and Meyers treat only marginally (and which are far less salient in the European context):

1) class disparities in existing access to work–family support, and
2) the influence of market fundamentalism, which is the key political impediment to legislative proposals in this area.

After briefly discussing each of these phenomena as they are manifested in the US as a whole, I turn to the case of California, the state that has made by far the most substantial breakthrough in work–family policy in recent years. California's new paid family leave program, established by a law passed in 2002 and implemented in 2004, offers a model of what might be possible elsewhere in the US—for the moment, in other "blue" states; and perhaps in the future at the federal level.[1] However, California's experience also presents a cautionary tale in regard to the ongoing challenges facing advocates of change in the work–family arena, at least in the absence of a broader macro-political and cultural shift that legitimizes state intervention in the workplace more generally.

CLASS DISPARITIES

In the US, social class profoundly affects both patterns of time use and access to existing (mainly employer-provided) benefits that facilitate work–family reconciliation.[2] Along both dimensions, professionals and managers (regardless of gender) are sharply differentiated from the rest of the workforce. As the *New York Times* recently reported, even pumping breast milk at work is an option available mainly to well-paid professional women, while for lower-income mothers it is "close to impossible." (Kantor, 2006)

Such class disparities are hardly new, but they have intensified in the past few decades as economic inequalities have grown—both within the employed female population and among men (Bianchi, 1995; McCall, 2001). The pattern is stark, with access to paid time off for caregiving purposes widely available to professionals and managers (albeit on a modest scale by European standards), and largely inaccessible to the rest of the workforce (Heymann, 2000). There is an intermediate group, comprised of unionized and/or public-sector employees, but this sector of the workforce is shrinking as economic polarization continues to reshape the US political economy (Mishel et al., 2005).

The limited wage replacement that is currently available for family-related absences from work in the US primarily takes the form of employer-provided benefits—ranging from paid sick leave and paid vacation or "paid time off" (which combines sick leave and vacation) to disability insurance (commonly used for pregnancy-related leaves). Some employers—often as a result of collective bargaining agreements—also provide paid maternity or parental leave benefits. Eligible workers typically draw on a patchwork of employer-provided benefits (in a few states supplemented by state-sponsored disability insurance programs[3]) for income support when the arrival of a new child or a serious family illness necessitates an absence from work for any significant amount of time. But for many, especially those outside the managerial–professional occupations, wage replacement for caregiving purposes is not available at all, since in the US even paid sick leave, paid vacation and similar employer-provided benefits are far from universal. Indeed, between 1996 and 2000, only 42 percent of US women who were employed during their first pregnancy received *any* type of paid leave when the child was born (Johnson and Downs, 2005: 9).

Prior to the early 1990s, the US lacked any formal policy provision for parental leave, apart from the 1978 Pregnancy Discrimination Act (PDA), which requires employers to offer wage replacement for pregnancy-related "disabilities" to the same extent as they do for other disabilities. This law did not mandate any disability coverage, however, and to this day many employers (especially smaller ones) provide none. The legal framework guiding the PDA was explicitly gender-neutral, reflecting concern among feminists at the time that sex discrimination might increase if leaves were provided only to mothers (Vogel, 1993).[4] Indeed, this longstanding concern has been borne out in recent years by evidence that mothers who take advantage of employer-provided "work–family benefits" suffer substantial wage penalties (Glass, 2004).

In the 1980s and early 1990s several states passed laws providing job-protected (but unpaid) family leaves, and the federal government followed suit in 1993 with the Family and Medical Leave Act (FMLA). That law guarantees job-protected, unpaid leaves of up to twelve weeks to eligible US workers who need time off to care for a new baby or for a seriously ill family member.[5] Yet FMLA is limited in several critical ways. First of all, not everyone is aware of its provisions. Survey data suggest that, as late as 2000, seven years after it became law, only about 60 percent of US workers knew that FMLA existed (Waldfogel, 2001). Secondly, less than half of all private-sector workers meet the FMLA's eligibility requirements: to be covered, workers must be employed in establishments with at least fifty employees within a seventy-five-mile radius, and must have worked at least 1,250 hours during the previous year. Less than a fifth of new mothers are estimated to be covered by the FMLA (Ruhm, 1997). Third, because it provides only unpaid leaves, even those who are covered often cannot afford to take advantage of the law.

Both the frequency and length of family leaves taken by new mothers in the US have increased significantly since the passage of the FMLA (although this has not been the case for new fathers, despite the gender-neutral character of the legislation). Leaves to care for seriously ill family members (especially parents) have also increased in this period (Han and Waldfogel, 2003; Waldfogel, 2001). And the number of mothers who quit their jobs or were fired as a result of a first pregnancy has declined since the FMLA's passage, from about 39 percent to 28 percent, according to US government data. However, the same data also show that over half of maternity leaves remain entirely unpaid. The percentage of new mothers taking paid leaves (including those financed by employer-provided sick pay or paid vacations, and/or maternity and other paid family leave policies), after rising slightly in the late 1980s, has stabilized (at about 42 to 44 percent) since the FMLA's passage (Johnson and Downs, 2005).

The data on such paid leaves vividly illustrate the salience of class disparities: between 1996 and 2000, 59 percent of college-educated women who were employed during pregnancy received some sort of paid leave after the birth of their first child, but only 18 percent of those with less than a high school education did so (Johnson and Downs, 2005: 12). All else equal, those workers employed by large firms have greater access to paid leave benefits than do those working in small and medium-sized businesses. With the important exception of unionized workers (a steadily declining group in the US), professionals, managers, more educated, and better-paid workers generally, are far more likely than non-supervisory, low-wage, less-educated workers to have access to any type of employer-provided paid leave benefits. Ironically, despite their limited participation in caregiving activities, male workers are also more likely to have formal access to such benefits than their female counterparts (Heymann, 2000; Milkman and Appelbaum, 2004).

Thus, more than a decade after the passage of the FMLA, many US workers have no access to family leave whatsoever. Even among those who are covered by the FMLA, in the absence of adequate provision for wage replacement, a large proportion cannot afford to take a leave from work for more than a brief period of time when caregiving needs arise. A survey of employees conducted for the US Department of Labor in 2000 found that among FMLA-eligible respondents who indicated that they had recently needed family leaves but could not take them, the vast majority reported that the reason was financial. The same survey found that, among those who did take FMLA-covered leaves, economic worries remained salient, with more than half of respondents (54 percent) expressing concern about lacking enough money to pay their bills. Over a third of the female leave-takers surveyed (38 percent), and 30 percent of male leave-takers, received *no pay* during their FMLA-covered leaves (Waldfogel, 2001).

Similarly, in a 2004 screening survey of California employees who either had recently experienced or expected soon to experience the triggering events that would qualify them for benefits under the state's new paid family leave program, 18 percent of respondents indicated that they had needed but not taken a leave to care for a new child or a seriously ill family member in the preceding two years. Once again, the most frequently cited reason for not taking the needed leave was financial. Within the group that needed leave but did not take it, 61 percent of respondents reported that they "definitely" would have gone on leave if they "could have received some income to make up for lost pay," and another 25 percent reported that they "probably" would have done so. Among female respondents earning $9 per hour or less within the group who needed but did not take leave, 100 percent indicated that they "definitely" would have gone on leave if they could have received wage replacement![6]

Not only is access to employer-provided benefits concentrated in the upper echelons of the labor force, but public discussion of work–family issues in the US also focuses primarily on the needs and dilemmas of the affluent. This phenomenon dates back at least to 1963, when Betty Friedan's best seller, *The Feminine Mystique*, highlighted the anomie of college-educated homemakers in the post–Second World War years, and urged them to embrace careers to solve "the problem that has no name." Millions of women have since followed Friedan's advice, and indeed today unprecedented numbers are employed in managerial and professional jobs.

Public attention to the work–family reconciliation dilemmas facing this elite group of women is extensive and growing (among many recent examples, see Blair-Loy, 2003; Mason and Ekman, 2007; Correll et al., 2007; Stone, 2007). But the far more difficult plight of the majority of the female workforce, toiling away in low-wage, gender-stereotyped "pink collar" jobs, remains largely invisible. Even Arlie Hochschild's insightful 1997 book, *The Time Bind*, sometimes fell into the trap of generalizing from the experience of women in managerial jobs to that of Everywoman.[7]

In fact, the character of work–family issues varies greatly by social class. As Jerry Jacobs and Kathleen Gerson (2004) have shown, managers and professionals (of both genders) in the US typically work far longer hours than lower-level employees. Although many non-supervisory workers would prefer to work *more* hours than are readily available to them (for an extreme example, see Lambert, 2007), those who aspire to successful careers in elite occupations are expected to work extremely long hours. This contrasts starkly with the European pattern, and is directly tied to the far higher level of inequality in the US earnings distribution, perhaps because the most elite US workers receive such disproportionately large returns for working extra hours (see Freeman 2007: ch. 4).

That the norm of extensive work hours is so deeply embedded in managerial and professional culture presents a poignant dilemma for mothers in elite occupations, particularly in view of the late-twentieth-century ideology of "intensive mothering" (Hays, 1996). That ideology has been disproportionately adopted by the nation's most affluent families, eager to reproduce their class position, as Annette Lareau (2003) has documented; by contrast, working-class parenting takes a very different form.

Ironically, the escalating time demands on the nation's upper-tier workers emerged just when large numbers of highly educated women first gained access to elite professional and managerial jobs. Mary Blair-Loy (2003) has starkly exposed the hegemony of the "male model" at the highest levels of the contemporary corporate world, where family involvement for women (as well as men) is effectively precluded by a deeply entrenched culture that demands total "24/7" commitment to the firm. The same problem, albeit in less extreme form, is pervasive throughout the managerial ranks in the US. Indeed, even when firms are putatively "family-friendly," available benefits often go underutilized for this reason (see Hochschild, 1997; Fried 1998; Glass 2004). As Blair-Loy observes, some top women managers respond by "opting out," abandoning their fledgling careers, or in some cases forgoing motherhood entirely (see also Stone, 2007). Others use their abundant financial resources to hire substitute caregivers (Hertz, 1986).

In contrast, low-income workers in the US are regularly forced to choose between economic security and providing vital care for family members. Parents who have access to paid sick leave or paid vacation are five times more likely to stay home with a sick child than are those who lack such benefits, and ill children recover more quickly when parents are present (American Academy of Pediatrics, 2003; Ruhm, 2000; Heymann, 2000: 57–59). Yet paid leave is disproportionately available to those with the greatest economic resources. One recent survey found that two-thirds of low-income mothers (compared to slightly over a third of middle- and upper-income mothers) lose pay when they miss work because a child is sick (Kaiser Family Foundation, 2003). Apart from lost income, missing work under such conditions often has other negative employment consequences.

At the other extreme, public welfare provisions for the indigent have been radically restructured so as to require workforce participation from poor single mothers who formerly had access to state assistance while caring for their children at home (Reese, 2005; Somers and Block, 2005). And the nation's large and growing disenfranchised population of unauthorized immigrants is often unable or unwilling to access even the meager public provisions that do exist (from FMLA, to state-sponsored disability programs, to what remains of "welfare").

Class disparities, then, are a key feature of the work–family landscape in the US. Although there are some exceptions (most notably, unionized workers who gain access to employer-provided family leave and related benefits through collective bargaining), on the whole professionals and managers enjoy far more extensive work–family options—including paid leave, flexible hours, and so on—than their counterparts in clerical, service, sales and other low-wage jobs. Such highly paid professionals and managers are also more able to afford the wide array of commodified services—from prepared meals to paid domestic labor and private child care—available on the open market, on which affluent families increasingly rely to reconcile the demands of work and family.

Elsewhere in the industrialized world, governments have long since established universal social benefits that support children and families, and that were from the start intended to moderate class disparities. The growing popular concern about work–family balance and the recent groundswell of public support for paid family leave suggest the prospect that such policies might finally have a chance to take root in the US. But for that to occur, a key obstacle must be overcome—namely the anti-statist market fundamentalism that is hegemonic among employers, and that also influences the wider political culture.

MARKET FUNDAMENTALISM

Popular support for national family leave legislation has been on the rise in the US since at least the 1980s. But even the comparatively minimalist FMLA became law in the face of sustained opposition from organized business interests, which effectively blocked its passage for many years. Earlier, the business lobby had also strenuously opposed the PDA (Vogel, 1993: 71); but they lost this battle in 1978. Passing such legislation became still more difficult in the period of conservative ascendancy that followed. Congress approved family and medical leave bills twice under the first President Bush, who vetoed the legislation both times. The issue was then debated in the 1992 election campaign, and a revised version of the legislation was passed by the new Congress in January 1993. A month later, the FMLA was signed into law by President Clinton—the very first bill he signed after taking office (Martin, 2000; Bernstein, 2001).

In the post-Clinton years, political momentum shifted to the state level. California passed the nation's first paid family leave law in 2002, and the program it established came into effect in mid-2004. In 2005, paid leave bills were introduced in twenty-six states (National Partnership for Women and Families, 2006). Despite business opposition, in Washington State, a paid family leave law was passed and signed in 2007, although funds have not yet been appropriated to launch the program. The state of New Jersey (which, like California, has a longstanding state disability insurance program) also created a paid family leave program through a law passed and signed in 2008, with program benefits starting on July 1, 2008. Similar programs are moving closer to passage in other states as well and federal legislation creating a national paid family leave program has been actively considered by Congress for the past few years as well.

The best-documented, and indeed prototypical case in the history of political contestation over work–family policy in the US is the seven-year campaign against the FMLA, led by the national Chamber of Commerce and small business groups. Cathie Jo Martin succinctly summarizes the arguments that business made against the bill at the time:

> Small business predicted dire economic impacts to companies from the high costs of hiring replacement workers [and] also argued that the new benefit would constrict the creation of jobs and hurt female workers by motivating employers to discriminate against women in hiring . . . and reduce the flexibility with which managers and workers could negotiate compensation packages. (Martin, 2000: 221–22)

It was perfectly acceptable for companies to offer such benefits voluntarily (as indeed many already did), but organized business passionately opposed any employer "mandate" in this (or any other) area. As Martin rendered the dominant business view: "Although parental and disability leaves are excellent employee benefits, Congress should not dictate benefits. Doing so is contrary to the voluntary, flexible and comprehensive benefits system that the private sector has developed" (Martin, 2000: 221). Similar arguments were advanced by business interests at the state level in response to proposals for paid family leave legislation (Koss, 2003, documents this for the case of California).

The specific claims of negative effects on business from employer mandates are largely unsustainable (see below); but this practical reality has yet to undercut the ideological framework that continues to dominate the business side of the policy debates. Indeed, market fundamentalism, or "the idea that society as a whole should be subordinated to a system of self-regulated markets" (Somers and Block, 2005: 261) is the most salient political obstacle to the development of work–family policy in the twenty-first century US. It has been the central trope of organized business opposition to the FMLA and subsequent legislative efforts to address work–family issues, and has increasingly penetrated the wider political culture as well. As Margaret Somers and Fred Block (2005: 282) argue, Anglo-American societies, with their Lockean legacy and long-standing distrust of the state, have been particularly influenced by this ideology since the 1970s, and among these societies the US is the most extreme case.

Business opposition to family leave legislation is part of a broader animus against "employer mandates," which are routinely denounced as "job-killers." This is a logical corollary of the broader ideology of market fundamentalism. With rare exceptions, employers consistently oppose—often on explicitly ideological grounds—virtually all labor and social legislation that would move the US toward European-style family policies, including even minimum- and living-wage laws. The New Deal order—let alone the corporate liberalism of a century ago—has in recent decades entirely lost any legitimacy it once enjoyed among employers. In my own fieldwork I have even encountered managers who, blissfully ignorant of practices in the rest of the world, assert that the introduction of paid family leave in the US would endanger the nation's global competitiveness. For example, one California manager, aghast at the state's new law, exclaimed, "That's why we moved our call center to Ireland!"—apparently unaware that paid family leave had existed in Ireland for half a century.

Although this ideological consensus has virtually no defectors at the public, political level, many employers' practical experience with FMLA and other work–family balance policies nevertheless appears to have been quite positive. Over a decade after the FMLA's passage, there is little evidence to support earlier concerns of business that its enactment would be highly burdensome. On the contrary, managers on the ground report little difficulty in adhering to the law's provisions. A 2000 US Department of Labor employer survey found that nearly two-thirds (64 percent) of respondents found it "very easy" or "somewhat easy" to comply with the FMLA, with even larger majorities (84 percent and 90 percent, respectively) reporting that the law had "no noticeable effect" or a "positive effect" on their productivity and profitability (US Department of Labor, 2001). Indeed, many employers expanded their own provision of family and medical leave benefits in the aftermath of the law's passage (Ruhm, 1997; Waldfogel, 1999, 2001; Han and Waldfogel, 2003). Administering such leaves is now a routine feature of the human resource management repertoire of many (though by no means all) large US companies.

Field interviews with managers—to be sure, mostly in large, family-friendly firms—echo the 2000 Department of Labor survey data in confirming that FMLA compliance has been unproblematic for most covered employers.[8] "Back when we didn't have [FMLA], if you told me this is what I had to do, I think I would have shot myself," one said. "But now that we do it on a day to day basis, it's no big deal." Many of these informants indicated that FMLA leaves related to pregnancy were especially easy to handle, since they could plan ahead to cover the work involved during an absence of predictable duration. In contrast, leaves tied to family medical crises took all concerned by surprise, but most interviewees viewed such events as an unavoidable part of doing business, and effectively manageable under the FMLA.

Most of those interviewed felt that the positive benefits of FMLA outweighed its drawbacks, and some were positively enthusiastic. "You always have perfunctory whining," one human resource manager at a nonprofit research firm told us. "But everyone has problems from time to time and we understand that employees need time off occasionally." And a manager at a computer chip design company defended the decade-old federal law against ongoing criticism from colleagues in the business world, asserting that, as far as productivity and profitability were concerned, FMLA was a "non-event." "When we're talking about bottom-line issues, I've never heard anyone say, 'The real problem is FMLA.' No one has ever said 'The share price of our stock stinks, and if we could only repeal this leave law we'd be doing better.'"

Several managers suggested that the availability of FMLA leaves had improved organizational morale, as well as facilitating retention of valued employees. "The people who get the leaves appreciate it," one manager at a large food processing firm asserted. "In the long term, we get better productivity, because employees feel they are supported by the company," a computing engineering firm manager reported. "Overall, it helps with the morale." And a manager at a large retailer (which offered paid time off only to the minority of its employees who were full-timers) noted, "Yes, people have the burden of picking up the slack for someone else on leave, but they also know that someone will do this for them if they need it." Still another manager at an entertainment firm commented, "Turnover would be much higher in the absence of FMLA leaves."

In keeping with the pragmatic approach of these on-the-ground managers in family-friendly firms who recognize the positive features of the FMLA and related policies, some work–family advocates have devoted a great deal of energy to advancing the "business case" for paid family leave and, more generally, for a family-friendly workplace. They point to the considerable costs associated with (a) employee turnover—i.e. the cost of recruiting and training new workers to replace those who quit for family-related reasons; (b) absenteeism; and (c) lost productivity associated with employees who remain at work while preoccupied with the unmet needs of their families, or while trying to juggle caregiving with paid work (see Levin-Epstein, 2006; Williams, 2006).

Although systematic evidence on these matters is difficult to obtain, some companies have done their own calculations, and have concluded that generous work–family benefits can indeed offer large cost savings. Merck, for example, estimated that its own six-month parental leave policy saved $12,000 per employee in turnover-related costs; similarly, Aetna reported saving $2 million in hiring and training costs, because 91 percent of its employees returned after taking family leave (Martin, 2000: 157).

In some cases, employer recognition of such costs has led them to improve their own benefit packages—especially in cases where this could improve retention of female professionals and managers with firm-specific training and/or for whom recruitment costs are especially high (such as recently feminized professions like law and accounting, or skilled occupational fields facing labor shortages, such as nursing). It may well be the case, as Williams (2006: 25–34) has so eloquently argued, that even employers in low-wage, female-dominated sectors like the retail or service industries—which rarely provide even health insurance or paid sick leave to their workers, much less paid family leave—would be economically better off if they devoted some degree of attention to work–family needs. But such low-road employers often appear to view high turnover positively, since it keeps the bulk of their payroll clustered at entry level and makes it easy to adjust to market fluctuations (see Lambert, 2009). And even in the case of managers and professionals in whom firms have sunk extensive training investments, and thus have a real interest in retaining, as Mary Blair-Loy (2003) has eloquently argued, ideology often trumps economic rationality.

The employers who do offer generous work–family benefits to their own employees nevertheless adamantly oppose legislative proposals that would require such provisions, standing in firm solidarity with the rest of the business community in opposing all legislative mandates. This is part of a broader commitment to market fundamentalism, and perhaps reflects concern that any concession to state intervention on one issue could become a slippery slope, legitimating state intervention on other fronts as well.

It follows that, as long as the ideology of market fundamentalism remains dominant (despite its retreat in the face of the current financial crisis, revival is not unlikely in the US context) efforts to appease business interests are not likely to be effective. The only hope of overcoming business opposition to paid family leave and other legislative proposals is to advance a competing, morally compelling narrative that can prevail over the anti-statist narrative of the fundamentalists. Such a narrative must emphasize the human needs left unmet in the absence of comprehensive policies for work–family support. Only on that basis will it be possible to mobilize enough political support to secure the passage of state-sponsored paid family leave and related work–family legislation in the face of business objections.

Indeed, that is how advocates finally won passage of both the FMLA (see Dark, 1999: 166; Martin, 2000; Bernstein, 2001: 125–26) and the California law (see Labor Project for Working Families, 2003). Both achievements, to be sure, were ultimately subject to political compromises, and included major concessions to the demands of organized business—although the business lobby nevertheless opposed them to the bitter end. In both cases, organized labor (also anathema to most employers in the US today, and to market fundamentalists generally) did much of the political strategizing and lobbying to win passage of the legislation, in coalition with women's rights groups and advocates for children, the elderly, and the disabled.

An effective coalition of this sort is possible, in part, because of the widespread public perception that work–family pressures are at a crisis point. Polls show overwhelming popular support for such measures as paid sick days and paid family leave laws, the hegemony of market fundamentalism notwithstanding. In a 2003 survey of California adults, for example, 89 percent of non-college-educated respondents supported paid family leave, compared to 82 percent of respondents with some college or higher levels of education (Milkman and Appelbaum, 2004: 53). The difference is statistically significant, but more surprising than the strong support among those who are least likely to have any access to employer-provided benefits is the high level of support among the more educated group, many of whom presumably have employer-provided benefits to draw on. This may reflect the fact that, in the absence of job security, even at the most family-friendly firms, managers and professionals often hesitate to take advantage of work–family benefits, fearing (with reason) that if they do so, they will be seen as lacking in career commitment (Fried, 1998; Hochschild, 1997; Glass, 2004). Universal state-supported paid family leave programs would level the playing field in this respect, so that more privileged workers would benefit too, even if the bulk of the material benefits would go to those who currently lack any paid leave options at all.

Some advocates feared that the 2003 California recall election removing Gray Davis from office and catapulting the pro-business Arnold Schwarzenegger into the governor's seat might lead to a rollback, or some sort of damaging modification of the California paid family leave program, which took effect just before the recall. But this has not occurred, perhaps because paid leave enjoys such broad popular support—both across the political spectrum and across class boundaries. As both this example and the widespread managerial complacency that set in shortly after the FMLA became law well illustrate, once business opposition to legislation of this type is successfully overcome, employers tend to accept defeat pragmatically, make the necessary adjustments in their day-to-day practices, and move on. All the more reason for advocates to concentrate on struggling for state intervention, rather than seeking to persuade or placate organized business.

CALIFORNIA'S PAID FAMILY LEAVE PROGRAM

The short history of California's paid family leave program—a key legislative success in the work–family area—is worth examining in a little more detail. Although its provisions are minimal by European standards, it nonetheless represents a breakthrough in the US context. The program is still too new to be definitively evaluated, but its political history is revealing, and some of its achievements and limits are already becoming evident.

When the California law was proposed in 2002, it faced intense opposition from the state's business lobby, just as the PDA and FMLA had on the federal level in earlier years. The California Chamber of Commerce and other business groups vigorously opposed the proposed bill. Ignoring the accumulated evidence from the previous decade's experience with the FMLA, they argued that a paid family leave program would impose excessive burdens on employers, especially small businesses (Koss, 2003).

Although organized business ultimately failed to block the bill's passage, it did win modifications to the initial version of the legislation, from which the final version differed considerably.[9] Nevertheless, on September 23, 2002, the nation's first comprehensive paid family leave program was signed into law by California's then-governor Gray Davis, and benefits became available to most employed Californians starting on July 1, 2004. The program provides up to six weeks of partial pay for eligible employees who need time off work to bond with a new child or to care for a seriously ill family member. It builds on California's longstanding state disability insurance (SDI) system, which for decades has provided income support for medical and pregnancy-related leaves. Like SDI, the paid family leave program is nearly universal in coverage: apart from some self-employed people, virtually all private-sector employees are included. (Public-sector workers are only included if they opt in through the collective bargaining process, but most already have access to paid leave benefits more extensive than those provided by the new law.)

Unlike the FMLA, then, California's paid family leave program covers all private-sector employees, regardless of the size of the organization they work for, including most part-time workers. (To be eligible, employees must have earned $300 or more during any quarter in the "base period" five to seventeen months before filing a claim). The program is thus especially valuable for low-wage workers, many of them female, who have limited or no access to employer-sponsored benefits providing any type of paid time off.

Even before the passage of this new law in 2002, California provided more income support for family leave than most other states. Under SDI, nearly all pregnant women employed in the private sector, as well as some in the public sector, could already receive partial wage replacement for four weeks before delivery, and for an additional six to eight weeks afterward.[10] California's paid family leave builds on the SDI model. As with SDI, there are no direct costs to employers: the benefit is funded entirely by an employee payroll tax (0.6 percent of wages). Eligible workers can receive, after a one-week waiting period, up to 55 percent of their normal weekly earnings, with a maximum of $959 per week in 2009 (the maximum is indexed to the state's average weekly wage) for up to six weeks a year.[11]

Eligible leaves include those for bonding with a new biological, adopted, or foster child; this benefit is available to fathers as well as mothers. For biological mothers, the new benefit supplements the pregnancy disability benefits previously available under SDI. Although it does not increase the amount of job-protected leave available to women who have given birth, paid family leave does provide six additional weeks of partial wage replacement. Also eligible are leaves to care for specified seriously ill family members (parents, children, spouses, or domestic partners). The law does not provide job protection, however; nor does it guarantee the continuation of health and/or pension benefits (although in many cases leave-takers have these additional protections under the FMLA or other laws). Employers may require workers to take up to two weeks of unused vacation leave before collecting paid family leave benefits.

Among the specific concerns business lobbyists cited in explaining their opposition to California's paid family leave legislation was that employers would incur significant costs in covering the work of absent employees, in the form of increased overtime payouts, payments for temporary replacements, additional training costs, and so on (Koss,

2003). Thus, the ways in which employers covered the work of those on leave in the period prior to the new law's implementation are of some interest. Our 2004 employer survey asked how the work of employees who went on family-related leaves for a week or more was covered. The most commonly reported method was to "assign the work temporarily to other employees." Fully 90 percent of employer respondents reported that this was the primary method they used to cover the work of nonexempt employees during family leaves, and the figure was only slightly lower (83 percent) for exempt employees.

While this suggests a homogeneity in approaches to the problem, field interviews revealed a rich variety of arrangements for covering the work of employees during both brief and extended absences. Virtually all the establishments we visited had developed systematic, often ingenious methods for handling such situations. Making provision for covering the work of absent employees is a business necessity, entirely apart from family leave. Managers constantly face the possibility that an employee may quit precipitously, become seriously ill and unable to work, enter the military, take an extended vacation or unpaid leave, and so on. Similarly, several informants mentioned that it was common for immigrant workers (who make up a substantial part of California's workforce) to make extended visits to their home countries—sometimes to care for an ill family member, but in other instances simply for a long visit. Under all these circumstances, many of which occur frequently but unpredictably, the work of absent employees needs to be covered. Thus, virtually all employers have long since developed mechanisms for ensuring that work will be covered during employee absences. In many cases they are able to do so with little difficulty, although sometimes the costs (in overtime pay, or fees to temporary employment agencies) can be significant. Still, these costs are modest relative to those associated with employee turnover, which is both more frequent than leave-taking or absenteeism, and generally more expensive for employers to address.

The consensus among our management interviewees was that more workers would go on leave as a result of the new state program, and that such leaves would be somewhat longer than in the past. "People will definitely take the full six weeks," one manager at a construction-engineering firm said. "Now, they only take what they can afford—less than six weeks in many cases." A public utility company manager agreed:

> Employees will take longer leaves since they will be able to combine the use of vacation pay with the new state benefit while their leave is job-protected [i.e. for the twelve weeks of job protection they have

under the FMLA]. Currently, they take less than the full amount since they typically do not have sufficient accumulated vacation and sick days.

Another manager at the corporate headquarters of a large food processing firm speculated: "It may become more legitimate for employees to take time off." This informant also thought younger workers might be especially affected, since in his view their mentality is different from that of many older workers, who view any absences from work as illegitimate. There were also predictions that male workers would take more time off than in the past. "More people will take advantage of this [law] and take more time off to bond with new babies," an insurance company manager stated. "Men in particular!"

Other managers—particularly those at enterprises with large numbers of well-paid professionals who already enjoyed paid leave benefits prior to the passage of the new state law—suggested that the program's impact would be modest. "People already take time off if they have a sick parent or child. They already take as much time as they can and that won't change," according to one law firm manager. A manager at a biotechnology firm agreed: "Most employees here already have a way to take paid leave—using state DI, or paid vacation." Similarly, at a computer engineering firm where most employees have high salaries and already enjoy extensive benefits, managers "don't expect the new paid leave to make a big change at this company," although they did expect that men would take advantage of the wage replacement for baby-bonding leaves, and go on slightly longer leaves than before.

The California program, despite its limitations, is a promising effort to institutionalize paid family leave in the inhospitable political setting of the US, and one that many other states are already seeking to replicate. But the practical impact of the California program has been constrained so far by two interrelated factors: a lack of awareness of its existence on the part of large segments of the state's population, and a low take-up rate in the initial phase of its implementation.

A survey conducted in fall 2003, about a year after the new law was passed, found that only 22 percent of adult Californians were aware of the paid family leave program's existence (Milkman and Appelbaum, 2004). In a follow-up survey in the summer of 2005, the figure was a somewhat higher 30 percent, but still well below the same respondents' awareness of the FMLA, which was 59 percent in the initial 2003 survey and 57 percent in the 2005 follow-up. In a 2007 follow-up survey, the awareness level had actually fallen slightly (but the difference between 2005 and 2007 was not statistically significant).

Moreover, those most in need of paid leave—low-income workers, those with limited education, and the foreign-born—were disproportionately represented among those who were unaware of the new program. In 2007, only 14 percent of respondents with household incomes of $25,000 or less were aware of the program, while 36 percent of those with household incomes over $75,000 knew of it. The program's potential as a social leveler cannot be realized if those who stand to benefit most remain unaware of its existence.

The business groups that opposed the California paid leave law warned that the costs of implementation might be higher than those the state had projected. So far, however, the opposite has been the case, partly because the take-up rate for the new program has been so modest. In the program's first year (July 1, 2004 to June 30, 2005), a total of 176,000 claims were received by the state, representing just over 1 percent of the 13 million eligible workers. The following year the number of claims actually fell slightly, to 137,000. Most of the claims (just under 90 percent) were for bonding with a new child, and of these bonding claims, over 80 percent were submitted by women. Among the non-bonding claims (those for leaves devoted to caring for a close relative), 70 percent were submitted by women (Employment Development Department, 2005). Only limited data are available on the take-up rate by income, but in general the profile of claimants by income seems to mirror the income distribution of the eligible workforce. The one exception is that workers earning $12,000 or less a year—about 20 percent of those eligible—are underrepresented among paid family leave claimants, making up about 16 percent, perhaps because they are least likely to be aware of the program (Sherriff, 2007: 7).

Over time, as public awareness grows, the take-up rate may rise, but the costs—which, as I have already noted, are borne entirely by workers themselves—are likely to remain manageable. Because the events that precipitate eligibility for leave are spread over the life course, a relatively small proportion of the workforce will go on leave from work to care for new children or ill family members at any one point in time. Indeed, California employers surveyed in 2004 (just before the new law took effect) reported that, in the previous year, an average of only 1.1 percent of their workers had taken a leave of more than one week due to childbirth or adoption, while just 1.8 percent had taken a leave of more than a week in order to stay home with a seriously ill child, parent, spouse or domestic partner.

Moreover, insofar as employers are able to coordinate their own benefits with the new state program, the more family-friendly firms might actually enjoy cost savings. As one manager predicted in an interview I conducted shortly before the program went into effect,

> Paid family leave in California was intended to help people who don't have any pay during maternity leave or medical leaves. But in fact the main beneficiaries will be higher-paid workers who already have paid sick leave and vacation and who will use the state program to top off their current benefits.

This is confirmed by the fact that, among the minority of adult Californians surveyed in 2007 who were already aware of the state program, 45 percent had learned about it from their employers; no other source of information was more frequently cited (though an equal proportion had learned about it from the mass media). If awareness of the program does not expand well beyond those workers whose employers are coordinating it with their own benefits, however, the new California law will do little to ameliorate the disparity between workers who already had access to paid leaves (via employer-sponsored benefits) and those who lacked such access.

Thus, the reality of California's paid family leave program is far less problematic for employers than the business lobbyists initially claimed. Not only are excellent systems already in place for covering the work of employees who are absent for extended periods, but the costs of those systems are modest, and counterbalanced by the savings associated with reduced turnover and absenteeism. Moreover, those employers whose employees use the state benefits instead of—or in tandem with—long-standing employer-financed benefits, are enjoying additional savings.

CONCLUSION

In the US, where market fundamentalism is a deeply entrenched feature of the political culture, organized business opposition to paid family leave and other legislative work–family "mandates" is likely to persist for the foreseeable future. This will be the case regardless of the practical, on-the-ground effects of such legislation, which might well be positive, as advocates of the "business case" maintain. Business resistance is rooted in a broader agenda of opposition to state regulation of all sorts, so that appeals to economic rationality—even if they are demonstrably correct—are unlikely to have much impact.

Rather than arguing within the terms set by business advocates, which are embedded in the larger market-fundamentalist narrative, those who favor public policy interventions to create paid leave programs and other work–family supports would do well to focus on two interrelated tasks. The first is to develop a strategy to surmount the organized lobbying efforts of business in the political arena, and the second is to advance an alternative moral narrative which reframes work–family issues in terms of human needs.

The strategic challenge is to build a coalition between labor unions, women's rights groups, senior organizations, those representing the disabled, and children's advocates—which collectively have the potential to exercise more political clout than the Chamber of Commerce and the rest of the business lobby. The legislative history of the FMLA and the California paid family leave program both suggest that this is a viable path to victory. Organized labor, which despite sharp declines in union density still has considerable political influence (see Dark, 1999) was particularly crucial in both these cases, and was further strengthened by its alliance with the other coalition partners. Both the FMLA and the California program became law because broad political coalitions were able to mobilize enough support for campaigns that successfully shaped the legislative process, and were strong enough politically to overcome the intransigent opposition of organized business.

As part of such an effort, claims that the proposed legislative initiatives for paid family leave and the like will have dire economic consequences can certainly be countered by the arguments that have already been developed by advocates of the "business case." Similarly, it is helpful to point out that decades of experience elsewhere show that government-mandated paid leave benefits far more generous than the ones now on offer in California are neither utopian nor incompatible with sustainable economic growth (as Gornick and Meyers have demonstrated in compelling detail). But under no circumstances will business relent in its opposition in response to such rational appeals. For an advocacy campaign to succeed, the defensive counterclaims must be coupled with an offensive strategy that frames the issue within an alternative moral narrative.

That alternative narrative should be focused on a straightforward insistence that paid family leave and other state-sponsored work–family policies deserve public support not on economic grounds (even if those too exist), but primarily because such policies meet urgent human needs. Those needs exist across class lines, even if they are especially pressing among the most disadvantaged populations. As noted above, polling data show overwhelming popular support for paid family leave programs, paid sick day legislation, and other work–family interventions, even among putatively conservative segments of the population. This popular support is rooted in the recognition that working families urgently need access to paid leaves and other types of family support, and that employers are not providing such access—especially not to those with the least ability to purchase substitute care in the marketplace.

The challenge, in short, is to outmaneuver the formidable business lobby politically. This is best accomplished not by engaging business on its own market-fundamentalist ideological terrain, but instead by appealing directly to the hearts and minds of the public with a moral narrative that focuses on the family-centered human needs of children, the seriously ill, and the elderly. Coupling such an alternative narrative with strategic coalition-building, as the recent success in California has shown, can be an extremely effective organizing approach. Winning work–family legislation on this basis in other states, and perhaps even at the federal level, is already within reach, even in the face of the nation's long-standing anti-statist tradition. Among other positive benefits, such efforts also promise to move the US in the direction of greater gender egalitarianism.

NOTES

1 In 2007, Washington State passed a paid family leave bill into law (although funding for it has not yet been appropriated) New Jersey passed a paid family leave bill into law in 2008, with benefits beginning in mid-2009. Similar efforts are underway in other states and also at the federal level.

2 The racial and ethnic disparities that are highly correlated with class are also salient, although I do not discuss them here, partly because of a paucity of data and partly because professionals and managers of color are treated quite similarly to their white counterparts in this particular arena.

3 State disability insurance programs, which can be used to support pregnancy-related leaves, have existed in California, Hawaii, New York, New Jersey, Rhode Island, and Puerto Rico for many years, but are absent in the rest of the US.

4 However, some states did enact legislation creating benefits exclusively for pregnant women in this period, later challenged in the courts by employers who argued that the PDA pre-empted such "special treatment." The Supreme Court ruled otherwise, however, in 1987. Vogel, 1993, offers an excellent analysis of this history.

5   The FMLA also mandates unpaid, job-protected leaves for an eligible employee's own illness, including pregnancy-related "disability."

6   These data are from a screening survey conducted in 2004 by the author and Eileen Appelbaum of employed Californians who either had recently experienced, or expected to experience in the near future, a life event such as the birth of a new child, or a serious family illness, triggering the need for family leave.

7   Hochschild's key finding was the counterintuitive and intriguing one that many women actually *preferred* to spend time at work rather than with their families, and thus often did not take advantage of the "family-friendly" policies provided by the firm that was the focus of her case study. However, the media spin on the book mainly focused on the ill effects for children and families of this preference, and of maternal employment more generally (see Milkman, 1997).

8   Eileen Appelbaum and I conducted management interviews and site visits to a convenience sample of nineteen establishments in California in 2003–04, and an additional thirteen in New Jersey in 2005, on which I draw here. The samples included firms in a variety of industries, but most were medium-to-large companies; indeed, all but four of the thirty-two were large enough to be covered by the FMLA. For more details on the New Jersey cases, see Appelbaum and Milkman, 2006.

9   Whereas the original bill had provided twelve weeks of paid leave, with costs evenly split between a tax on employers and one on employees, business won elimination of the employer tax. Ultimately employees alone were saddled with the full cost of the program, and the benefit was cut back to six weeks. Business pressure also led to an amendment providing that employers could require employees to use up to two weeks of paid vacation time before receiving the state-paid family leave benefit. With these modifications, the California bill was passed in August 2002 by a legislature with a strong Democratic majority, and signed into law by then-governor Davis the following month (Labor Project for Working Families, 2003).

10   In addition, since the late 1970s, the California Fair Employment and Housing Act (FEHA) has guaranteed women who are disabled because of pregnancy, childbirth, or related conditions, the right to up to four months of job-protected leave. The California Family Rights Act (CFRA), passed in 1991 (two years before the FMLA), provided additional rights; it was amended in 1993 to conform to the federal FMLA. Used together, FEHA and CFRA permit a pregnant woman disabled by pregnancy to take up to four months' leave, as well as an additional (unpaid but job-protected) leave for bonding with a new child extending beyond what the federal law provides, up to a total of four months. A 1999 amendment to the state's FEHA requires employers with five or more workers to provide reasonable accommodations

to pregnant women. And a 1999 "kin care" law requires California employers who provide paid sick leave to allow workers to use up to half of it each year to care for sick family members (see Milkman and Appelbaum, 2004).

11 These family leave benefit payments (unlike SDI benefits) have been deemed taxable by the US Internal Revenue Service—a development that was not anticipated by those who crafted the legislation.

REFERENCES

American Academy of Pediatrics, Committee on Hospital Care, 2003, "Family-Centered Care and the Pediatrician's Role," *Pediatrics* 112: 691–96.

Appelbaum, Eileen, and Ruth Milkman, 2006, *Achieving a Workable Balance: New Jersey Employers' Experiences Managing Employee Leaves and Turnover*, New Brunswick, N.J.: Center for Women and Work, Rutgers University.

Bernstein, Anya, 2001, *The Moderation Dilemma: Legislative Coalitions and the Politics of Family and Medical Leave*, Pittsburgh: University of Pittsburgh Press.

Bianchi, Suzanne, 1995, "Changing Economic Roles of Women and Men," in Reynolds Farley, ed., *State of the Union: America in the 1990s*, vol. 1, New York: Russell Sage Foundation, 107–54.

Blair-Loy, Mary, 2003, *Competing Devotions: Career and Family among Women Executives*, Cambridge: Harvard University Press.

Correll, Shelley J., Stephen Benard, and In Paik, 2007, "Getting a Job: Is There a Motherhood Penalty?" *American Journal of Sociology* 112: 1,297–338.

Dark, Taylor, 1999, *The Unions and The Democrats: An Enduring Alliance*, Ithaca: Cornell University Press.

Employment Development Department, State of California, 2005, unpublished data in author's possession.

Freeman, Richard B., 2007, *America Works: Critical Thoughts on the Exceptional US Labor Market*, New York: Russell Sage Foundation.

Fried, Mindy, 1998, *Taking Time: Parental Leave Policy and Corporate Culture*, Philadelphia: Temple University Press.

Friedan, Betty, 1963, *The Feminine Mystique*, New York: W. W. Norton.

Glass, Jennifer, 2004, "Blessing or Curse? Work–Family Policies and Mothers' Wage Growth over Time," *Work and Occupations* 31: 367–94.

Gornick, Janet, and Marcia Meyers, 2003, *Families That Work: Policies for Reconciling Parenthood and Employment*, New York: Russell Sage Foundation.

Han, Wen-Jui, and Jane Waldfogel, 2003, "Parental Leave: The Impact of Recent Legislation on Parents' Leave Taking," *Demography* 40 (1): 191–200.

Hays, Sharon, 1996, *The Cultural Contradictions of Motherhood*, New Haven: Yale University Press.

Hertz, Rosanna, 1986, *More Equal than Others: Women and Men in Dual-Career Marriages*, Berkeley: University of California Press.

Heymann, Jody, 2000, *The Widening Gap: Why America's Working Families Are in Jeopardy—and What Can Be Done about It*, New York: Basic Books.

Hochschild, Arlie, 1997, *The Time Bind: When Work Becomes Home and Home Becomes Work*, New York: Metropolitan Books.

Jacobs, Jerry, and Kathleen Gerson, 2004, *The Time Divide: Work, Family, and Gender Inequality*, Cambridge, MA: Harvard University Press.

Johnson, Julia Overturf, and Barbara Downs, 2005, *Maternity Leave and Employment Patterns of First-Time Mothers: 1961–2000*, Current Population Report P70–103.

Kaiser Family Foundation, 2003, *Women, Work, and Family Health: A Balancing Act*. Menlo Park, CA: Kaiser Family Foundation, online: http://www.kff.org/womenshealth/loader.cfm?url=/commonspot/security/getfile.cfm&PageID=14293.

Kantor, Jodi, 2006, "On the Job, Nursing Mothers Find a 2-Class System," *New York Times*, September 1: 1.

Koss, Natalie, 2003, "The California Temporary Disability Insurance Program," *Journal of Gender, Social Policy and Law* 11: 1,079–87.

Labor Project for Working Families, 2003, *Putting Families First: How California Won the Fight for Paid Family Leave*, Berkeley: Labor Project for Working Families, online: http://www.laborproject.org/publications/pdf/paidleavewon.pdf.

Lambert, Susan, 2009, "Making a Difference for Hourly Employees," in Ann C. Crouter and Alan Booth, eds., *Work-Life Policies*, Washington, D.C.: The Urban Institute Press, 169–195.

Lareau, Annette, 2003, *Unequal Childhoods: Class, Race, and Family Life*, Berkeley: University of California Press.

Levin-Epstein, Jodie, 2006, *Getting Punched: The Job and Family Clock*, Washington: Center for Law and Social Policy.

Martin, Cathie Jo, 2000, *Stuck in Neutral: Business and the Politics of Human Capital Investment Policy*, Princeton: Princeton University Press.

Mason, Mary Ann, and Eve Mason Ekman, 2007, *Mothers on the Fast Track: How a New Generation Can Balance Family and Careers*, New York: Oxford University Press.

McCall, Leslie, 2001, *Complex Inequality: Gender, Race and Class in the New Economy*, New York: Routledge.

Milkman, Ruth, 1997, "A Dream Come True [review of Hochschild, *The Time Bind*]," *The Women's Review of Books* 15 (1), October.

Milkman, Ruth, and Eileen Appelbaum, 2004, "Paid Family Leave in California: New Research Findings," *The State of California Labor* 4: 45–67.

Mishel, Larry, Jared Bernstein, and Sylvia Allegretto, 2005, *The State of Working America 2004/2005*, Ithaca: Cornell University Press.

National Partnership for Women and Families, 2006, "Where Families Matter: State Progress Toward Valuing America's Families: A Summary of 2005 Initiatives," online: http://www.nationalpartnership.org/ site/PageServer?pagename=library_pl_PaidLeave/.

Reese, Ellen, 2005, *Backlash Against Welfare Mothers: Past and Present*, Berkeley: University of California Press.

Ruhm, Christopher, 1997, "Policy Watch: The Family and Medical Leave Act," *Journal of Economic Perspectives* 11: 175–86.

——— 2000, "Parental Leave and Child Health," *Journal of Health Economics* 19: 931–60.

Sherriff, Rona Levine, 2007, *Balancing Work and Family*, Sacramento: California Senate Office of Research.

Somers, Margaret R., and Fred Block, 2005, "From Poverty to Perversity: Ideas, Markets, and Institutions over 200 Years of Welfare Debate," *American Sociological Review* 70: 260–87.

Stone, Pamela, 2007, *Opting Out: Why Women Really Quit Careers and Head Home*, Berkeley: University of California Press.

US Department of Labor, 2001, *Balancing the Needs of Families and Employers: Family and Medical Leave Surveys, 2000 Update*, Rockville, MD: Westat.

Valian, Virginia, 1998, *Why So Slow? The Advancement of Women*, Cambridge: MIT Press.

Vogel, Lise, 1993, *Mothers on the Job: Maternity Policy in the US Workplace*, New Brunswick: Rutgers University Press.

Waldfogel, Jane, 1999, "Family Leave Coverage in the 1990s," *Monthly Labor Review* 122 (10): 13–21.

——— 2001, "Family and Medical Leave: Evidence from the 2000 Surveys," *Monthly Labor Review* 124 (9): 17–23.

Williams, Joan C., 2006, *One Sick Child Away from Being Fired: When "Opting Out" Is Not an Option*, San Francisco, CA: Work Life Law, UC Hastings College of the Law, online: http://www.uchastings.edu/site_files/WLL/onesickchild.pdf.

16

The Normative and Institutional Embeddedness of Parental Employment: Its Impact on Gender Egalitarianism in Parenthood and Employment

Rosemary Crompton

INTRODUCTION: A CRITIQUE OF THE "CONTINUUM"

There can be little argument that, as Gornick and Meyers argue, a dual-earner/dual-caregiver society would be good for gender equality, good for children, and (probably) good for men. However, the model is "utopian," and the problems and pitfalls in achieving it are immense. Identifying these problems, however, is a necessary exercise if they are to be tackled. In this chapter, therefore, I will begin by identifying some of the difficulties with the framework and associated continuum that Gornick and Meyers have drawn upon in making their arguments.

Figure 16.1

Beyond the 'Male Breadwinner' Model (Crompton, 1999)

Traditional	←	→	Less traditional
1	2	3	4
Male-breadwinner/female-caregiver	Dual-earner/female part-time-caregiver	Dual-earner/state-caregiver *or* Dual-earner/marketized-caregiver	Dual-earner/dual-caregiver

Described as a "flexible framework" rather than a "static taxonomy," this continuum was originally developed in the concluding chapter of a book (Crompton, ed., 1999) that reported on the Gender Relations project—a comparative cross-national study of changing gender relations that included data from Britain, France, Norway, the Czech Republic, and Russia.[1] The simple idea contained in Figure 16.1 was that gendered divisions of care and market work would be associated with varying degrees of traditionalism in gender relations. This broad term recognizes that "gender" is structured by different institutions (generated by states, markets and families), and at different levels (through legislation; by organizations, households, and in couple relationships). The move through from box 1 to box 4 in this figure was explicitly seen as a move towards more gender equality.

From the very first, however, and in the light of the interviews gathered within the Gender Relations project, there were problems with this suggested trajectory, largely in respect of box 3. In the 1990s, four of the countries studied (Norway, the Czech Republic, Russia and France)— either at that time or in the very recent past—had reasonably extensive state child-care provision. None of the countries in our comparison were characterized by a high level of marketized care in the 1990s.[2] However, the "outcomes" of state-provided child care, in terms of equality in gender relations, and particularly in the domestic sphere, were rather different.

In Norway, as in other Scandinavian countries, state assistance with child care is associated with greater overall equality in gender relations—and indeed, these policies were explicitly developed as part of the "state feminist" equality agenda (Hernes, 1987; Ellingsæter and Leira, 2006). In the Scandinavian countries, state-provided child care can be seen as part of a move in the direction of a dual-earner/dual-caregiver model. By contrast, in Russia and the Czech Republic, state child care was provided so that women could fulfill their public duty— employment. Although gender equality was an official state goal in state socialist countries, this was understood entirely in terms of access to paid employment—for example, Stalin described the "woman question" as "solved" when women achieved parity in employment with men (Einhorn, 1993). However, the everyday reality of gender relations in the Eastern bloc was (and is) rather traditional. Within the Gender Relations project, our qualitative work–life interviews in Eastern Europe described quite blatant instances of discrimination in employment, and it was clear that domestic work and child care were seen as almost entirely the responsibilities of women. Quantitative data (from the Czech Republic) revealed very traditional attitudes to gender roles (particularly among men), and a correspondingly traditional division of domestic work in the home—despite the fact that Czech women usually worked full-time (Crompton and Harris, 1999).[3] In these circumstances, state-provided substitute care had not been associated with greater equality in gender relations.

The case of France added further complexities. State child-care provision in France is relatively generous, and long-established. As a consequence, French women have been enabled to work full-time, and had performed rather better in the labor market than those in Britain—for example, in reaching managerial positions (Hantrais, 1990). Indeed, France has been described as a "modified male breadwinner" welfare state (Lewis, 1992). However, our interviews suggested that the domestic division of labor in France was rather traditional, as were gendered workplace relations.

Considerable caution, therefore, was expressed in relation to box 3, as follows: "Women's full-time work in combination with substitute care . . . is more likely to result in less traditional gender relations and greater gender equality—with the important proviso that this economistic association is by no means automatic" (Crompton, ed., 1999: 206–7). In a similar vein, it was emphasized that "gender cultures have to change, as well as the gender division of labor in employment."[4]

What goes on in box 3, therefore, is absolutely crucial in influencing trajectories in the direction of a dual-earner/dual-caregiver society. Box 2 is associated with continuing, albeit modified, gender traditionalism—for example, studies of the domestic division of labor have demonstrated that women's part-time employment has relatively little impact on the domestic division of labor in the home (Coltrane, 2000; Crompton and Lyonette, 2008). However, even when women are in full-time employment, if caring and associated domestic work are simply shifted elsewhere (usually to another woman), then gender relations in the home may remain very traditional. Box 3, therefore, represents a transitional state, from which gender relations might either shift in a less traditional direction, or remain relatively traditional.[5] If, therefore, we want to understand the difficulties associated with a move to box 4 (and therefore make suggestions as to how they might be overcome), the more we can understand the particular circumstances of box 3 "cases," the better.

In this chapter, therefore, I will first examine in more detail two box 3 cases: France and Portugal. I will draw on the findings of a further cross-national quantitative study (the "Employment and the Family" project). This drew upon the 2002 Family and Gender Roles module of the International Social Survey program (ISSP). The countries studied included Britain, France, Finland, Norway, and Portugal.[6]

One of our major foci was the topic of work–life conflict—that is, the difficulties faced by dual-earner couples, given that it can no longer be assumed that women are available for unpaid domestic work.

THE CASE OF FRANCE

France is included as one of Gornick and Meyers' "exemplar" countries. However, it will be argued that, in some important respects, gender equality has advanced rather less in France than it might have done, despite the long-term presence of policies friendly to working mothers.

As Gornick and Meyers demonstrate, France is characterized by extensive supports for mothers' employment, having generous maternity and parental leaves, a statutory thirty-five-hour working week, and universal, publicly funded early-years child care and education facilities.[7] Elements of these policies have been in place for many years. Historically, they were introduced in response to labor shortages, in combination with a sensitivity to the impact of maternal employment on birthrates, rather than in response to gender equality concerns (Jenson, 1986; Lewis and Astrom, 1992). Indeed, largely because of the French tradition of republican universalism, "equality" for women as such has not been particularly prominent (and indeed has sometimes been resisted) in French policy development. Gender equality in the workplace, for example, has not progressed to the same extent as in Britain (Crompton and Le Feuvre, 2000). Employment rates among French women are not particularly high. Despite mother-friendly policies, rates of employment among French women were around the EU (fifteen-country) average (57.8), at 58.5 percent, in 2005—compared to 70.4 percent in Sweden, 71.9 percent in Denmark, 71.7 percent in Norway, and 65.8 percent in the UK (Eurostat, Employment Rate by gender, LFS adjusted series).[8] Moreover, the under-representation of French women in political life (French women only won the vote in 1944) became something of a national scandal at the end of the twentieth century.[9] As many commentators noted, the political under-representation of French women was exceeded within the EU only by Greece.

Nevertheless, in the "Employment and the Family" project (Crompton, 2006; Crompton and Lyonette, 2006b), we anticipated that the relatively good dual-earner policies to be found in France would have a positive impact on work–life balance. A work–life conflict scale was constructed using four items from the ISSP survey:

I have come home from work too tired to do the chores which need to be done.
It has been difficult for me to fulfil my family responsibilities because of the amount of time I spent on my job.
I have arrived at work too tired to function well because of the household work I had done.
I have found it difficult to concentrate at work because of my family responsibilities.

Respondents were asked to indicate, for each item, whether this occurred several times a week, several times a month, once or twice, or never. Higher scores indicate higher work–life conflict.[10] On the basis of a review of policies in respect of dual-earner families in these five countries, we expected Norway and Finland to demonstrate the lowest levels of work–life conflict and Britain and Portugal the highest, with France somewhere in the middle (this association might also have been predicted on the basis of the cross-national data summarized by Gornick and Meyers). What we found was that, as anticipated, Norway and Finland had measurably lower levels of work–life conflict than the other countries, even when a range of other factors were controlled for—thus, a Scandinavian "societal effect" (Gallie, 2003) could be argued to be in operation. As far as work–life conflict was concerned, however, France was in the same country cluster as Britain and Portugal (Britain having the highest level of work–life conflict among full-time employees).

When we explored further this example of "French exceptionalism," we found that, in the case of France in particular, traditionalism in the domestic division of labor was a factor significantly associated with a higher level of work–life conflict. A domestic division of labor (DDL) index was computed from five questions from the ISSP survey:

In your household, who usually does the:
    Laundry
    Cares for sick family members
    Shops for groceries
    Household cleaning
    Prepares the meals
(always me, usually me, about equal, usually spouse/partner, always spouse/partner)

Table 16.1

Means of Work–Life Conflict for Congruence Categories, France (Full-time Employees Only)

	More liberal divisions of domestic labor	More traditional divisions of domestic labor
Liberal gender role attitudes	Mean=6.71 SD=2.24 N=151	Mean=7.69 SD=2.45 N=237
Traditional gender role attitudes	Mean=8.42 SD=(2.65) N=32	Mean=7.98 SD=2.48 N=125

Notes: ANOVA F = 11.365; p <0.001. Post-hoc tests showed that congruent liberals had significantly lower work–life conflict scores than both other groups. In fact, levels of domestic traditionalism are relatively high in France compared to Britain, Finland and Norway, as can be seen from Table 16.2.

By convention, these would be considered "women's" tasks. Scores were allocated in accordance with this assumption. DDL scores could range from 5 to 25, and higher scores indicated a more traditional DDL.[11] A regression analysis on the French data (Crompton and Lyonette, 2006b) demonstrated that, the more traditional the domestic division of labor (DDL), the higher the level of work–life conflict reported.[12]

We were also concerned to explore whether a disjunction between attitudes and behavior had an impact—for example, an individual might be involved in a very traditional division of domestic labor, but if they think this is "the right thing to do," this might not necessarily be a source of conflict. We therefore developed a variable that combined level of traditionalism in gender role attitudes (indicated by the extent of agreement with the statement "a man's job is to earn money, a woman's job is to look after the home and family") with level of traditionalism in the domestic division of labor.[13] This produced some very striking results in the French case. The level of work–life conflict for "congruent liberal" French respondents (that is, liberal gender-role attitudes in combination with lower levels of domestic traditionalism) was 6.70, whereas for "congruent traditionals" (less liberal gender role attitudes with a traditional division of domestic labor) the average score was 7.98 (Table 16.1). Moreover, those with "incongruent" attitudes and behavior had work–life conflict scores that were comparable to the "traditionals," rather than the "congruent liberals."

Table 16.2

Mean Scores of Domestic Division of Labor (DDL) for Each Country (Full-Time Respondents Only)

Country	N	Mean (SD)
Britain	514	18.61 (3.23)
Finland	452	18.23 (2.67)
France	575	19.23 (3.22)
Norway	545	18.19 (2.67)
Portugal	276	20.49 (3.18)
Total	2,363	18.81 (3.08)

Notes: ANOVA F = 35.066; p<0.001. Post-hoc tests showed that Portugal and France had significantly higher DDL scores than the other three countries.

In fact, levels of domestic traditionalism are relatively high in France compared to Britain, Finland and Norway, as can be seen from Table 16.2.

A comparative analysis using our DDL measure revealed that the two Scandinavian countries had the least traditional DDL scores. As demonstrated in Table 16.2, in respect of the domestic division of labor, post hoc tests showed that France was closer to Portugal (which has the most traditional division of domestic labor) than to Britain, and that the difference between the DDL means of France and Portugal and the other three countries was statistically significant. In a similar vein, Windebank's qualitative comparative study of domestic labor and parenting in Britain and France found that French men contributed less than British men:

> [I]n the French sample, there were numerous men who were available to look after children during the week when their partner was employed (e.g. teachers who did not work in the school holidays or on a Wednesday afternoon) but nevertheless, did not take responsibility for childcare even when they were free. This was not the case in any of the British sample where sequential scheduling of jobs was used to minimise formal childcare provision. . . (Windebank, 2001: 287).

Windebank suggests that the greater involvement of British men in child care and domestic work is in fact a consequence of the greater flexibility in labor markets and poorer support for child care in Britain than in France. She suggests that British men have been in a sense "forced" into domesticity in order to enable their partners to work, which is increasingly becoming a financial necessity for British households. In contrast, French men have been enabled to "fall back" on state child-care provision if their partners are in employment.

Policies to support employed mothers in France do not, therefore, seem to have had much of an impact on gendered divisions of labor in the home. Indeed, if Windebank's argument is valid, their impact might even have been counter-productive. In fact, it would be widely acknowledged in France that family (or work–life) policies are directed largely at labor market objectives, rather than being concerned with gender egalitarianism as such (Le Feuvre and Lemarchant, 2007). For example, the introduction of the APE ('allocation parentale d'éducation'—1985, reformed 1994), a monthly benefit paid to a non-employed parent of more than two children was seen as a measure to reduce rates of unemployment, rather than to promote gender equality. In fact, its introduction meant that between 1995 and 2001, and for the first time in forty years, the activity rates of mothers with two children and a youngest child aged less than three years dropped from 69 percent to 53 percent (98 percent of APE recipients are women).[14] Moreover, women who had been unemployed before the birth of their second child and/or had only a low level of education, are proportionately over-represented among APE recipients. The impact of this policy, therefore, will be to increase inequalities between women as well as households.

The example of France, therefore, has been used to make the argument that, as far as gender egalitarianism is concerned, the impact of state policies in supporting families and working parents is highly mediated by the gendered division of labor in the home, which is rather traditional in France. It is not being argued that this exception "disproves the rule" that family leave provisions, the regulation of working time, and good early childhood education and care policies are highly beneficial for working parents and their children. Family poverty is relatively low in France, and rates of mortality for French children are lower than in the US. Rather, the example is being used to support the more general argument that gender egalitarianism in parenthood and employment will require transformations in gendered divisions of labor in employment and at home, and that variations in these divisions can have an impact on policy outcomes in respect of gender equality.

DOMESTIC WORK: NATIONAL VARIATIONS

It is not necessary to labor the point that domestic sharing is crucial to gender equality. Fraser (1994) has argued that gender equality is not possible unless men become "more like women," and combine market work, domestic work, and caregiving. In a similar vein, Lewis and Guillari (2005: 94) argue that women's responsibilities for care restrict their agency freedom, and thus their "choices":

> [T]he key issue is not how to make women more self-interested . . . but rather how to promote conditions that foster responsibility for sharing care between men and women and that enhance women's agency freedom by making men more accountable for their responsibility to care for others.

Caregiving and domestic work are normatively assigned to women, and whether they perform paid work full-time, part-time, or not at all, women do more domestic work than men. As the summary of Coltrane (2000: 1,209) states:

> In general, women have felt obligated to perform housework, and men have assumed that domestic work is primarily the responsibility of mothers, wives, daughters and low-paid female housekeepers. In contrast, men's participation in housework has appeared optional, with most couples . . . characterising men's contributions as "helping" their wives or partners.

These responsibilities mean that, in practice, many women do not compete on equal terms with men in the labor market. Others, however, have argued that many (if not most) women "choose" to retain the major responsibility for domesticity, and are in fact happier when they do so (Hakim, 2004; but see Crompton and Lyonette, 2005). In fact, as women have entered the labor force, so men have increased their share of housework—although this seems to have reached a plateau in the 1990s. However, the major reason for the closing of the gendered domestic labor "gap" since the 1960s is that, as women have entered employment, they have reduced their domestic work hours (Coltrane, 2000; Bianchi et al., 2000).

Comparative cross-national research on variations in levels of domestic traditionalism has produced some interesting findings. First, it has been demonstrated that the domestic division of labor in the Scandinavian countries, where governments have actively promoted gender equality in the home (Brandth and Kvande, 2001; see also Ellingsæter and Leira, 2006), is not significantly less traditional than in neoliberal countries such as Britain and the US, where governments have not pursued such policies (Gershuny and Sullivan, 2003; Geist, 2005). Our results, summarized in Table 16.2, confirm these arguments. Nevertheless, the finding that the domestic division of labor is generally more traditional in conservative or "corporatist" regimes (Geist, 2005; see also Korpi, 2000) that have developed policies that reflect and give priority to women's domestic responsibilities, is generally supportive of the argument that state policies do have an impact on the gendered division of labor in the home.[15]

Moreover, it may be suggested that the finding of similar levels of domestic traditionalism in the Scandinavian and neoliberal countries is a case of "plural causation" (Pickvance, 1995); that is, that different explanatory factors are in operation within the two different regime clusters. In the relatively unregulated labor markets of neoliberal regimes, there are few barriers to the employment of women. Employers are free to develop non-standard jobs (such as part-time employment, nonstandard hours of work) that are attractive to women with domestic responsibilities. Downward pressures on wages in neoliberal regimes mean that, for many families, dual earning becomes increasingly necessary. As Gornick and Meyers have demonstrated in relation to the US, there are few if any state supports available for working mothers and dual-earner families. Thus, in aggregate (as Windebank has argued in her comparison between the cases of France and Britain), men find themselves constrained to give domestic assistance to their partners if their partners are to be enabled to generate much-needed income for the family. In contrast, in the Scandinavian countries, the level of mothers' employment is high, and good dual-earner state family supports are available. These supports would facilitate mothers' employment even if domestic assistance were not forthcoming from male partners. Nevertheless, men in the Scandinavian countries contribute as much by way of domestic support as do men in neoliberal regimes (in fact, slightly more), where dual-earner supports are not available. This argument suggests that state-sponsored efforts to persuade men in the Scandinavian countries to contribute to domestic work have, in fact, met with some degree of success.

State policies, therefore, can have an impact on the domestic division of labor, but these policies themselves are reflective of national "path-dependencies" that have significant impacts on gender cultures and gender regimes. In particular, all of the major religions incorporate an essentialist view of women that argues (among other things) that they are particularly suited to caring and domesticity.[16] Very obviously, there are considerable differences in the impact of religious beliefs and organizations between nation-states; "corporatist" welfare regimes have been much affected by Catholic ideology, for example (see Korpi, 2000). There will also be national cultural variations in culinary standards and fashions in household décor that will have an impact on the amount of domestic work that needs to be carried out. Although "culture" is a notoriously slippery term, its impact and effects simply cannot be factored out, particularly as far as gender relations are concerned.[17]

Nevertheless, empirical research has demonstrated that a range of similar factors have an impact on variations in levels of domestic traditionalism in all countries. These include the presence or absence of children in the household, the extent and level of the woman's employment, her earnings, level of education (and the closely related factor of occupational class), age, and attitude to gender roles. However, even when these factors are controlled for, the extent of domestic traditionalism is still greater in some countries than in others (see Crompton, 2006). As we have seen, among the countries we studied, Portugal had the highest level of domestic traditionalism. Moreover, Portuguese women reported many more hours of domestic work than women in the other countries studied. Average hours of household work (not including child care) reported by women in Britain, Finland, France and Norway were just over thirteen a week; but Portuguese women reported twenty-six hours a week.

As has been argued above, some countries are more gender-traditional than others, and much of this variation will be a consequence of specific historical factors. In the particular case of Portugal, under the Salazar regime (which lasted until 1974), women were legally subject to their husbands (and legally responsible for housework), and formally barred from a wide range of occupations.[18] There have been very substantial changes in legislation and attitudes to women since Salazar left power, but nevertheless, as Wall (2006) has argued, Portugal "still has to deal with the legacy of authoritarian values which still permeate society and many institutional settings, as well as the problem of a civil society bogged down for forty years." Thus, for example, in the ISSP surveys 34 percent of Portuguese respondents agreed that "a man's job is to earn money, a woman's job is to look after the home and family," compared to only 10 percent of the Norwegian sample and 18 percent of the British (Crompton, 2006: 145). In all countries, levels of gender traditionalism vary by age, but in Portugal, even among the 18–34 age group, in 2002 14 percent still agreed that the "man's job" was to earn money, compared to only 5 percent in

Norway and 7 percent in France, Finland, and Britain. Similarly, in a comparison between Britain and Portugal, whereas 56 percent of Portuguese men and women in full-time employment agreed that "what women really want is a home and family," only 17 percent of full-time British men and women held to this view. Levels of employment among mothers of young children (under three) in Portugal are high, at 69 percent. Nevertheless, in the ISSP surveys, 79 percent of Portuguese women *in full-time employment* thought that a preschool child suffered if his or her mother went out to work, compared to 25 percent of similar British women (Lyonette et al., 2007).

Variations in national occupational structures also contribute to national variations in both attitudes and behavior in respect of gender roles. In general, as we have seen, both gender role attitudes and levels of traditionalism in the domestic division of labor are associated with class and educational levels, in that professional and managerial groupings are more gender-liberal than the "lower" occupational groups. Occupational structures vary from country to country, and richer countries will have higher proportions of managers and professionals (as well as higher educational levels). Portugal was the poorest of our sample of five countries, and in aggregate the most gender traditional in attitude.[19] But there were highly significant class differences in "general" gender role attitudes in Portugal—for example, whereas 87 percent of managerial and professional women in Portugal disagreed with the statement that a "man's job" was to earn money, only 57 percent of women involved in manual work did (Lyonette et al., 2007). Portugal has a smaller proportion of managerial and professional employees (21 percent, compared to 37 percent in the British ISSP sample), and on the "gender roles" question, the higher level of aggregate gender-traditionalism might to some extent be explained by this occupational imbalance. However, on a range of other attitudinal statements, including "what women really want is a home and children," "watching children grow up is life's greatest joy," and the claim that both family life and preschool children will suffer if the woman is in employment, employed managerial and professional men and women in Portugal were significantly more traditional and family-oriented than similar respondents in Britain (Lyonette et al., 2007: 290–91).

Although Portuguese men in the managerial and professional groupings are highly supportive of "general" gender role liberalism, the ISSP data suggest they contribute very little to domestic work (Lyonette et al., 2007). However, the same data suggest that about a third of professional and managerial women in Portugal have help with domestic cleaning, washing and ironing. If a "bought-in" household employee replaces an employed woman's domestic input, there will be little need or incentive for men to share in domestic tasks—particularly in rather traditional countries like Portugal—and gender relations in the home will remain traditional.

There are significant regional variations in the hiring of domestic workers. In Scandinavia, paid domestic help is relatively uncommon (it is a very small occupational category, and ISSP data suggest that very few respondents used paid help for domestic chores). Paid domestic help becomes more common as one moves south through Europe, and in Portugal, ILO data reveal that it is the largest single category of female employment. The relative national availability of low-cost domestic help, therefore, is another factor that has an impact on the kinds of trajectories out of box 3 of Fig. 16.1.

The purpose of our discussion of these cross-national differences has not simply been to draw attention to country-specific problems in achieving a dual-earner/dual-caregiver society—this has, in any case, been extensively demonstrated in another contribution to this volume (Morgan). Nor has it been only to make the (important but obvious) point that shifts in the gendered domestic division of labor are essential in order to make a successful transition to box 4 of Fig. 16.1. Rather, our purpose has been to explore, however briefly, the roots of gender-traditionalism. In the case of both France and Portugal, these may be at least partly explained by historic circumstances in which particular national traditions relating to gender and gender equality have been important.

A rather simple explanation of gender-traditionalism is available—the persistence of patriarchy (see Walby, 1990). It cannot be denied that, globally, women are still dominated by men, as they have been throughout recorded history. However, "patriarchy" can be a dangerous concept for feminists: if male domination is viewed as being somehow inevitable, then the essentialist trap—the idea that men are inherently oppressive—is all too easy to fall into. Patterns of gender equality have been decisively shaped by two major sets of gender-essentialist normative assumptions. The first is masculine supremacy. Men have been regarded for millennia as superior to women, and accordingly as better suited for positions of authority and domination. This ideology of masculine supremacy has been buttressed by the second set of assumptions—normative ideas about the "proper" roles of men and women (Charles, 2005). In the second part of the twentieth century, the ideology of masculine supremacy has been successfully challenged in Western societies, and women have been formally recognized as the equals of men. What have proved to be much more enduring, however, are deep-seated norms and cultural beliefs about what men and women are good at and how they should behave. As we have seen, these essentialist gender norms and, more importantly, associated behaviors, have been more persistent in France and Portugal than in the other three countries studied in the "Employment and the Family" project. As far as gender equality is concerned, changing these norms and the behavior associated with them is as important a task as developing institutions that support gender egalitarianism.

As my discussions of France and Portugal have suggested, the model described in Fig. 16.1 may be defended as a useful heuristic device, but is by no means an accurate description of trends in gender relations. Indeed, one of its major uses might be in stimulating discussion and debate as to how and why "positive" transitions out of box 3 might *not* be achieved. In addition, as in Gornick and Meyers' elaboration of the model, it is useful in thinking through the varying ideological emphases on employment, caregiving and gender relations that are assumed by the different "stages" (boxes 1 to 4) within it. Nevertheless, as was cautioned when it was originally formulated, on its own Fig. 16.1 is excessively "economically deterministic," and it is vital that its "embeddedness" in both particular normative contexts and particular state welfare and labor market institutions should be continually emphasized.

Despite the fact that we live in an era of globalization, national differences still count as far as gender egalitarianism is concerned. Among the factors I have discussed in this chapter are specific historical features (including legacies such as fascism, or the dominance of particular religious creeds) that have affected state policies in relation to women and the family. There are persisting national differences in the extent to which child care and domestic work are normatively assigned to women, even in countries where women have achieved formal equality with men. There are also persisting national differences in the structuring of labor markets, giving rise to variations in the availability of "good" and "bad" jobs, and opportunities for flexible working (Soskice, 2005). National policies also affect the extent to which low-cost labor—particularly migrant labor—may be used to replace women's unpaid domestic labor as women enter employment (Ehrenreich and Hochschild, 2003).

Part-time work in Britain may be used as a "worked example" to illustrate this general argument. One major reason why part-time work for women emerged as a "British solution" to the problems of the integration of employment and family life from the 1960s onward was that, as the British labor market was relatively unregulated, employers were at liberty—indeed, were encouraged—to introduce short-hours working that could be fitted in around conventional family arrangements. An example would be the "twilight shift," in which women are employed from early to late evenings, when their partners are available to look after the children. Part-time workers are cheap to employ, which is just one of their advantages from an employer's point of view (Purcell et al., 1999).[20] However, in more regulated labor markets in Europe, such as France, job protections made it much more problematic to develop part-time employment; indeed, in France part-time employment is still seen by many as a dangerous innovation that may lead to excessive flexibilization and a reduction in labor-market protections (see Morgan, this volume).

Policies designed to normalize part-time work—that is, to give it similar rights and protections to those of full-time employment—have been introduced widely in Europe, particularly as a consequence of EU policy directives. Nevertheless, the hourly rates of part-time workers remain substantially less than those in full-time employment, and part-time work has a strongly negative impact on career development at all levels of employment. Putting it bluntly, getting promoted requires working full-time (Crompton et al., 2003). Part-time work is overwhelmingly "women's" employment, and is an important factor that contributes to gender inequality in employment (O'Reilly and Fagan, eds, 1998). Thus, even when part-time work is instituted ostensibly for the "right" reasons—as in the Netherlands, where the right to part-time work was introduced for men and women in order to facilitate a combination of employment and family life—it is overwhelmingly women who choose this option, and bear the subsequent negative consequences (see Morgan, this volume).

Does the fact of the embeddedness of couples' earning arrangements in particular normative and institutional patterns lead us to advocate any major changes in the policies recommended by Gornick and Meyers? I would suggest not. But embeddedness does mean that careful thinking has to take place about strategies for the implementation of these policies. Work–family policies intersect with both existing beliefs about gender roles and the care of children (Pfau-Effinger, 1999), as well as established national institutional frameworks. Thus, in France, and in the countries of the Soviet bloc, where policies to facilitate mothers' employment (rather than "work–family balance") were introduced in the earlier part of the twentieth century—before the impact of "second-wave" feminism—they had little impact on prevailing domestic gender norms.[21] In contrast, work–family policies introduced and developed with gender equality as a specific goal, as in the Scandinavian countries, are much more likely to effect a successful transition from box 3 to box 4 of Fig. 16.1.

Finally, in thinking about these issues, I am often reminded of Folbre's

(1994) observation to the effect that although the male-breadwinner model of the division of labor between men and women was not "fair," at least it underwrote human reproduction. One of the arguments that underpins Gornick and Meyers' recommendations is that, with the erosion of the male-breadwinner model, human reproduction is *not* best left to individualized, marketized care arrangements—hence their emphasis on the role that state ("collective") provisions have to play in their policy prescriptions. However, given that we are in an era in which neoliberal political and economic thinking is in the ascendant, the redirection of resources toward collective provision is going to be a difficult task. On the other hand, women's employment is on the increase in all Western countries, and issues of gender equality and work–life balance have moved toward the upper reaches of policy agendas (see, for example, Esping-Andersen et al., 2002). It is vital, however, that an explicit goal of gender equality remains central to the debates over policies facilitating adaptations to an increase in women's employment. Policies emphasizing the importance of parental "choice" are presented as gender-neutral; but even Esping-Andersen (Esping-Andersen et al., 2002: 91), who is formally committed to gender equality, endorses Hakim's arguments relating to maternal "choice," and makes the essentialist assumption that women's choices will naturally differ from those of men. Gender equity in parenthood and employment does not necessarily mean that men and women will behave in exactly the same way, but it does mean that women should be enabled to make choices independently of the gendered normative constraints that have for so long been attached to parenting and domestic work.

NOTES

1   The project began in the late 1980s. In each country, fifteen qualitative work–life interviews were carried out with female medical doctors, and with banking and finance sector managers. We also had access to ISSP data (see note 5, below) for Britain, Norway, Russia and the Czech Republic (see Crompton, ed., 1999). Russia was "under-represented" in our final discussions, largely because of problems with the quantitative materials available (which in the event were not used), together with difficulties in maintaining contact with Russian colleagues in what were fast-changing times (to put it mildly).

2   The level of state child-care provision in Norway was lower than in the other Scandinavian countries, although it was increasing rapidly. Parents in Norway have a strong preference for state child care, and although provision is generous, shortages are still perceived (Ellingsæter, 2006). Universal state

child care was a feature of "state socialist" economies, and although it was being cut back in the early 1990s, was still generous. The level of provision in Czechoslovakia was somewhat lower than that of other Eastern bloc countries (Heitlinger, 1979), though still good by Western standards.

3   This analysis has been updated using 2002 data (see Crompton et al., 2005). Czech men remain highly traditional, although the attitudes of Czech women have changed considerably.

4   Indeed, it was argued that, as gender systems and arrangements are multidimensional, the "continuum" was not in fact a continuum, "although its heuristic value may still be defended" (Crompton, 1999: 207).

5   Men *do*, in aggregate, carry out more domestic work when their partners work full-time.

6   Acknowledgements and thanks to the ESRC for two grants: R000239727: "Employment and the Family," and R000220106: "Families, Employment and Work–Life Integration." For a description of the ISSP program, see Davis and Jowell (1989). In 2002, interviews were carried out with a stratified random sample of 2,312 in Britain, 1,353 in Finland, 1,903 in France, 1,475 in Norway, and in 1,092 in Portugal. Questions on work–life conflict were only asked of those in employment, and numbers will vary.

7   There are, however, considerable regional variations in child care provision in France. Indeed, it has been argued that one of the intentions of the APE (see below) was to "encourage" mothers of young children to withdraw from the labor market in regions with below-average child care provision (see Le Feuvre and Lemarchant, 2007).

8   Eurostat European Commission, http://epp.eurostat.ec.europa.eu/.

9   Following the 1997 legislative elections, women were 10.9 percent of deputies, but only 5.9 percent of senators. In 1999, the French Constitution was amended to actively promote the political participation of women.

10   Cronbach's alpha: 0.73; factor analysis showed one factor with an eigenvalue of 2.2, explaining 56 percent of variance.

11   Factor analysis showed one factor, eigenvalue 2.699, explaining over 54 percent of the variance. Cronbach's alpha for all five items: 0.7860.

12   A similar association was also found in the other countries, but the difference was statistically significant only in France.

13   The DDL scale was dichotomized and cross-tabulated with a dichotomized version of the gender role question, generating four categories.

14   The level of the APE is approximately 50 percent of the national minimum wage.

15   Using the definition very loosely, both France and Portugal might be described as "corporatist."

16   For example, the "Letter to the Bishops of the Catholic Church on the Collaboration of Men and Women in the Church and in the World" (Offices

of the Congregation for the doctrine of the Faith, May 31, 2004, written by the present pope) asserts that a woman, "in her deepest and original being, exists 'for the other'," linked to her "physical capacity to give life." Furthermore, women live the "dispositions of listening, welcoming, humility, faithfulness, praise and waiting," with "particular intensity and naturalness."

17   Indeed, following the "cultural turn" within the social sciences, "gender" is frequently discussed as a largely "cultural" phenomenon. For an interesting discussion, see Fraser, 2000.

18   Official explanations of French women's exclusion from political life similarly draw on historical factors, including Salic law, which excluded women from succession to the throne, and the French Revolution, which excluded them from citizenship. See France Diplomatie, http://www.diplomatie.gouv.fr/.

19   Figures for 2001 show that, compared with an EU-15 gross earnings average of 31,910 euros for full-time employees in enterprises with ten or more employees, Portugal was much lower, with an average of 13,338 euros.

20   Short-hours working was also encouraged by the fact that, until recently, short-hours part-time work in Britain was not liable for National Insurance contributions.

21   It is of interest that in France, women's "right to employment" is widely accepted, although domestic gender norms, and ideas about "suitable" work for women, remain rather conventional (see Crompton and Le Feuvre, 2000).

REFERENCES

Bianchi, S. M., M. A. Milkie, L. C. Sayer, and J. P. Robinson, 2000 "Is anyone Doing the Housework? Trends in The Gender Division of Household Labor," *Social Forces* 79 (1): 191–228.

Brandth, B., and E. Kvande, 2001, "Flexible Work and Flexible Fathers," *Work, Employment and Society* 15 (2): 251–67.

Charles, M., 2005, "National Skill Regimes, Postindustrialism, and Sex Segregation," *Social Politics* 12 (2): 289–316.

Coltrane, S., 2000, "Research on Household Labor: Modelling and Measuring the Social Embeddedness of Routine Family Work," *Journal of Marriage and the Family* 62 (4): 1,208–33.

Crompton, R., ed., 1999, *Restructuring Gender Relations and Employment*, Oxford: Oxford University Press.

———2006, *Employment and the Family*, Cambridge: Cambridge University Press.

Crompton, R, M. Brockmann, and C. Lyonette, 2005, "Attitudes, Women's Employment and the Domestic Division of Labour: A Cross-National Analysis in Two Waves," *Work, Employment and Society* 19 (2): 213–33.

Crompton, R., and F. Harris, 1999, "Attitudes, Women's Employment and the Changing Domestic Division of Labour," in Crompton, ed., *Restructuring Gender Relations and Employment*.

Crompton, R., and C. Lyonette, 2005, "The New Gender Essentialism: Domestic and Family 'Choices' and Their Relation to Attitudes," *British Journal of sociology* 56 (4): 601–20.

——— 2006a "Some Issues in Cross-National Comparative Research Methods: A Comparison of Attitudes to Promotion, and Women's Employment, in Britain and Portugal," *Work, Employment and Society* 20 (2): 389–400.

——— 2006b "Work–Life 'Balance' in Europe" *Acta Sociologica*, December.

——— 2008 "Who Does the Housework? The Division of Labour within the Home," British Social Attitudes 24th Report, London: Sage.

Crompton, R., and N. Le Feuvre, 2000, "Gender, Family and Employment in Comparative Perspective: The Realities and Representations of Equal Opportunities in Britain and France," *Journal of European Social Policy* 10 (4): 334–48.

Crompton, R., S. Lewis. and C Lyonette, eds, 2007, *Women, Men, Work and Family in Europe*, London: Palgrave.

Crompton, R., J. Dennett, and A. Wigfield, 2003, *Organisations, Careers and Caring*, Bristol: Policy Press.

Davis, J. A., and R. Jowell, 1989, "Measuring National Differences," in R. Jowell, S. Witherspoon, and L. Brook, eds, *British Social Attitudes: Special International Report*, Aldershot: Gower.

Ehrenreich, B., and A. R. Hochschild, 2003, *Global Woman*, London: Granta Books.

Einhorn, B., 1993, *Cinderella Goes to Market*, London: Verso.

Ellingsæter, A. L., and A. Leira, eds, 2006, *Politicising Parenthood in Scandinavia*, Bristol: The Policy Press.

Ellingsæter, A.L., 2003, "The Complexity of Family Policy Reform: The Case of Norway," *European Societies* 5 (4): 419–43.

——— 2006, "The Norwegian Childcare Regime and its Paradoxes," in Ellingsæter and Leira, eds, *Politicising Parenthood*.

Esping-Andersen, G., D. Gallie, A. Hemerijck, and J. Myles, 2002, *Why We Need a New Welfare State*, Oxford: Oxford University Press.

Folbre, N., 1994, *Who Pays for the Kids? Gender and the Structures of Constraint*, London: Routledge.

Fraser, N., 1994, "After the Family Wage," *Political Theory* 22: 591–618.

———2000, "Rethinking Recognition," *New Left Review* May/June.

Gallie, D., 2003, "The Quality of Working Life: Is Scandinavia Different?" *European Sociological Review* 19 (1): 61–79.

Geist, C., 2005, "The Welfare State and the Home: Regime Differences in the Domestic Division of Labour," *European Sociological Review* 21: 23–41.

Gershuny, J., and O. Sullivan, 2003, "Time Use, Gender and Public Policy Regimes," *Social Politics* 10 (2): 205–28.
Hakim, C., 2004, *Key Issues in Women's Work*, London: GlassHouse Press.
Hantrais, L., 1990, *Managing Professional and Family Life: A Comparative Study of British and French Women*, Aldershot: Dartmouth.
Heitlinger, A., 1979, *Women and State Socialism*, London: Macmillan.
Hernes, H., 1987, *Welfare State and Woman Power*, Oslo: Norwegian University Press.
Jenson, J., 1986 "Gender and Reproduction," *Studies in Political Economy* 20: 9–46.
Korpi, W., 2000, "Faces of Inequality," *Social Politics* 7 (2): 127–91.
Le Feuvre, N., and C. Lemarchant, 2007, "Employment, the Family and 'Work–life Balance' in France," in Crompton et al., eds, *Women, Men, Work and family in Europe*.
Lewis, J., 1992, "Gender and the Development of Welfare Regimes," *Journal of European Social Policy* 2 (3): 159–73.
Lewis, J., and G. Astrom, 1992, "Equality, Difference and State Welfare: Labor Market and Family Policies in Sweden," *Feminist Studies* 18 (1): 59–87.
Lewis, J., and S. Guillari, 2005, "The Adult Worker Model Family, Gender Equality and Care: The Search for New Policy Principles and the Possibilities and Problems of a Capabilities Approach," *Economy and Society* 34 (1): 76–104.
Lyonette, C., R. Crompton, and K. Wall, 2007, "Gender, Occupational Class and Work–Life Conflict: A Comparison of Britain and Portugal," *Community, Work and Family* 10 (3): 281–306.
O'Reilly, J., and C. Fagan, eds, 1998, *Part-Time Prospects*, London: Routledge.
Pfau-Effinger, B., 1999, "The Modernization of Family and Motherhood in Western Europe," in Crompton, ed., *Restructuring Gender Relations*.
Pickvance, C., 1995, "Comparative Analysis, Causality and Case Studies in Urban Studies," in A. Rogers and S. Vertovec, *The Urban Context*, Oxford and Washington: Berg.
Purcell, K., T. Hogarth, and C. Simm, 1999, *Whose Flexibility?* York: Joseph Rowntree Foundation.
Soskice, D., 2005, "Varieties of Capitalism and Cross-National Gender Differences," *Social Politics* 12 (2): 170–79.
Sullivan, O., and J. Gershuny, 2001, "Cross-National Changes in Time Use," *British Journal of Sociology* 52 (2): 331–47.
Walby, S., 1990, *Theorizing Patriarchy*, Oxford: Basil Blackwell.
Wall, K., 2006, "Family Change and Family Policies," in S. Kamerman and A. Kahn, eds, *Family Change and Family Policies in Southern Europe*, Oxford: Clarendon Press.
Windebank, J., 2001, "Dual-earner Couples in Britain and France," *Work, Employment and Society* 15 (2): 269–90.

17

Fatherhood, Gender and Work–Family Policies

Scott Coltrane

What fathers and mothers do—or don't do—with and for their families typically defines who they are as gendered adults. When a woman changes her baby's diaper, comforts her crying toddler, or serves a nutritious family meal, her actions are seen as expressions of motherhood. When a man sits at the head of the family table, plays catch with his son, or takes an extra job to afford a new house, his actions are seen as expressions of fatherhood. But, contrary to popular cultural stereotypes, the activities associated with mothering and fathering are converging, and their symbolic meanings are constantly undergoing change. What constituted the ideal father in colonial America is different from the family breadwinner model of the 1950s, and both diverge from current images of nurturing, caregiver fathers. Not only are human parenting behaviors and family practices learned rather than instinctual; they vary considerably across time and place, and have always responded to the complex and shifting demands of the natural environment, economics, politics, culture, personal history, individual temperament, and couple dynamics (Coltrane and Adams, 2008). Over the past half-century, women's increased employment has been the primary engine driving changes in marriage and family life, though cultural ideals have also shaped what we consider appropriate behaviors for mothers and fathers.

In this essay I describe how social and economic forces have influenced men's family involvements over the past few decades, and document how work–family issues have become more similar for men and women. In so doing, I begin to assess whether the goal of gender symmetry envisioned by Gornick and Myers is worthy and practical. If these policies were implemented, would fathers take advantage of new opportunities to balance their family and work lives? Whose needs would be met by the various policies, and which men might be expected to accept or resist them? What impact might these policies have on the gendered division of labor within families, and how much sharing is it realistic to expect? Finally, which policies and programs carry the most potential for furthering the goal of gender equality?

RECENT TRENDS IN MEN'S FAMILY INVOLVEMENT

To assess whether Gornick and Meyers' proposed policies might be adopted by men, it is useful to review recent changes in family composition and the division of labor within two-parent households. Research in the US reveals two contradictory tendencies—more father involvement within two-parent families, but fewer father-present families in the population. These trends mirror popular culture stereotypes of "good dads" (those who marry the mother, care for the children, and support the family) and "bad dads"—those who don't marry the mother, participate in child care, or pay child support (Furstenberg, 1988). Although this good–bad dichotomy is too simple, many scholars concur that fatherhood has gained symbolic importance in the past few decades precisely because men's family participation has become more voluntary, tenuous, and conflicted (Coltrane, 1996; Griswold, 1993; LaRossa, 1997).

The trend toward fewer two-parent families in the population is driven by declining marriage rates, relatively high divorce rates (though falling since the 1970s), an increasing number of births to unmarried mothers (for all race and ethnic groups), and an increasing number of single-mother households. The entry of significant numbers of mothers into the permanent labor market and the weakening of the male-only breadwinner ideal, coupled with trends in fertility, marriage, divorce, and custody, has resulted in the average American man spending fewer years living with children than in the past (Eggebeen, 2002), and has also resulted in more American children spending time in a family without a co-resident father. Though marriage rates have been declining slightly in the US, belief in marriage and the likelihood of marrying continue to be higher in the US than in most other countries (Cherlin, 2005).

As families were becoming less likely to contain fathers in the 1970 and 1980s, a "new father" cultural ideal emerged in which men were expected to be nurturing and to share most aspects of routine child care with their wives (Coltrane, 1996; Furstenberg, 1988). This ideal has gained wide acceptance in popular culture, with American men ranking marriage and children among their most precious goals. For example, in a 2007 survey, 80 percent of US fathers ranked their relationships with their children (under eighteen years old) as very important to their personal happiness and fulfillment (rating it 10 out of a possible 10). Similarly, 81 percent of the men ranked their relationships with their wives as very important, compared to just 21 percent who rated their jobs or careers using this top category of importance (Pew Research Center, 2007). Similar shifts in men's attitudes and in father imagery have occurred in England and Europe (Sullivan, 2006). Changes in popular ideals about fathers have not been uniform, with the result that there are now many different versions of fatherhood ideals at play in developed nations. Nevertheless, most recent fatherhood imagery suggests that it is now considered masculine to be a nurturing and involved father. In relation to the Gornick–Meyers proposal, it is worth investigating the extent to which the emergence of these new fatherhood ideals can be linked to empirical changes in practice.

Fathers in two-parent households now spend more time with co-resident children than at any time since such data have been collected, and the number of single-father households has increased dramatically—though they still constitute only about one in five US single-parent families (Pleck and Masciadrelli, 2003). Men's absolute level of unpaid family work in two-person households has increased significantly over the past few decades, especially for direct parenting and housework, and somewhat less for managing or planning those activities (Coltrane, 2000; Pleck and Masciadrelli, 2003). As noted below, researchers show that these increases in men's family labor are statistically significant, but are they meaningful in the context of gender relations within households?

Studies show that men's family labor continues to lag well behind women's, especially for routine housework. Men's share of the work has risen faster than their hourly contributions, primarily because the women they live with have decreased the number of hours they devote to these routine activities. Even in two-parent households where gender convergence is most evident, large differences remain in the type of work that men and women perform. The average married father continues to spend significantly more time in paid employment and less time in unpaid family work than the average married mother (which is no doubt related to the fact that men earn significantly higher average wages than women). And most men still contribute only about a third to half as much time as women to unpaid family work. In summary, although men are doing more domestic chores than ever, recent changes in family life have been driven primarily by women increasing their labor force participation, and by women cutting back their contributions to housework.

Because men's contributions to parenting and housework lag behind those of women, it is difficult to evaluate the significance of recent changes and to estimate how much more might be achieved with policies designed to encourage more equal sharing. In order to address those questions, we need to disaggregate the changes that are occurring. Which men are doing more, and how do their individual contributions compare to those of their partners? How are mothers and fathers in different types of families responding similarly or differently to the work and family dilemmas they face? Past research suggests that we are seeing some unprecedented changes in the direction of de-gendering various household and childrearing tasks, yet it also reveals that systems of gender hierarchy still operate in and through divisions of paid and unpaid labor. Will the proposed policies strategically undermine those systems of gender hierarchy or inadvertently sustain them?

PREDICTORS OF MEN'S INVOLVEMENT IN FAMILY WORK

Under what conditions do men do more family work? Research shows that there are differences in the predictors and outcomes associated with men's participation in child care versus housework, although the more routine aspects of each are highly correlated. In addition, researchers attempting to predict absolute hourly contributions to housework and child care by men and/or women often come up with different findings from those who use relative measures—i.e. the amount of sharing within the couple. I focus this discussion on men's and women's proportion of family work within households because this approach has the simplest and most direct relevance to issues of gender equality as framed by Gornick and Meyers (but this does not imply that domestic labor in single-parent households, same-sex couples, or other family forms is any less important). In other words, what factors have researchers found to be associated with men in heterosexual couples sharing more family work with their partners?

Variables associated with women's initiative and enhanced

bargaining position, such as more education and higher relative earnings, tend to predict shared housework better than shared child care, though the more mundane aspects of parenting can also be predicted by women's resources and time availability. Shared involvement in parenting, in contrast, appears to be especially responsive to men's availability, initiative and gender ideals. The latest research shows that men do more housework and routine child care when they are employed fewer hours and their wives are employed more hours. Men also tend to do more housework when they are more highly educated and their wives earn more of the family income, though results here are more mixed, as discussed below.

Although both men and women tend to be committed to raising children when their offspring are conceived, most studies conclude that the arrival of children shifts the couple toward more conventional gender-based allocations of family work. Having children tends to increase women's family and household work, whereas men's hourly contributions to family work traditionally remain about the same after the children arrive—though their hours of paid work tend to increase. In the US, having a child means working about three more hours on the job per week for men; but for women it has been associated with spending about an hour less in the paid labor force each week, while putting in significantly more time on housework and child care. These gender-linked patterns of paid and unpaid labor allocation are the target of the Gornick–Meyers proposal, and beg the question of how these new policies might change the domestic labor allocation process in two-parent families. To assess prospects for change, I review findings on the influence of employment, earnings, education, and attitudes on the sharing of family work. Because most of this research is based in North America, I also provide a brief review of some recent cross-national research on men's sharing of household labor and child care, focusing on the potential influence of national differences in work–family policy regimes. I follow this with a discussion of women's patterns of labor force attachment in relation to men's paid and unpaid work. At the end of this essay I offer some predictions about men's likelihood of using the new programs, as well as prospects for men (and women) resisting equal sharing of family work. I conclude with a discussion of the need for embracing gender-egalitarian goals, even if they may be utopian for some families.

Employment

Research shows that employed mothers do less housework and child care than those who are not employed, and consequently share more family work with their male partners. I discuss women's employment more fully below, but here I focus on findings about men's family participation in relation to their own employment demands, as well as their wives'. Employment schedules are perhaps the most consistent and important predictors of housework-sharing that researchers have documented (Coltrane, 2000).

When men are unemployed or working part-time, some studies show that they perform more household labor, but some show that they do less (Brines, 1994; Shelton and John, 1993). Most research does find that, when employed, a father's employment hours are a strong predictor of his involvement in both housework and child care. When mothers of preschool children are employed, a father's time availability, measured by employment hours, predicts whether he will serve as a primary caregiver. Fathers and mothers with non-overlapping work shifts are the most likely to share child care. When mothers of school-aged children are employed for more hours, their husbands tend to do a greater portion of the child care and housework, and fathers tend to be more involved to the extent that they view their wives' career prospects more positively. And although some early research from the 1970s and 1980s suggested that men's "free" time was not readily convertible to domestic labor, men's time seems now to be more fungible. For example, US fathers in the late 1980s and 1990s were likely to use non-working discretionary hours for child care, whereas previously (from the 1970s to early 1980s) they tended to use those hours for other activities.

Although many researchers have reported that middle-class men are most likely to embrace nurturing fatherhood ideals, some recent data suggest that working-class fathers have changed more than their more privileged counterparts. Focusing on longitudinal data from England, Sullivan (2006) showed that men assumed more responsibility for family work if their jobs were in the manual or clerical category. Other data suggest that, whereas managerial and professional couples were the most likely to share family work in the 1970s and 1980s, by the 1990s and 2000s the most change (and sometimes the most sharing) occurred in couples with blue-collar or pink-collar jobs (Coltrane and Adams, 2008).

Earnings

Most researchers find that when wives have higher relative earnings, or when the gap between husbands' and wives' earnings is smaller, there is a more equal division of labor. Others focus on the independent influence of wives' earnings on their own hours of housework, rather than relative measures, suggesting that the economic influence comes from wives' absolute contributions and autonomy, rather than from bargaining influence (Bittman et al., 2003; Gupta, 2006. Thus, researchers typically find that earnings influence women's household labor (by reducing it), but that women's absolute or relative earnings do not automatically increase men's household labor.

Women's higher occupational status and income (but not men's) are strongly associated with the purchase of domestic services. Results from sample surveys and historical or ethnographic studies converge on a general finding: women's economic resources allow them to reduce their own housework contributions and "buy out" of gendered domestic obligations. Upwardly mobile and well-educated women are the most likely to purchase domestic services, whether performed in their own homes or embedded in the food and products they purchase for the family from outside the home. It is predominantly white, middle-class women who consume these services and products, and it is immigrant, ethnic minority, and working-class women who produce and provide them. This gender-, class- and race-based allocation of paid domestic work is an additional area in need of policies to promote social justice.

Education

Findings about the influence of education on family work are also somewhat mixed, with patterns sometimes differing for men and women and for housework versus child care. Many studies show that women with higher levels of education do less routine housework (cooking, meal clean-up, shopping, house-cleaning, and laundry), perhaps because, as noted above, they tend to hire others to do the work. A few studies show that men with higher levels of education do less housework and have spouses who do more of it, but most studies indicate that men with higher levels of education do more overall household labor and child care and that couples with more education share more household labor, partly because education is associated with more egalitarian gender ideals, which in turn are associated with men doing more family work.

Attitudes

Research shows that women's egalitarian gender ideology is a consistent predictor of shared housework, though women's attitudes are a less consistent predictor of shared child care. When wives feel more strongly that both paid work and family work should be shared, and when they agree more fully with statements about equality between women and men, they are typically more likely to share housework with husbands. Many studies also show that men with more egalitarian attitudes share more housework or child care than more traditional men but questions remain about whether gender attitudes should be considered as causes or consequences of such sharing (Coltrane, 1996, 2000; Sullivan, 2006).

Attitudes about sharing child care or housework operate in tandem with self-images, proportionate earnings, and job-schedule pressures, and these tend to shift as couples confront new challenges and opportunities. As the emerging gatekeeping literature attests, if women hold to strong separate-spheres ideals in the face of increased demand for women to work and men to "help" at home, such sharing can be seen as coerced, and father involvement in routine tasks can be interpreted as interference rather than helpfulness (see also Macdonald, this volume). In general, if family members want fathers to be more involved, and if they agree that women should share breadwinning (arguably now the norm), their participation in routine family work is evaluated positively. In contrast, if family members feel that mothers should not work outside the home and that fathers should not be expected to change diapers or do laundry, then such practices can cause stress. Nevertheless, interview studies show that the ideology of intensive mothering that leads some mothers to feel totally responsible for children and to resist sharing with their male partners often gives way to new ideals about the benefits of sharing the emotional as well as the mundane aspects of parenting (Coltrane, 1996; Doucet, 2006).

Ideals about marriage and marital status also matter. Proving that housework is not *inherently* gendered, studies have shown that men do more housework before they are married than they do afterwards. Once married, however, they tend more easily to label domestic chores as "women's work," and turn more of them over to their wives. And when couples have children, a combination of gender attitudes and practical choices coalesce to shape decisions that increase men's employment hours and increase women's domestic chores. This research shows that culture and attitudes are influential in how parents think and talk about their family lives, but my reading of the research findings in this area does not support the supposition that gender attitudes determine family practices. In fact, I would suggest that material concerns often override abstract ideals, so that gender attitudes are often overlooked or modified to accommodate shifting practical realities (vivid examples from my own research include Evangelical Promise Keepers and Mexican immigrants who maintain beliefs in male family headship and male breadwinning, even when wives' jobs or superior earnings would seem to undermine them). Such findings raise issues about how gender attitudes and domestic labor allocation are related, and suggest that work–family policies directed toward married couples with children are an ideal focus for future initiatives to promote gender equality.

Types of parental involvement

Some researchers also make a distinction between routine parenting (including helping with dress, hygiene, or homework; general supervision and monitoring, putting to bed, driving to school, and so on) and more enrichment or leisure activities (playing games; coaching or supervising children's sports; accompanying children to museums, parks, recitals, concerts or sporting events; engaging in creative activities such as arts, theater, or music; participating with children in youth groups; overseeing religious activities). In general, routine parenting is more likely to be associated with everyday housework and home maintenance activities, which are also more likely to be shared by men when they are employed for fewer hours, have more education, and have wives who are employed for more hours and make more money. In contrast, if men participate in enrichment or leisure activities with children they are not necessarily more likely to share routine domestic work with their wives (and such men have been found to be *less* likely to do cooking and cleaning—see Coltrane and Adams, 2008). In the discussion that follows, I focus on the more routine aspects of housework and child care (including especially cooking, cleaning and child supervision), because they are the most time-consuming and most likely to be allocated on the basis of gender. In addition, these are the tasks that, when shared, are the most likely to relieve stress and help women feel appreciated and supported. If the Gornick–Meyers proposals are to advance the cause of gender equality, men will need to perform a greater share of these routine tasks.

CROSS-NATIONAL TRENDS IN MEN'S HOUSEWORK

Recent research using cross-national time-diary data from twenty countries in Europe and North America documents a significant increase between 1960 and 2000 in men's share of housework and child care (Sullivan and Gershuny, 2001). For routine housework (cooking, cleaning, and clothes care), employed women's time went down (just under one hour per day) and men's went up (around twenty minutes per day). These data, based on time diaries (widely considered to be the most accurate measure of time use), show men's share of the routine housework increasing substantially (from 15 percent to 25 percent of the total), but still lagging behind women's. Results differ for shopping, driving children, and leisure activities with children, with both women and men spending significantly more time doing these things. For general child care, employed women increased their time commitments between 1960 and 2000, and, to a lesser degree, so did men (this finding held both for those employed full-time and part-time; for those with preschoolers as well as those with school-aged children). These general changes apply regardless of national context and across employment and family status (Sullivan, 2006; for comparison, Bianchi, 2000, reports that US women's time in child care was relatively constant over this period). The greater time spent on childrearing shown in this multi-nation study may result, at least partly, from a decline in normatively backed "mandatory parenthood." As fewer people opt to have children, existing parents include a higher proportion of those who affirmatively and deliberately choose to have children. Thus, time spent with children might be expected to increase for both mothers and fathers, and child care might correspond more closely to deeper preferences than in the past.

Comparative time-use data from developed countries shows that there has been a general decline in hours of paid work for both men and women over the past thirty years or so. This finding appears to be at odds with those of commentators who focus on the "time-poverty" or "time-bind" faced by modern parents (Hochschild, 1997; Jacobs and Gerson, 2004). The former finding is derived from structured time-diary data, whereas many of the later findings are based on interviews with parents who express feelings of intense pressure to fill their children's lives with structured leisure and enrichment activities. As the Gornick–Myers paper reminds us, the former findings are also based primarily on data from countries where sick leaves are automatic, parental or family leaves are ensured, vacation time is guaranteed, and the average work week is limited to less than forty hours per week. For overall time in all forms of paid and unpaid work in these developed nations, full-time employed women with school-aged children reduced their hourly contributions, but part-time employed women with preschool children showed no change (Sullivan and Gershuny, 2001). Women employed in low-wage part-time work face the most severe time pressures, and tend to have the least leisure time. Although aggregate trends are similar across employment categories, individual women's employment does make a difference within the family. Women employed full-time for more years have male partners who do more housework, and a transition to full-time employment for the woman is typically associated with the man taking on more of the routine family work (Sullivan, 2006).

To assess the gender-equality goal of the Gornick–Meyers paper, changes in labor force participation and domestic work allocation must be assessed with reference to sharing within the couple. In the Sullivan (2006) analysis of cross-national data, in nearly one-third of couples with two full-time workers, men were contributing more time to domestic work than their female partners. This is a significant change from past decades, and suggests that work schedules (and perhaps relative earnings) are increasingly important to couples' work–family allocation strategies. Sullivan (2006) found that there has been a general decline in the percentage of couples with a gendered division of domestic labor and an increase in the percentage of couples with more equal divisions of labor. This increase in sharing is directly linked to women's labor force participation. Among couples with part-time employed mothers, 41 percent did over 70 percent of the domestic labor, whereas among couples with non-employed mothers, 54 percent did over 70 percent of the domestic labor (Sullivan, 2006). And changes over time have been significant, if still limited: women (overall) were previously doing three-fourths of the domestic work, whereas they are now doing about two-thirds of it.

Sullivan suggests that findings of increasing amounts of time spent on child care are most interesting because they happened during the period when media concern over a shortage of time devoted to children in developed countries was growing. Sullivan found that the increase in time devoted to child care is consistent across countries with different subsidies, policies and regulations governing child care. Interpreting time-diary data from the US, Bianchi suggests that employed mothers attempt to maximize their time with children by reducing time spent in other activities, such as housework. Participation in child-related activities (homework, lessons, skill-building and so on) has received more attention from researchers in recent decades, and parents report spending more time doing these activities for and with children. And enrichment activities of this sort are increasingly linked to social class and "cultural logics" of childrearing (see Hays, 1997; Macdonald, this volume). Annette Lareau (2003) reports how middle-class mothers and fathers (regardless of race) engage in practices of "concerted cultivation" by fostering and assessing their children's talents, opinions, and skills. They schedule their children for a myriad of activities, reason with them, hover over them, intervene on their behalf outside the home, and make deliberate and sustained efforts to stimulate their cognitive and social skills (Lareau, 2003: 238). Poor and working-class parents, in contrast, frequently talk about money in the face of severe economic constraints, focus on providing for their children by giving them food and shelter, and tend to view their children's development as unfolding spontaneously, spending less time engaging in the enrichment activities that preoccupy aspiring middle-class parents. Changes in the meanings of these child-enhancement activities have likely influenced parents' reporting rates, so it is difficult to make precise judgments about actual time spent in these activities over time (Sullivan, 2006). In addition, rather than viewing child-care hours as a zero-sum calculation, recent research shows that the more time mothers spend with children, the more time fathers spend with children (Yeung et al., 2001), adding further support for the symbolic valuation of children in two-parent families as this family form becomes somewhat less prevalent in the population at large, and as middle-class family size continues to shrink.

As Gornick and Meyers suggest, cross-national differences in policies and employment patterns can also predict men's family involvements (see also Cooke, 2006). In a cross-national study of twenty industrialized countries, Jennifer Hook (2006) found that in nation-states with higher levels of maternal employment, men did more unpaid work in the home. If countries had generous maternal leave programs, men tended to do less; but when those leaves were available to fathers as well, men in general tended to perform more hours of household and family work (these data did not allow for testing the recent "daddy day" parental leave options discussed by Gornick and Meyers). And in general, the provision of publicly supported child care did not suppress men's contributions to unpaid domestic labor.

Supporting the main Gornick–Meyers' thesis, Hook suggests that individual-level theories of unpaid work behaviors ignore how national context can affect men's and women's time-allocation decisions by influencing the benefits of specialization, the terms of bargaining, and the ease or difficulty of adhering to gender norms. She found that there is a direct effect of women's labor force participation on men's unpaid work that affects all men—men married to employed women, men married to non-employed women, and even single men. In contexts where women are more involved in the public sphere, men are more involved in the private sphere, not necessarily because of household bargaining or other household-level processes, but because of societal shifts in gendered behavior" (Hook, 2006: 655).

Asking related questions, Iversen and Rosenbluth (2006) found that, in countries supporting general labor market skills, public sector jobs, and work–family policies such as child care, women have more power at home and shoulder less of the domestic labor. Similarly, in an analysis of Germany and the US, Cooke (2006) concluded, "the slow evolution in the division of domestic tasks observed over the past half century may not result from persistent gender differences, but from continuing institutional reinforcement of the gendered division of labor". In an analysis of US couples, Cooke (2007) found that interstate differences in poverty, public transfers, child support and family law, along with more typical measures of income and education, shaped the division of housework within couples, presumably because these factors influenced women's alternatives to marriage. Research of this sort supports the idea that public policies contribute to the gender-balance of power within couples—even in the US, where state supports are relatively meager compared to European-style welfare states. As noted above, an emerging body of cross-national research also suggests that government policies providing paternal, as well as maternal, leaves and other family supports can influence the normative and behavioral dimensions of gender relations in housework and parenting.

MOTHERS' EMPLOYMENT, MALE-BREADWINNER ASSUMPTIONS, AND GENDER EQUITY

The Gornick–Meyers goal of gender equality assumes that women's labor force participation is the key to parity with men, but does not specify the various mechanisms through which their labor and earnings might influence family dynamics. Why have women entered the labor market in record numbers, and how do their jobs alter the balance of power in family negotiations over domestic labor? Some women take jobs for reasons of personal fulfillment, for career motivation, or to be able to afford luxury items; but most women go to work for wages out of necessity. Demographers note that the need for women to work for basic living expenses has increased dramatically in the past few decades, and national surveys find that over 80 percent of Americans agree it takes two paychecks to support a family (Jacobs and Gerson, 2004). Over a quarter of all US children need a mother's income to lift the family out of poverty.

Although women are more likely to be employed than before, it is still men who tend to be identified most strongly with paid work. Masculinity and men's authority are still associated with success on the job. Even though male-breadwinner families with stay-at-home wives are now vastly outnumbered by dual-earner families, the man's work still tends to count (in some peoples' eyes) for more than the woman's. This is partly because full-time-employed workers who are male continue to be paid about 25 percent more than full-time-employed workers who are female. There are two contradictory patterns concerning employment and wages of US women: although they now make up 47 percent of the labor force, stay employed when they become mothers, and are earning more than they used to, on average, women continue to be employed slightly less and to earn significantly less than men.

With two earners in most families, however, the provider role has undergone some changes, and most families now give recognition to women whose incomes are essential. Nevertheless, men tend to retain symbolic responsibility for earning money, and often get more credit for doing so than their equal-earning female partners. Many men are still reluctant to accept wives as equal providers, even when both spouses are working full-time. In working-class couples, where it is evident that wives take jobs out of financial necessity, they are more likely to see themselves—and are more likely to be seen by their husbands—as sharing the provider responsibility. This is particularly so when wives' earnings approach husbands'. Among all married-couple US families in which both the wife and husband work, about one-fifth of the wives earn more than their husbands (US Department of Labor, 2005). And the trend toward more equal earnings continues: in over a third of all US couples, wives make at least 40 percent of the couple's income (Raley et al., 2006). Although American couples in which women's earnings exceed men's are more likely to divorce than others, this tendency is eliminated when men share half of the housework (Cooke, 2006).

Within couples, the wage gap is smallest, on average, between working-class spouses. Nevertheless, most studies of work–family issues in two-earner families have been conducted with middle-class samples. Considerable research attention has been paid to upwardly mobile professional couples who focus on their careers and espouse egalitarian beliefs. Some researchers conclude that such marriages are "more equal than others" (Hertz, 1986). Nevertheless, professional men's salaries are usually considerably higher than their wives', so the women may have a harder time receiving recognition as providers than their working-class counterparts. It may be that well-educated professional couples talk more about the importance of sharing, which leads researchers to report more equality than actually exists (Coltrane, 1996).

Today, most people say they hold jobs to make money, but the majority also report that they derive personal satisfaction from their jobs and careers. This is now as true for women as it is for men. Satisfying, well-paid work is related to enhanced well-being for both men and women. The only exception seems to be when people— especially mothers—believe that they should *not* be working, but circumstances force them to take jobs or work longer hours than they want. This is especially stressful for mothers who work exceptionally long hours, bring work home, or have nonstandard shifts, and for those who generally feel under pressure at work (Jacobs and Gerson, 2004). In general, however, as men's and women's jobs and work histories begin to look more alike, they are also likely to share similar family concerns. Recent polls find that over 60 percent of both American men and women would like to work fewer hours on the job (Jacobs and Gerson, 2004). In addition, 60 percent of men and 55 percent of women say they experience conflict in balancing work, personal, and family life (Bond et al., 1998), and the majority of both men and women report that they feel torn between the demands of their job and wanting to spend more time with their family. Workplace factors such as flexibility in scheduling work hours, increased autonomy, and a supportive supervisor are associated with both men and women workers reporting less work–family conflict, interference and stress (Jacobs and Gerson, 2004).

Because of an older ideal of separate work and family spheres, it has been easier for men to feel that they are fulfilling their family commitments by working and being a financial provider. Women, on the other hand, have had to justify why having a job does not make them a bad mother. Pleck (1977) suggests that the boundaries between work roles and family roles are "asymmetrically permeable" for men and women. Men have typically been able to keep family commitments from intruding on their work time, and have been able to use job demands to limit family time. In contrast to men, women's family obligations have traditionally been allowed to penetrate into their workplace. It is usually mothers who take time off from work when a child becomes ill, though we are seeing a small increase in the number of fathers doing this. The typical pattern has been for women, more than men, to move in and out of the labor force, regulating the number of hours they are employed in response to child-care demands and other family needs (Moen, 2003).

Social scientists have often reproduced assumptions about separate spheres for men and women in the ways they have defined work–family research questions. For example, research before the 1980s tended to conceive of men's non-employment as a problem, whereas women's employment was seen as a potential problem for the family and for children's development. More recently, the issue of "working families" has been defined by researchers as one of overload and "balance". Some work–family researchers have labeled the lockstep model of continuous full-time employment exemplified by the male-breadwinner model as "the career mystique," noting that this ideal is still dominant not only for men, but also for the few women (often single or childless) who can now pursue it (Moen, 2003; Moen and Roehling, 2004). Most researchers also point out that it is still women who tend to do the balancing, by scaling back on their occupational aspirations or hours of paid work, thus perpetuating the asymmetrical permeability between work and family roles for men and women (Williams, 2000). As Hochschild (2003) phrased it, this has resulted in a "stalled revolution," fundamentally changing women's equal access to primary-sector careers, but not fundamentally challenging the social organization of those careers. With equal opportunity in the labor market as the major focus, all adults in families, and especially women, are expected to pursue long-hour, lockstep occupational careers (Moen, 2003; Williams, 2000).

Researchers have attempted to measure people's work and family attachments by asking questions about how committed they are to each. Although somewhat superficial, answers to these survey questions indicate whether someone gains special meaning from family and work activities, and how willing they might be to cut back on one or the other. Both men and women say they are strongly committed to both family and work. Nevertheless, on average, men tend to be slightly more identified with work than with family, and women to be slightly more identified with family than work. Men's commitments to paid employment have remained relatively stable or declined slightly over the last few decades, but women's have continued to increase. Overall gender differences in commitment to paid work are thus diminishing.

As women receive more education, and as job opportunities and rewards open up to them, they become more attached to their careers. If women have work statuses and experiences similar to men's, and have the opportunity to identify as strongly with the work as men, gender differences in commitment to work and family begin to disappear (Jacobs and Gerson, 2004). In recent studies, job conditions and opportunities are the strongest determinants of work commitment, with marital and family status having little, if any, impact (Jacobs and Gerson, 2004). Although there is much less research on the family side, there is also evidence that, when men have household responsibilities similar to those of women, they are as strongly committed to the family as are women. This seems to be especially true if men take advantage of paternity leave or otherwise arrange to spend significant amounts of time with their children when they are young (Coltrane, 1996).

Against an optimistic vision of gender convergence in work and family roles, some scholars cite difficulties faced by fathers that are similar to dilemmas faced by mothers with careers (Sullivan, 2006). Others focus on high divorce rates, an increasing number of single-mother families throughout Europe and North America, and levels of children's contact with their birth fathers that are moderate at best (Eggebeen, 2002). Some social scientists suggest that recent small changes in the domestic division of labor "should be better understood in terms of a largely successful male resistance" (McMahon, 1999: 7). Why are men resisting? The short answer is that it is in men's interest to do so, as it reinforces a separation of spheres that underpins masculine ideals and perpetuates a gender order privileging men over women (Adams and Coltrane, 2004). Early work–family research suggested that the most resistance would come from working-class men, who would defend their patriarchal privilege, though more recent findings suggest that male wage-workers (rather than upwardly mobile professionals) will be the most likely to take advantage of such policies (without necessarily embracing the feminist or egalitarian principles underlying them).

WILL THE POLICIES WORK?

Gornick and Meyers present a range of policies to encourage father involvement, and I predict that all would promote more sharing of family work (with the exception of promoting part-time work for women and the provision of universal child care, both of which could have the opposite effect). I discuss each proposal in turn, making predictions about possible uptake by men.

Shorter work week

Limiting weekly employment hours and setting normal full-time weekly hours in the range of thirty-five to thirty-nine hours per week (as is standard in several European countries today) would affect men more than women. Though not all fathers would use the increased non-work time to do more with their children, recent research suggests that a significant proportion of men would use the time to participate more in family life. As noted above, one of the most consistent predictors of men sharing housework and child care is their own hours of employment. As Gornick and Meyers suggest, limiting the standard full-time week to below forty hours would grant fathers more time for children on a daily basis. I agree that limiting men's time in the labor market (and limiting mandatory overtime work), would raise the likelihood that men would share more family work with their partners. If most men had employment that was "full-time," but at less than forty hours, men who left work to be with their families would be less likely to be sanctioned or passed over for promotions. Evidence suggests that dual-earner couples who each work thirty hours per week experience less stress and report higher family satisfaction (Hill, et al., 2006).

Paid time off

A month of paid time off per year would guarantee workers a substantial number of paid days off each year, and would very likely be used by men in a wide range of occupations. As Gornick and Meyers suggest, the right to paid time off would alleviate some of the burden of arranging child-care coverage during summer and other school breaks, and would grant parents needed periods of uninterrupted family time. Fathers with vacation time, sick time, and personal time now take time to spend with their children, and an increased amount would undoubtedly increase their time spent with children. As noted in the literature review above, men's paid work hours are a consistent predictor of their family work performance, most men say they would like more time off, and reductions in work time have been linked to increases in men's child care.

Scheduling options

Increasing the availability of flexible work scheduling, telecommuting, and other individualized control over the timing of work, would also be used by many fathers in the US. Studies show that men who use these options report greater job satisfaction and better relations with their children (Hill, et al., 2006).

AVAILABILITY OF PART-TIME WORK

The proposal to ensure all workers the right to formally request a shift to reduced-hour or flexibly scheduled work, subject to employer agreement, is clearly advantageous for parents and children, and on that basis is a worthy policy objective. Access to part-time work would allow some men to become primary parents and others to adopt co-parenting more fully. As the earnings of men and women become more similar and as their career trajectories converge, there will be more men who will opt for part-time work when they become parents, and this will allow them more time to devote to child care and housework. Nevertheless, previous research suggests that men will be less likely to pursue such options than will women. Seeking pay and benefit parity for part-time workers will benefit parents and children in general, but because uptake will be greater among women than men, this provision will do less to promote the goal of gender equality within the couple. In fact, making long-term, well-paid part-time work readily available to all workers may actually reduce the amount of sharing between individual mothers and fathers, as many couples will decide for financial reasons that only one spouse should pursue such an option, and that spouse will most often be the woman. If women's and men's wages were equal, then instituting this initiative would carry less potential for reinstituting separate career paths for women and men.

Paternity leave

In the countries discussed by Gornick and Meyers, national maternity leave policies grant nearly all employed mothers several weeks or months of job security and wage replacement around the time of childbirth or adoption. Some offer the leave to either men or women in a family, and some also offer special paternity leave that is only available to men. Because few firms now provide paternity leave in the US, it is difficult to assess the extent to which men would take advantage of these leaves. Modest leave periods (one to two weeks, for example) with wage replacement would be very likely to be used by the majority of US men. A survey of leave-taking in California before the new paid family leave program was operating showed that men took as many leaves as women, though often for shorter periods (Milkman and Appelbaum, 2004). The new California paid family leave program and the national Family and Medical Leave Act (FMLA) have nontransferable benefits of the type proposed by Gornick and Meyers and, as they note, this provision would promote men's utilization better than a European-style family-based allocation of a set number of weeks for parental leave to be used by either parent. Gornick and Meyers note that Swedish and Norwegian fathers' use of paternity leave increased exponentially when they instituted nontransferable benefits for men ("daddy days"). Interview studies in Canada and the US show that leave-taking around the birth of a child has helped many fathers to develop stronger attachments to their newborns, and afforded them opportunities to develop competencies that would not be possible if only mothers had taken parental leave (Coltrane and Adams, 2008; Doucet, 2006).

Paid family leave

The Gornick–Meyers proposal calls for six months of family- or child-related leave with wage replacement for men (as well as women). I suspect that the majority of men will take a week or two at the time of the birth (or adoption) of a child, but will probably take the bulk of their paid leave time as children grow older and as mothers exhaust their leave benefits. This fits a general pattern of men being secondary caretakers for infants, even when they attempt to share parenting equally with the mother. Although some men are actively involved in infant care, more begin to share significant amounts of child care when their children become toddlers, and become more comfortable as routine caregivers when their children are school-aged. With nontransferable benefits for each parent, it is likely that mothers will use their leaves around the birth and during infancy (when many are breastfeeding). Because children routinely and repeatedly get sick, need doctor and dentist visits, and have gaps in their care provision, it is likely that men will use this leave in short spurts to cover routine emergencies of child care and health care. If leave allotments can be taken for a period of eight years, as proposed by Gornick and Meyers, and if male leave-taking becomes normative, fathers will use their time to attend preschool and elementary school conferences, performances, and other activities as their children mature. With full wage replacement and strong job protection provisions, most men would use the leaves, though undoubtedly at somewhat lower levels than women.

With the proposed means-tested earnings cap, working-class men would receive a greater portion of wage replacement. Because men with more education and higher-status occupations are already more likely to espouse sharing ideals and embrace new fathering models, they may need less monetary incentive to take these leaves. And if the leave policies were utilized widely, even men with partial wage replacement would be more likely to take them than currently, partly because workplace culture will be more accepting of men utilizing such leaves. Spreading the cost for the leave programs between employers and employees should make employers less likely to discourage men from taking the leaves. Using funding mechanisms that resemble existing unemployment insurance programs (as the new California family leave program does) is especially promising. As Gornick and Meyers note, publicly financed "leave for family reasons" would ensure that parents could meet children's needs when unpredictable but routine "emergency" situations arise. Importantly, the policy would extend benefits to low-wage workers, whose jobs and employers typically grant the fewest options for parents who need to make short-term changes in work scheduling. Most American parents would heartily welcome this policy, and, as recent research on working-class fathers attests, these men are definitely committed to caring for their children, and are poised to utilize the leaves if they were to receive wage replacement and if they knew their jobs were secure. I predict that a majority of fathers who are hourly wage workers would utilize family leaves, typically for a few days at a time and as their children reached school age, but longer when their children or other family members had special needs. Previous research suggests that the ability to adjust work schedules to meet child care or medical care needs leads to better mental health among parents, and presumably this will lead to more effective parenting and better child outcomes.

Child-care provision

The Gornick–Meyers proposal calls for the provision of non-parental care for children of various ages in various locations and configurations. Although high-quality child care is probably more expensive than the various parental leave and work schedule options they propose, a combination of the two will benefit both children and parents. As with the promotion of part-time work possibilities for mothers, full provision of state-subsidized high-quality child care could undermine the goal of including more men in the provision of routine child care, if couples used the child care in place of men's contributions. But by changing women's alternatives outside of marriage, universal child care could also improve women's bargaining position within the couple.

An addition to the child-care proposal might include an explicit focus on child care that also trained fathers in parenting skills. As the research on father involvement shows, more education is a key predictor of greater father involvement. Recent efforts by the federal Head Start program could provide a model, especially because the target populations are men with less education and social capital, but who nonetheless have a strong desire to be good fathers. Men have few opportunities to learn how to care for children, yet they respond well to institutionalized instruction, particularly in the company of other men. I favor new initiatives to promote subsidized child care that also maintain the goal of gender equity between men and women. Such programs could include child-care skill-building for adolescent boys (and "home economics" for boys in middle or high school), birthing classes for new fathers delivered through hospitals and medical clinics, parent education classes and support for fathers' groups, and cooperative child-care centers where fathers are encouraged to participate in routine on-site care, and in so doing are taught new skills. Research shows that most fathers want to be involved in their children's lives, but that they feel unprepared and inadequate. More state resources devoted to the development of men's nurturing capacities would benefit mothers, fathers and their children.

Because categorical beliefs in parenting and gender differences mask relations of power and inequality, asking men to do more family work is both discomforting and necessary (Coltrane, 1996). Policies designed to help families should assume that both men and women want to contribute to their families through both breadwinning and the provision of everyday care and unpaid support work. I suspect that it is unrealistic to assume that men will do half the parenting and housework in the majority of families, but, with Gornick and Meyers, I do not believe we should set significantly lower standards for fathers than for mothers. We need to stop assuming that men are incapable of nurturing children or doing housework, or that women cannot be primary breadwinners (see Brighouse and Wright, this volume). The Gornick–Meyers policy proposals have a realistic chance of helping men and women to negotiate new patterns of sharing for both paid and unpaid work.

American men and women need policies to promote parental leave when children are born, to allow for paid leave to care for children or other family members as needed, to shorten the work week, to guarantee longer vacations, to ensure living wages, to set pay equity standards for women, and to support subsidized child care. Instead of allowing these proposals to be seen as attacking "the family," we should think about how we might utilize the power of cultural symbols of "motherhood," "fatherhood," "family," and "children" to promote gender equality. If policies are to increase men's participation in family work, they might neutralize the ambivalence that many women and men feel about bringing men into a realm considered by many to be "the woman's domain." They might do this by drawing on American ideals of individual rights and equal opportunity. Although I formerly questioned the wisdom of using rhetoric from the women's movement to champion fathers' rights, the Gornick–Meyers policies could easily be promoted on the basis of full parenting rights for every individual, whether woman or man, married or single, gay or straight (see also Hobson, 2002). Children do benefit when they have loving and committed fathers in their lives, and these policies are designed to create more fathers (and mothers) who fit this profile. In addition, these policies are designed to maximize the chances that fathers and mothers will participate as equal parents, by balancing their commitments to paid employment and unpaid family work. If men would thus be encouraged to assume more responsibility for routine child care and housework, we might approach the necessary conditions for more egalitarian gender relations in society at large. This is, indeed, a worthy goal.

REFERENCES

Adams, M., and S. Coltrane, 2004, "Boys and Men in Families: The Domestic Production of Gender, Power, and Privilege," in R. W. Connell, J. Hearn, and M. Kimmel, eds, *The Handbook of Studies on Men and Masculinities*, Thousand Oaks, CA: Sage Publications.

Bianchi, Suzanne M., 2000, "Maternal Employment and Time With Children: Dramatic Change or Surprising Continuity?" *Demography* 37: 401–14.

Bittman, M., P. England, N. Folbre, L. C. Sayer, and G. Matheson, 2003, "When Does Gender Trump Money? Bargaining and Time in Household Work," *American Journal of Sociology* 109: 186–214.

Bond, J. E. Galinsky, and J. Swanberg, 1998, *The 1997 National Study of the Changing Workforce*, New York: Families and Work Institute.

Brines, J., 1994, "Economic Dependency, Gender, and the Divison of Labor at Home," American Journal of Sociology 100: 652–88.

Cherlin, A. J., 2005, "American Marriage in the Early Twenty-First Century," *The Future of Children* 15: 33–55.

Coltrane, S., 1996, *Family Man*, New York: Oxford University Press.

——— 2000, "Research on Household Labor," *Journal of Marriage and the Family* 62: 1,209–33.

——— Coltrane, S. and M. Adams, 2008, *Gender and Families*, Lanham, MD: Rowan and Littlefield.

Cooke, L. P., 2006, "'Doing' Gender in Context: Household Bargaining and Risk of Divorce in Germany and the United States," *American Journal of Sociology* 112: 442–72.

——— 2007, "Policy Pathways to Gender Power: State-Level Effects on the US Division of Housework," *Journal of Social Policy* 36: 239–60.

Deutsch, F., 1999, *Halving It All*, Cambridge, MA: Harvard University Press.

Doucet, A., 2006, *Do Men Mother? Fathering, Care, and Domestic Responsibility*, Toronto: University of Toronto Press.

Eggebeen, D., 2002, The Changing Course of Fatherhood, *Journal of Family Issues* 23: 486–50.

Furstenberg, F. F., 1988, "Good Dads—Bad Dads," in A. Cherlin, ed., *The Changing American Family and Public Policy*, Washington, DC: Urban Institute Press.

Griswold, R. L., 1993, *Fatherhood in America: A History*, New York: Basic Books.

Gupta, S., 2006, "Her Money, Her Time: Women's Earnings and Their Housework Hours," *Social Science Research* 35: 975–99.

Hays, S., 1997, *The Cultural Contradictions of Motherhood*, New Haven: Yale University Press.

Hertz, R., 1986, *More Equal than Others: Women and Men in Dual-Career Marriages*, Berkeley: University of California Press.

Hill, E. J., N. T. Mead, R. D. Ludas, D. M. Hafen, R. Gadd, A. A. Palmer, and M. S. Ferris, 2006, "Researching the 60-hour Dual-Earner Workweek," *American Behavioral Scientist* 49: 1,184–203.

Hobson, Barbara, ed., 2002, *Making Men into Fathers*, Cambridge/New York: Cambridge University Press.

Hochschild, A., 1997, *The Time Bind: When Work Becomes Home and Home Becomes Work*, New York: Metropolitan Books.

——— 2003, *The Second Shift*. New York: Penguin.

Hook, J., 2006, "Care in Context: Men's Unpaid Work in 20 Countries, 1965–2003," *American Sociological Review* 71: 639–60.

Iversen, T., and F. Rosenbluth, 2006, "The Political Economy of Gender: Explaining Cross-National Variation in the Gender Division of Labor and the Gender Voting Gap," *American Journal of Political Science* 50: 1–19.

Jacobs, J. and K. Gerson, 2004, *The Time Divide: Work, Family and Gender Inequality*, Cambridge, MA: Harvard University Press.

Lareau, A., 2003, *Unequal Childhoods*, Berkeley: University of California Press.

LaRossa, R., 1997, *The Modernization of Fatherhood: A Social and Political History*, Chicago: University of Chicago Press.

McMahon, A., 1999, *Taking Care of Men: Sexual Politics in the Public Mind*, Cambridge, UK: Cambridge University Press.

Milkman, R., and E. Appelbaum, 2004, "Paid Family Leave in California," *The State of California Labor* 4: 45–67.

Moen, P., 2003, *It's About Time: Couples and Careers*, Ithaca: ILR Press.

Moen, P. and P. Roehling, 2004, *The Career Mystique*, Lanham, MD: Rowman & Littlefield Publishers.

Pew Research Center, 2007, "As Marriage and Parenthood Drift Apart, Public is Concerned about Social Impact, online: http://pewresearch.org/pubs/526/marriage-parenthood (accessed July 24, 2007).

Pleck, J. H., 1977, "The Work–Family Role System," *Social Problems* 24: 417–27.

Pleck, J. H., and B. P. Masciadrelli, 2003, "Paternal Involvement: Levels, Sources, and Consequences, in M. E. Lamb, ed., *The Role of the Father in Child Development*, ed., New York: John Wiley.

Raley, S. B., M. J. Mattingly, and S. M. Bianchi, 2006, "How Dual are Dual-Income Couples? Documenting Change from 1970 to 2001," *Journal of Marriage and the Family* 68: 11–28.

Shelton, B. A., and D. John, 1993, "Does Marital Status Make a Difference? Housework among Married and Cohabiting Men and Women," Journal of Family Issues 14: 401–20.

Sullivan, O., 2006, *Changing Gender Relations, Changing Families: Tracing the Pace of Change over Time*, Lanham: Rowman & Littlefield.

Sullivan, O., and J. Gershuny, 2001, "Cross-National Changes in Time-Use *British Journal of Sociology* 52: 331–48.

US Department of Labor, 2005, "Employment Characteristics of Families," Table 5, online: http://www.bls.gov/cps

Williams, J., 2000, *Unbending Gender*, New York: Oxford University Press.

Yeung, W. J., J. F. Sandberg, P. E. Davis-Kean, and S. L. Hofferth, 2001, "Children's Time with Fathers in Intact Families," *Journal of Marriage and the Family* 63: 136–54.

18

What's Culture Got to Do with It? Mothering Ideologies as Barriers to Gender Equity

Cameron Macdonald

Janet Gornick and Marcia Meyers have offered reasoned and idealistic suggestions for the creation of institutional supports to assist working parents while simultaneously creating gender equity. Generous paid parental leaves that provide incentives for gender-equitable parenting; policies that limit working hours, and that create fair wages and benefits for part-time workers; and universal child care—all are important steps toward improving the lives of working families. In this essay, I raise the issue of culture, and particularly of ideologies concerning the "good mother," as a potential barrier to the kind of social change Gornick and Meyers envision. I argue that making significant workplace changes in parenting arrangements without also addressing the dominant mothering ideology is short-sighted, and thus risky. Too little regard for the power of gender ideologies in general, and of mothering ideologies in particular, may lead a set of overtly progressive policies to produce regressive results.

I draw on my own research on working mothers and a review of the extensive literature on mothering to raise two questions. First, given the contemporary norm of the "good mother" as an "at-home mother," will women take up parental leave and, more crucially, part-time work at a much higher rate than men? Doing so would entrench a "mommy track" within a set of policies designed to be *both* family-friendly *and* gender equitable. Second, given that gender intersects with race and class will mothers of different backgrounds respond to the proposed policies, and in particular to publicly provided child care, in class- and race-based ways that reproduce existing inequalities among children? I limit my discussion of Gornick and Meyers' proposals to those aimed at improving the conditions of part-time work and at instituting publicly provided child care, because these two social policies risk the most regressive consequences, given the nature of contemporary mothering norms. I focus mainly on the US context because, although widespread, childrearing norms are contextually specific.

MOTHERING AND CULTURE

Since I accept the utopian mandate that informs this volume, I leave aside thorny questions concerning whether or not policy-makers would support or enact the proposed changes, and move directly to exploring the cultural and social belief systems in which actors are embedded. A clear understanding of context is essential. In order for any policy change to be effective, individuals have to be willing to implement it in their daily lives. Borrowing from sociologists Mary Blair-Loy (2003: 115) and William Sewell (1992: 27), I suggest that social structures are composed of "mutually sustaining cultural schemas and sets of resources that empower and constrain social action and tend to be reproduced by that action." Further, these schemas "help define and make sense of what [one] finds desirable and compelling."[1] In the US, working-class and middle-class mothers are expected not only to raise their own children using their own resources, but also to *want* to provide this mother-care, particularly during the period from birth to age three. Mothering action takes shape within these cultural constraints, as mothers choose which aspects of existing norms to embrace and which to resist. How might Gornick and Meyers' proposed policies fare in this context?

The current cultural climate is particularly hard on mothers, pitting them against one another along a rigid mother-care/other-care binary, and giving rise to the so-called "mommy wars" (Johnston and Swanson, 2004). Swidler (1986, 2001) makes the case that, in times of social upheaval, common-sense knowledge or cultural "taken-for-granteds" often harden into dogma. It is this dynamic that underlies the "mommy wars." Evidence of the increasingly dogmatic approach to mothers' roles and responsibilities is evident in the strident nature of debates over childrearing. For example, even the panel of experts in a 1997 government-sponsored study intended to resolve debates regarding the value of mother-care versus child care (NICHD Early Child Care Research Network, 1997, 1998) could not reach consensus.

Accusations of bias created deep divisions among panel members (Arnst, 2001; Birns, 1999; Bruer, 1999; Chira, 1998; Lamb, 1990). The surge in the number of advice books on parenting that has accompanied the significant rise in mothers' participation in the labor force is another indicator of polarizing perspectives. Five times as many childrearing advice books were published in 1997 as in 1975 (Hulbert, 2003).

The US can be said to be in the midst of an epoch of unsettled mothering, in which ideological views on good mothering have both hardened and proliferated. Here I refer to ideology not in the Marxian sense (which can be interpreted to entail some degree of intention on the part of knowledge-producers), but rather in the Weberian or Foucauldian sense of expert discourse that filters through the capillaries of popular culture and social structures, forming a general consensus concerning what is normal or abnormal. As I will discuss below, mothering ideologies are produced by experts—typically, pediatricians, neurologists, and child development researchers—and circulated through conferences and research papers. Experts' views are then interpreted and disseminated via mass media such as newspapers, popular magazines, and childrearing advice books. Different groups of mothers consume this information at different rates and act on it to different degrees. The result, however, is a widespread acceptance of the current state of expert ideologies concerning childrearing and maternal obligations. Pediatricians and child psychologists do not set out to make mothers miserable when they formulate the latest version of what children need, but this is the net effect of their pronouncements. It is impossible to write about what children need without simultaneously implying what mothers "ought."

Likewise, many commentators who write about working mothers seem unable to avoid blaming the victim, or assuming some degree of "false consciousness" among women who try simultaneously to emulate the "good mother" and the "unencumbered worker" (Williams, 2000). I reject these views and instead endorse Nancy Folbre's argument (this volume: 111–119) that good childrearing is both publicly valuable and intrinsically fulfilling work. At the same time, it is important to recognize that the contemporary mother-blame rhetoric has reached levels of near hysteria. The views of child development specialists, the content of advice books, and the shifting tides of public opinion combine to pressure all mothers to maintain their status as primary parent. It is not surprising, then, that so many mothers strive to adhere to some version of what Hays (1996) has termed "intensive mothering."

Other essays in this collection (see the contributions by Scott Coltrane and Ruth Milkman) also address the problem of ideology and motivation. Scott Coltrane approaches the problem from the fathers' side, while Ruth Milkman examines the employers' perspective. These are important areas, as is demonstrated by the need for incentives and sanctions to promote employer and paternal participation in countries that already have enacted family leave policies. However, most work–family studies assume, somewhat uncritically, that mothers will embrace the dual-earner/dual-caregiver model—particularly the earner component—whether that means increasing their hours at work if high-quality care is provided, or welcoming fathers and other loving adults into the parenting endeavor. In practice, though, it may instead mean continuing to work more, as contemporary mothers do, without reducing their own hours in child care (Bianchi et al., 2006). Or it may mean, as it has in some European countries, switching to a 1.5-earner model, in which men work full time and women remain in the part-time workforce for the duration of their childrearing years. Finally, it may mean that mothers will adapt to publicly provided child care slowly and in ways that reproduce both class and gender inequalities. If well-off women can "buy their way out" of working full-time, or can supplement or replace publicly provided child care with privately purchased services aimed at enhancing their children's cognitive and social development, can a national child-care program succeed? The question I raise, then, is not the ubiquitous "Can men mother?" (Risman, 1998); rather, it is the somewhat more complex, "Can/will women father?"

THE INTENSIFICATION OF "INTENSIVE MOTHERING"

Never before in American history have the daily lives of so many mothers been so at odds with beliefs about children's needs. Previous historical periods, such as the mid-to-late nineteenth century, or the period immediately following the Second World War, produced large amounts of mother-centric childrearing advice, but these ideological phases were in line with the homebound behavior of a plurality of mothers.[2] Today, although 70 percent of US mothers work outside the home, prevailing beliefs about childrearing are, if anything, even more firmly based on the ideal of the ever-present, continually attentive, at-home mother. Scholars agree that contemporary child development research, advice books, parenting magazines, and general cultural sentiment have converged to raise the bar on expectations for mothering young children so high that even full-time, at-home mothers would be hard-pressed to meet them. For working mothers, these expectations, which *require* the presence of a full-time mother as the primary caregiver, are by definition impossible to meet. Nevertheless, as Hays (1996) convincingly shows, while the ideology of intensive mothering is at odds with the market rationality usually associated with the successful worker, this ideology holds sway among working mothers and at-home mothers alike.

Based on her analysis of childrearing literature, and of both middle- and working-class mothers' interpretations of that literature, Hays defines "intensive mothering" as "child centered, expert-guided, emotionally absorbing, labor intensive, and financially expensive," and points out that "the task of child rearing is considered primarily the responsibility of the mother" (Hays, 1996: 69). Although authors of contemporary childrearing manuals make efforts to include fathers, and often use the gender-neutral term "parents," they direct their advice almost exclusively to mothers, and suggest that "consistent nurture by a single primary caregiver is crucial," ideally for the first three years of a child's life (Hays, 1996: 53). Further, according to these experts, a good mother is "not a subject with her own needs and interests" (Bassin et al., 1994: 2). Therefore, a belief in the value of intensive mothering inherently supports both the ideal of nuclear family self-sufficiency and of the gender inequities inherent in this ideal. Intensive mothering also places working mothers squarely in the crosshairs of two incompatible ideals: the unencumbered worker and the ever-present mother.

In the years since Hays published her analysis of the effects of childrearing advice on mothering practices, early childhood development researchers have produced new ideological strands that combine to create notions of child perfectibility, and the attendant need to produce the perfect child. In 1980, Jerome Kagan stated with some prescience that "the question of how to rear the better baby is so glamorous, so attractive to Americans and so fraught with emotionalism, that it invites judgments and ungrounded speculations" (quoted in Hulbert, 2003: 313). As it turned out, 1997 was the halcyon year for that prediction. The release of the first findings from the National Institute of Child Health and Human Development's (NICHD) attachment study, the publication of the Families and Work Institute's *Rethinking the Brain: New Insights into Early Development*, and the Clinton administration–sponsored Carnegie Corporation program, Starting Points, which focused on the birth-to-three period, all occurred that year. They also all produced the same result: media hysteria about mothering.

The issue of *Newsweek*, "Your Child from Birth to Three," which documented the findings of Starting Points, sold 1 million copies, setting a record for the magazine (Hulbert, 2003).

The NICHD attachment study,[3] while producing reassuring findings about the benefits of high-quality child care, ultimately devolved into an argument between those researchers who had a "mother is best" bias and those who wanted to prove that quality child care could be as salutary as good mothering. The media contributed to the general confusion by publishing only the negative findings on the effects of institutional child care. For example, instead of disseminating the key early finding from the first wave of the study, which showed positive outcomes for children in child care, the *New York Times Magazine* drew on the NICHD findings to draw parallels between American children in child care and Romanian orphans who developed "attachment disorders" because they were left to lie face down in cribs all day and deprived of human contact (Talbot, 1998).

During the same period, emerging research in neurology claimed to show that the human brain created its primary neural pathways from birth to age three, and that a child's long-term cognitive functioning depended in large part on the kinds of cognitive stimulation he or she received during this period. As Harvard child psychiatrist Felton Earls proclaimed,

> A kind of irreversibility sets in. There is this shaping process that goes on early, and then at the end of this process, be that age 2, 3 or 4, you have essentially designed a brain that probably is not going to change very much more. (Quoted in Bruer, 1999: 23)

These arguments produced predictable results. After the findings were made public, a nationally representative survey of parents with children under three found that 92 percent of respondents believed that their children's educational successes would be influenced by their birth-to-three cognitive experiences, and 85 percent feared that if they did not provide proper stimulation, their babies' brains would not develop properly (Bruer, 1999: 52).

The take-away message from these studies, and of the advice books and magazine articles that interpreted and popularized their findings, was that by working outside the home, mothers risked depriving their children of essential emotional security and cognitive stimulation, especially during the preschool years. These media messages coincided with strong opinions and deep ambivalence among Americans about mothers and employment. For example, a poll conducted in 2000 found that 80 percent of mothers aged between eighteen and twenty-nine preferred to stay home (Public Agenda, 2000). The general public seemed to concur. A separate poll, conducted the same year, indicated that 75 percent of Americans surveyed agreed that children *already* spent too much time in child care or with babysitters, and 80 percent of Americans agreed that while "it may be necessary for the mothers to be working because the family needs money, it would be better if she could stay home and take care of the house and children" (*Washington Post*, 2000). Rather than leading to discussions of how to maximize the benefits of quality child care, the cultural fallout from the NICHD attachment studies and the new claims in neurology added fuel to already-heated debates on the effects of maternal employment on child development, representing a worst-case scenario for advocates of gender-equitable policies: research intended to reassure the public and invoke support for publicly funded child care instead raised the stakes for mother-only care.

In evaluating the cultural impact of the child development research leading into the twenty-first century, it is important to assess critically both their research design and the framing of research questions. As Max Weber pointed out, scientific researchers use the methodological tools at hand to solve problems that are socially and culturally relevant to their historical period (Weber, 1949). In this case, the movement of mothers of young children into the paid labor force is the socially relevant historical problem, and tools such as the "strange situation test" and new techniques in neuroscience are the favored tools to hand. In child development research, questions are repeatedly framed in terms of the effects of maternal absence on cognition, emotional stability, and social adjustment. The prevalence of this kind of framing is significant. It creates normative discourse around early childhood development that is predicated on the mother-care/other care binary. Findings based on this narrow research frame are then transmitted to the general public through an upsurge in advice books and magazine articles aimed at anxious mothers. In light of the staying power of the mother-care/other-care binary, it is not clear that the proposals suggested by Gornick and Meyers would reshape child development research or popular culture in ways that would help families move beyond this binary into a model of childrearing that embraces the presence of other caring adults.

MOTHERS INTERPRET IDEOLOGY: PUTTING CULTURE INTO ACTION

How do mothers interpret and implement current childrearing discourses? Here I draw on Michele Lamont's (1992) perspective on the impact of culture on social action. She rejects ideological determinism, but also tempers the "voluntaristic" view proposed by "tool kit" theorists (Swidler, 1986, 2001):

> [T]he multicausal explanation I propose takes into consideration how remote and proximate structural factors shape choices from and access to the tool kit—in other words, how these factors affect the cultural resources most likely to be mobilized by different types of individuals and what elements of tool kits people have most access to given their social positions. (Lamont, 1992: 135)

Mothers, therefore, will interpret dominant childrearing ideologies based on their exposure to these discourses, and based on their ability to implement the dictates of experts. They will also filter the dominant childrearing ideologies through their own cultural and class backgrounds, their aspirations for their children, and their own experiences of being mothered. Still, since childrearing ideologies are as ubiquitous as they are unrealistic, most mothers must at least take them into account and "be accountable" to them (West and Zimmerman, 1987).

In the US cultural context, intensive mothering ideologies are a powerful motivator. This does not mean that all mothers *automatically* enact this ideal. It means that the attitudes and actions of mothers, and the responses of public opinion to mothers, take this ideology into account. Research on social class and intensive mothering indicates that, while not all US mothers have the resources to fulfill the ideals of intensive mothering, most are aware of the ideal and use it as a standard to which they compare their own mothering practices. Hays (1996) interviewed both middle-class and working-class mothers, and found that they held themselves equally accountable to the ideology, even if they were not always able to enact it. As she notes,

> Working-class, poor, professional-class, and affluent mothers alike nearly all believe that childrearing is appropriately child-centered and emotionally absorbing. And, practically speaking, this common attitude means that they understand that good childrearing requires the daty-to-day labor of nurturing the child . . . and placing the child's well-being ahead of their own. (Hays, 1996)

The distinction between mothers of different classes is not in how much they feel responsible for being home, but, as will be discussed below, in how much flexibility they can afford and in how much they can supplement their own care with enrichment activities and child-care services.

The working-class and middle-class working mothers interviewed by Anita Garey also stressed "doing motherhood" in a way that emphasized "maternal visibility" and "being in the mother-appropriate place at the mother-appropriate time" (Garey, 1999: 29, 32). These symbolic expressions emphasize the women's awareness of being "in interaction with dominant-culture conceptions of mother-appropriate activities, and [their understanding that] it is *as mothers* that their actions are assessed" (Garey, 1999: 26–27). The strategies working mothers used included working the night shift so that they could be at home and available during the day, or taking time off from work to attend a school outing. Garey points out that

> in going on the field trip, a mother is also indicating to herself and others that she is the *kind of mother* who acts to keep her child safe, or the *kind of mother* who is involved in her child's education, or the *kind of mother* who is not too busy to do her part to support school activities. (Garey, 1999: 29)

These examples indicate the power of intensive mothering as a cultural context in which even mothers who lack the financial resources, time, flexibility (or sleep) to approximate the at-home mother will go to great lengths to *produce the image* of the at-home mother. They produce the image because, in addition to being accountable to others, they are accountable to themselves and to the ideal of motherhood they hold.

In other studies, women interpreted the content of intensive mothering in class-based ways, but held themselves no less liable for its enactment. The single mothers Margaret Nelson interviewed, for instance, reinterpreted intensive mothering as "practical motherhood":

> Each woman makes central to her account of mothering the efforts that go into simply keeping her children alive and safe. Each woman also highlights the extra challenge incurred because of limited human and financial resources. As they do, the women acknowledge that their efforts might compete with, and occasionally cause them to diminish the range of what they believe their children deserve. (Nelson, 2005: 128)

What these women felt their children deserved was the time, attention, and "emotion work" that intensive mothering entails. While they acknowledged that they had good reason not to provide that intensity of care, they were left with feelings of guilt, inadequacy, and uneasiness. This sense of accountability held true regardless of social class. Further, other work suggests that working-class mothers may be *more* drawn toward home because unfulfilling and low-paying jobs may cause them to identify more closely with motherhood than with working as a primary role (see Gerson, 1985; van Wel and Knijn, 2006).

In my own study of professional-class working mothers in dual-earner families, I found mothers to be deeply attached to the intensive mothering ideal. I found this surprising, because initially I had believed that women who had broken the glass ceiling surely would have left outmoded mothering ideologies behind. Not so. For example, Jessica, a corporate consultant, and the highest earner in my study, was responsible for 80 percent of the family income. And yet, she explained that even though her husband was an actively involved parent, and even though Anabel, the caregiver they employed, was the "dream *au pair*," she intended to leave her job. Jessica described a

> deep, deep hurt that even to this day, Sammy wants Anabel, or he wants Jack, and I'm third. And I worry. I feel like, 'Is our relationship ever gonna recover from that? Is he ever gonna be more mommy-oriented? I hope so.

Jessica felt that she was failing on two fronts—she was no longer the unencumbered worker that her "male-pattern career" demanded, and she was not the omnipresent mother that the stacks of advice books she read told her she should be.[4] Feeling inadequate as a mother was the norm in the 60 child-care arrangements I studied, and anxiety over being adequate as a mother played out in my respondents' mothering practices and in their work–family balancing strategies.[5]

These findings also raise questions about how mothers would adapt to sharing the primary parent role with fathers or with childcare providers. Over half of the mothers I interviewed had second-shift-sharing husbands. Yet this created more, not less strain in family life. Significantly, those mothers with husbands who had more flexibility at work and were able to stay home more sometimes envied the time their husbands had at home. Other mothers felt threatened when a child preferred "daddy" to them. Some of fathers' second-shift work frequently entailed helping mothers have quality time with their children. Suzanne, a corporate executive, expressed envy because her husband had more time at home with the baby when she was first born because he was in school. He did not have the responsibility of being the primary caregiver—the nanny had that responsibility—but he did have, as Suzanne noted, the "at-homeness" that she missed:

> Well, my husband's been in sort of a unique situation in that he was in school when Lindsay was born, and so for a year and a half, kind of had that at-homeness, and he's just transitioned into working and he, uh, keeps on joking that he'd like to stay home. I told him that's not an option [laughs].

Suzanne gratefully acknowledged that her husband often did the cooking in the evenings, in order to give her "face time" with their baby, since she had the more demanding work schedule. However, when they discussed the possibility that one of them might take time off from work, she made it clear that she considered it her turn to be at home with Lindsay, and her chance to catch up on the "face time" she had missed.

This kind of behavior has been termed "emotional hoarding" (Hochschild, 1989) as well as "maternal gatekeeping" (Allen and Hawkins, 1999; Gaunt, 2008), and is viewed as a barrier to gender-equitable parenting. Research on maternal gatekeeping defines this behavior as: "a) a reluctance to relinquish family responsibility by setting rigid standards; b) a desire to validate maternal identity; and c) differentiated conceptions of family roles" (McBride et al., 2005: 362). Some of this literature takes a "blame the victim" approach toward mothers. Still, it does demonstrate that the more salient motherhood is to a woman's identity, the more likely she is to expect motherhood to be her sole domain.

Research on mothering identities indicates that mothering is a more powerful aspect of identity than either marital status or occupation (Rogers and White, 1998). As Susan Walzer's (1998) study of men and women preparing for parenthood indicates, the social-psychological process of becoming a mother and "thinking about the baby" in itself increases the salience of both gender and maternal identities. Among the time-deprived professional-class mothers I interviewed, the increased importance women accorded their maternal identity also arose from insecurity regarding the mother's place in the child's psychological life. Among working-class women, a lack of stimulation or nourishment at work may increase the salience of maternal identity. In either case, I would argue that anxiety concerning maternal identity is a potential barrier to equal uptake of part-time work, even if parental leave is equalized. The widespread belief in mother-only attachment—the dominant ideology among mothers across social classes—needs to be overcome in order for gender-equitable work–family balance policies to succeed.

IMPLICATIONS FOR POLICY IMPLEMENTATION

Scaling back at work and ramping up at home?

Current time-use data for the US and for parts of western Europe show that, regardless of whether women increase or reduce their time at work, *and* regardless of whether men do or do not increase their time in child care, women's time spent in child care remains stable or increases. These findings raise concerns regarding the possibility of mothers of young children "opting out" of full-time work if part-time options become more attractive.[6] In the US, women work part-time at rates double those of their male peers, and most do so for child-care-related reasons. Improved benefits for part-time workers would certainly better the lot of those working families who already rely on 1.5 incomes. Would it, though, lead to gender equity? Given the current ideological climate in the US and the data on current time use by American working mothers, I do not share Gornick and Meyers' optimistic view that improved part-time working conditions will "provide incentives for more men to participate in part-time employment" (this volume: 24). Rather, I suggest that such a move, without a corresponding change in definitions of motherhood, would result in a part-time ghetto for mothers, while men and childless women would enjoy the benefits of a full-time career track.

The pull toward home for mothers is documented in recent studies of time-use diaries of dual-earner families. In the US and in selected European countries, the overall trend in the past twenty years has been toward more time with children for both mothers and fathers. What is especially significant in these findings, however, is the fact that mothers' time with children has remained steady or increased, even though their working hours have increased dramatically (Bianchi et al., 2006). They achieve this feat by cutting back on housework, time alone with spouses, time for themselves, and sleep. In fact, among school-aged children, the differences in time spent with employed mothers versus unemployed mothers is "reassuringly small" (Bianchi et al., 2006: 156).[7] In the US, despite working more outside the home and having fewer children inside it, working mothers have not reduced the hours they spend on child care compared to that of their own mothers.[8] More strikingly, mothers' time in child care continues to increase, regardless of the fact that fathers' time in child care has also increased. In 1965, fathers reported spending about half the amount of time on it that mothers did; by 1998, this ratio had increased to two-thirds (Bianchi, 2000: 411).

The take-away message from time-use studies is that women are spending more time with fewer children, regardless of their own work hours and regardless of the parental involvement of their partners.[9] While such findings are reassuring to demographers, they are not sufficient to reassure working mothers, who continue to report feeling guilty about not spending enough time with children. Among married women, this feeling of guilt is attributable almost exclusively to time spent at work: 47 percent of employed married mothers reported feeling guilty about depriving their children of time with them, compared to only 18 percent of at-home mothers (Bianchi et al., 2006: 133).

In the US, would changes in the structure of work significantly change working mothers' attitudes toward and time investment in caring for their children? Trends in Europe are suggestive. In the EU, laws have been passed that offer part-time workers job quality (wages, career development, benefits) commensurate with that of full-time workers. Since the enactment of these laws, part-time workers have been significantly more likely to be women. In 2001, the EU average for female part-time employment was 35 percent and the male rate a mere 6.2 percent. Further, the majority of this part-time work is described as voluntary. While there are vast discrepancies in the amount of part-time work in different EU countries,[10] the EU in general has witnessed overall increases in part-time employment rates, and in all of the countries with the highest rates the majority of workers are female (Buddelmeyer et al., 2004). Women in the US already work part-time at higher rates than men, and mothers with children under age six work part-time at higher rates than any other group of women: "By far the modal experience, at least for a married mother of a preschooler, is to be working either less than 35 hours per week or not at all" (Bianchi 2000: 407–8).

What might the European experience tell us about the impact of mothering ideologies? How much do what others frequently term "traditional cultures of care" shape the part-time employment strategies observed on the other side of the Atlantic? The Netherlands passed a law in 2000 that gives all employees the right to request reduced working hours, with the hope that this policy would a) aid working families and b) create more gender-equitable parenting (see Morgan, this volume). Since the passage of that law, 86 percent of partnered working mothers have worked part-time. "Among dual-earner couples, with young and school-aged children, a one-and-a-half earner family (the man works full-time, the woman part-time) is the most dominant type" (van Wel and Knijn, 2006: 634). In van Wel and Knijn's research, this was not only the dominant form of work–family arrangement—among all but the most educated group of women, it was deemed the *most desirable*. Why? The nature of Dutch mothers' participation in part-time labor "is not determined currently by external obstacles but by a cultural factor: the care culture" (van Wel and Knijn, 2006: 648). In this study of 1,285 Dutch mothers, the "care culture" is defined as the extent to which women feel that home and child care are more important to them than paid employment. Findings from studies like these raise the possibility that progressive policies with respect to part-time work may have the unintended consequence of producing a new stage in the evolution of dual-earner families: the emergence of a 1.5-earner or "neo-traditional" family form (Moen, 2003; van Wel and Knijn, 2006).

There is some hope for progressive developments in the fact that well-educated women are not satisfied with staying in part-time work roles. Significantly, although 55 percent of the highly educated women in the Netherlands study lived in 1.5-earner families, 50 percent of them viewed a dual-earner family as their ideal (van Wel and Knijn, 2006). Whether they could act as the leading edge of cultural change that would lead to more equitable division of full-time and part-time work remains to be seen. In the US context, women already "relinquish the goal of equality with men in the workplace, in favor of more hours at home when their children are young," even though most reduced-hours employment is underpaid and insecure, and carries poor benefits (Bianchi et al., 2006: 175). What is clear is that family-friendly policies like these part-time work regulations need to be explicitly aimed, not just at helping families meet caregiving needs, but at achieving gender equity in the home and in the workforce as a public good.

However, even in Scandinavian countries, where work–family policies are explicitly designed to create gender-equitable working and parenting, ideologies promoting maternal sacrifice show remarkable staying power. Research conducted in Sweden[11] demonstrates that mothering ideologies remain strong. Although working full-time is acceptable for Swedish mothers, they do so for the express benefit of their children. This discursive position also coincides with competing positions that frame the mother's well-being as existing for the good of the child, and frame motherhood as a context in which the "mother exists for the child" (Evlin-Nowak and Thomsson, 2001: 423). Further, although there is a high rate of full-time labor participation among Swedish mothers, they spend as much time as they can with their children as a way of "immunizing them" against future troubles, framing the "child's being as the project for the future" (Evlin-Nowak and Thomsson, 2001: 414–15). Even in a country with progressive work–family and child-care policies framed with an explicit gender-equity intent, mothers struggle to reconcile deep-seated beliefs about good mothering with their beliefs in the benefits of working and gender-equitable parenting.

SOCIAL CLASS, RACE/ETHNICITY, AND USE OF PUBLICLY PROVIDED CHILD CARE

Although most mothers in the US believe in the value of at-home mother-care and embrace some version of intensive mothering, how they interpret these ideologies varies by social class and race. Similarly, public attitudes toward mothers sort them into those who ought to stay home and give their children the benefit of their time and attention, and those who ought to work, and give their children the benefit of enriching activities like Head Start. This class- and race-based ambivalence about mothering is most clearly articulated when it comes to poor mothers. A survey showed that 86 percent of parents with children under age five agreed that it was more important for mothers receiving public assistance to work than to stay home with their children, even if that meant the children would be in child care (Farkas et al., 2000). Although the belief in at-home mothering is strong, so is the belief child improvement. Not long after the passage of the Personal Responsibility and Work Opportunity Act, 74 percent of respondents in a Pew Research Center study favored increased spending on child care for low-income families (Sylvester, 2001).[12] Some children, it seems, are better off with their mothers, while others would benefit from professional care, and these children are categorized by race and class.

Based on these differences in expectations for middle-class, working-class, and poor mothers, two questions seem salient. First, how do these class- and race-based strains in mothering ideologies translate into individual mothering beliefs and practices? And second, what implications might these beliefs and practices have for the ways mothers would respond to the publicly provided child care proposed by Gornick and Meyers?

In answer to the first question, in the US context, we see the greatest resistance to intensive mothering coming from immigrant communities and communities of color. According to Patricia Hill-Collins (2000), mother-work among African-American women primarily involves teaching children how to cope with inequality, and ensuring family and racial survival, and inculcating a positive ethnic identity. Further, black women's mothering includes the involvement of "other-mothers"—be they relatives, friends, or neighbors—who actively participate in childrearing because it is assumed that most biological mothers will have to work to support their children. As Terry Arendell (2000: 1,199) points out, "African American mothers' employment rates have been higher for a longer period of time and are recognized within the community as being essential to family survival."

Likewise, Denise Segura studied the effects of ethnic culture on mothering beliefs by comparing Mexicana and Chicana mothers. Her findings reinforce the significance of the at-home mother as an ideal in developed countries. The Mexicana mothers she interviewed, who had migrated from Mexico as adults, were accustomed to "a world where economic and household work often merged" (Segura, 1994: 219). They did not view work and family as separate spheres, and therefore they experienced very little internal conflict in combining working and mothering. Chicanas, on the other hand, born in the US, drew on the cultural binaries of mother/worker prevalent in US culture. They therefore approached combining motherhood and employment with much greater ambivalence than the Mexicanas. Her findings and those concerning African-American mothers suggest that, the more a woman frames her identity in terms of "mainstream" American cultural ideals, the more likely she is to feel conflicted over combining work and mothering.

These subcultures represent counter-hegemonic challenges to the idealized at-home mother that stem from economic need and from embeddedness in specific sub-cultures, rather than from ideological preference. In Segura's study, the more Americanized Chicanas quickly embraced the at-home mothering ideal, even if they could not afford to provide it. Likewise, in Annette Lareau's (2003) study of parenting practices among blacks and whites in the middle and lower classes, class, not race, was the decisive factor in determining parental culture. Middle-class African-American parents embraced the same activity-laden, mother-intensive practice of "concerted cultivation" as their white class peers.

It may be that class trumps race in parenting style because long-standing and pervasive individualism in the US has given rise to "the rhetoric of competitive mothering" (Hondagneu-Sotelo, 2001: 26). Each family, and indeed each mother, is expected to marshal and transmit the economic, social, and cultural resources needed to reproduce or enhance children's class status. In her study of executive women, Blair-Loy found that those who "opted out" of their careers were "busily engaged in transmitting an upper-class capital to their children" (Blair-Loy, 2003: 54). By comparison, recent welfare reform laws and public opinion about welfare-to-work policies indicate that poor women should provide their children with access to middle-class cultural capital by putting them in child care where, presumably, their life skills and educational preparedness would be enhanced by care received from others. With the exception of mothers in poverty, who are expected to work, it seems clear that most mothers feel strong pressure to be at home with their children, and that pressure has significant implications for how work–family policies are likely to be implemented.

More educated mothers may also be married to higher-earning husbands who can "buy them out" of the labor force; more highly educated women also read more advice literature (Arendell, 1997); and, finally, higher education may coincide with the ways middle- and upper-class women use "mothering as a means of transferring middle-class status to children" (Johnson and Swanson, 2006: 510). In my own research with middle-and professional-class mothers and their child care providers, I found that mothers worried significantly less about their children's physical safety in their absence than they did about whether the nanny could provide appropriate intellectual stimulation, arrange social interactions with the "right" playmates, and transmit class-based cultural values. In other words, highly educated women worry about how to delegate the transmission of middle- and upper-class habitus through an intermediary. This worry was a key factor in their preference for a nanny over a child care center, and was the most frequently cited reason for nanny turnover. These findings suggest that educated middle- and professional-class women may opt out of publicly provided child care in favor of scaling back to part-time work themselves, or by hiring a suitable mother-substitute to provide their children with the appropriate class-based cultural and social capital.

Differences in mothering practices across class are complex. While the bulk of research shows that mothers of all classes and races prefer to stay home with their children,[13] middle- and upper-class mothers have the added pressure of preparing their children for a competitive school and work environment and of believing that they ought to provide this preparation themselves—or if they cannot, that they should purchase the appropriate enrichment activities and services. At the other end of the spectrum, poor mothers are pressured to model "self-sufficiency" for their children by working outside the home, and to give their children middle-class advantages by sending them to publicly provided preschool and subsidized child care (when they can get it). This equation is similar to the ways that public education has played out in the US. Parents who can afford to do so frequently opt out of the public system in favor of private schooling, or pay for supplemental lessons. They then feel less accountable to the public school system and less likely to support it politically or financially, leaving behind families who are economically restricted and have no other options.

For the range of publicly provided preschool child-care services to avoid the fate of public schooling in America, parents of all class backgrounds would have to "buy in" to the services and to see them as more beneficial to their children's advancement than privately provided alternatives. In my own research, mothers chose nannies over any other form of child care because they believed that a "home-centered" childhood provides the optimal environment for early childhood development. Further, they justified the significant extra cost of a nanny because they believed that one-on-one care would give their children a "leg-up" when it came time to compete for a spot in the most prestigious preschools. While these mothers clearly represent an elite minority among full-time working mothers, I would argue that it is just such elites who would need to embrace publicly provided child care. If they do not, the system of options outlined by Gornick and Meyers is likely to lack sufficient political and financial support, and to be seen as a "second-class" form of care (which, more than likely, would continue to be staffed by "second-class" workers—namely women). This dystopian possibility reproduces not only gender inequalities, but also existing class inequalities, sending public preschool care down the same sad road already traveled by US public education as a whole.

Nancy Fraser (1997) argued that men need to become more "like women are now." Here, I raised the question of how policy and changes in ideology can encourage women to become more like men are now. If we cannot accomplish this transformation, we are likely to see even the progressive policy changes proposed by Gornick and Meyers take a decidedly regressive turn. Middle- and upper-class families could opt out of the new child-care supports either by purchasing one-on-one substitute mother-care or by "buying the mother out" of the workforce—a move that would reinforce both class and gender inequities. In either case, the pressure to transmit middle-class habitus and its attendant upward mobility will drive middle-class mothers to participate in "competitive mothering," unless upward mobility and mother-care are somehow decoupled in the public imagination.

Garey (1999: 9) has argued that "we need a way of thinking about women's employment that doesn't presume a zero-sum relationship between women's commitments to their employment and to their families." While this may seem self-evident to some, creating that way of thinking—indeed, creating a new mothering ideology—is more difficult than one might expect. As Rosemary Crompton points out, while the ideology of masculine supremacy has been successfully challenged inside and outside of dual-earner families, "[w]hat have proved to be much more enduring, however, are deep-seated norms and cultural beliefs about what men and women are good at and how they should behave." (this volume: 377–378) I would add that these gender-specific norms are at their most powerful in the realm of mothering. While the male-breadwinner role is on the decline, there is no similar decline in the female-caregiver role. This is due partly to the ways that women's self-interest is continually framed in opposition to the interests of their children and to the collective interests of the family—whether in child development studies, historical accounts, or even in popular family sociology textbooks (Cherlin, 2006; Degler, 1980). Motherhood seems to be the ideological sticking point in attempts to encourage gender equity in the uptake of family-friendly policies.

Gornick and Meyers present a compelling structural view of social change: build the social supports, and change will come. Yet I believe this view underestimates the force of culture in motivating action. The persistence of American individualism, competitive mothering, and intensive mothering indicates the need for broad changes in belief systems. These are possible, but are only likely to accompany a social movement or a change in expert discourse, or both. Deborah Stone (2000) and Evelyn Nakano Glenn (2000) have both argued persuasively for a care movement. They call for mobilization around the rights of care-recipients and those of paid and unpaid caregivers across the dependency spectrum. This would be a start, but it would also have to include advocacy for the positive effects on children that result from care provided by multiple adult caregivers. This last challenge is particularly difficult, especially in light of expert advice that calls for maternal self-sacrifice as the key to producing perfect offspring. Ultimately, we need a care movement that would embrace as a positive social good the equitable sharing of child care, not only between fathers and mothers, but also between family members and paid caregivers, and across settings. Only then will we be able to embrace family policies that do not continue to disadvantage women in the name of raising healthy children.

NOTES

1 Blair-Loy (2003). Blair-Loy breaks these into "devotion to family" and "devotion to work" schemas. While I disagree with her oversimplification of this binary (which she also views as an ideal typical analytic tool), her interpretation of how cultural schemas influence action is compelling.

2 For more on motherhood during these periods, see Ammott and Matthei (1996) and Kessler-Harris (1982). On the other hand, poor women, mothers from racial minorities and immigrant groups have always had to work to make ends meet. See, for example, Leonard (1997). The significant difference today is that middle- and upper-class women do not conform to the ideal.

3 This was a longitudinal study of over 1,000 families diversified by race and social class. Researchers followed children who were cared for at home by a parent and those who were cared for in various child-care settings. The children were followed through elementary school.

4 Interestingly, the recently released Pew Study on Women, Family, and Work found that most mothers judged themselves inadequate as mothers. The least satisfied mothers were college-educated, with 72 percent of at-home mothers in this group "less satisfied" with their mothering skills, and 68 percent of the working mothers unsatisfied. Mothers without college degrees were not pleased with themselves as mothers, but they were less self-critical than those with college degrees. In this group, 62 percent of working mothers and only 54 percent of at-home mothers reported dissatisfaction with their own mothering (Bianchi, 2000).

5 I refer to 60 *arrangements* because, although I interviewed eighty women (fifty child-care providers and thirty working mothers who employed them), many of the women were interviewed as worker–employer dyads. Therefore, among eighty women, there were sixty child-care relationships.

6 I am not suggesting that improved pay and benefits for part-time workers would necessarily harm the interests of women workers, who make up the majority of part-time employees in general. Rather, I question whether such a policy would lead to gender equity.

7 Time-diary data for US mothers with preschool children indicate that these mothers tend to reduce their time in paid work until their children reach school age (National Center for Health Statistics, 2000, 2006).

8   The average number of live births per woman in the US was 3.6 in 1960 and 2.1 in 2005 (Buddelmeyer et al., 2004).

9   These data vary significantly for single mothers, who must provide all the income and all the care for their families. However, since the proposed policies are designed primarily to benefit dual-earner families, I focus my discussion on the time use patterns of these families.

10 The Netherlands has the highest rates, followed by the UK, Germany, France, and Sweden, with Italy and Greece showing the lowest rates of part-time work (Buddelmeyer et al., 2004).

11 Sweden has "moderate" part-time work rates, with over 30 percent of women working part-time and approximately 20 percent of men working part-time (Pew Center for People and the Press, 1998).

12 See Farkas et al. (2000).

13 For example, 80 percent of mothers of children under age five "would prefer to stay home with children when they are young, and 63 percent of parents of young children surveyed disagree that the care and attention children get from a 'top-notch day care center' is as good as what they would receive at home from a parent."

REFERENCES

Allen, S. M., and A. J. Hawkins, 1999, "Maternal Gatekeeping: Mothers' Beliefs and Behaviors that Inhibit Greater Father Involvement in Family Work," *Journal of Marriage and the Family* 61: 199–212.

Ammott, T., and J. Matthei, 1996, *Race, Gender, and Work: A Multi-Cultural Economic History of Women in the United States*, Boston: South End Press.

Arendell, T., 1997, "A Social Constructionist Approach to Parenting," in T. Arendell, ed., *Contemporary Parenting: Challenges and Issues*, Thousand Oaks, CA: Sage Publications.

———2000, "Conceiving and Investigating Motherhood: The Decade's Scholarship," *Journal of Marriage and the Family* 62: 1,192–207.

Arnst, C., 2001, "Relax Mom, Day Care Won't Ruin the Kids," *Business Week*, May 7.

Bassin, D., M. Honey, and M. M. Kaplan, 1994, "Introduction," in D. Bassin, M. Honey, and M. M. Kaplan, eds, *Representations of Motherhood*, New Yaven, CT: Yale University Press.

Bianchi, S., 2000, "Maternal Employment and Time with Children: Dramatic Change or Surprising Continuity?" *Demography* 37: 401–14.

Bianchi, S., J. P. Robinson, and M. A. Milkie, 2006, *Chaging Rhythms of American Family Life*, New York: Russell Sage Foundation.

Birns, B., 1999, "Attachment Theory Revisited: Challenging Conceptual and Methodological Sacred Cows," *Feminism and Psychology* 9: 10–21.

Blair-Loy, M., 2003, *Competing Devotions: Career and Family Among Women Executives*, Cambridge, MA: Harvard University Press.

Bruer, J. T., 1999, *The Myth of the First Three Years: A New Understanding of Early Brain Development and Lifelong Learning*, New York: Free Press.

Buddelmeyer, H., G. Mourre, and M. Ward, 2004, "Recent Developments in Part-Time Work in EU–15 Countries: Trends and Policy," Bonn, Germany: Institute for the Study of Labor.

Cherlin, A., 2006, *Public and Private Families: An Introduction*, New York: McGraw-Hill.

Chira, S., 1998, *A Mother's Place: Choosing Work and Family Without Guilt or Blame*, New York: HarperCollins Publishers.

Degler, C. N., 1980, *At Odds: Women and the Family in America from the Revolution to the Present*, NY: Oxford University Press.

Evlin-Nowak, Y., and H. Thomsson, 2001, "Motherhood as Idea and Practice: A Discursive Understanding," *Gender & Society* 15: 407–28.

Farkas, S., A. Duffett, and J. Johnson, 2000, *Necessary Compromises: How Parents, Employers and Children's Advocates View Childcare Today*, New York: Public Agenda.

Fleischer, V. E., 1996, "Separating from Children," *Columbia Law Review* 96: 375–517.

Fraser, N., 2000, "After the Family Wage: A Postindustrial Thought Experiment," in Barbara Hobson, ed. *Gender and Citizenship in Transition*, New York: Routledge.

Garey, A. I., 1999, *Weaving Work and Motherhood*, Philadelphia: Temple University Press.

Gaunt, R., 2008, "Maternal Gatekeeping: Antecedents and Consequences," *Journal of Family Issues* 29: 373–95.

Gerson, K., 1985, *Hard Choices: How Women Decide about Work, Career, and Motherhood*, Berkeley: University of California Press.

Glenn, E. N., 2000, "Creating a Caring Society," *Contemporary Sociology* 29: 84–94.

Hays, S., 1996, *The Cultural Contradictions of Motherhood*, New Haven, CT: Yale University Press.

Hill-Collins, P., 2000, *Black Feminist Thought: Knowledge, Consciousness, and the Politics of Empowerment*, second ed., New York: Routledge.

Hochschild, A., with Anne Machung, 1989, *The Second Shift: Working Parents and the Revolution at Home*, New York: Viking.

Hondagneu-Sotelo, P., 2001, *Domestica: Immigrant Workers Cleaning and Caring in the Shadows of Affluence*, Berkeley: University of California Press.

Hulbert, A., 2003, *Raising America: Experts, Parents, and a Century of Advice about Children*, New York: Knopf.

Johnson, D. D., and D. H. Swanson, 2004, "Moms Hating Moms: The Internalization of Mother War Rhetoric," *Sex Roles* 51: 497–509.

———2006, "Constructing the 'Good Mother': The Experience of Mothering Ideologies and Work Status," *Sex Roles* 54: 509–19.

Kessler-Harris, A., 1982, *Out to Work: A History of Wage-Earning Women in the United States*, New York: Oxford University Press.

Lamb, M. F., 1990, "New Approaches to the Study of Day Care," *Human Nature* 1: 207–25.

Lamont, M., 1992, *Money, Morals and Manners*, Chicago: University of Chicago Press.

Lareau, A., 2003, *Unequal Childhoods: Class, Race and Family Life*, Berkeley, CA: University of California Press.

Leonard, M., 1997, "Mother's Day: A Guilt-Edged Occasion," *Boston Globe*, May 11: E1.

McBride, B., G. Brown, K. Bost, N. Shin, B. Vaughn, and B. Korth, 2005, "Paternal Identity, Maternal Gatekeeping, and Father Involvement," *Family Relations* 54: 360–72.

Moen, P., ed., 2003, *It's About Time: Couples and Careers*, Ithaca, NY: Cornell University Press.

National Center for Health Statistics, 2000, "Vital Statistics of the United States, Volume 1: Natality," National Center for Health Statistics, Washington, DC.

———2006. "Births: Preliminary Data for 2005," *National Vital Statistics Reports*, p. 55.

Nelson, M., 2005, *The Social Economy of Single Motherhood: Raising Children in Rural America*, New York: Routledge.

NICHD Early Child Care Research Network, 1997, "Familial Factors Associated with the Characteristics of Nonmaternal Child Care," *Journal of Marriage and the Family* 59: 389–408.

———1998, "Early Child Care and Self-Control, Compliance and Problem Behavior at Twenty-Four and Thirty-Six Months," *Child Development* 69: 1,145–70.

Pew Center for People and the Press, 1998, *Deconstructing Distrust: How Americans View Government*, Washington, DC: Pew Center for People and the Press.

Public Agenda, 2000, *Child Care: Red Flags*, Washington, DC: Public Agenda.

Risman, B. J., 1998, *Gender Vertigo: American Families in Transition*, New Haven, CT: Yale University Press.

Rogers, S. J., and L. K. White, 1998, "Satisfaction With Parenting: The Role of Marital Happiness, Family Structure, and Parents' Gender," *Journal of Marriage and the Family* 60: 293–308.

Segura, D. A., 1994, "Working at Motherhood: Chicana and Mexican Immigrant Mothers and Employment," in E. N. Glenn, G. Chang, and L. R. Farrey, eds, *Mothering: Ideology, Experience, and Agency*, NY: Routledge.

Sewell, Jr, W. H., 1992, "A Theory of Structure: Duality, Agency, and Transformation," *American Journal of Sociology* 98: 1–29.

Stone, D., 2000, "Caring by the Book," in M. H. Meyer, ed., *Care Work: Gender, Class, and the Welfare State*, New York: Routledge.

Swidler, A., 1986, "Culture in Action: Symbols and Strategies," *American Sociological Review* 51: 273–86.

——2001, *Talk of Love: How Culture Matters*, Chicago: University of Chicago Press.

Sylvester, K., 2001, "Caring for Our Youngest: Public Attitudes in the United States," *The Future of Children* 11: 53–61.

Talbot, M., 1998, "Attachment Theory: The Ultimate Experiment," *New York Times Magazine,* June 21: 10.

van Wel, F., and T. Knijn, 2006, "Transitional Phase or New Balance? Working and Caring by Mothers With Young Children in the Netherlands," *Journal of Family Issues* 27: 633–48.

Washington Post, 2000, *Issues in the 2000 Election: Values*, Menlo Park, CA: Kaiser Family Foundation.

Walzer, S., 1998, *Thinking about the Baby: Gender and Transitions to Parenthood*, Philadelphia, PA: Temple University Press.

Weber, M., 1949, *The Methodology of the Social Sciences*, New York: Free Press.

West, C., and D. Zimmerman, 1987, "Doing Gender," *Gender & Society* 1: 125–51.

Williams, J., 2000, *Unbending Gender: Why Family and Work Conflict and What to Do About It*, New York: Oxford University Press.

===================== 19 =====================

Further Thoughts
Janet C. Gornick and *Marcia K. Meyers*

In our 2003 book, *Families That Work*, we first presented our collaborative work on policies for reconciling parenthood and employment. During the course of writing our book, we understood that we were making an ambitious policy proposal, and that we had embedded it in a radical end-vision, but we did not overtly conceptualize these components as utopian.

In extending the analyses of that earlier work for this book in the Real Utopias Project series, our first task was to identify what exactly defined "our" Real Utopia. As we saw it, and still see it, our Real Utopia is defined by the end-vision of the dual-earner/dual-caregiver (henceforth, "earner–caregiver") society. The earner–caregiver society is defined by gender symmetry in work and care; by the participation of both mothers and fathers in the care of their own children; by high-quality care for all children, whether by parents or well-trained and well-compensated non-parental caregivers; and by the socialization of a portion of the costs of raising children through redistributive social policies. To advance these ends, we recommend a package of work–family reconciliation policies that we believe would, in the short run, enable individuals and families to care for their children and live more gender-egalitarian lives and, in the longer run, to increase the value that society places on caregiving work, and greatly reduce, and ultimately dissolve, the gendering of divisions of labor.

Erik Olin Wright, in his discussion of emancipatory social science, charges us to develop coherent, credible theories of the alternatives to existing institutions and social structures that would advance the goals of social and political justice.[1] We take up this charge in this essay by organizing our comments to address two of the three criteria he recommends for evaluating social alternatives: the *desirability* of the ends, imagined without the constraints of feasibility; and the *viability* of the proposed social and institutional approaches to achieve these ends. The third of Wright's three criteria, *achievability*, involves the "practical work of strategies for social change" within the contingencies of present and future conditions. For the purposes of this essay, as for most of the essays in this volume, the question of achievability is largely left aside to make room for the central questions posed by the Real Utopias Project: What are the ideal ends? And what would be the institutional designs to achieve them?

DESIRABILITY

As Wright defines it, the project of imagining a Real Utopia begins with the specification and defense of the desired outcomes. Our earner–caregiver society imagines four social outcomes: gender symmetry in market and care work; extensive parental involvement in caregiving, particularly during children's early years; high-quality, non-parental care for children, provided by well-compensated careworkers; and the socialization of a portion of the costs of raising children. Are these outcomes in fact desirable? The essays in this volume pose two especially thought-provoking challenges to the desirability of the earner–caregiver society that we envision.

First, several essays in this volume argue that these outcomes may be desired by some individuals, but that there is enormous diversity in family forms, allocations of time to market and caregiving work, and beliefs about gender roles. Ann Orloff takes us to task for not sufficiently respecting the merit to be found in "the different visions of the good held by members of the polity, that is, in pluralism"; our utopia, she adds, is not defined in terms of choice. Michael Shalev argues that, although the majority of women from all class backgrounds reject the male-breadwinner model of gender roles, there are also systematic differences by education and occupational class. In Shalev's view, our proposals are most consistent with the orientations of relatively privileged women. Rosemary Crompton also reminds us that attitudes toward gendered divisions of domestic labor vary widely within and across societies. Lane Kenworthy draws out the practical implications by arguing that our proposal for equal and nontransferable leave benefits may be unacceptable for many families in which mothers want to take longer leaves than do their male partners.

In short, these critics argue that, by specifying the earner–caregiver society as an end-goal, we may be imposing "one size fits all" social arrangements that run roughshod over individual preferences and social and cultural diversity. This criticism could be leveled at each of our utopian outcomes. Some parents may not want to devote time and energy to caring for young children. Others may not want to place their children in any non-parental care arrangements. A fair number of individuals, especially those with abundant private resources, may object to socializing the costs of raising children. Most commonly, however, the critique that our proposals involve social engineering targets the outcome of gender symmetry in both market and caregiving work.

To some extent, these criticisms overstate the extent of social engineering in our policy proposals. When we envision an earner–caregiver society, it is one in which men and women share equally in market and caregiving work *on average*, and in which children receive intensive parental care and high-quality substitute care *as appropriate*. Our Real Utopia does not require adults in all dual-parent families to allocate exactly the same time to market and care work, nor does it require all families to use the exact same combination of parental and non-parental care for their children.

That said, we readily admit that our proposed policies do require state action to redistribute resources and secure workplace rights. More subtly, some specific policy features are intended to apply what Norwegian sociologist Arnlaug Leira calls "mild structural coercion" to de-gender caregiving and encourage parental care. Most notably, non-transferable, individual leave rights are intended to create incentives for equal participation by mothers and fathers. At the same time, generous wage replacement for paid leaves enables parents to reduce paid hours of work in the first year after the birth or adoption of a child. Limiting paid leaves to six months, and subsidizing non-parental care, makes it feasible for all parents to enter or return to employment shortly after childbirth or adoption.

Can this institutional coercion be reconciled with respect for individual choice and diversity? It can if we recognize that these policies are means to an end, not an end in themselves. Our proposed work–family reconciliation policies are designed to create *options* for combining market and caregiving work, and parental and non-parental care. In a world in which all adults had these options, unconstrained by gender or private resources, we would be agnostic about the actual distribution of these choices. In the real world, in which gender and parental identities are socially constructed within historical and social contexts that are inegalitarian and overwhelmingly patriarchal, we are not agnostic. While respecting diversity, we cannot and should not interpret existing distributions of family forms and gender relations as revealed preferences—that is, as the "true" distribution of how men and women would choose to spend their time and organize the provision of care in the absence of institutional and normative constraints.

Individuals cannot make unconstrained choices until they have both realistic opportunities and social approbation for those choices. Work–family reconciliation policies can increase parents' choices by, for example, replacing wages during parenting leaves and subsidizing non-parental care. In the absence of changes in social norms about gender, work and caregiving, however, parents' choices will remain constrained by their own constructed identities as "male breadwinner" or "female caregiver." Through the gentle coercion of incentives—for example, for more paternal leave-taking and for higher levels of maternal employment—social policies can also contribute to changes in social and gender norms that allow meaningful choices. As Harry Brighouse and Erik Wright argue, policies operate not only by changing opportunities and incentives, but also by reinforcing or challenging social norms that inform both public behaviors, such as employment decisions, and private identity formation.

A second, and very important, critique of the desirability of our Real Utopia is that the outcomes are limited to de-gendering child care and improving the quality of care for children. As several critics point out, social and gender inequalities result from what Nancy Folbre terms "the general social organization of care," not just the care of children. Heidi Hartmann and Vicky Lovell, likewise, argue that both moral and practical concerns require us to broaden our policy package to extend support for other forms of caregiving. Johanna Brenner also urges us to go further "toward socializing and democratizing the organization of care over the life-cycle." Myra Marx Ferree places this argument squarely in the American context: "Rather than expanding maternalism to encompass men in families, as the more progressive elements of the European systems have done, American feminists should expand the concept of 'social security' to be more truly inclusive across gender and generational lines."

In our original formulation of the earner–caregiver society we argued that the provision of care for children in families headed by two heterosexual parents provided the most pertinent "test case" for gender-egalitarian policy design. The birth or adoption of children is particularly disruptive for women's employment, and an especially crucial moment for the negotiation of gender roles in heterosexual couples. We were also persuaded that the "public goods" dimension of child-rearing, and the lifelong consequences of poor-quality early care, elevated the importance of child care issues.

The essays and discussions provoked by the Real Utopias Project have challenged our thinking on this formulation. As Folbre argues, arrangements to care for other dependents are often intertwined with care for children, and pose many of the same dilemmas, including the limited substitutability of paid and unpaid care work, the economic vulnerabilities for both paid and unpaid caregivers that result from prisoner-of-love dilemmas, and the regressive distribution of private support for caregiving. Efforts to "de-gender" caregiving for children while ignoring other forms of care are unlikely to bring about the social transformations that we envision.

We have been persuaded that the desired ends of the earner–caregiver society would include de-gendered caregiving for all dependents; realistic opportunities for men and women to be involved in all forms of caregiving for loved ones; high-quality and well-compensated substitute care arrangements for the elderly and disabled, as well as for children; and greater socialization of the costs of these care arrangements.

Broadening the focus of our analysis raises the question of normative justification. The "public goods" argument typically justifies distributing the costs of raising children more broadly on both efficiency and equity grounds because "well-raised" children are expected to be economically productive workers in the future. This instrumental justification could be more difficult to apply to the case of other dependents, such as the disabled and elderly, whose current and future economic contributions are usually limited. As Folbre argues in this volume, children represent a specific kind of public good "but care in general also has public good aspects and spillover effects that make it vulnerable to undervaluation by the market. Children cannot exercise consumer sovereignty—neither can other dependents." (this volume: 107).

In the end, the strongest justification may be that of social rights: everyone should have the right to care for loved ones and the right to be cared for. In a Real Utopia, these rights would be protected for all, and their costs, in terms of time and money, would be shared between men and women and between the family and the state.

VIABILITY

Wright argues that the viability of all proposals for utopian institutional development or reform must be assessed, because "not all desirable alternatives are viable." He suggests several criteria for assessing the viability of proposed reforms. First, we should be concerned with "whether, if implemented, they would actually generate in a sustainable, robust manner, the emancipatory consequences that motivated the proposal." Second, we should question whether there are "contextual conditions-of-possibility" that are needed for the proposed policies to achieve the desired outcomes. Finally, we should consider whether there are potential "perverse" unintended consequences that could actually subvert or prevent the achievement of these outcomes.

Several of the essays in this volume raise important questions about the viability of our proposals for gender-equalizing work–family reconciliation policies. We consider three compelling questions below: whether the proposed policies could substantially affect the gendered distribution of work; whether some policies might actually exacerbate gender divides; and finally, whether these policies are only viable in the rich countries and might, in fact, contribute to the exploitation of the developing world.

First, several authors argue that the policies we propose are simply too weak to advance gender equality because men and women will be unwilling to relinquish the immediate rewards of existing gendered divisions of labor. Ann Orloff is especially pointed in her critique of our analysis of the persistence of gender roles. While she recognizes that both men and women are invested in existing gender relations, she emphasizes men's recalcitrance, in particular, because men stand to lose the most from a realignment of gender roles:

> To my mind, [Gornick and Meyers] take too lightly the deep investments people have in gender
>
> . . .
>
> Of particular concern for the prospects of a gender-symmetric utopia that will depend on men's recruitment to caregiving, men's attachment to the powers and privileges of masculinity seems to be underplayed in Gornick and Meyers' account. I am thinking here of men's attempts to maintain gendered divisions of labor by avoiding dirty work at home and in the workplace, or by excluding women from favored positions in the paid labor force through sexual and other forms of harassment, or through discrimination in hiring, pay, or occupational access (this volume: 137–139).

Cameron Macdonald makes a somewhat parallel argument about the powerful hold that mothering has on many women, perhaps even more so in the US than elsewhere. Macdonald argues that the

> power of intensive mothering as a cultural context in which even mothers who lack the financial resources, time, flexibility (or sleep) to approximate the at-home mother will go to great lengths to *produce the image* of the at-home mother. They produce the image because, in addition to being accountable to others, they are accountable to themselves and to the ideal of motherhood they hold (see p. 419).

Macdonald concludes that institutional change cannot be sufficiently powerful to alleviate the fear of being an inadequate mother that plagues so many women. Thus, large numbers of mothers will resist relaxing their intense engagement with their children, regardless of public policy supports.

We agree that both men and women are invested in existing gender roles. Men's power is bound up with their disproportionate engagement in employment and commerce, and they reap benefits from their higher-status jobs and their greater levels of income and wealth (relative to women's), and from the various forms of power and control that those resources confer. Many women find deep satisfaction in caregiving, and their greater investment in care work (relative to men's) provides other forms of status, legitimacy and power within the family and society. There is no question that preferences for employment and caregiving vary across individuals and sometimes on the part of individuals over time. As we argue above, however, it is impossible to know the extent to which the gendered distribution of these preferences is socially constructed by material conditions as well as social norms. If we believe that gendered identities are socially constructed we must also acknowledge the possibility that they would be different in the context of different conditions and norms.

We are not policy determinists; we know that policies operate alongside many political, social, economic, and psychological factors that shape preferences and inform behaviors. But to the extent that gender identities, expectations and preferences are socially constructed, social policy is one of the factors that influence them. Orloff and others in this volume remind us, however, that this understanding of the socially constructed nature of gender, and the capacity of social institutions to change existing norms, may fail to address the strength of existing power and privilege. Power differentials between men and women remain large, and history suggests that existing systems of power and privilege are not easily disrupted. The "mild structural coercion" of policy reform may not be enough to alter the gendered divisions of labor without more direct and forceful action by the state and polity.

On the other hand, we are perhaps more optimistic than Orloff about men's commitment to current arrangements. Our optimism is shared, to some extent, by Scott Coltrane. In this volume, Coltrane reviews a substantial literature on men's involvement with caregiving. Coltrane is not sanguine about men's willingness to alter domestic divisions of labor. He notes that many men resist change because "it is in men's interest to do so ... as [current divisions of labor reinforce] a separation of spheres that underpins masculine ideals and perpetuates a gender order privileging men over women" (see p. 401). However, Coltrane also finds evidence that new "fatherhood ideals" are emerging in many of the rich countries; substantial numbers of men show signs of willingness to invest more time at home. Synthesizing recent research, Coltrane reports that, "as men's and women's jobs and work histories begin to look more alike, they are also likely to share similar family concerns" (this volume: 399). He notes that, in the US, over 60 percent of both men and women report that they would like to work fewer hours on the job, while 60 percent of men and 55 percent of women say that they experience conflict in balancing work, personal, and family life. The majority of both men and women also report that they feel torn between the demands of their jobs and wanting to spend more time with their families. Coltrane concludes that there is good reason to believe that employer and state policies are important influences on men's engagement in caring and other domestic work. In the end, he says, "[p]olicies designed to help families should assume that both men and women want to contribute to their families through both breadwinning and the provision of everyday care and unpaid support work" (this volume: 406).

The formidable challenge of changing gender roles is closely related to a second especially compelling question raised by several essays in this volume. A number of authors argue that, in the absence of a major realignment of gender roles, policies that enable parents to take breaks from paid labor or to reduce working time could actually cause more gender inequality by exacerbating gendered divisions of labor and slowing women's labor market advancements.

Barbara Bergmann argues that our policy proposal is, in a word, dangerous. She believes that women will always take up options such as paid family leave and part-time work at higher rates than men. As a result, enacting or strengthening policies that support these options "would have adverse effects on gender equality in the workplace as well as the home" (this volume: 64). The only way to ensure an equal labor market is to restrict these options—for intermittent and reduced-hour work—for both women and men.

Michael Shalev raises a related set of concerns. Shalev draws on his own comparison of labor market outcomes in the US compared to Sweden, as well as on a growing cross-national empirical literature on this question, and concludes that highly educated, highly skilled women in settings with generous work–family policies might face a lower and more impenetrable glass ceiling than will women where policy supports are more limited. Where policy offerings are generous and take-up is disproportionately female, employers are motivated to statistically discriminate against women. That discrimination will be most intense with respect to women in (or seeking) upper-level occupations, because their temporary labor market absences are understood to be especially costly. Shalev cites a recent finding that women's probability, relative to men's, of having a managerial occupation is more than 80 percent greater in the US than in Sweden.

Kimberly Morgan adds to this chorus of worries the possibility that countries could start the process of implementing gender-egalitarian policy packages, but then get stuck with a partial package that could cause harm. "Rather than arriving at a set of gender-egalitarian arrangements for work and care," she notes, "countries may stall halfway there in a modified male-breadwinner model" (this volume: 316). A country might, for example, adopt generous paid family leave but lose the gender-egalitarian requirements and incentives—a result, she argues, that would undermine gender equality. Finally, Kathrin Zippel warns that, without effective anti-discrimination and affirmative action policies, the policy package that we propose could create more damage than good. She argues specifically that workplace inequalities will foreclose the intended positive effects of work–family policy: "Given the persistence of gender inequalities at work, optional leave and the reduction of working hours are likely to be taken up by mothers, and to reinforce rather than ameliorate inequality in workplace and home" (this volume: 213).

We consider the claim that, in the absence of major transformations in gender roles, our proposals for paid leave and reduced-hour work would do more harm than good to be one of the most serious and worrisome critiques in this volume. These concerns about the possibility of worsening gender inequality have pushed us to think more analytically about the potential hazards, and to disaggregate the underlying causal arguments more carefully.

While we are sympathetic with Bergmann's overall logic that higher take-up of these benefits by women is problematic, we are at least somewhat optimistic that this risk can be minimized through policy design. As she hints in the title of her essay—"Long Leaves, Child Well-Being, and Gender Equality"—Bergmann's main concern is that long leaves will encourage women to leave employment for long periods of time, with a consequent erosion of human capital and increased risk of being shunted by employers into low-quality jobs. In light of these concerns, and of empirical evidence that suggests that long leaves are associated with greater labor market inequalities, we specifically limit the duration of paid leave to six months following the birth or adoption of a child. Short, highly paid leaves have been shown to increase women's employment rates, to increase their likelihood of returning to work within a year after birth or adoption, to raise the chances that women return to the same employer, and to diminish the wage penalties associated with childbearing. All of these factors ultimately narrow, not widen, gender gaps in employment.

We find Shalev's argument about statistical discrimination (presumably associated even with short leaves) and its impact on the glass ceiling for women to be more challenging. As with Bergmann's argument, the concern that high-achieving women will hit the glass ceiling (due to adjustments that they make for caregiving) assumes that women will be much more likely than men to take up paid leaves and opportunities for reduced-hour employment. Shalev, and others contributing to this growing literature, suggest that, if gendered differentials in take-up persist, employers will impose limits on women's advancement because they assume that women will be more costly employees than men.

There is no question that this is a worrisome scenario. As we see it, this underscores the enormous importance of policy design. If "god is in the details" in any policy arena, it is surely true in the case of work–family policies. Peter McDonald argues persuasively in this volume that "good ideas can founder on matters of detail"; we agree wholeheartedly. Policies that support parents' caregiving time are not necessarily gender-egalitarian, but the converse is true as well: they can be designed to maximize incentives for gender-egalitarian take-up and outcomes. If men's take-up increases substantially, the glass ceiling may remain in place for parents, but it will become de-gendered. (We return to this below, when we reflect on anti-discrimination protections for caregivers.) Arguments about incentives for statistical discrimination also remind us that we need to evaluate our policy designs constantly so as to ensure that they subject employers to as little hardship as possible; strains and costs for employers can be alleviated through required notification periods, cost-sharing mechanisms, and the absence of experience rating.

We are also particularly challenged by the political hazards raised by Morgan. The passage and enactment of "half of a policy loaf" could in fact be worse than no policy change at all. Introducing generous leaves for women without options and incentives for men, for example, or without ample quality child care, could have the perverse effect of creating incentives for women (but not men) to withdraw from the labor market. Raising the availability of part-time work without raising its quality could have the perverse effect of further feminizing part-time work and entrenching the existing part-time compensation penalty. In advancing reform proposals, it is crucial to think not only about the design of each but about potential interactions between policies that have the capacity to further or impede progress toward an earner–caregiver society.

The possible synergy between policies underscores the importance of Zippel's emphasis on anti-discrimination and affirmative action policies. We agree fully that such policies are part of a comprehensive approach to gender-equalizing work–family policies. To the extent that they protect women's right to participate on an equal footing with men in the workplace, these laws promote gender equality and reduce the risk that work–family reconciliation policies will have perverse, unintended effects. That said, anti-discrimination laws based on gender may not be enough to reduce the risks associated with supporting parents in their caregiving activities. Our reading of the literature leads us to conclude that it is no longer gender per se, but gendered divisions of caregiving labor—especially mothers' withdrawals and reductions in employment—that are the primary cause of continued male–female disparities in wages and occupational attainment.

Zippel's argument prompted us to think again about how anti-discrimination policies should be constructed and targeted. We have come to agree with the many social activists in the US and Europe now calling for anti-discrimination protections aimed at caregivers (men as well as women) as an important complement to protections targeted on women. Employment penalties associated with caregiving harm men's employment prospects, and women's even more so. However, even if the (unfair) discrimination against caregivers per se were successfully eliminated, caregivers might still command less compensation and fewer advancement opportunities than non-caregivers. That would be the case if caregivers are less productive in their paid work, all else equal, due to the extra demands on their time and attention. (Whether caregivers are less productive is an empirical question—one that has not yet been resolved). If they are less productive, the overall question might be: how large a productivity-related penalty is fair? In many rich countries, this penalty may simply be too high now. Equity and reproductive concerns might suggest that states should offer some compensatory support.

A third, particularly compelling, question about the viability of our proposals is raised by Shireen Hassim in her essay, "Whose Utopia?" She argues that, given the existing distribution of resources and state capacities, our proposed work–family reconciliation policies are simply not viable in much of the world without radical changes in economic and institutional arrangements. Even more problematically, the implementation of these policies in rich countries might depend on continued exploitation of the developing world.

In making her case that our proposed work–family reconciliation policies are not viable in much of the world, specifically the global South, Hassim describes formidable barriers to the development of gender-equalizing, redistributive work–family reconciliation policies. Formal economies are dwarfed by informal economies in much of the developing world, while work-based benefits are rare and inequitably distributed to privileged elites. Possibilities for de-gendering market and caregiving work are hampered by both traditional gender expectations and the exclusion of women from the formal economy. Weak and unstable government institutions greatly limit the capacity of the state to redistribute resources, regulate private employers, or extend social protections. The globalization of capital, production and labor markets has exacerbated the problems of the developing world, as have demands by supranational and international financial institutions that poor countries forgo the development of state-centered social protections in order to grow their labor and export markets.

We agree with Hassim that some level of economic and state development is a critical precondition for the implementation of the work–family reconciliation policies that we propose. But this would preclude the development of gender-equalizing work–family policies only if these preconditions can never be achieved. Given the necessary economic and institutional capacity, there is no reason to conclude that currently developing countries will not have the political will to pursue these policy developments. In fact, many developing countries do provide some protections for working parents, if only in the formal economy. Jody Heymann and her colleagues have studied work–family policies in 173 countries, and found evidence of relevant policy developments globally.[2] Heymann's team reports, for example, that 169 countries offer some guaranteed leave with income to women in connection with childbirth; 66 countries ensure that fathers either receive paid paternity leave or have a right to paid parental leave; at least 107 countries protect working women's right to breastfeed; 137 countries mandate paid annual leave; at least 134 countries have laws that fix the maximum length of the working week; and at least 145 countries provide paid sick days for short- or long-term illnesses.

As Hassim points out, these protections are limited when only a small portion of the workforce participates in the formal economy. Many are also maternalist, reinforcing gender inequalities by increasing the costs of employing women relative to men. However, although they are far from complete, the adoption of policies protecting the health and time of working parents in so many countries, rich and poor, suggest that there is no absolute North–South divide in the political will to develop work–family policies.

A potentially more damning charge against our blueprint is that it actually depends on the continued impoverishment and exploitation of poor and developing countries. In the broadest terms, this critique suggests that the wealth of the rich countries would not be possible without continued economic imperialism. More narrowly, the argument advanced by Hassim and others is that of a "global care chain" in which the equalization of labor market opportunities for women in rich countries depends on the exploitation of low-wage, often immigrant, female workers who forgo the care needs of their own families to work as caregivers for affluent families in rich countries.

The existence of global care chains that exploit female workers from poor countries is well documented. We would argue, however, that the policies that we propose challenge rather than reinforce these arrangements. By valuing caregiving labor, increasing public financing, and regulating the quality of non-parental care, our proposals will increase the skills needed by, and the wages provided to, non-parental caregivers. In the rich countries, these changes hold promise for reducing severe gender imbalances in the paid caregiving workforce and for encouraging workers to shift from the informal to the formal economy, thereby improving their conditions of work. Higher wages for caregivers in the rich countries will also reduce the demand for low-skilled, low-wage labor from developing countries. Whether these policies reduce total demand for non-parental caregiving labor by immigrant and non-immigrant women is an empirical question. Giving parents the right and opportunity to care for their own children is likely to reduce demand for non-parental care for infants, but this may be offset by an expansion of subsidized care for preschoolers, and of before- and after-school care for older children. Whether or not these policies would reduce the importation of caregivers, they promise to reduce the exploitation of these workers as cheap alternatives to parental labor.

Higher wages for caregivers in the rich countries may weaken the links in the global care chain. They will not directly improve conditions for women in poor countries (including those who may be effectively expelled from care work in the rich countries). For parents and children in the developing world to benefit from gender-equalizing reconciliation policies, the rich countries of the world will need to invest more directly and much more generously in the development of the state, market and civil society institutions that are a prerequisite to the effective adoption of these policies in developing countries.

Hassim describes one intriguing mechanism for redistribution, first proposed by Ruth Pearson: a "Maria Tax." Such a tax could be imposed on the value of exports to reflect the proportion of women in the export labor force. It could be levied by governments (on, for example, producers or importers) and reinvested in initiatives to achieve gender equity for women workers. The raised revenues could be spent on child-care facilities, health-care facilities and insurance, and on educational and social welfare programs.

Less directly, it is reasonable to believe that the adoption of more egalitarian policies in the global North is consistent with, and may even encourage, investments in the developing world. To the extent that we can promote the adoption of egalitarian, non-exploitative work–family policies in the rich countries, we can hope to delegitimize continued economic imperialism, slow the exportation of neoliberal social reforms to the global South, and reduce international pressures on poor countries to delay investments in their social and educational infrastructures. The more egalitarian Nordic countries contribute more to international aid, as a share of their GDP, than do the less egalitarian rich countries. Rather than intensifying global inequalities, a more egalitarian and gender-equalizing organization of caregiving within the rich countries is compatible with, and might advance, a commitment to greater global redistribution and equality.

As we explain in the essay opening this volume, our work on the earner–caregiver society was motivated in part by our observation that scholars and policy makers have been engaged in at least three parallel but distinct conversations about work and family life. We hoped to stimulate conversations that link concerns about child well-being in high-employment societies to the problem of work–family balance and to long-standing feminist demands for gender equality in the home and workplace. We had a critical breakthrough in our thinking when we recognized that the apparently competing interests of women, men and children reflected the failure of social, market and policy institutions to address adequately the care of children in high-income societies. The insight that the solution to the triad of problems had to involve men as well as women, and the state as well as the family, informed our subsequent analyses and recommendations for policies that, we believe, promise simultaneously to reduce gender inequalities and improve care for children.

In this essay we have considered a few of the penetrating critiques and challenges to these proposals that were raised by our colleagues during the Real Utopias Project process. Although we remain convinced that the earner–caregiver society offers both a worthwhile long-term ideal and a useful framework for policy development in the short term, grappling with these issues has been a daunting task.

One of the issues raised by a number of the participants also gives us renewed optimism about the desirability, viability, and ultimate achievability of a more gender-egalitarian, caring society. We are persuaded that expanding the focus of policy development to include care for all family members and loved ones—including the disabled, the ill and the elderly, along with children—is normatively and strategically sound. It forces us to rethink the justification for these policies and to de-emphasize instrumental concerns in favor of the more basic claim that, in a just society, all individuals should have the right to provide care and the right to be cared for. Expanding the focus of concern to include other dependents knits together even more clearly the interdependences within and between families, employers and the state. Recognition of the commonalities in the interests of adults caring for the youngest and the oldest, often at the same time, holds promise for building broader and more effective coalitions in support of gender-equalizing reconciliation policies. Ruth Milkman's essay in this volume further encourages us; she demonstrates the possibility of successful coalition-building in support of policy reforms that meet the "human needs of children, the seriously ill, and the elderly." As Folbre astutely observes, there is also a potential political alliance between paid and unpaid caregivers. Acknowledgement of the common interests and continuing exploitation of caregivers—in the home and in the market, in the rich countries of the North and in the developing countries of the South—offers even greater promise for advancing political demands that call for the recognition, honoring and support not only of earning but of caregiving as well.

NOTES

1 See Erik Olin Wright, forthcoming, *Envisioning Real Utopias*, chapter 1, Erik Olin Wright's Home Page, University of Wisconsin – Madison Social Science Computing Cooperative online: http://www.ssc.wisc.edu/~wright

2 See Jody Heymann, Alison Earle, and Jeffrey Hayes, 2007, *The Work, Family, and Equity Index: How Does the United States Measure Up*? McGill University: Institute for Health and Social Policy.

Index

abortion, 147, 319
absenteeism, 350. *See also* "presenteeism"
administrators and managers. *See* managers and administrators
adoption, 273, 357, 403
advice books for parents. *See* parenting advice books
Aetna, 351
affirmative action, 209–25 passim, 291
Africa, 95. *See also* sub-Saharan Africa
African Americans, 216, 301
  women, 217, 272, 289, 430
  mothers, 430
after-school care, 25, 26, 327, 334n7
aggressiveness in children, 75–76 passim
Aid to Families with Dependent Children, 140
AIDS, 99
altruism, 91n8
anti-discrimination policies, 209–25 passim

APE (allocation parentale d'education), 372, 381n7
Arendell, Terry, 427
Asian women workers, 103
Aspen, Colorado, 181
attorneys. *See* lawyers
Australia, 111, 167–70 passim, 213
Austria, 330

"Baby UI," 234
Bacchi, Carol, 222
Belgium, 18, 29–42 passim, 48, 326, 334n4
  male workweek, 10
Bergmann, Barbara, 112, 219, 246, 442
Berkovitz, Nitza, 293
biological difference, 91n7
birth. *See* childbirth
birthrate, 431n8
Bittman, Michael, 213
Blair-Loy, Mary, 345–46, 430n1
Blau, David, 205
Block, Fred, 346
blue-collar workers, 224, 390

Bollier, David, 184
books for parents. *See* parenting advice books
Borchorst, Anette, 320
Boulder, Colorado, 181
brain development, 13
breastfeeding, 118, 153n15, 164, 168
 legislation, 311
 Norway, 321
 paid leave and, 404
 Sweden, 321
 work and, 339, 448
Breen, Richard, 215
Brenner, Johanna, 438
Brighouse, Harry, 438
Britain. *See* United Kingdom
Bureau of Labor Statistics (BLS), 241, 242, 249n5
Bush, George H. W., 347
business opposition to state regulation, 348–53 passim, 358

California, 235, 245, 352, 361n8–10 passim
 Chamber of Commerce, 353
 family leave law, 347
 public opinion in, 330
 state disability insurance, 353
California Fair Employment and Housing Act, 361n10
California Family Rights Act, 361n10
care services, 111–24 passim
care workers, 112, 114, 149. *See also* child-care providers; domestic workers (hired help); health-care workers
"caregiver parity" model, 136–37
Catholic ideology, 375, 381n16

Chamber of Commerce, 348, 353, 359
Chang, Mariko-Lin, 273
Chicana mothers, 426
child care
 child development and, 13
 consequences of, 74
 cost of, 259–61, 270
  Norway, 53n19
 cross-national comparison, 62
 employers and, 28
 for one- and two-year-olds, 195–205 passim
 for three- and four-year-olds, 162
 France, 366, 379
 New Zealand, 167
 policy, 18–27
  financing: cross-national comparison, 63
  Europe, 32–43
  state-subsidized, 406
 See also crèches; family-provided child care; infant care; public child care
childbirth, 237, 243, 293. *See also* maternity leave
child-care providers
 cross-national comparison, 64
 education and pay, 39, 173, 270
child development, 168–69, 186, 429
 mass media and, 413
child mortality, 372
child perfectibility, 415
child poverty, 285
child psychologists, 413
child well-being, 11–14 passim, 67, 193–95 passim

childlessness, 118–119
childrearing advice books. *See* parenting advice books
children as public good, 19, 113, 165
Christian Democratic parties, 326
Chronicle of Higher Education, 77
citizen's wage (proposed), 149
Civil Rights Act (1964), 216, 217, 291
  Title VII, 220, 225
Civil Rights Act (1991), 218
class, 140–47 passim, 180–81, 239, 255–75, 339–47 passim
  housework and, 394
  mothering and, 412 passim, 429
classism, 255, 277n22
Clinton, Bill, 334
cohousing, 178, 179–82
collaborative governance of public schools, 186
collective bargaining, 236, 342, 346, 354
collectivism, 179
college education. *See* higher education
colleges: women professors and, 70–71
Coltrane, Scott, 442
commons, 184, 188
communes, 181
"competitive mothering," 427, 429
consensus decision making, 181
consumer choice. *See* parental choice
Cooke, Lynn, 215

Cooperative Housing Association Law, 181
cooperatives. *See* worker cooperatives
corporate boards, 225
costing, 171
crèches. *See* public crèches
Crompton, Rosemary, 15, 17–18, 136–137, 436
cultural norms. *See* social norms
Czech men and women, 381n3
Czech Republic, 366, 380n1
Czechoslovakia, 381n2

"daddy leave." *See* paternity leave
Dahlgren, Hoa-Hoa, 320
Davis, California, 180
Davis, Gray, 352, 381n6
Deepening Democracy (Fung and Wright), 185, 188
Democratic Party, 321, 322
Denmark, 7, 10, 18, 28–42 passim, 319–24 passim
  cohousing, 178–79
Deutsch, Francine, 22
developing countries, 94–108 passim, 446
"difference feminism," 152n10
disability insurance. *See* temporary disability insurance
District of Columbia. *See* Washington, DC
diversity, 144
diversity training programs, 220
divorce, 292, 300, 319, 386
  income inequality and, 117
Dodd, Christopher, 236, 243, 244
domestic work. *See* housework

domestic workers (hired help), 99, 377. *See also* nannies

Earls, Felton, 416
early childhood education and care. *See* child care; preschool
"early childhood education and care" (term), 52n13
earning gap. *See* income inequality
Eastern bloc. *See* Soviet bloc
"educare" systems (Nordic countries), 35, 320, 327
education, 133
  domestic traditionalism and, 373
  gender egalitarianism and, 257–60 passim, 378
  housework and, 389–90
  income inequality and, 117
  men and, 403
  See also higher education; private schools; public schools; religious education
Ehrenreich, Barbara, 241
elder care, 231, 248, 265. *See also* nursing home care
elder cohousing, 190n3
Ellingsaeter, Anne Lise, 50n4
employee payroll taxes. *See* payroll taxes
employee turnover, 350
employers
  benefits of, 350
  child-care policy and, 27 passim, 168, 327
  costs, 447
  fathers' family leaves and, 405
  California, 352–56 passim
employment rates, 9
  of French women, 368
employment training. *See* on-the-job training
England, Paula, 19
entitlements for publicly supported early childhood education and care: cross-national comparison, 62
Equal Credit Act, 291
Equal Employment Opportunity Commission, 219
equal pay for equal work law, 217
Equal Rights Amendment (proposed), 291, 311n2
Esping-Andersen, G., 199–200
Estevez-Abe, Margarita, 264
ethics, 120
EU. *See* European Union
Europe, 317–33
  adult literacy inequality, 199–201
  fertility rates, 173
  See also Nordic countries; *names of individual countries*
European Union, 30, 102, 217
  anti-discrimination efforts, 209, 216, 221, 291
  Directive on Equal Treatment of Race/Ethnic Minorities, 223
  Directive on Equal Treatment of Women and Men, 223
  Directive on Parental Leave and Leave for Family Reasons, 30

Directive on Part-Time Work, 34
Directive on Working Time, 32–33
paid vacation standard, 244
executives, 225

Fair Labor Standards Act (1938), 76n2
Families That Work (Gornick and Meyers), 275, 435
"family" (definition), 238, 312n8
Family and Medical Leave Act (1993) (FMLA), 41, 146, 232–34 passim, 295, 343
  employees' own illnesses covered, 361n5
  non-transferability of entitlements and, 52n10
  proposed changes and, 412
  Social Security and, 296, 303–04
Family and Medical Leave Allowances (proposed), 305
family leave, 22–24 passim, 118
  breastfeeding and, 168
  business lobby opposition to, 347–52 passim
  class and, 376 passim
  cross-national comparison, 53
  differentiated from maternity leave, 91n4
  Europe, 22–32, 52n12, 317, 327–30
    Germany, 330
    Nordic countries, 46, 133, 151n8, 318–23
    Iceland, 153n20, 318
  feminist opposition to, 139
  Kenworthy on, 193
  loan system for, 167
  parent-to-parent transfer, 170
  public opinion, 323, 330
  See also fathers: family leave and; maternity leave; paternity leave; unpaid leave
Family Leave Insurance Act (proposed), 236, 243–45 passim, 249n3, 347, 360n1
family-provided child care, 68
fathers, 385–414
  "daddy-track" jobs, 211
  family leave and, 51, 442
    European policy, 49, Denmark, 31, 319–20
    Iceland, 318, 324–28
    Norway, 381n6
    Sweden, 31, 39, 69, 89, 211, 319–20, 443
    statistics, 244
  fathering and, 153n18
  housework and, 10, 69, 293, 393–97, 402
  income, 113–15
  on time with family, 11, 195
  vacation leave and, 354
  work hours, 23
  See also paternity leave; single parents: fathers; working-class men: fathers
Fechner, Holly, 239
fees, 36, 37, 98
The Feminine Mystique (Friedan), 345
feminism and feminists, 140 passim, 274–93 passim
  ideology and, 414
  Nordic countries, 96
  state and, 102

Sweden and, 320
  See also "difference feminism";
    second-wave feminism
Feminist Party (Sweden), 322
Ferree, Myra Marx, 438
Ferrera, Maurizio, 141
fertility rates, 42–43, 162, 173,
    295, 318
Filipina domestic workers, 99
Fineman, Martha, 295
Finland, 16, 18, 28–42 passim,
    52n16–18, 320–22
    passim
  "Employment and the
    Family" study and,
    367–68 passim, 378,
    381n6
first child, 170
flexible work hours, 403
Folbre, Nancy, 19, 413, 428, 438
food stamps, 243
foster children, 354
frames and framing, 283, 284,
    287, 295, 296
  motherhood and, 426
France, 18, 29–42 passim, 48,
    52n16, 276n11, 326–28
    passim
  Gender Relations project and,
    366 passim
  universal early childhood
    education, 333
  See also APE (allocation
    parentale d'education)
Fraser, Nancy, 136
Friedan, Betty, 345
Fung, Archon, 185

Garey, Anita, 419
gay marriage, 312n8
Geist, Claudia, 215
gender essentialism, 378

gender inequality, 6, 44–47. *See
    also* income inequality
gender neutrality, 154n27,
    292–93
gender symmetry, 17, 43, 129–49
    passim
gender wage gap. *See* income
    inequality
General Social Survey, 196,
    257
Germany, 10, 53n19, 212, 284,
    327–30 passim. *See
    also* West Germany
Gerson, Kathleen, 196, 345
"glass ceiling," 49, 268, 270,
    444
Glenn, Evelyn Nakano, 429
government policy, 112 passim,
    124, 172, 216–19,
    292–320 passim
  costing, 171
  domestic division of labor
    and, 373
  Europe, 22–43, 96, 101,
    317–33
  loans for parental leave, 165
  sick leave, 242–51 passim
  See also affirmative action;
    anti-discrimination
    policies; minimum-
    wage laws
government workers, 301
  SDI and, 353
  sick leave and, 242
Graefe, Peter, 188
Great Britain. *See* United
    Kingdom
Greece: male workweek, 10
Gross Domestic Product (GDP),
    124
guilty feelings, 420

Habitat for Humanity, 181
Hakim, Catherine, 47, 259
Hartmann, Heidi, 438
Hassim, Shireen, 446
Hays, S., 418
Head Start, 308, 406, 425
health and inequality, 118
health-care workers, 99, 103
health insurance, 122, 309
Healthy Families Act
    (proposed), 238–44
    passim, 249n4
Heymann, Jody, 239, 446
higher education, 112, 173, 274
    paid leave and, 443
Hill-Collins, Patricia, 426
hired help. *See* domestic workers
    (hired help)
Hispanics, 301. *See also*
    Chicana mothers;
    Mexicana mothers
HIV/AIDS, 99
Hochschild, Arlie, 103, 340, 346, 400
Holland. *See* Netherlands
"home care allowances," 201, 321
homework, 102
Hook, Jennifer, 213, 396
horizontal equity, 164–65
housewives: gender ideologies
    of, 259
housework
    division of labor and,
        271, 328
        fathers/men and, 292,
            334n3, 407
        mothers/women and, 11,
            426
        national variations, 222,
            376 passim
    housework services, 265

working time and, 372
See also domestic workers
    (hired help)
housing, 179–80 passim
human brain development. *See*
    brain development

Iceland, 153n20, 318
ideologies, 257, 411. *See also*
    Catholic ideology;
    mothering ideologies
immigration and immigrants,
    132
    Asian, 301
    assimilation, 285
    California, 353
    Nordic countries, 318
    paid domestic work and, 391
    state assistance and, 346
income, 171, 389
    public vs. private employees,
        268
    Sweden, 266–68 passim
    Portugal, 381n6
    See also citizen's wage
        (proposed); living-
        wage movement
income ceiling (Social Security),
    304–05
income inequality, 117, 118, 241
    long work hours and, 345
    Sweden, 221, 266
    trend toward equality, 398
income-sharing proposals,
    312n7
individualism, 107, 143, 153,
    292, 302 passim
    mothering and, 429–30
inequality and health, 117
infant care, 322
infant formula, 118
infant mortality, 285

informal labor market, 100
Institute for Women's Policy Research (IWPR), 239
insurance, 115, 120. *See also* Family Leave Insurance (proposed); health insurance; social insurance; state disability insurance; temporary disability insurance
"intensive mothering," 418–25
International Adult Literacy Survey, 199
International Social Survey Program (ISSP), 257, 330, 367
Ireland: male workweek, 10
Italy, 187

Jacobs, Jerry, 196, 345
Japan, 103
Journal of Health Economics, 114

Kagan, Jerome, 415
Kennedy, Edward, 239
Kenworthy, Lane, 436

labor force
  age of, 174
  participation rates by gender, 212
  women, 245
Labour Party (UK), 123
lactation. *See* breastfeeding
Lamont, Michele, 418
Landsorganisationen i Sverige, 324
Lareau, Annette, 426
Latin America, 95 passim
Latinos. *See* Hispanics

lawsuits, 293
lawyers, 225
Leira, Arnlaug, 437
Lenhoff, Donna, 234
Levitsky, Sandra, 294
liberalism, 291, 295. *See also* neoliberalism
literacy, 199
Littleton, Christine, 122
living-wage laws, 349
living-wage movement, 241
loans, 170
Lovell, Vicky, 438
low-income women. *See* poor women
low-wage jobs, 240

Macdonald, Cameron, 441
MacKinnon, Catharine, 139
male power, 441
male privilege, 92n10, 138, 442
male supremacy. *See* masculine supremacy
managers and administrators, 219–20, 267–69, 277n20, 348, 376
  shared family work and, 388
mandatory overtime, 402
"Maria Tax," 106, 448
market fundamentalism, 348–49
marriage: taxation and, 300–3
Martin, Cathie Jo, 348
Marxism, 132, 135, 150n3
masculine supremacy, 377
"maternal gatekeeping," 421
maternal identity. *See* mothers: identity
maternalism, 286–87 passim, 438
maternity leave, 28, 70–80, 90n2, 403
  Australia, 167

cross-national comparison, 53
Europe, 32, 33, 326
    France, 366
    Sweden (abolished), 318
    UK, 330
housework and, 395
unpaid, 343
US, 233
    Family Leave Insurance (proposed) and, 243
    See also family leave
McCall, Leslie, 218
McDonald, Peter, 42, 444
men. *See* fathers
men's power. *See* male power
Merck, 351
Mexicana mothers, 426
middle-class parents, 396
    African-American, 426
    mothers, 419–23
Middle East, 102
migrant labor, 103, 378
Milkman, Ruth, 449
minimum-wage laws, 349
minorities, 216, 244, 430n2. *See also* women of color
moral narrative, 359, 360
Morgan, Kimberly, 443, 445
mothers
    African-American, 426
    Chicana, 426
    employment, 10, 51n8
        child well-being and, 11
        public opinion, 330
        statistics, 7, 9
    identity, 426
    "maternal gatekeeping," 421
    Mexicana, 426
    "mommy tax," 9, 212
    "mommy track," 67, 210, 290, 411
    mothering ideologies and, 413–25 passim
    self-judgment, 430n4
    See also maternity leave; middle-class parents: mothers; poor women: mothers; rich mothers; single parents: mothers
Muir Commons, 180
musicians, 216

nannies, 117, 168, 270, 272, 304, 328, 428
    class and, 429
    France, 326
    pay of, 149
National Commission for Employment Policy, 240
National Institute of Child Health and Human Development (NICHD), 74, 419–21 passim
National Longitudinal Survey of Youth, 239
National Organization for Women, 277n23, 293
National Partnership for Women and Families, 234
national policies. *See* government policy
National Study of the Changing Workforce, 261
National Welfare Rights Organization, 140
needs, 151n5
Nelson, Margaret, 419
neoliberalism, 293
Netherlands, 10, 16, 53n19, 212, 326, 327–29 passim

part-time work, 378
  legislation, 375
neurology, 416, 417
New Jersey, 235, 361n8
New Zealand, 104
New York Times Magazine, 416
newborns, 234, 235
  fathers and, 406
Nickel and Dimed (Ehrenreich), 241
non-parental care. *See* child care
nonprofit enterprises, 123
Nordic countries
  class equality and, 270
  "educare" systems, 35, 37
  family leave and, 51, 120
  feminist gains/gender equality and, 91, 95, 140–41
  Gornick and Meyers's proposals and, 123, 151n8, 152n14
  housework and, 373
  occupational segregation and, 49
  See also names of individual countries
North–South relations, 94
Northern Ireland, 222
Norway, 18, 28–41 passim, 53n17–18, 53n22, 319–24
  Gender Relations project and, 366
  parliament, 225
  public opinion, 323, 330
nurses, 112, 113, 117, 118, 324
nursing home care, 112, 243

off-the-books work, 312
Old Age and Survivors Insurance. *See* Social Security

on-the-job training, 276n16
one-and-a-half-earner model, 271
one-year-olds, 195–205 passim
Organization for Economic Cooperation and Development (OECD), 50n2, 326
organized labor. *See* unions
Orloff, Ann, 222, 273, 284, 440, 441, 442
orphans: Romania, 416
Osberg, Lars, 44
overtime work, 210. *See also* mandatory overtime

paid domestic help. *See* domestic workers (hired help)
paid time off from work. *See* family leave; sick leave; vacation leave
Papua New Guinea, 98
"parent track," 116, 211. *See also* mothers: "mommy track"
parental choice and child-care policy, 46, 187 passim, 307, 308, 380
  Europe, 329–30
  Nordic countries, 139, 151n8, 319
  "home care allowances" and, 201
parental fees. *See* fees
parenting advice books, 417–24 passim, 431
parenting leave. *See* family leave
parents and school governance, 185
part-time employment, 23, 24, passim, 201–03 passim, 266, 422

INDEX 461

Europe, 33–34, 48, 52n12,
    376–77, 423
feminization of, 108
Healthy Families Act
    (proposed) and, 239
involuntary, 324
men and, 48, 287, 323
right to, 168, 235, 320, 324,
    329
  cross-national comparison,
    61
women and, 14, 22, 439, 443
  maternal identity and, 421
paternity leave, 22, 31, 401–3
  commitment to family and,
    400
  cross-national comparison, 53
  number of countries with,
    449
  Sweden, 31, 39, 69, 89, 211,
    263
  UK, 330
  See also fathers: family leave
    and
patriarchy, 377
pay equity laws, 211
payroll taxes, 243
Pearson, Ruth, 98, 101, 448
pediatricians, 413
pension benefits, 354
people of color. *See* minorities
Personal Responsibility and
    Work Opportunity
    Reconciliation Act,
    241
Pew Research Center, 425
Pew Study on Women, Family,
    and Work, 430n4
Philippines, 118
physicians, 413. *See also*
    pediatricians
pink-collar jobs, 390

PISA (Programme for
    International Student
    Assessment), 327
pluralism, 148
polls, 352, 399
poor countries. *See* developing
    countries
poor women, 147, 295
  mothers, 285, 343, 429, 435
poor working parents, 240
Portugal, 367–69 passim, 373–80
    passim
power, 441
pregnancy, 136, 139, 234–35, 243
  disability benefits, 354
Pregnancy Discrimination Act,
    237, 291, 342
  opposition to, 348
preschool, 26, 34–38 passim,
    191, 260
  cross-national comparison, 62
  Europe, 326
  Portugal, 375–78
"presenteeism," 242
private schools, 428
privatization, 183, 187
productivity, 349
Promise Keepers, 393
protectionism, 285
public child care, 16, 201, 329
public crèches, 329
public schools, 185, 187, 310
public employees. *See*
    government workers

Quebec, 187, 188

race, 147, 285
  mothering and, 412
Reich, Rob, 148
religions: view of women, 374
religious education, 334n5

462 INDEX

Rethinking the Brain, 415
retirement, 303
retirement communities, 180
rich countries, 94–103 passim, 442, 446, 448–49 passim
rich mothers, 418, 422
rights, 151n5, 163, 168–69, 232, 294
   care-recipients' and care-givers', 429, 449
   fathers', 329
   right of working women to breastfeed, 447
   right to employment, 382n21
   right to parental access to care services, 332
   right to parental leave, 274
   right to part-time work, 170, 246, 324, 379
Roberts, Dorothy, 147
Robeyns, Ingrid, 107
Roman Catholic ideology, 375, 381n16
Russia, 366, 380n1

S-CHIP (State Children's Health Insurance Program), 309
Sachs, Albie, 108
same-sex couples, 6, 168, 388
Sayer, Andrew, 271
Scandinavia. *See* Nordic countries
Schwarzenegger, Arnold, 352
scientists, 71, 224–25, 401
Scott, Joan, 138
SDI. *See* state disability insurance (SDI)
second child, 166
second-shift work, 420
second-wave feminism, 255, 341, 379

Segura, Denise, 426
Self-Employed Women's Union, 108
self-help books for parents. *See* parenting advice books
service industry, 266–77, 251
sexual harassment, 210, 217
   laws against, 85
Shalev, Michael, 436, 443–44
sick children, 239, 242
sick leave, 231–33, 306, 342, 346, 351, 394
   number of countries with paid sick leave, 362
   public opinion, 330
single parents, 6, 52n9, 168, 180, 197, 307
   fathers, 385
   mothers, 179, 239, 284, 293, 343, 385, 431n9
six-hour day, 318
sleep, 419, 422
social class. *See* class
social democratic parties, 319
   Finland, 332
   Sweden, 320
social insurance, 120, 161, 243, 292
social norms, 86–87 passim, 110, 208, 212, 213, 375, 445
   excessive work hours, 345
   mothering and, 411–16 passim
   policy and, 428
   working-class, 269
Social Security, 237, 272, 285–88, 293–314 passim
solidarity, 101, 107, 141, 178–89 passim, 272
Somers, Margaret, 348
South Africa, 103, 108

Soviet bloc, 379
Spain, 7, 10
Stalin, Joseph, 366
standard of living, 44
Starting Points, 415–16
state child care. *See* public child care
state disability insurance (SDI), 353–54 passim, 360n3
statistical discrimination against women, 81, 90n4, 92n12, 134, 139, 444
stepparents, 168
stereotypes and stereotyping, 81, 86, 92n12, 210, 214, 216
stigmatization, 294, 296
Stone, Deborah, 429
sub-Saharan Africa, 95, 97, 100
subsidies, 26 passim, 181, 248, 262, 310
   Europe, 222, 326
      France, 326, 329
   low-income households and, 262
   tax subsidies, 270
subsistence economies, 97
substitute care. *See* child care
Supreme Court, 225, 285, 291, 299, 360n4
Survey of Income and Program Participation (SIPP), 239–40
Svallfors, Stefan, 257
Sweden, 99, 179, 187, 263–70 passim, 277n20, 318–24
   affirmative action seen as unnecessary in, 220
   "cash for care" policy, 145
   feminists and, 322
   gender and labor force, 70, 96
   women's employment rate, 7, 203
   gender inequality in, 84, 211
   wage inequality, 218, 221
   Gornick and Meyers's proposals and, 79–80 passim, 130, 151n9
   model for US policy, 311n1
   mother's share of parental earnings, 10
   mothering ideologies, 424–25
   part-time work rates, 427
   paternity leave, 31, 58
   public opinion, 330
   subsidized day care, 76n1
   tax rebates, 276n14
   working time, 195, 203
"Swedophilia," 150n2
symphony orchestras, 216

taxation, 101, 122, 124, 223
   child care and, 256–60 passim, 270
   deductibility for children, 168
   family-care insurance and, 243
   family leave benefits and, 354
   progressive, 260, 288
   proposed "Maria Tax," 106, 448
   rebates, 276n14
   Social Security and, 297–304
   tax partnerships (proposed), 303 passim, 312n8–9
   US public opinion, 183
   See also off-the-books work; payroll taxes
telecommuting, 403
Temporary Assistance for Needy Families (TANF), 243, 306

temporary disability insurance (TDI), 235, 243
Therborn, Göran, 104
The Time Bind (Hochschild), 345
time-poverty, 3, 45, 290, 394
time-use studies, 10, 11, 423
  mothers and, 11, 427
Title VII. *See* Civil Rights Act (1964): Title VII
trade unions. *See* unions
Treaties of Rome (1957), 217
two-year-olds, 191–205
Tyson, Laura D'Andrea, 119

UK. *See* United Kingdom
undocumented workers, 117
unemployment: child care and, 35
unemployment benefits, 9, 123
  Australia, 111
  "Baby UI," 234
unions, 97, 102, 152n14, 183, 186, 274–75
  Europe, 222, 317
    Sweden, 221, 321
  family leave legislation and, 349, 354
  government workers and, 301
  paid leave and, 246
    sick leave and, 242
  teachers', 327
  See also collective bargaining
United Kingdom, 16, 53n19, 117
  anti-discrimination laws, 222
  Gender Relations project and, 366 passim
  male workweek, 10
United States, 10, 20, 41
  inequality and, 135
  male workweek, 10
  public opinion of mothers' employment, 330
  See also Bureau of Labor Statistics (BLS); Supreme Court
upward mobility, 429
"universal caregiver" model, 136, 137
universities: women professors and, 70–71
unpaid leave, 80, 343
unpaid work, 103, 114, 213, 289, 329. *See also* housework
upper-class mothers. *See* rich mothers
upper-class women. *See* rich women
Urban Institute, 261
urbanization, 301
US. *See* United States
utopians, 143

vacation leave, 354
  cross-national comparison, 61
  fathers and, 406
  number of countries with mandated leave, 447
vertical equity, 162, 165–68
voters, 172, 238
vouchers, 183, 205

wage gap. *See* income inequality
Wal-Mart, 249n1
Walzer, Susan, 421
Washington, DC, 237
Washington State, 249, 347, 360n1
Weber, Max, 417
welfare, 240, 241, 285, 286, 427. *See also* Temporary

Assistance for Needy Families
West Germany, 223
white-collar workers, 259
white families, 295
white women, 140
widows, 312n5
Willett, Cynthia, 142
Williams, Joan, 70, 247
Windebank, J., 371, 374
women: statistical discrimination against. *See* statistical discrimination against women
women executives, 225
Women, Infants, and Children program (WIC), 118
women lawyers, 225
women managers and administrators, 219, 268, 346
  career abandonment, 346
  Portugal, 375
  retention of, 350
women musicians, 216
women of color, 140, 147, 189. *See also* African-Americans: women; Chicana mothers
women physicians, 413
women scientists, 71, 225
Women's Legal Defense Fund, 234
work hours. *See* working time
work productivity. *See* productivity
workday, 72. *See also* six-hour day
worker cooperatives, 186–87
worker-owned day-care centers, 188
worker turnover. *See* employee turnover
workforce. *See* labor force
working at home. *See* homework
working-class conservatism, 257
working-class couples, 398
working-class men, 401
  fathers, 388, 403–04
working-class mothers, 418–21 passim
working-class parenting, 345
working conditions, 105
working time, 195–96, 332, 372
  regulation, 23, 203, 205
  Europe, 32–34
  See also flexible work hours; workday; workweek
workweek, 48, 170, 203, 248, 394, 402
  cross-national comparison, 61
  dual-earner couples, 42
  Europe, 32–33
  managers' and professionals', 267, 345, 351, 352, 376
  men's, 10
  regulation, 23
    France, 48, 366
Wright, Erik Olin, 435

Zippel, Kathrin, 248, 443